Tending Call

TENDING CALL

A Liberation Theology of Vocation

L. Callid Keefe-Perry

Maryknoll, New York 10545

Founded in 1970, Orbis Books endeavors to publish works that enlighten the mind, nourish the spirit, and challenge the conscience. The publishing arm of the Maryknoll Fathers and Brothers, Orbis seeks to explore the global dimensions of the Christian faith and mission, to invite dialogue with diverse cultures and religious traditions, and to serve the cause of reconciliation and peace. The books published reflect the views of their authors and do not represent the official position of the Maryknoll Society. To learn more about Maryknoll and Orbis Books, please visit our website at www.orbisbooks.com.

Copyright © 2026 by L. Callid Keefe-Perry

Published by Orbis Books, Box 302, Maryknoll, NY 10545-0302.

All rights reserved.

All Vatican documents are available online at Vatican.va.

Scripture quotations are from the New Revised Standard Version Updated Edition, copyright © 2021 National Council of the Churches of Christ in the United States of America. Used by permission. All rights reserved worldwide.

No part of this publication may be reproduced or transmitted in any form or by any means, electronic or mechanical, including photocopying, recording, or any information storage or retrieval system, without prior permission in writing from the publisher.

Queries regarding rights and permissions should be addressed to: Orbis Books, P.O. Box 302, Maryknoll, NY 10545-0302.

Manufactured in the United States of America

Library of Congress Cataloging-in-Publication Data

Names: Keefe-Perry, L. Callid author
Title: Tending call : a liberation theology of vocation / L. Callid Keefe-Perry.
Description: Maryknoll, NY : Orbis Books, [2026] | Includes bibliographical references and index. | Summary: "Helps to discern vocations in life with attention to communities, power structures, and relational well-being"— Provided by publisher.
Identifiers: LCCN 2025033872 (print) | LCCN 2025033873 (ebook) | ISBN 9781626986602 trade paperback | ISBN 9798888661147 epub
Subjects: LCSH: Vocation—Christianity | Liberation theology
Classification: LCC BV4740 .K44 2026 (print) | LCC BV4740 (ebook)
LC record available at https://lccn.loc.gov/2025033872
LC ebook record available at https://lccn.loc.gov/2025033873

To the memory of Dr. Hugh Morgan Hill, our Brother Blue,

who lived so fully into his call that he transformed.

If you ever meet me, feel free to ask me about him.

I'll tell you a story.

Contents

Practices x
Acknowledgments xi
Introduction xiii

Part I Seeds

What We Find in the Soil 3

1. **Vocation** 5
   Perspectives and Definitions 6
   Moral Orientation and the Shape of Vocation 18
   Experiences of Call 23
   Consequences of Call 32
   Reaching an Equilibrium 36
   Questions for Reflection 44

2. **Discernment** 46
   Discernment: Definitions and Perspectives 49
   Individual Discernment 56
   Communal Discernment 64
   Constant Attunement and Calibration 72
   Questions for Reflection 73

3. **Formation and Reflection** 75
   The Practice of Theological Reflection 77
   Considering Spiritual Formation 84
   The Living Ecosystem of Tradition 91
   The Challenges and Opportunities of Tradition 95
   Questions for Reflection 103

Part II Growth

What We Do Not See 107

4. **Systems Thinking** 111
    - *The Power of Systems* 114
    - *Bowen Family Systems Theory* 119
    - *Systems in Scripture and Theology* 135
    - *How the Stars Are Named* 144
    - *Questions for Reflection* 147

5. **Joy and Lament** 149
    - *Bumps on the Road* 151
    - *What Psychology Says* 156
    - *Theological Insights* 162
    - *Fostering Space for Rejoicing and Lamentation* 167
    - *Valleys and Peaks* 172
    - *Questions for Reflection* 174

6. **Identity and Belonging** 176
    - *A Fragmented Framework* 179
    - *The Impact of Fragmentation on Identity and Belonging* 191
    - *When Communities Collide* 194
    - *Whose Table?* 199
    - *From Table to Bed* 202
    - *Questions for Reflection* 205

Part III Abundance

What the Farmers Knew 209

7. **Accompaniment** 213
    - *Listening into Action* 214
    - *Toward a Three-Dimensional Model of Accompaniment* 225
    - *Practical Guidance for Accompaniment* 228
    - *A Possible Practice* 237
    - *The Power and Limits of Silence* 242
    - *Questions for Reflection* 243

8. Storytelling ... 245
- Theological Perspectives on Storytelling ... 248
- Context Collapse and Re-Narration ... 255
- Exploring the Future ... 261
- More Than a Wish ... 268
- Questions for Reflection ... 271

9. Ministry ... 272
- Servitude, Power, and the Call to Serve ... 274
- Scriptural Foundations of Christian Ministry ... 278
- The Historical Evolution of Ministry ... 283
- Contemporary Understandings of Ministry ... 290
- Ministry in a Changing Spiritual Landscape ... 300
- Implications of Emphasis ... 303
- Ministry as Manifestation of Call ... 309
- Questions for Reflection ... 314

In Closing ... 316

How to Listen for What Comes Next ... 317

Appendix ... 319
- Theological Reflection in Practice: A Step-by-Step Guide ... 321
- Set Your Sliders: A Tool for Assessing Spiritual Formation Dimensions ... 353
- System Mapping Me: A Visualization of Vocational Influences ... 359
- Organizational Boundary Audit Worksheet ... 363
- Trauma-Informed Culture Self-Assessment Tool: "4 People Encounter 5 Values in 4 Places" ... 367
- Sample Scenario: Alex and a Trauma-Informed Admissions Process ... 373
- Group Reflection on the NEPER Practices ... 377
- Seeding Change with Story ... 383

Index ... 391

Practices

Life Review	12
Leave the Cave	16
Tracing the Call	28
Condensed Examen	60
Theological Reflection	84
Set Your Sliders	90
Systems Mapping Me	119
Seeing Angels	145
Double Journal	162
Failure Fridays	170
A Fragment Inventory	191
Tending the Web	198
Witness and Walk	226
Re-Frame and Re-Tell	262
Your Ministry Recipe	299

Acknowledgments

This book was not written alone. It's the fruit of more than a decade of teaching, failing, learning, listening, and showing up again. So much of what I know about vocation has been shaped by those who have entrusted me to walk alongside them in seasons of discernment, confusion, and transformation. To all my students over my years at Boston University and Boston College: you have been among my greatest teachers.

I am similarly humbled by the extraordinary group who gathered for a consultation at Boston College to give me feedback on a cold February day in 2025. I'm grateful to the support of the Provost's office at Boston College that allowed me to be able to bring everyone together while the book was still in development. Thanks to Eileen Daily, rose j. percy, de'Angelo Dia, Joe Penny, Anastasia Kidd, Robert Dove McClellan, Zachary Moon, and Kristina Lizardy-Hajbi. Your presence was a gift and your insights a blessing. And a particular mark of gratitude to Nick Fagnant, Sangwon Yang, and especially Sarah Miller. It felt like a gift that you all showed up as fully as you did while managing the demands of your doctoral studies. The day we spent together was everything I had hoped it would be: a convergence of wisdom, laughter, challenge, and care. To sit in a room with people so deeply committed to liberative education and vocational clarity, and to have you turn your attention so generously toward my work, was profoundly moving.

Thanks as well to my colleagues at Boston College's School of Theology and Ministry, especially Theresa O'Keefe. The story of how we came to be coworkers has a number of twists and turns for sure, but what I'm profoundly grateful for is that I've found a colleague upon whom I can depend completely. Thank you for reminding me (over and over) that faithfulness and institutional life don't have to be at odds.

To Zachary: few people have helped me name the shape of my own vocation as clearly as you have. Your friendship and theological insight show up between the lines of nearly every chapter in this book. Here's to more experiments and more walking forward with integrity. There's good work to be done, and I hope I get to do some of it with you.

To the members of my Care & Accountability Committee at Fresh Pond: many thanks for the ongoing ways in which you remind me that even though occupation and vocation are not the same thing, they can overlap. Similarly, thanks to the Friends at the Obadiah Brown Benevolent Fund, whose support on the production of this book is greatly appreciated.

To Nahar: it has been great to live and think alongside you as you increasingly ask great questions. Your deepening commitment to capoeira and Portuguese has rekindled my own interest. Thanks for that. And thanks for being the reason I got to learn more about quilombos, an important part of my thinking these days. It is great to be your Papa and have you be my kid.

Finally, thanks to Kristina Keefe-Perry, whose faithfulness in ministry is a constant inspiration. You live your call with such a fierce grace that it's possible to believe that liberation is not only achievable, but already underway. I'm glad for your patience with others (and me!), especially for the ways in which that space allows for people to shift toward their better selves. This book bears your imprint in more ways than most will ever know. I'm glad you encouraged me to write it.

Introduction

The landscape of ministry is shifting rapidly, inviting diverse individuals and communities to reimagine service and leadership in ways that meet their unique challenges and opportunities. While some pursue this calling through formal theological education with the intention of becoming ordained, many others answer God's call to ministry by other means, bringing vital service to their communities through diverse paths. These changes give rise to new challenges and opportunities for all those seeking to discern and live out their vocations. As a theological educator, I have witnessed firsthand the growing diversity of students' backgrounds, experiences, and hopes. I have also seen the urgent need for a more inclusive, contextual, and justice-oriented approach to ministerial formation beyond the walls of traditional seminaries and divinity schools.

In Catholic contexts, Pope Francis established the formal ministry of catechist and officially extended the functions of acolyte and lector to women, signaling a broader recognition of the vital contributions of lay ministers. Among Protestants, there is an increasing trend toward viewing pastoring as a bivocational role, combining ministry with other forms of work to meet both personal and community needs. Across many traditions, lay ministry is no longer seen as secondary but as a vital expression of the church's mission, reflecting the diverse ways people live out their faith in their everyday lives. For everyone, the advent of powerful systems of generative artificial intelligence means that access to knowledge is easier than ever, but it comes without an increase of access to intentional formation or opportunities to increase actual skills. These shifts challenge traditional paradigms of theological education and ministry, inviting a deeper exploration of how diverse individuals and communities discern their callings and contribute to God's transformative work in the world.

At its core, this book offers a liberation theology of vocation: a vision of calling that emerges from the lived experience of people navigating unjust systems and struggling to live meaningfully in community. Drawing on the pedagogical insights of Paulo Freire, the spiritual traditions of communal discernment, and the political commitments of liberation theology, it proposes a way of thinking about vocation that is as much about moral orientation and collective transformation as it is about individual direction. Rather than separating spiritual formation and theological reflection, this book holds them together in a kind of double helix: entwined practices that help us listen for God's voice and respond with integrity, courage, and care.

Inspired by Freire's liberative pedagogy, I view theological education not as a mere transfer of knowledge or skills, but as a means to empower students. This involves critical reflection on their social location, discerning their unique gifts and callings, and becoming agents of personal and systemic transformation. This requires a significant reconsideration of many paradigms of theological education, as well as vocation and ministry. Throughout them all, there is a need for a deepening commitment to centering the voices and experiences of those who have been historically marginalized in the church and the academy. If you've ever longed to see your own experiences and realities reflected in the books you read, this book was written with you in mind.

Just as Freire's approach to education emphasizes the importance of students' lived experiences and the need for critical reflection, the process of vocational discernment requires a similar attentiveness to context and a willingness to engage in ongoing growth and transformation. In this spirit, I settled on the title *Tending Call*, as it emphasizes the ongoing, organic process of nurturing and discerning one's vocation.

During the revision process, I convened a consultation of a dozen or so trusted colleagues, including pastors, educators, organizers, and scholars, whose vocational lives embody the commitments this book tries to honor. I invited them to offer candid critique of the manuscript in its early form, including the title, which was then *Cultivating Call*. Their feedback was both incisive and generous. Several participants raised thoughtful concerns about the connotations of "cultivation," noting how, in contemporary usage, it often evokes mechanistic, industrial agriculture. That approach is more concerned with mass production, control, and commodification than with relational care. I was deeply grateful for this critique. It helped me realize that, while the book itself resists those logics, the title could unintentionally reinforce them. In discerning a better name, we practiced the very things this book invites: communal discernment, attentiveness to context, and a willingness to change.

I believe "cultivation" is a term worth redeeming, though. As I explore in the fourth chapter, drawing on the work of Walter Wink, distorted systems are not inherently evil. Instead, they are good things that have lost their way. The same can be said of the idea of cultivation. For thousands of years, cultivation has been an embodied, adaptive, and often sacred practice: farmers as stewards rather than extractors, growers in deep relationship with land and community. It includes foraging, seed saving, tending wild edges, and attuning to what the land could give, not just what it could be made to produce: a kind of cultivation that didn't rely on domination.

That vision of cultivation still matters, but I also came to see that the word might be carrying too much baggage for some readers. *Tending Call* offers a way forward. We tend gardens, yes, but also fires, wounds, friendships, sorrows, joys, and sacred commitments. "Tending" names the kind of responsive, humble, and non-coercive relationship I believe we are called to have with vocation, and with each other. It is, in that way, the truer name for what this book seeks to cultivate.

The subtitle, "A Liberation Theology of Vocation," names the theological heart of this project. Liberation theology, as I understand and draw upon it here, is not a fixed system but a method, specifically a way of doing theology that begins in the observable and lived experiences of the marginalized and insists that faith must be practiced through critical engagement with the social, political, and economic realities of the world. It involves what Paulo Freire called praxis: a cycle of reflection and action grounded in context, aimed at transformation. Liberation theology challenges us to consider not only who is speaking but also who is being heard and, importantly, who is missing from the conversation.

This challenge is not about abandoning cherished values but about seeing more clearly how those values call us to respond to a world marked by inequity, considering how even our most beloved traditions might inadvertently obscure the full dignity of all people. It means interrogating structures of power and privilege, naming how they deform our sense of call, and lifting up the wisdom, resilience, and creativity of communities that have long had to discern vocation in the face of structural sin.

While some liberation theologies engage in large doctrinal reinterpretation, offering liberative Christologies, ecclesiologies, or pneumatologies, this book does not take that path. Instead, it offers a liberation theology of vocation. That is, it takes the question of calling as its starting point and seeks to reframe it through the lens of structural critique, communal discernment, and liberative pedagogy. By focusing on how people make meaning and act with purpose in unjust worlds, this approach expands the theological conversation about vocation beyond personal fulfillment, toward shared responsibility and transformative presence.

In that spirit, readers can expect this book to differ from many traditional approaches to vocation. It is not primarily a guide to finding personal fulfillment or uncovering an abstract "life purpose." Instead, this book invites readers to explore vocation as a dynamic process of moral orientation and relational responsibility, always situated in context, always shaped by systems, always open to disruption and renewal.

Whether you are discerning your first steps in ministry or reimagining your call after years of faithful labor, the reflections and frameworks here are meant to help you attend to the wild, sacred, and often messy process of listening for God's voice in the world as it actually is. Throughout, I hope to make space for the complexities of real life. Room for grief, injustice, ambiguity, and, yes, joy. This is a book that invites you to consider a liberating vision of vocation that is as much about collective transformation as it is about personal calling.

How I Got Here

At one level, this book emerges from more than a decade of experience with courses designed to prepare students for ministry in master's programs. These classes, bearing titles like "Integration of Theology and Practice," "Theological Reflection for Ministry," and "Contextual Education," typically have two interwoven aims: to help students wrestle with the question of what they feel called to do, and to equip them for that work with both theological grounding and practical skills. In teaching this material I've learned a lot about what folks find useful, so it felt like the time to make sure that what I've learned can be shared beyond me and the rooms I'm in. But that's not really the full story.

I was raised without religion. My parents both had childhoods that heavily featured the Catholic Church and left them with enough of a negative experience that they decided their children wouldn't need religion to be good people. And I think they were right. You don't need religion to be good. But goodness isn't all religion is about. I didn't learn that until later.

When I was nine, my father's job evaporated because of changing national politics and budget cuts. My father's lack of a college degree made it hard for him to find work, and so our family of five moved in with family so that debt wouldn't swallow us whole. That early taste of insecurity lodged deep: hard work is no guarantee of safety. There is a precariousness that shapes how you look at the world. It made me suspicious of any story that equates virtue with stability or blessing with effort.

College sharpened that wariness. I was a first-generation college student and sometimes felt like that place wasn't built for me. Opportunity was everywhere, but so were the velvet ropes that decide who gets invited in and who gets studied as a "case." The kind that say, "this is for people like you," or, "you're lucky to be here, so don't ask too many questions." I cobbled together an interdisciplinary major because the standard tracks seemed designed for someone else's questions. Eventually, I got good at playing the games of the academy, but it never felt like home.

After college, and after a season when depression nearly convinced me the world would be fine without me, I ended up connecting with The Religious Society of Friends. In worship there, it felt like someone had turned off the background hum of annoyance and I could enter into what my mind and spirit were supposed to feel like. Here was a community whose reflex was to listen first, then act together, and to measure faithfulness not by external orthodoxy but by whether their lives bent toward peace and equity. The Friends' witness, tax resistance to fund abolition, jail time for suffragists, quiet accompaniment of conscientious objectors, matched many of the questions that had been gnawing at me too: Who is deemed expendable? Who gets protected? Why?

Religion, it turned out, didn't have to be a prize for the already good; it was the shared work of naming what harms and imagining what might heal.

Much to the frustration and confusion of my parents, I eventually realized that membership in a religion was right for me. Even more confusing was that my community named gifts in me that suggested I shouldn't just be a member, but a public minister, someone called to teach and give vocal ministry beyond the local congregation. What followed were years of deepening study (and bivocational ministry) on the side while my income came from elsewhere. I ended up a public-school social-studies teacher.

There, I saw too many colleagues burn out under policies that reduced children (and teachers) to data points. Their moral unmooring became one of my central research questions: What happens when people who enter a profession as a vocation can no longer recognize their own work as good?

I discovered that the harm is rarely a single dramatic betrayal; it is a thousand ordinary concessions. A teacher shaves five minutes from recess to drill another worksheet. A nurse skips the comforting conversation because the electronic-health-record timer is blinking. A pastor shortens a prophetic sermon so the livestream won't exceed its algorithm-approved length. No one sets out to wound children, patients, or parishioners; yet the slow accretion of policies, metrics, and market logics turns living persons into performance indicators.

This is the texture of what the philosopher Hannah Arendt called the "banality of evil," the everyday pressures that keep fundamentally decent people compliant with a status quo that frustrates their deepest hopes for healing and liberation. Most vocational failures are not spectacular collapses; they are the quiet moments when gifted practitioners are blocked, again, from doing the good they know how to do. That dissonance, more than any blatant wrongdoing, became the lens through which I now examine vocation, moral agency, and the systems that shape, or misshape, our sense of call across every field.

The vocational tumblers finally clicked when I returned to graduate school. Research let me name what I had been grappling with most of my life: the way systems form, or deform, our moral imagination.

My first academic love story was with Rubem Alves, who spoke of a "theology of human hope" that refused the false peace of resigned cynicism and insisted on imagining alternatives even when the data say none exist. Alves was the first to help me see that theology could begin in longing: not in answers, but in an ache for something more. It was Alves who helped me find words for a feeling I carried long before I knew its name: *saudade*.

This untranslatable Portuguese term speaks of a deep, almost melancholic yearning, a poignant ache for what is absent, for a wholeness that feels just out of reach, perhaps for a future that has not yet been born but which the heart insists is possible. Alves understood this *saudade* not as a passive despair, but as the very wellspring of hope, the engine of imagination.

For Alves, *saudade* was an embodied reality, not an abstracted concept. It was important not to shy away from this longing, but to truly know it, to feel its contours in one's own life. He often reminded readers that, in his native Portuguese, "tasting (*sabor*) and knowing (*saber*) have the same origin. To know something is to feel its taste, what it does to my body."[1] To know *saudade*, to truly know and inhabit this longing, is to recognize the profound, embodied yearning that fuels our theological questions and our quest for a more liberated existence. It is the ache that propels us beyond the merely given, into the poetic and prophetic engagement with life.

Imagination is not a luxury, but a survival tool. Calling isn't just about what you do when things go well, but how you remain faithful when they don't. Alves cracked open the possibility that theology rooted in ordinary lives could powerfully rise to prophetic vision. He taught that such vision begins not with certainty, but with yearning. Longing itself can be a kind of knowledge. To feel *saudade* is to know, in your bones, that another world is possible. And to refuse to relinquish that ache is, in his view, a form of faith. Not naïve optimism, but a stubborn, critical, and hard hope that insists: something more is still worth imagining.

And then came Paulo Freire. If Alves gave me the language of longing, then Freire gave me the language of praxis: the cycle of reflection and action, rooted in lived experience and aimed at transformation. His pedagogy taught me that education is never neutral: it either domesticates or liberates. That means that teaching itself can be a sacred act of accompaniment. In Freire, I recognized the tools I needed not just to think about vocation but to teach it. To form people who could listen for God in the world as it is, and who might have the courage to imagine what could be otherwise.

Freire said that, no matter what particular calling someone has, underneath it there is always one that is shared across humanity. He said the "ontological vocation of humanity is to become more."[2] The word "ontological" here means that, in our very being, we are called to "become more." This "become more" is a funny phrase in Portuguese too. He makes the word up in a way, turning "to be more" into a noun.

---

1 Rubem A. Alves, *The Poet, the Warrior, the Prophet* (London: SCM Press, 1990), 122.

2 The original Portuguese is "a vocação ontológica e histórica dos homensa—do ser mais." Paulo Freire, *Pedagogia do Oprimido* (Rio de Janeiro: Editora Paz e Terra, 1974), 45.

I sometimes translate it as "the being-more," which I think gives it the right feel. The point is, for Freire, humans are incomplete. Our story isn't done. Deep within our very being, we're called to a deeper way of being with one another. I think it is resonant with Augustine's declaration that "You have made us for yourself, Lord, and our heart is restless until it rests in you."[3] In both cases, there's a holy restlessness, an ache not to possess more, but to become more fully who we are meant to be, in communion with others and with God. That is, "being more" isn't about accumulating possessions or status, but about deepening endlessly into what more God might have envisioned for us. It is about striving against all that dehumanizes and diminishes our capacity to act upon and transform our present into something more just and more supportive of human flourishing.

This "being-more" is fueled by our awareness of our own incompleteness, not as a flaw, but as the very engine of our creativity and freedom. It's a call to move from being objects in the world, conditioned by oppressive structures, and pushed around by the powers that be, to becoming Subjects of our own history, actively and critically shaping a more just and liberated existence for all. This is a call to reclaim our agency, to understand that the world is not fixed but can be remade. This remaking is the ethical and political heart of Freire's entire life's work. It has become mine as well.

Together, Alves and Freire ushered me into the wider stream of liberation theology. Through their work, I came to understand that vocation is always entangled with power; that our deepest sense of calling must include an account of the systems that constrain it; that discernment without analysis risks becoming complicity. Liberation theology taught me that God's call is not just about who we are becoming and where we are headed: it's about who is being left behind, and what it will cost to change that.

In my doctoral program, I discovered "contextual education" might be a home for me. While some colleagues and mentors looked at it as a sideline to "real" academic work, for me it came into focus as the heart of it all. This was the place where all those threads—vocational clarity, social analysis, spiritual formation, and public witness—could be woven together. In contextual education, I found a pedagogy that refused abstraction and demanded presence. A place where call could be tested, refined, and reimagined in community. And a place where the classroom could spill out into the world, and the world could speak back.

For over a decade now, I've accompanied students as they enter sites of ministry—hospitals, parishes, food justice collectives, mutual aid hubs—and then gathered with them to reflect on what their experiences reveal about call, power, and faithfulness. Over and over, I've seen how formation takes root not just in books, but in practice: in the tension between what people believe and what they're allowed to do. This

---

3 St. Augustine, *The Confessions*, trans. Maria Boulding (Hyde Park, NY: New City Press, 2002).

book is an attempt to distill those years of learning into something usable. It's for students and seekers, pastors and practitioners. It's for anyone who's ever felt the pull of a calling and then smacked hard into institutions that make living it out seem impossible. And it's offered in the spirit of those who taught me to believe that, even when the way seems blocked, there may still be some new thing to try: there is always more life to tend.

So, that's how I got here. This book is my way of sharing what I've learned with others trying to live out their call in a world that doesn't always make it easy.

Goals of This Book

The primary goal of this book is to offer a comprehensive, practical, and justice-oriented guide to vocation that speaks to the evolving landscape of ministry. Historically, students entered theological education with the clear goal of becoming clergy. While that remains true for some, today's students come with a wide array of motivations, backgrounds, and vocational aspirations. Plus, lots of folk who faithfully serve their communities receive formal theological education but still want to read and learn. This book reflects a commitment to both traditional and emerging forms of ministry and is grounded in the conviction that all people, regardless of their background, professional role, or formal credentials, have the capacity to live into a meaningful and transformative sense of call.

One of the things that makes this text distinct is its integrated and liberative approach. It weaves together theological reflection and spiritual formation as mutually reinforcing practices—what I describe as a "double helix"—and situates that dynamic within a framework of liberation theology that presumes that you, the reader, already have a wealth of wisdom and valuable experience you're bringing to the table. This approach also intentionally nurtures holistic ways of knowing, integrating heart, body, and spirit alongside the mind, recognizing these as crucial for discerning and living into faithful callings. Vocation here is not merely about personal fulfillment or professional identity, but about the ongoing work of discernment within real communities, social structures, and histories. Attending to this interplay allows for a vocational vision that is both theologically grounded and practically responsive.

Another central aim is to foreground how power, privilege, and systemic inequity shape the possibilities people have for responding to call. This book insists that vocation cannot be meaningfully addressed without a clear-eyed look at the social, cultural, and political forces that limit access to discernment, formation, and flourishing. It also carries a quiet eschatological claim: that the work of discernment is not just preparation for some future world, but participation in the one being born around and among us now. As such, it reframes vocational discernment not only as an individual spiritual process, but also as a communal act of resistance and critical hope.

This book also introduces the concept of a Moral Orienting System (MOS), a framework that helps readers explore how their sense of moral meaning, coherence, and responsibility develops over time and in response to changing circumstances. The first chapter lays the foundation for this concept, showing how MOS can clarify the inner dynamics of calling, especially in moments of moral disorientation or transition. Threaded throughout the volume, MOS becomes a quiet partner in the book's wider argument: that vocation is not just about what we do, but how we navigate, embody, and reorient our moral lives across time in relationship with others and tradition.

Rather than reinforcing overly individualistic notions of "finding one's call," the book emphasizes the vital role of relationships, tradition, and community in shaping how we listen for and respond to God's invitation. I see communal discernment and accompaniment at the center of vocational formation. Discernment, in this view, is a shared endeavor: a lifelong, lived process that requires mutual support, courageous reflection, and deep listening. Furthermore, this book seeks to equip readers not only for their own discernment but also for the practice of accompaniment, of traveling faithfully alongside others in their vocational journeys. It also means listening for the ways in which tradition can be held up in ways that are life-giving and, at times, stifling to new growth.

In addition, this book aims to expand the definition of ministry itself. Rather than narrowing the focus to traditional, church-based roles, I present a broad and inclusive vision that encompasses activism, caregiving, chaplaincy, creative expression, and work in secular institutions as vital expressions of call. Ministry, here, is understood as a consequence of call, a way of participating in God's healing and justice-making work in the world, wherever that work takes place.

Finally, this book takes a practical theological approach, rooting every chapter in the wisdom of lived experience. It honors the complexity of real vocational journeys: complete with contradiction, ambiguity, joy, lament, failure, and discovery, and seeks to accompany readers through their own processes of discernment and growth. It is unapologetically committed to the flourishing of all people and to the transformation of the systems and structures that constrain that flourishing.

In all of these ways, I want to invite you to tend to your own sense of call with intention, humility, and courage. This book is for those who wonder how their lives might matter, how they might serve, and how they might live faithfully into the sacred invitation to participate in the world's healing. It is a guide for students, ministers, seekers, and communities who long not just to discover a call, but to tend it as something living, growing, and real.

Vocation and the Evolving Nature of Theological Education

The landscape of theological education has evolved significantly over the centuries, reflecting the diverse motivations and aspirations of modern students. Historically, students entered theological institutions primarily to become pastors and serve within church settings. In the early seventeenth century, theological education in the United States began with Protestant churches at institutions like Harvard and Yale. This education was initially intended for young white men who would do their theological reading in the final year of what we now consider a bachelor's degree. Following graduation, these hopeful ministers would be apprenticed under established pastors.

In the early nineteenth century, the model of theological education transformed with the founding of seminaries, which institutionalized these apprenticeship opportunities. By the mid-1800s, further changes led to the form of theological education that persists today. The creation of the University of Berlin in 1810, led by the philosopher Wilhelm von Humboldt, was pivotal. Humboldt, along with theologian Friedrich Schleiermacher, redefined theology's place in the university, proposing it as both a practical discipline for pastoral care and a general branch of scholarship with the same research potential as the hard sciences.[4]

Schleiermacher's influence led to the "Berlin Model" of theological education, which emphasized a fourfold curriculum: Biblical studies and languages, theology, history of Christianity, and practical theology. This model, still used today, sought to tie all aspects of theological education to practice, aiming to improve general pastoral care. However, over time, this framing has often resulted in the fragmentation of learning, where practical or pastoral studies are undervalued compared to biblical studies, theology, and history. Things like "Supervised Ministry" or "Contextual Education" have in some places become an afterthought rather than a central feature of ministerial preparation. This is unfortunate because now, perhaps more than ever before, there is a need to contextualize and provide guidance that is adapted to current realities.

Importantly, this model's influence extends far beyond formal theological education. The fourfold division of biblical studies, theology, history, and practical application has "leaked" into how churches, lay ministry programs, and even informal religious groups organize their learning and understanding. You can see it in how many churches structure their adult education programs, how Christian publishing houses categorize their books, and how lay ministry training programs divide their curriculum. Even Bible study groups often unconsciously follow this pattern,

---

4 Edwin D. Aponte, "Friedrich Schleiermacher," in *Beyond the Pale: Reading Theology from the Margins*, ed. Miguel A. De La Torre and Stacey M. Floyd-Thomas (Louisville, KY: Westminster John Knox, 2011), 105–14.

separating scriptural analysis from historical context, theological interpretation, and practical application.

While this organization can be helpful, it can also create artificial divisions in how we understand and live out our faith. For those called to ministry, this inherited pattern might feel restrictive or suggest that deep engagement with faith requires formal academic training. However, recognizing this influence can help us intentionally integrate these aspects of faith and ministry in ways that better serve our contexts and callings. Many effective ministers naturally weave together scripture, theology, history, and practice in their service, demonstrating that, while the Berlin Model has shaped our thinking, it need not constrain how we live out our vocations.

Indeed, the desire to move beyond such fragmentation has been evident in various traditions. For instance, the Catholic Church in the United States, for at least two decades, has actively cultivated a broader vision of theological education. As early as its 2001 edition of the *Program for Priestly Formation*, the Church sought to place the purely intellectual components of theological training within a wider, more integrated perspective, identifying four crucial pillars for priestly formation: human, spiritual, intellectual, and pastoral.[5] This more holistic, four-pillar model was later extended to encompass lay ministry formation with the United States Conference of Catholic Bishops' publication of *Co-Workers in the Vineyard of the Lord* in 2005.[6] Such an emphasis on intellectual, spiritual, human, and pastoral formation as interconnected aspects of a single journey signals a commitment to forming ministers prepared for the multifaceted realities of service.

This movement toward a more integrated understanding of formation is not unique to Catholic contexts. Many Protestant traditions and institutions have also been actively seeking to cultivate more holistic approaches to theological education, recognizing that deep learning and faithful ministry require more than intellectual acuity alone. These efforts often emphasize the intentional weaving together of academic study with spiritual maturity, personal character development, and practical wisdom.

Some seminaries, for example, now articulate their educational mission around distinct commitments to academic excellence, spiritual formation, and community engagement, aiming to transform lives rather than merely transfer knowledge. Others champion "missional spirituality," which forms leaders by integrating theological knowledge, practical skills, and missional attitudes, all oriented toward participating

---

[5] United States Conference of Catholic Bishops, *Program of Priestly Formation,* 5th ed. (Washington, DC: United States Conference of Catholic Bishops, 2006).

[6] United States Conference of Catholic Bishops, *Co-Workers in the Vineyard of the Lord: A Resource for Guiding the Development of Lay Ecclesial Ministry* (Washington, DC: United States Conference of Catholic Bishops, 2005).

in God's work in the world. The ongoing conversation about how best to achieve such integration across courses, curricula, and institutional cultures is robust, as evidenced by collaborative scholarly works like *Integrating Work in Theological Education*, which explores these very challenges and possibilities from diverse Protestant and ecumenical perspectives.[7] While specific language and frameworks vary, the underlying impetus is similar: to form leaders whose hearts and hands are as well prepared as their minds, capable of navigating the complexities of ministry with integrity, compassion, and skill.

Beyond these structural and curricular reforms within individual academic institutions, the broader landscape of theological education has also been enriched by dedicated organizations and movements fostering more reflective and integrated pedagogical practices. For example, within the academic sphere, entities such as the Wabash Center for Teaching and Learning in Theology and Religion play a crucial role by supporting faculty development and encouraging a style of teaching that is contextual and integrative.[8] Parallel to this, numerous church-based and denominational initiatives actively work to equip congregations and lay leaders for deeper, more integrated faith formation. These might include comprehensive discipleship programs that weave together study, spiritual practice, and community action, or networks that supply local churches with tools for communal discernment and reflective learning. Such initiatives, whether academic or congregational, recognize that forming faithful and effective people for ministry (in all its varied forms) requires not only well-designed curricula or programs but also well-supported, critically reflective, and practically skilled guides who can help individuals and communities make vital connections among knowledge, faith, and a lived experience of community. These efforts to deepen and broaden theological formation are timely, as they respond to and intersect with a notable diversification in what draws individuals to theological study in the first place.

Given the history of theological education writ large, literature on vocation and discernment long defaulted to a norm that presumes a predominantly middle-class, male, white, college-educated audience. This demographic skew can be traced back to the origins of many theological institutions in Western countries, which were established during times when higher education was largely inaccessible to marginalized communities. These institutions were often founded and led by white men who shaped the curriculum and dominant narratives within theological education.

---

7 Kathleen A. Cahalan, Edward Foley, and Gordon S. Mikoski, eds., *Integrating Work in Theological Education* (Eugene, OR: Pickwick Publications, 2017).

8 "About," Wabash Center for Teaching and Learning in Theology and Religion, accessed March 17, 2025, https://www.wabashcenter.wabash.edu/about/.

Consequently, the literature on vocation and discernment has predominantly reflected the experiences and assumptions of white men with social power, overlooking the diverse experiences of many who now pursue theological education. Today, there is a growing recognition of the need to include voices and perspectives from a broader spectrum of cultural, racial, and socioeconomic backgrounds.[9] This book seeks to address these contemporary realities and add to the literature that offers insights and guidance that is inclusive and reflective of the diverse community of learners engaged in theological studies.

Today, the motivations driving people to theological education are far more varied than they were in Berlin's 1810. Many students are driven by a desire to engage deeply with their faith and address contemporary issues of social justice, environmental stewardship, and interfaith dialogue. Others pursue theological studies for personal spiritual growth or to develop skills for "nontraditional" forms of ministry like chaplaincy, counseling, work in the arts, or community organizing. Additionally, some individuals, such as successful business professionals, might seek to integrate theological insights with their secular careers, enhancing their work in fields such as education, healthcare, and social services. For example, it wasn't long ago that I had a student who was a full-time hospital administrator and had no intention of leaving her career. She was studying to think more deeply about how it was that her work was a form of ministry for her. This broader understanding of vocation reflects the diverse ways people find meaning and purpose in their lives.

As we explore the evolving landscape of theological education and its implications for vocation, it's important to acknowledge the limits of what any single book or perspective can achieve. While the challenges and opportunities facing theological education as a whole are vast and complex, my aim in this book is to focus on the areas where I have the most direct experience and expertise: contextual education, supervised ministry, and vocational discernment. These areas are particularly relevant in addressing the challenges outlined above, as they provide opportunities for students to integrate their learning with real-world contexts, grapple with questions of identity and social location, and discern their unique callings in a diverse and changing world.

Drawing on my years of teaching and mentoring students in these areas, I hope to offer insights and guidance that are grounded in the realities of today's diverse and changing student body. By focusing on these specific aspects of theological education, I believe we can make a meaningful contribution to the larger conversation about the

---

9 See, for example, Bonnie Miller-McLemore's *Follow Your Bliss and Other Lies about Calling* (New York: Oxford University Press, 2024); the work of Patrick Reyes; as well the multi-author volume *Explore: Vocational Discovery in Ministry*, ed. Kristina Lizardy-Hajbi and Matthew Floding (Lanham, MD: Rowman and Littlefield, 2022).

future of ministry and religious leadership. As Bonnie J. Miller-McLemore notes in *Follow Your Bliss and Other Lies about Calling*, popular approaches to vocation often romanticize it as a blissful, individual pursuit, ignoring the burdens and sacrifices inherent in calling.[10] I entirely agree with her call for "truth-telling" about the complexities of vocation. This book takes a step further by situating vocation itself within systems of power, privilege, and liberation.

In the chapters that follow, I explore how those who are feeling called into service can integrate theological insight with contextualized experience and reflect on their unique callings and contexts. At the same time, I grapple with the complexities of vocation in a world marked by inequality, diversity, and rapid change. I explore how factors such as race, gender, class, and sexuality shape the contours of vocation and how we can cultivate a more expansive and liberative understanding of what it means to be called to ministry and service.

By grounding the discussion in these specific areas of contextual education, supervised ministry, and vocational discernment, I hope to offer a valuable resource for students, educators, and leaders who are seeking to navigate the challenges and opportunities of theological education today. Although the scope of this book is necessarily limited, I believe that by focusing on these critical aspects of formation and discernment, I can make a meaningful contribution to the ongoing work of preparing leaders for changing contexts of faith.

Approach and Assumptions

At the heart of this book's approach is the recognition that living into one's vocation is a deeply spiritual process, one that involves attentiveness to our experience of God in our lives. Through prayer, reflection, and engagement with our faith traditions, we begin to discern the unique ways in which we are called to serve and live out our purpose. This book assumes that spirituality is not separate from the work of social transformation but is intimately connected to it. As we grow in our relationship with God, we are invited to participate in the ongoing work of creating a more just and compassionate world. By exploring the intersections of faith and social justice, this book seeks to offer a holistic approach to vocation that honors the deep interconnections between our spiritual lives and our actions in the world.

My approach to theological education is greatly indebted to the work of Paulo Freire and what came to be known as "critical pedagogy."[11] Freire's perspective assumes

---

10 Miller-McLemore, *Follow Your Bliss and Other Lies about Calling*.

11 This is most famously represented in Freire's *Pedagogy of the Oppressed*, but a great introduction to his work is Antonia Darder's *Freire and Education* (New York: Routledge, 2014).

that education is most effective when it is participatory, reflective, and rooted in the lived experiences of students. This pedagogy emphasizes dialogue, critical reflection, and the acknowledgment of students' cultural and personal backgrounds as valuable sources of knowledge. Applying this perspective to theological education means fostering environments where students' diverse backgrounds and insights are integral to the learning process.

This commitment to participatory and reflective education finds a powerful corollary in the Latin American and US Latinx tradition of "*testimonio*."[12] Rooted in liberation theology and taken up especially by Chicana and Latina scholars, *testimonio* is a narrative form that foregrounds personal experience not as mere anecdote, but as a political and theological act of truth-telling. It is a mode of speaking that bears witness to oppression while inviting solidarity, and it insists that lived experience, especially the experience of those marginalized by systems of power, is a source of insight and transformation. Like Freire's pedagogy, *testimonio* is dialogical and democratizing; it calls forth agency in both speaker and listener. Throughout this book, such narrative forms are not decorative. They are integral. Stories, memories, and reflective accounts function as theological texts in their own right, helping to illuminate vocation and ministry not from above, but from within the lives of those who are discerning what faithfulness looks like.

Building on this narrative and liberative grounding, the book's understanding of ministry embraces a wide and evolving range of expressions. These range from theological sources like the priesthood of all believers and Catholic lay ecclesial ministry, to grassroots practices of community care, creative expression, advocacy, and organizing. In addition to my own Quaker tradition's teaching, Jesuit perspectives on discernment, scriptural visions of service, and Spirit-given gifts across traditions all inform this mosaic. But the thread that runs through them all is a commitment to ministry as a response to vocation: a way of participating in God's healing and justice-making wherever one is called. This includes roles both within and beyond formal church structures, and honors the real-life complexity of those living out ministry in workplaces, families, hospitals, streets, and sanctuaries alike. Rather than offering a single model, this book cultivates a theology of vocation and ministry that arises from dialogue that occurs between traditions, between communities, and between lived experience and theological reflection.

A core assumption guiding this book is that theological education must integrate spiritual formation and contextual education, recognizing that students' lived

---

12 A great read on this is Kathryn Blackmer Reyes and Julia E. Curry Rodríguez, "*Testimonio*: Origins, Terms, and Resources," *Equity & Excellence in Education* 45, no. 3 (2012): 525–38, https://doi.org/10.1080/10665684.2012.698571.

experiences hold profound wisdom and are vital for uncovering deeper meanings about God's work in the world. This Freirean approach directly connects to the need for institutions to better prepare students for modern ministry, advocating for educational practices that are adaptive, inclusive, and reflective of the complexities of contemporary life. Following this, a key assumption is that vocational exploration must engage with the need for systemic transformation, acknowledging that existing structures may need to change to allow diverse voices and leadership styles to thrive.

This vision is grounded in a theological framework that draws deeply from liberation theology and is animated by a framework that takes seriously the sacredness of everyday life and the moral weight of our collective choices. Paulo Freire's pedagogy of critical consciousness and Rubem Alves's invitation to theopoetics are central to this task, both of which remind us that theology must not only interpret the world but imagine it otherwise. Through this lens, vocation becomes a communal and justice-seeking practice. It is less about individual fulfillment and more about faithful participation in God's unfolding call toward healing, liberation, and beloved community.

From this vantage, theological and contextual education has a profound responsibility and opportunity to prepare students for transformative roles. This involves recognizing that vocational discernment is not simply about finding a slot within the current model but also about curating an educational environment that encourages critical reflection on these structures and supports students in envisioning and enacting transformative change. Too often, vocational discernment is framed as fitting into existing systems, which inherently maintain the status quo. Instead, we must foster spaces that allow students to wrestle with questions of anger and the need for systemic change, recognizing that some are called to prophetic work that challenges and transforms current structures.

This Freirean approach to theological education aligns with what Alves called a "theology of human hope." This perspective sees theological reflection not just as academic exercise, but as vital engagement with material reality. He argued that faithful theological reflection must begin with the concrete situations of human suffering and struggle, while simultaneously maintaining an openness to new possibilities.

> Hope is a beautiful thing, which I love. But ... dreams of gardens were not enough for me: it was necessary to know which gardens could and would be planted. Love of gardens had to become a gardening manual.[13]

This perspective sees theological reflection not just as academic exercise, but as vital engagement that can spark systemic change. Alves insisted that hope becomes real

---

13 Rubem Alves, "Sobre Deuses e Caquis," *Comunicações do ISER* 7, no. 32 (1988): 29.

Introduction xxix

when it leads to action in the present moment; this happens when our visions of a better future shape how we live and work today. This understanding helps us see vocational discernment as both deeply personal and inherently political, involving collective movements toward justice and liberation as well as individual choices.

As religious leaders, those new to ministry will encounter a wide range of backgrounds, experiences, and needs, requiring skills in active listening, critical reflection, and cross-cultural engagement. This approach fosters adaptability and resilience, enabling emergent ministers to draw upon diverse perspectives and resources in their service. Additionally, by prioritizing inclusivity and systemic transformation, theological education can empower ministers from all backgrounds to lead and advocate for change, amplifying the voices of marginalized communities and working collaboratively to dismantle unjust structures. This allows them to live out their vocational callings with greater integrity and impact, contributing to the collective work of healing and transformation.

Ultimately, embracing a holistic and inclusive approach to vocational discernment is not only about creating space for marginalized students to thrive but also about recognizing their leadership and contributions as integral to fostering a more vibrant, meaningful, and transformative theological education for all. Too often, books about "social justice" presume that the people reading them are going to be allies to the "people who need help." This book challenges that assumption. It invites all readers, including those from marginalized communities, to know themselves as leaders and co-creators in the work of justice and liberation. By creating spaces where every student's experiences and insights are valued and integrated into the learning process, we can cultivate a new generation of religious leaders who are equipped to meet the urgent needs of our world with wisdom, courage, and compassion. This vision of vocation can lead to flourishing for all students, regardless of their background. It also probably means that some of "the way things are done" may well need change.

This work isn't only for students. Educators, too, are implicated, called not just to guide discernment but to remain active within it. Teaching about vocation and justice ought never be a matter of simply assigning the right readings or facilitating the right reflections. We who teach are also being formed, also discerning, also reckoning with our own participation in the systems we critique. To teach this material with integrity means doing the work alongside our students, not excusing ourselves from the process, but entering into it with courage and humility. When we do, the classroom shifts. It becomes a space where everyone is practicing, everyone is listening, and no one is pretending to be finished.

For those of us who are Christian, we are called to this work in community as the Body of Christ. Engaging with diverse perspectives allows everyone to critically examine their own positions of power and privilege and to build coalitions and collaborations that are vital for change work. Learning alongside individuals from different life experiences helps develop a more nuanced and compassionate approach to ministry and leadership, prompting us to confront our biases and deepen our commitment to justice and inclusivity as a unified community. This inclusive approach to vocation prepares all students to navigate an increasingly diverse and complex world.

In the chapters that follow, I explore how these key approaches and assumptions can inform our understanding of vocation and guide our practices of discernment. By grounding the discussion in the realities of today's diverse student body and the challenges of modern ministry, this book aims to offer valuable insights and practical tools for navigating the evolving landscape of ministry, faith, and theological education.

A Note on Audience

Many people use "theological education" as a shorthand for "doing graduate-level studies at a school where you can get a degree, usually a master's degree." But really, theological education is just a phrase meaning education that is theological. And you know what? Most theological education doesn't take place in theological education institutions. Many people are educated about God and faith at kitchen tables and in places of worship, never setting foot in an institution of higher education. Understanding that "theological education" extends far beyond the confines of graduate-level studies at seminaries or divinity schools is crucial for this book.

While formal theological education is a significant aspect, it represents only a fraction of the broader spectrum of learning and spiritual growth. Recognizing this broader definition is vital for appreciating the diverse contexts and experiences that contribute to theological education. This perspective aligns with the book's goal to honor and incorporate varied educational experiences, acknowledging that theological education can happen anywhere and is accessible to all.

The likelihood is that many people who read this will do so as part of their own wrestling with vocation within the context of formal graduate study. That's great! But I also hope those who are being educated by other means find some use in it as well. And I hope that we can learn to recognize that theological education, in its broadest sense, encompasses any form of learning that engages with questions about God, faith, and spirituality. This kind of education happens in many contexts beyond the walls of seminaries and divinity schools. It occurs in churches, community centers, homes, workplaces, and countless other spaces where people gather to reflect on their beliefs and how those beliefs inform their lives.

Consider the wisdom passed down in families, the insights gained from personal spiritual practices, and the profound learning that happens in community activism and social justice work. These are all forms of theological education, even though they might not come with formal credentials. They involve the same deep engagement with questions of meaning, purpose, and ethics that characterize any rigorous theological inquiry. Recognizing that God helps us in our learning in many spaces is vital to accept for all of us. It is lived out in daily experiences, in the ways people respond to challenges, and in their efforts to make sense of the world through the lens of their faith. This kind of education is dynamic, contextual, and deeply rooted in the lived realities of individuals and communities. Recognizing and valuing these diverse forms of theological education broadens our understanding of what it means to learn and grow theologically. This book aims to honor and incorporate these varied educational experiences, acknowledging that formal theological education is just one part of a much larger tapestry of learning and spiritual growth.

My hope is that this book will be useful to all kinds of people interested in theological education, regardless of their educational backgrounds or professional aspirations. Whether you are a student in a formal theological program, a layperson seeking to deepen your understanding of your faith, a community leader working toward social justice, or someone exploring spirituality in your daily life, this book offers insights and tools that can support your journey. For students in traditional theological programs, this book provides a framework that connects academic study with real-world application, encouraging a holistic approach to ministry that integrates personal, spiritual, and communal dimensions. It challenges the notion that theological education is confined to the academy and invites students to see their entire lives as spaces for theological reflection and growth.

For all readers, this book seeks to foster a sense of connection and shared purpose. It recognizes that theological education, in its many forms, is a communal endeavor that benefits from diverse perspectives and experiences. By exploring themes of vocation, discernment, and ministry from multiple angles, this book encourages readers to engage with their own journeys and with each other in meaningful and transformative ways. In essence, this book aims to provide a space where readers can reflect on their own journeys, informed by a Christian perspective.

By drawing on a rich tapestry of experiences, traditions, and insights, the book seeks to illuminate the many ways in which people can live out their callings in ways that are rich with meaning and purpose. Whether you find yourself within the Christian tradition or outside it, whether you are in a formal theological program or learning through life's daily experiences, this book is for you. It is an invitation to explore, to question, and to grow. Together, we can foster a more just, compassionate, and spiritually enriched world through our shared journey of theological education.

How This Book Works

This book is organized into three main parts: "Seeds," "Growth," and "Abundance." These parts offer a spacious, cyclical way of engaging the vocational life. Although the titles may suggest a linear arc, they are not meant to chart a straight line from beginning to end. Instead, they reflect recurring movements: invitations to begin again, to deepen in new ways, to bear fruit that nourishes others and can be sown the next season. This structure resists mechanistic or developmental assumptions and instead honors vocation as an unfolding process shaped by context, disruption, relationship, and renewal. These three parts provide a flexible framework for attending to vocation in all its messy beauty, always grounded in liberation, attuned to power, and open to surprise.

Part I: Seeds

The first part, "Seeds," establishes the foundational framework through which I examine vocation throughout the book. These aren't just introductory chapters laying groundwork to be left behind. Instead, they are fertile ground in their own right. The ideas planted here will keep resurfacing, sprouting new insights as they interact with later chapters and your own unfolding reflections. It is also the case that there is a lot here even for folks who are long-experienced with the work in ministry, especially if they are looking for new ways of thinking about their work.

Beginning with the first chapter's exploration of vocation as a dynamic, evolving journey rather than a static destination, Part I moves through the second chapter's examination of both individual and communal approaches to discernment, drawing on insights from Ignatian spirituality and liberation theology. The first part concludes with the third chapter's investigation of how spiritual formation and theological reflection work together to deepen our understanding of calling. You'll see this play out especially in the first chapter, where I introduce the idea of a Moral Orienting System (MOS). This framework helps name what's happening when we feel disoriented, called, or changed. That concept echoes throughout the book, offering language for how our moral and spiritual intuitions are shaped over time.

Part II: Growth

The middle part of the book, encompassing the fourth, fifth, and sixth chapters, examines how our vocational understanding grows through engagement with broader systems and relationships. This is the stretch of the journey where things deepen, tangle, and stretch. The seeds planted earlier push up against real-world complexity here, rooting into relationships, power structures, and the emotional terrain of formation.

The fourth chapter introduces systems thinking as a vital lens for understanding vocation, exploring concepts from Bowen Family Systems Theory and concepts from adrienne maree brown's work on emergent strategy. The fifth chapter investigates the deep connection between identity and belonging, drawing particularly on Willie James Jennings's work on fragments and Ubuntu theology. The sixth chapter then explores the necessary interplay of joy and lament in vocational journeys, examining how both celebration and sorrow shape our understanding of calling while introducing trauma-informed approaches to ministerial formation. These chapters work together to show how vocational discernment involves navigating complex systems, building meaningful community, and holding space for the full range of human experience.

Part III: Abundance

The final part of the book, comprising the seventh, eighth, and ninth chapters, focuses on practices that help us live into our vocational callings with greater fullness. Although this part may feel like a turn toward application, it is not a conclusive "harvest" of earlier insights; rather, it extends the invitation into deeper, riskier, and more embodied engagement with call. In fact, abundance in this framing doesn't mark the end of the journey, but instead circles back to seeds, each one a small, brave act of attention and commitment that continues to take root and grow over time.

The seventh chapter examines accompaniment as a dynamic practice involving three key dimensions: Companioning, Disruption, and Witness. It also introduces practical tools like the "Stewarding Leadings and Gifts" workshop. The eighth chapter explores the power of storytelling and re-narration in vocational discernment, engaging with concepts like "context collapse" and prefigurative politics to show how sharing our stories can shape both present action and future possibilities. The book concludes with the ninth chapter's examination of ministry itself, wrestling with scriptural metaphors of service while offering a vision of ministry that balances personal growth with systemic transformation. These chapters provide concrete practices and perspectives that help readers move from discernment into active engagement with their callings.

The Interludes

Before each part, you'll find a short piece of writing that aims to capture something of the next part's spirit. These aren't summaries or teaching tools in the traditional sense. Rather, they serve as threshold moments, places of playing between, an invitation for you to pause and shift your attention before entering the chapters that follow. Like clearings in a forest where you might stop to get your bearings, these interludes offer space for contemplation and reorientation. I wrote them to ground the conceptual work that follows in image and metaphor, speaking to both heart and mind. You may find it helpful to return to these poems throughout your reading, allowing their imagery to deepen your engagement with the themes and ideas in their respective parts. They are meant to be companions on the journey and questions to consider, not signposts pointing the way.

Questions for Reflection

At the end of each chapter, you will find "Questions for Reflection" designed to help you engage deeply with the material. These questions are intended to prompt personal introspection and facilitate meaningful discussion, whether you are reading alone or in a group. You don't need to address all of them, but I've provided a wide range to ensure there is something for everyone to wrestle with intellectually and spiritually. I encourage you to take the time to journal your responses, discuss them with peers, or meditate on them in prayer. This reflective practice is vital for integrating the concepts discussed in the book with your own experiences and for fostering a deeper understanding of your vocational journey. Use these questions as a tool to explore your thoughts, feelings, and insights, allowing them to guide you toward a more profound and personal discernment of your calling.

Call-Out Boxes

Throughout the chapters, you'll also find "Call-Out Boxes" offering practical exercises to help bring the book's concepts into your daily life. These boxes introduce specific practices, ranging from reflective journaling to group activities and personal inventories, each an invitation to engage actively with the material. Each exercise is designed to deepen your exploration of the chapter themes and to help you embody the ideas in ways that resonate with your unique journey.

Some exercises are simple reflections; others may encourage you to organize a small group activity, start a new journaling practice, or experiment with a creative approach to vocational discernment. I encourage you to try those that resonate most with you, and perhaps revisit others over time as your journey unfolds. You'll find additional guidance for some practices in the appendix, providing detailed steps to ensure you get the most from each exercise. I hope you can let these call-out boxes serve as opportunities to experiment, reflect, and integrate the concepts in practical, meaningful ways, helping you bring the journey of vocational discernment into the reality of everyday life.

Appendix

At the end of the book you will find an appendix filled with resources to support and deepen your exploration of the themes discussed in the chapters. The appendix includes tools and exercises designed to complement the book's content and provide practical guidance for your journey of vocational discernment and spiritual growth. These resources are organized by chapter themes, offering diverse perspectives and approaches that invite you to engage with the material in new ways.

Whether you are looking for theological insights, practical applications, or reflective exercises, the appendix serves as a companion to help you integrate these ideas into your life and work. I encourage you to explore the sections that resonate with you and to revisit the appendix as your journey unfolds. Each resource has been chosen to inspire, challenge, and equip you for the ongoing work of cultivating your calling. Let this appendix be a space where you can continue the conversation, expanding your understanding and enriching your practice in meaningful ways.

A Prayer for Readers

In the next chapter, I dive into the very concept of vocation itself. I explore its historical and theological roots, its contemporary relevance, and its potential for shaping a more just and compassionate world. As we explore these roots, let us remember that this exploration is not merely an intellectual exercise but a deeply personal and communal one. May you emerge from these pages with a deeper understanding of your calling and a renewed commitment to living it out with courage and love.

My prayer for you, reader, is that you find both guidance where you need help seeing your next step and tension where you realize something has to change in you first. May you feel God's presence deeply in your life, helping you see clearly the gifts and passions you possess and how best to use them in service to others.

For those learning outside traditional institutions, may you find validation and encouragement in your experiences, recognizing that divine truth is revealed in many ways. For those in formal theological education, I pray you gain the insight to connect your academic pursuits with applications that reflect love and justice beyond the institution that will grant you a degree and credential.

For all readers, I hope this book serves as a source of inspiration and practical guidance, fostering a deeper connection to God, to others, and to the communities you serve. May it help us all to cultivate a more just, compassionate, and spiritually enriched world.

PART I

SEEDS

Many vocations begin in mystery: a hint of something not yet visible, a seed nestled in the soil. These opening chapters plant the foundational questions and frameworks that make vocational reflection possible. We begin with the unseen: formation, discernment, and the conditions that allow a sense of call to emerge and take root.

When we think of tending plants, it is with some concern and care. It is personal. We water what we hope will grow. We return, again and again, even when there's little to show. Vocation asks something similar of us: attention, patience, and trust in what is not yet fully formed.

Seeds don't grow by force. They need the right relationships: with water, with warmth, with time. Likewise, vocational life begins not with certainty, but with curiosity, attention, and care. These early explorations may feel small, even tentative, but they carry within them the shape of what may one day bloom. What follows is not a blueprint but a fertile ground from which your own questions and commitments might grow.

What We Find in the Soil

Sometimes, people think that the way to avoid offending people is to be abstract and vague. *If we are careful enough*—these people think—*we can say something that everyone can agree on, and no one will be upset by.* But it hardly ever works out that way, does it? The things we reference give away our presumptions and directions. How can a book that is framed with the words *tending*, *seeds*, *growth*, and *abundance* appeal to people who are not farmers and do not work the soil? Isn't it biased to frame a book on call in an agricultural metaphor at a time when the cost of land to grow in prevents many from doing just that? And shouldn't we talk about whose land this actually is? And how exhausted many of us come to most conversations? Yes.

Sometimes, I think we're best served by being rooted in tradition and reaching to a future we can imagine only the barest shape of. When I do that, I try to imagine what it would be like to have someone in the future point back to me now and think about it as historical tradition. In the 1700s, the poet William Blake said, *We become what we behold.* Later, the philosopher Ludwig Feuerbach wrote, *Der Mensch ist, was er ißt*, which has some great letters in it and means *Man is what he eats*. And that's true but not the whole story.

    The whole story is too large to consume. We'd need something larger to take it all in, and I'd worry about that something if we found it. In the 1960s, the media theorist Marshall McLuhan used to say that *First we make our tools and then our tools make us.* The things we use to work with work on us. Days of shoveling mark us with calluses and strength in the back. I've heard of people who feel the buzz of their phone's vibration in their pocket even when they don't have their phone on them. Our bodies have come to want the feeling of something to pay attention to: someone or something reaching out. The internet also thinks Tupac said, *Reality is wrong. Dreams are for real*, but, when you try to find out where and when Pac dropped that line, the details slip away. Water into the sand.

Sometimes, when I scroll past another Instagram post of a white woman in a flowing dress holding a basket of sun-ripened tomatoes, I think about Karen Washington laughing. I don't know if she's a laugher that way, but I imagine she is. Not because there's anything wrong with white women growing tomatoes, but because of how thoroughly she refuses to let that image be the only story farming tells. *When I put my hands in the soil,* Washington says, *and I look at that brown skin, I say:* "Hello ancestors; thank you, thank you." That is the work happening at Rise & Root Farm.

Resistance is not always signs and shouts and raised fists. Those things matter, but, sometimes, the work is teaching people to grow collards in the Bronx or founding a farmers' market in a neighborhood that grocery stores decided wasn't worth their time. Sometimes, the work is a shift to speaking about food *apartheid* instead of food *deserts* because deserts are natural and life-supporting, but there's nothing natural about industrial decisions about who gets fresh vegetables and who doesn't. That's why Washington and her partners insist that farming isn't just about production or pastoral aesthetics. It's about healing historical wounds and feeding present communities. *This, too, is farming.* These urban plots, these Black and brown hands, these bodies working the land—this, too, is agriculture. This, too, is growing food. This, too, is connecting with the earth.

Sometimes, I think about an old story I know about burning bushes and bare feet on holy ground. I wonder if holiness isn't just in the flame. Maybe it's in the ground itself, in the hands that work it, and in the communities that eat from it. Maybe, other times, that voice might not come from above but burst forth from the ground, life abundant. It might be an invitation to breathe deeply—the Jewish storyteller David Abrams once told me he was taught that YHWH is the sound of Creation breathing. So put your hands in soil—whatever soil you have—and grow what your people need. And remember that growing isn't neat. Plants are not machines. Knowledge of the seed shouldn't just be so that we get to eat the fruit. Not everyone tills the earth, but everyone needs what soil yields. No language is universal but hunger and love. Let us grow something worth sharing.

1

Vocation

Before I can tell my life what I want to do with it, I must listen to my life telling me who I am.

—Parker Palmer

For us, the solitary human being is a contradiction in terms.

—Desmond Tutu

This chapter is a lens through which to read the rest of the book. It lays the groundwork for understanding how vocation infuses every aspect of our lives, guiding us in our search for meaning and faithful purpose. As we explore the living nature of vocation here, we'll keep in mind the role that discernment plays in sustaining this journey, a process that, as we'll discuss in the second chapter, helps us identify what to carry forward and what to release as we answer our evolving call. I invite you to consider the dynamic nature of vocation not as a static destination but as an evolving journey that shapes, and is shaped by, our experiences, communities, and the world around us. Reflecting on vocation helps individuals understand who they aspire to be, how they connect with their communities, and what trajectory their lives might take moving forward.

The journey of vocational discernment often oscillates between deep personal reflection and communal engagement. While Parker Palmer encourages us to listen to our life telling us who we are, Desmond Tutu reminds us that this listening always happens within a web of relationships that shapes both what we hear and how we interpret it.[1]

---

[1] Desmond Tutu, "Ubuntu: On the Nature of Human Community," in *God Is Not a Christian: And Other Provocations*, ed. John Allen (San Francisco: HarperOne, 2011).

By exploring and discerning vocation, people can align their daily actions with their deepest values, increasing the likelihood that their life's work resonates with their sense of God's call. Through this lens, we will navigate the complexities of discerning our paths and responding to the calls that beckon us forward.

While these ideas sound appealing, it's important to remember that life unfolds at the ground level amid the everyday messiness we all experience. Vocation, like a seed waiting to sprout, contains within it both the potential for growth and the need for proper conditions to flourish. Thus, while we will engage with big theological ideas, I will equally focus on how these ideas manifest in everyday life. I want us to look at how people navigate their vocational journeys amid the stuff of everyday life. The chapter is divided into three sections: first, we clarify what we mean by "vocation"; second, we explore how people experience vocation; and third, we discuss the consequences of taking vocational discernment seriously, reflecting on the multiple things that call to us for attention.

Perspectives and Definitions

Too often, writing on vocation and discernment sounds like something from a fantasy novel or a superhero movie. There are perspectives that frame the concept of a calling as if God places knowledge of our future fully formed in our hearts and minds, waiting to be discovered through the right kind of praying and quiet sitting. After we find *it*, we have unlocked some new knowledge of self and can serve in new ways. Parker Palmer is emblematic of this approach, writing beautifully about a deep contemplative search for call. Palmer writes:

> Vocation ... comes from listening. I must listen to my life and try to understand what it is truly about—quite apart from what I would like it to be about—or my life will never represent anything real in the world, no matter how earnest my intentions.... Before I can tell my life what I want to do with it, I must listen to my life telling me who I am. I must listen for the truths and values at the heart of my own identity, not the standards by which I must live—but the standards by which I cannot help but live if I am living my own life.[2]

There is nothing in Palmer I actively disagree with on the surface, but the idea that vocation is "truly about" something can feel like what you are called to is one single unchanging thing. I can support that idea if the "one thing" is something broad, like how Catholic teaching suggests there is a "universal call to holiness" and vocation is

---

[2] Parker J. Palmer, *Let Your Life Speak: Listening for the Voice of Vocation* (San Francisco: Jossey-Bass, 2000), 4.

"a call from God to a distinctive state of life, in which the person can reach holiness."[3] That is broad enough that I can get behind it, but its broadness often offers little specific guidance for life outside explicit religious roles.

This gap was significantly addressed during the Protestant Reformation, particularly through the work of Martin Luther. He radically redefined vocation (*Beruf*), arguing that God's call extended beyond the monastery or priesthood into all legitimate spheres of human activity, from farming and parenting to governing.[4] For Luther, these secular stations were not lesser paths but holy ground, places where individuals could faithfully serve God and neighbor through their daily labor and relationships.[5] This theological move profoundly democratized the concept of calling, investing ordinary life with divine significance, though subsequent thinkers would continue wrestling with how one discerns and lives into such a call amid life's complexities.

I also wrestle with Presbyterian theologian Frederick Buechner's definition of vocation. He wrote that "the place God calls you to is the place where your deep gladness and the world's deep hunger meet."[6] While these "big picture" definitions may be poetic, inspiring, and true, they also remain somewhat vague regarding practical application. They invite us to consider the intersection of our passions, the needs of the world, and our desire to move toward holiness, but they don't always provide the clarity needed for specific life choices. More is often required.

For many, discerning what exactly constitutes their "deep gladness" or identifying the "world's deep hunger" can be an ongoing, complex process. When a vocation is defined too broadly, it may become abstract and challenging to apply to the concrete decisions and actions of everyday life. For instance, knowing that one's ultimate goal is holiness does not necessarily help discerning specific career choices, relationships, or personal commitments. Individuals can struggle to translate this general call into specific, actionable steps.

Drawing on the insights of Ada María Isasi-Díaz, whose theology emerges from Latina women's experiences, we might say that discerning vocation begins not with abstraction but in "*lo cotidiano*," the everyday realities where ordinary people encounter meaning.[7] Here, call is most often discerned, heard, and lived. Rather than

---

3 This teaching is rooted in scripture (1 Thess 4:3; Eph 1:4) and is prominently articulated in the Second Vatican Council's Dogmatic Constitution on the Church, *Lumen Gentium,* chap. 5.

4 Robert Benne, "Martin Luther on the Vocations of the Christian," in *Oxford Research Encyclopedia of Religion* online (August 31, 2016).

5 Gene Edward Veith, "Vocation: The Theology of the Christian Life," *Journal of Markets & Morality* 14, no. 1 (Spring 2011): 119–31.

6 Frederick Buechner, *Wishful Thinking: A Seeker's ABC* (New York: HarperOne, 1993), 118–19.

7 Ada María Isasi-Díaz, "Lo Cotidiano: A Key Element of Mujerista Theology," *Journal of Hispanic/Latino Theology* 10 (2002): 5–17.

waiting for a grand, singular moment of revelation, this approach invites us to notice what is already present in our daily lives: the patterns of joy and frustration, the places we show up again and again, the relationships that shape us, the injustices we can no longer ignore.

Is vocation a calling? Yes. Do concrete circumstances and the systems and structures of the world affect the ways in which I can respond to that calling? Also yes.

Vocation, then, is not a treasure buried deep within or a path hidden in the clouds: It emerges through the possibilities, constraints, and choices of our lived realities. This shift in approach to vocation also helps us recognize how not all constraints are inherently negative. Many of the structures and relationships in our lives provide the very stability and support that make discerning and living a calling possible. Rather, it's about recognizing how these realities (both challenging and supportive) become the sacred soil where we make our choices, and where God's invitations are often found.

This understanding of vocation, as something actively constructed within the givens of life, finds a powerful philosophical echo in the words of French philosopher Paul Ricœur. Reflecting on his own faith near the end of his life, Ricœur wrote that Christianity was "a chance transformed into destiny through continuous choice."[8] Born into a Huguenot (French Protestant) family in 1913, at a time when France was overwhelmingly Catholic, Ricœur would have inherited a faith tradition profoundly shaped by centuries of persecution and resilience. This historical legacy, a core element of Huguenot identity passed down through family and community, formed part of the complex chance of his existence: an unchosen circumstance, a specific set of possibilities and constraints defining his religious and cultural inheritance. Yet, for Ricœur, this was not where the story ended.

Vocation, like faith, is not found in remaining a passive subject of such givens, whether they be minority status or the weighty memory of historical suffering. Rather, vocation is realized through the active and ongoing "continuous choice" to engage with these inherited realities, a daily affirmation that the road before us is ours to walk. This persistent agency allows one to interpret these circumstances, to make commitments within them, and thus to weave them into a meaningful "destiny," into a vocational path that is neither wholly predetermined by the initial "chance" of birth, nor merely accidental, but is consciously and continuously authored over time. This transformation converts what began as circumstantial chance into something profoundly intentional: a calling we actively embrace rather than passively receive.

---

8 In his original French: "*Un hasard transformé en destin par un choix continu.*" Paul Ricœur, *La Critique et la Conviction: Entretien avec François Azouvi et Marc de Launay* (Paris: Calmann-Lévy, 1995), 219.

Yet where is God in this interplay of circumstance and agency? If vocation is a calling, then the "chance" circumstances of our lives, the very stuff of *lo cotidiano*, can be understood as a place to encounter God. Our calls do not often arrive as a disembodied voice from on high. More routinely, they are the felt whispers that bubble up through the concrete possibilities and limitations of our lives: through the needs we discern, the injustices that stir us, the relationships that shape us, and the surprising opportunities that emerge from seemingly random events.

The chances of life are not devoid of divine presence; they are the raw material through which God invites response. Our continuous choice is not a solitary act of self-creation, but a co-creative process of discerning and responding to the divine invitations embedded in the everyday. God is not only the one who calls from beyond, but also the one who accompanies us within: within the givenness of history, the layered texture of memory, the daily choices through which we construct meaning. Vocation, then, is neither imposed nor invented from scratch. It is a co-authored life, unfolding between divine invitation and human participation, where the Spirit moves not only in moments of revelation, but also in the faithful tending of what chance has placed in our care.

Ricœur's vision of faith as a chance transformed into destiny through continuous choice thus enriches our understanding of vocation not as a static discovery but as an ongoing, dynamic process of co-creation with the Divine, deeply embedded in the particularities of our lives. This resonated profoundly with my own journey. In full disclosure, I'll say that this idea of "continuous choice" isn't just a concept I admire: It's something I've lived. As someone raised outside of any faith tradition, in a time and place where the dominant cultural trends were moving away from religion, there was never any outward momentum pushing me toward the Church. And inwardly, I've never felt like I was discovering some buried, essential version of myself, as if there were a single right answer to the question of who I'm supposed to be. Have there been moments that felt profoundly powerful? Absolutely. Did they offer real guidance about how I wanted to live my life? Without a doubt. But did they reveal a total and complete "real me" that had previously been elusive? No.

What has felt true is this: the shape of my life has come through repeated choosing, sometimes with clarity, often in uncertainty, always with intention. There are parts of who I am that were given: context, history, family, body. But there is also the person I have worked to become, chosen to become, again and again. In the language of early Quaker minister Isaac Penington, I've known moments when I felt "the life and power flowing in upon me from the free fountain."[9] And I've known long, weary

---

9 Isaac Penington, "Some Directions to the Panting Soul." Originally published 1661, in Early English Books Online 2, University of Michigan Library Digital Collections, accessed May 11, 2025,

periods without a fountain or spring in sight. I think that's why Ricœur's phrase lands so deeply with me: My faith, too, is a chance transformed into destiny through continuous choice. It gave a name to something I'd already been living. That kind of choosing doesn't feel like self-invention; it feels like faithfulness: staying with the questions, honoring the givens, and participating in something larger than myself by choosing, again and again, to try to stay close to the living water.

I don't expect these particular framings to be everyone's touchstone, nor do I think my experience of call is universal. Rather, I offer my personal resonance with Ricœur's idea of continuous choice as an example of how theological concepts can sometimes land with such force because they give language and shape to an already lived reality. Sometimes, naming an experience well can be transformative on its own. In this spirit of connecting personal experience to broader theological currents, and understanding how we each make meaning within our unique contexts, we turn to the vital question that such an embodied understanding of vocation raises.

With my understanding that vocation is rarely a static blueprint of life discovered whole, vocational discernment is not passive waiting. Vocation emerges from the concrete, often messy, particularities of our daily lives, complete with its systemic influences, possibilities, and constraints. Vocational discernment, then, is a faithful, grace-filled, and increasingly conscious praxis: an ongoing embodied response to the divine invitations we encounter within the very texture of our lived experience and relationships. This understanding leads to a deeper question: If this is how calling emerges, then whose realities, whose particularities, and whose praxis are we centering in our theological reflection and action?

If God's invitations are indeed woven into the daily, embodied, and relationally embedded experiences of all people, then any theology of vocation aiming for integrity must take with utmost seriousness the concrete conditions, systemic pressures, and lived stories of all, especially those historically pushed to the margins and whose agency is most often constrained. Liberation theology shifts the frame precisely from this contextual and justice-oriented foundation, insisting that God's call is not only personal but profoundly social and political, emerging with particular clarity and power through sustained, humble engagement with the suffering, resilience, creative resistance, and transformative wisdom of those whose voices are not usually centered.

Although traditional theologies often root vocation primarily in God's initial salvific call (the study of which we technically call "soteriology") or in roles within the Church ("ecclesiology"), a liberation theology of vocation argues that, in our contemporary context, understanding God's call requires beginning with the lived experience of those navigating unjust systems. Praxis becomes the necessary starting point for discerning both the saving and the serving dimensions of vocation. Grounded in these lived realities, the challenge lies in discerning which specific path aligns best with one's gifts, circumstances, and the needs of one's community. This indicates that the concept of vocation requires constant tending. Let me give an example via metaphor.

If you are in someone's home and they say, "I love this piece of art," chances are that what you are looking at will be the same next time you visit. Conversely, if they take you into their garden and say, "I love this persimmon tree," you know that the tree will continue to grow and change over time. The tree is no less a "loved thing" than the art, but it is a changing, growing thing. What is loved now is not exactly what was loved before. Similarly, I think that vocation is a living thing.

Just as the tree requires nurturing and adapts to the seasons, so does our vocation evolve with our experiences and insights. Even as it changes and grows, the tree is still the tree. So, too, with vocation. This dynamic nature of vocation means it is not a fixed commodity or role, but a journey of continual growth, adaptation, and willingness to see what new thing God is creating in our midst. Pope Francis has some language that is resonant with this:

> A vocation is a fruit that ripens in a well cultivated field of mutual love that becomes mutual service in the context of an authentic ecclesial life. No vocation is born of itself or lives for itself. A vocation flows from the heart of God and blossoms in the good soil of faithful people, in the experience of fraternal love. Did not Jesus say: "By this all men will know that you are my disciples, if you have love for one another"? Let us dispose our hearts therefore to being "good soil," by listening, receiving and living out the word, and thus bearing fruit.[10]

Recognizing the ripening of the fruit of vocation can free us from the pressure of finding a single, unchanging calling and open us to the possibilities of transformation and discovery. Approaching vocational discernment and looking for unchanging certainty may work for some, but for many, the process is sloppy, less certain, and tinged with doubts, imposter syndrome, and mistakes.

Framing vocation as dynamic and evolving allows us to be more patient with and forgiving of ourselves and others. This perspective encourages us to remain open to new experiences and insights, understanding that our callings may shift and grow as we do. The more we pay attention to the present, the more likely it is that we will see the beginning of what comes next as it is still small. Whatever comes next has

---

10 Francis, "Message of Pope Francis for the 51st World Day of Prayer for Vocations," Vatican.va, January 15, 2014. Accessed August 4, 2024.

already started. With this mind-set, we can approach vocation with curiosity and adaptability, ready to embrace the unexpected turns our journeys might take. We will explore discernment in the next chapter, but it's important to note here that I see it as intimately tied to calling.

> A Practice to Consider:
> ## Life Review
>
> *Our lives are marked by moments that reveal who we are and who we might become. Reflecting on these pivotal points can illuminate the paths we are called to walk.*
>
> 1. Identify three moments from your life that particularly help to explain how it is that you got to this moment.
> 2. For each of them, ask yourself what qualities or actions did these moments bring out in you? How might they illuminate your evolving sense of purpose? Do they provide any insight into any current questions you have?

In my view, discernment is an intrinsic part of what we're called to do. Perhaps this is part of what a universal call to holiness means: a universal call to listen. This principle is well established in Jewish thought, exemplified by the prayer, "Shema Yisrael," which means "Hear, O Israel." The Shema is one of the most important prayers in Judaism, calling the faithful to listen and respond to God's commandments. Given Jesus's Jewishness, I think remembering the importance of the call to listen is vital. It underscores the importance of attentive listening to cultivate a relationship with God and live out one's faith with intention and purpose.

None of us is granted the luxury of figuring everything out once and never having to reassess or seek deeper understanding. In this regard, I am greatly influenced by the work of Brazilian liberation educator Paulo Freire and his idea that the fundamental human vocation is to become more human.[11] For Freire, becoming more human meant developing our capacity to think critically about our world and to act consciously to transform it. He believed that, as we learn to read both words and our world more deeply, we endlessly become more fully ourselves and more capable of relationship with others.

As beloved children of God, we are constantly unfolding, revealing ourselves to ourselves and others, with God guiding us toward greater possibilities for us as

---

11 Paulo Freire, *Pedagogia do Oprimido* (Rio de Janeiro, Brazil: Paz e Terra, 1987), 52; "vocação ontológica e histórica de ser mais."

individuals and within our communities. However, this doesn't mean that we are perpetually seeking without ever finding. There is an equilibrium to find. We can achieve clarity during discernment and then settle into that understanding, growing roots while listening and remaining open to new insights. It's important not to confuse continuous discernment with the inability to find stability. Sometimes, things will be quiet and deepening, other times more raucous and turbulent.

As a member of the Religious Society of Friends, I'm used to a quiet way of approaching my search for a call. We are oriented to listen for God's still, small voice in a contemplative way. That works for some people, including me, most of the time. But I'm deeply aware that this quiet and reflective mode of listening doesn't hold a monopoly on methods of discernment. Both my Quaker tradition and the Ignatian tradition of the Catholics tend to be relatively subdued affairs, with lots of silence and listening. Because people from these traditions are some of the ones who have written about discernment the most, our perspectives dominate the literature on the topic. But this is not the only way.

Years ago my friend Patrick Reyes playfully mentioned that he was glad that silent prayer worked for me, but he usually found that a loud table full of friends and family was more beneficial for him. He found more clarity about his calling in the tears and laughter surrounding a kitchen table. Amen. Hearing vocation may happen in the midst of rowdy conversations just as well as in an hour of silent prayer.

For those of us who are Christian, part of what we are looking to do ought to be trying to be more Christlike in our actions.[12] Based on my reading of the Gospels, part of that seems to be trying to meet people where they are, working with them on their terms rather than your own or the norms of the dominant society. In our context, that means not presuming that everyone will have a single experience of vocation. Do some people discern a clear, step-by-step plan that leads to a straightforward job and task they are called to? Yes, sometimes that does happen. Is it common? No. Much more often, people experience vocation directionally.

We are called *toward* something rather than to a specific point. Standing in Los Angeles and feeling called "eastward" is quite different from feeling called to Boston. What I find helpful to remember is that something important might happen in Detroit or in the airport en route. Vocation as direction means that being in motion *toward* what I feel called to is being faithful to the calling. If only the goal concerns me, then all the miles between LA and here can feel like obstacles to my "real" vocation. And, of course, this isn't just about geography and travel: What we "move toward" can be new parts of our lives, not just new places. I think that Reyes is excellent on this point.

---

12 1 John 2:6; John 13:14–15; 1 Corinthians 11:1; Ephesians 5:1–2; etc.

His perspective allows for a more flexible and expansive approach to discerning our purpose, acknowledging that meaningful experiences and growth often occur along the way. He writes that his definition of Christian vocation is "God's call to new life for all creation."

> Vocation has meant God calling me to live. Only when I was finally given the freedom and space to discern what living into full human flourishing looks like was I able to discern a call to do or be anything other than just alive.[13]

This spotlight on new life is a powerful way to think about what vocation is. It is helpful on its own and as a lens with other perspectives. Let's consider teachings from Ignatian spirituality and what Reyes's perspective adds to it.

Ignatian spirituality offers a rich perspective on vocation, emphasizing the interplay between "freedom from" and "freedom for." This tradition teaches that discernment involves being liberated from internal obstacles like disordered attachments, sin, and guilt. Ignatius encouraged a detachment from these hindrances to cultivate a state of indifference: not apathy, but a profound openness to whatever God wills. This is important for freeing oneself from fears and anxieties that might prevent a wholehearted response to God's call. The "Suscipe" prayer of St. Ignatius captures this sentiment:

> Take, Lord, and receive all my liberty, my memory, my understanding, and my entire will. All I have and call my own, You have given to me. To You, Lord, I return it. Everything is Yours; do with it what You will. Give me only Your love and Your grace, that is enough for me.[14]

Once freed from the "disordered affections" that impede our faithfulness, Ignatian spirituality turns toward "freedom for," which focuses on embracing and pursuing a life aligned with God's will. This includes discerning God's specific intentions for our lives, which often emerge not through grand revelations but through subtle movements of the heart.

Reyes's perspective adds an important dimension to this understanding. He emphasizes that vocation involves living into the fullness of human flourishing, seeking "new life for all creation." This view broadens the scope of vocation beyond

---

[13] Patrick B. Reyes, *Nobody Cries When We Die: God, Community, and Surviving to Adulthood* (St. Louis: Chalice Press, 2016), 13.

[14] David Coffey, "The Ignatian Suscipe Prayer: Its Text and Meaning," *Journal of Jesuit Studies* 5, no. 4 (2018): 511–29.

individual spiritual fulfillment to encompass the entire community's well-being. He wants our freedom to be yoked to the freedom of others. Sometimes, people need freedom from more than internal struggles. Sometimes, people need freedom from external circumstances. Sometimes, people need freedom from hunger and the fear that their family will go hungry. Sometimes, people need freedom from addictions to substances or consumerism. Sometimes, these are situations of self-denial, but, many times, people need self-love.

The story of the prophet Elijah vividly illustrates the journey of vocation, emphasizing the importance of openness and community. Elijah, convinced he is the only faithful prophet left, flees to a cave on Mount Horeb.[15] He cries out to God, saying, "I alone am left, and they are seeking my life, to take it away."[16] There aren't stage directions written into scripture, but I've always felt that Elijah's tone is a mix of despair and whine. "I'm the only faithful one. Harumph."

God repeatedly comes to Elijah in the cave, trying to draw him out of his despair. Despite witnessing a powerful wind, an earthquake, and a fire, Elijah remains in the cave, steadfast in his belief that he is alone. It isn't until Elijah hears a gentle whisper that he finally steps out of the cave. God then gives Elijah a directive: "Go, return on your way to the wilderness."[17] God also reassures Elijah, revealing that, though he feels alone, once he begins his journey again, he will find seven thousand more faithful still in Israel.[18] Only when Elijah gets back on the road, following God's instructions, does he begin to realize that he is not alone. This isolation is something I am deeply familiar with.

Images of the "self-made man" and people who can "pull themselves up by their bootstraps" exist as cultural images of self-sufficiency, especially popular in dominant cultural contexts in the United States. Reyes rightly critiques this kind of thinking as a form of the "hero's journey" framework, which isolates purpose as an individualistic pursuit rather than understanding it as inherently communal and relational.[19] I think that these kinds of stories about ourselves rarely have their roots in God's work. This is challenging because much of higher education, theological education, and American culture cultivate this prideful individualism. As theologian Willie James Jennings has argued, "White self-sufficient masculinity is the quintessential image of an educated person, an image deeply embedded in the collective psyche of Western education and

---

15 1 Kings 19.
16 1 Kings 19:10.
17 1 Kings 19:15.
18 1 Kings 19:18.
19 Patrick B. Reyes, *The Purpose Gap: Empowering Communities of Color to Find Meaning and Thrive* (Louisville: Westminster John Knox Press, 2021), 33–34.

theological education."[20] Jennings will show up more in the sixth chapter's discussion of identity and belonging, but it is worth introducing his awareness of cultural norms that make it such that it takes intention and energy to resist isolation, especially in the context of vocation.

God had to persistently call Elijah out of his isolation, showing him that a fuller understanding and fulfillment of his calling could only be realized in motion and community. This story reminds us that, even in moments of deep doubt and solitude, stepping out in faith and following God's call can lead us to discover that we are part of a larger, faithful community. Elijah's journey from isolation to the rediscovery of community teaches us that our sense of vocation is deeply intertwined with those of others. The path of vocation, while challenging, ultimately leads to greater connection and collective purpose.

A Practice to Consider:

Leave the Cave

Sometimes we find ourselves stuck in places of fear or isolation, believing we must journey alone. Yet the gentle whispers of God and the support of others call us forward into community and purpose.

1. Identify a "Cave": Name what holds you back. Fear, exhaustion, or the belief you must do it alone. Where are you stuck?
2. Listen for the Whisper: Notice small nudges or encouragements inviting you forward. What calls you forward?
3. Take One Step: Act this week. Reach out, join a group, or offer your gifts. What small thing can be done?
4. Look for Companions: Who will you find when you begin to move? How can you contact them for support?

Vocation is finding a way to live in the freedom that comes when our liberation is bound up with the liberation of others. Discerning vocation involves a dynamic interplay between being freed from what hinders us and embracing what calls us forward. This "interplay" unfolds throughout one's life. It is not a once-and-done kind of thing, but a continuous process done in the context of community. I think the "bands of prophets" that Elijah finds likely had to ask themselves collectively, "What

---

[20] Willie James Jennings, *After Whiteness: An Education in Belonging* (Grand Rapids, MI: William B. Eerdmans, 2020), 32.

is God calling us to?" That is, vocation isn't just a calling I need to consider for myself but for my community as well.

> Vocation is the long arc of a life spent searching for purpose and acting out call, and it applies to individuals as well as collectives. While vocation often appears more clearly as one looks back, discerning one's next steps toward a life of meaning and purpose is the ongoing work of vocation.[21]

If vocation is about how I am called by God and how my "I" is connected to a community, then the freedom I am called to is a freedom for us all.

I see in this idea echoes of the Bantu concept of Ubuntu: "I am because we are."[22] There is often an inherent mutuality in the callings placed on our lives. Is it possible that sometimes someone can be called to solitude away from community? I think so, but I don't think it is expected, *and* ... when it does happen, it isn't accompanied by Elijah's sense of despair and lament. Living into vocation is often accompanied by a sense of rightness and connection. Pope Francis is again helpful here:

> The Lord's call is not an intrusion of God in our freedom; it is not a "cage" or a burden to be borne. On the contrary, it is the loving initiative whereby God encounters us and invites us to be part of a great undertaking. He opens before our eyes the horizon of a greater sea and an abundant catch.[23]

Understanding vocation as a dynamic, evolving journey rather than a fixed destination invites us to embrace the unfolding nature of our callings. This perspective allows us to recognize that vocation is not merely about arriving at a particular role or position but about engaging in a continuous process of discovery and reorientation to what new things God is doing in our midst.

Moral Orientation and the Shape of Vocation

If vocation is not simply a role or job, but a way of being in the world, a way of responding to what matters most, then it is inseparable from our moral life. What we name as "call" is often the felt pull to align our life with what we believe to be right, good,

---

21 Stephen Lewis, Matthew Wesley Williams, and Dori Grinenko Baker, *Another Way: Living and Leading Change on Purpose* (St. Louis: Chalice Press, 2020), 49.

22 Sheila A. Otieno, "Ethical Thought of Archbishop Desmond Tutu: Ubuntu and Tutu's Moral Modeling as Transformation and Renewal," in *The Palgrave Handbook of African Social Ethics* (Springer International, 2020), 589–604, https://doi.org/10.1007/978-3-030-36490-8_32.

23 Message of His Holiness Pope Francis for the 2019 World Day of Vocations.

sacred, or necessary. That alignment, however, does not happen in isolation. It is shaped by our histories, our communities, our wounds, and our hopes. One way to understand this deeper structure of calling is through the lens of what I call a Moral Orienting System (MOS), a term from my colleague and friend, Zachary Moon, a pastoral theologian and chaplain.

As Moon frames it, there are four vital aspects to know about a MOS.[24] First, it is a "meaningful matrix of values, beliefs, behaviors, and relationships."[25] This means that our moral sense of who we are and what we are called to do does not arise from a single source but from the dynamic interplay of what we hold true (our beliefs), what we cherish (our values), how we act (our behaviors), and the people and communities to whom we are connected (our relationships). These elements are constantly shaping one another, and together, they form the structure through which we interpret our lives and respond to what matters most.

When this matrix is in sync, we tend to feel morally grounded and vocationally clear. When any part of it is thrown off, when our values are in conflict with our actions, or when our relationships no longer support our deepest convictions, we may begin to feel lost or fractured. Importantly, this disorientation is not a sign of failure. As Moon and others remind us, moral stress can be a faithful response to a world that no longer aligns with our sense of what is good. It may be the signal that our MOS is doing its job, refusing to let us remain comfortably aligned with incoherence, hypocrisy, or systems doing harm.

Reorientation, then, is not about returning to a previous state but about discerning what remains trustworthy and beginning again from a place of deeper integrity. In this sense, vocation is not rooted in any single dimension but in the convergence of what we believe to be good, how we try to live it, and who we live it alongside. When these elements cohere, we often experience clarity. When they diverge, we may feel disoriented or estranged from the very source of our call.

Second, a MOS is "socially and culturally informed by family, friends, mentors, religious traditions, and other significant communities, seeking confirmation and validation within situations and working to assimilate and accommodate experiences within its structure of expectation."[26] This means our MOS is not something we invent out of thin air, but something we inherit, assemble, and adapt through our formation in community. Our families, faith traditions, cultural narratives, mentors, and communities all contribute to the structure of our moral expectations.

---

24 Zachary Moon, *Warriors between Worlds: Moral Injury and Identities in Crisis* (Lanham, MD: Lexington Books, 2019).

25 Ibid., 25–27.

26 Ibid., 27–29.

These expectations include both what we think we should do and who we believe we are supposed to be. Consequently, the discernment of vocation is never just a personal or private affair. It is embedded in social structures and cultural meaning-making. It also means that misalignment between our evolving sense of call and the expectations of our communities can provoke conflict, guilt, or shame. Still, that tension can also be holy. It may invite us to reexamine who gets to name what is "moral," and whether the MOS we inherited can bear the weight of our lived experience.

Third, our MOS is "vulnerable to situations or events that overwhelm existing boundaries and assumptions, producing moral stress."[27] Our systems for knowing what is right can be disrupted by experiences that overwhelm its assumptions. Sometimes this happens suddenly, sometimes slowly. Both are moments of moral stress: when something happens that we cannot make sense of with the tools and frameworks we've been using.

That disruption might come from betrayal, disillusionment, failure, or violence. But it can also emerge from clarity: when we suddenly realize that our inherited system has been complicit in harm, or when we witness a truth that reveals our previous understanding to be insufficient. In these moments, the very compass we've used to orient ourselves begins to spin. When that happens, vocational discernment becomes less about identifying a new direction and more about surviving the storm of not knowing which way is true.

Fourth and finally, our MOS is dynamic and can be resilient, gaining stability especially when we seek "to relieve stress through reconnection in meaningful relationships."[28] Though disorientation is painful, it is not inherently pathological. In fact, moral stress may be a sign of deep engagement, evidence that a person is trying to live with integrity in a morally incoherent world. Reorientation, then, becomes a process of repair: of reconnecting with people and practices that help us tell the truth about what has happened and discern how we are called to respond.

This often requires community and spaces of compassion, accountability, and imagination where our disrupted MOS can be re-formed. Through story, accompaniment, and small acts of reconnection, we may begin to find coherence again, not by returning to the old system unchanged, but by integrating what we've learned into a new, more spacious moral framework. And from there, call emerges anew.

Together, these four aspects of MOS show us that moral orientation is not a static possession, but a dynamic, lived process. It is fragile but resilient, shaped in context, and essential to how vocation is discerned, disrupted, and renewed. I believe this frame helps us approach vocation as both a matter of direction (what should I do?) and as a matter of moral location (where am I? with whom? and what is being

---

27 Ibid., 30–31.
28 Ibid., 31–33.

asked of me here?). It recognizes that calls emerge in particular histories, bodies, and communities, and that disruptions in our sense of orientation can provoke vocational crises as well as vocational clarity. When people feel "lost" in their vocation, they are often not simply lacking a plan: They are trying to find coherence again in a disordered moral landscape.

Within this framework, moral disorientation is not reducible to trauma, guilt, or internal conflict (though it may include all three). It is the felt unraveling of one's ability to act, belong, or believe in the ways one once did. It can come from an acute rupture, like a betrayal, failure, or moral injury. It can also come from chronic exposure to systemic injustice, spiritual estrangement, or enduring contradictions between one's values and the world as it is. In these moments, call becomes something we tend instead of chase: We ask, how do I live faithfully in the midst of disorientation?

The MOS framework helps make sense of these experiences. It allows us to understand that vocational clarity is not simply a matter of inner peace or external confirmation. It is a matter of moral coherence, built and rebuilt across time through practices of repair, reflection, and relationship. Instead of merely finding a new role when our call feels fractured, we must work to participate in a process of moral reorientation, to reconnect with what is good, to reclaim moral agency, and to reengage with the communities and traditions that help us make meaning.

This process involves many layers: telling and retelling our stories (narrative reconstruction), practicing moral discernment in conversation with others (moral dialogue), engaging in concrete acts of repair and solidarity (reparative action), and reclaiming a sense of moral belonging within our communities and traditions. These are not ancillary to vocation: They are central to it. They are how call is lived, questioned, stretched, and renewed.

Through the MOS framework, vocation appears as a dynamic response to how one is morally situated in the world. Unlike more static or linear models of call, which assume that vocation is discovered once and followed with fidelity, the MOS perspective understands vocation as unfolding through an ongoing interplay of beliefs, values, behaviors, relationships, and meaning-making. Each of these dimensions can stabilize or destabilize one's moral clarity, and each contributes to the coherence (or disorientation) of vocational discernment.

For example, when a person's core beliefs and values come under strain, their sense of what is right and good may start to unravel. This can come about because of a betrayal by a trusted institution, a theological shift, or the pressure of systemic injustice. In response, a person may feel unable to act in ways that feel congruent with who they are. This is where the behavioral dimension of the MOS becomes important: When people can no longer embody their values in action, the dissonance can trigger feelings of guilt, shame, or self-doubt. They may continue performing the tasks associated with their vocation, but internally feel like a fraud, or like they've lost the thread of what once animated their sense of call.

This disorientation deepens if relationships begin to fracture. The relational dimension of MOS reminds us that vocation is never a solo project. It is nurtured, affirmed, and challenged in community. When those communities no longer feel safe, or when people experience alienation from their mentors, peers, or moral communities, they can begin to feel exiled from the very sources that once sustained their calling. These relational disruptions can erode a person's sense of meaning and purpose, leaving them adrift, unsure whether what once gave their life coherence still holds.

Moon's framework becomes especially helpful as it gives language to what often feels intangible, experiences like when people say they're burned out, uncertain, or misaligned but can't name why. Rather than treating moral disorientation as a vague spiritual malaise or personal failure, MOS invites us to ask which part of the system is under strain. Especially for those whose sense of vocation has been distorted or denied by racism, sexism, colonization, or other systemic forces, the MOS framework can provide language for understanding that disorientation as a response to unjust moral ecologies instead of a personal shortcoming. Rather than pathologizing these experiences, it recognizes them as signs of deep engagement with the complexity of moral life. It allows us to ask: What have they seen or been through that shifted their moral system and sense of trust? What relationships have been strained or lost? What values feel under threat? What meanings need to be reexamined or reimagined? And most importantly, how might the person begin to find footing again? How can they acknowledge they will not be able to return to what was, but can still participate in a process of moral reorientation?

Moral reorientation, crucially, is not a process of "getting back on track." It is about listening for what remains trustworthy, seeking out companions who can hold space for ambiguity and repair, and taking steps (however small) toward reconnection. Moral reorientation may involve telling one's story anew, finding new ways to enact one's values, or embracing new communities that can sustain moral belonging. In vocational terms, this may mean a recommitment to one's original path, a shift in how one understands their role, or even a transformation in the direction of their life's work. Whatever the outcome, the MOS framework offers language for understanding these shifts as part of the ongoing, sacred work of responding to call in a world that does not always make it easy to be faithful.

The MOS model also helps account for why people can feel called and disoriented at the same time. A person might still have clarity about what they are meant to do but find themselves unable to enact it because the system that once supported them has changed or crumbled. For example, a teacher may still feel called to educate and nurture young people but lose their footing because the institutional practices around them have become morally incoherent or unjust. Their disorientation is not a sign that they lack a calling. It is a sign that their moral landscape has shifted in ways that make it harder to act faithfully within it. MOS helps us name that tension.

Further, MOS allows us to see that reorientation is not always an individual journey. Because our moral lives are shaped in relationship, vocational repair often requires communal processes of listening, support, and rebuilding. This is where discernment and accompaniment take on their full moral weight. They are more than just spiritual practices; they are acts of moral care, helping individuals navigate the messy, embodied, and often painful work of finding coherence again. In communities that have long had to discern vocation under conditions of threat or exclusion, communal discernment itself can become a liberative practice, one that insists on the dignity, giftedness, and sacred purpose of the people we love and serve, and who love us.

While reorientation can heal individuals, it is equally about resisting and repairing the systems that fracture moral coherence in the first place. It involves reclaiming one's moral footing for both personal clarity and for the sake of others and the world. For some, vocation will mean tending to themselves and those closest to them, practicing healing, accompaniment, and presence in the midst of fractured realities. For others, it will mean challenging unjust systems, building new institutions, or reimagining communal life in ways that nourish integrity and flourishing. In both cases, the work of vocation is never only about self-actualization. It is about responding to the conditions of our time with moral imagination and faithful resistance.

Throughout this book, the concept of a Moral Orienting System will appear as a kind of quiet companion, a framework to help interpret the moral and theological complexity of vocational life. While its full theoretical depth is rooted in interdisciplinary research, including moral psychology, trauma studies, theology, and ethics, what matters here is this: Vocation is about how we stay morally located in a world that constantly disorients us as well as what we are called to do. Tending that orientation is vocational work, especially when done through relationship, reflection, and action. It is the slow, sacred work of living one's call in a world that does not make faithfulness easy.

Experiences of Call

While it is interesting to talk about *what* vocation is, I have always felt that discussing *how* it is experienced is also important. Sometimes, the how of a thing shapes its what. If we only tend to what a thing is, ignoring what it feels like to encounter it (or what to do when we come across it), we run the risk of our knowledge never connecting with practice. To that end, I think there are two dimensions of calling that deserve discussion as well. First, vocation can be experienced as arising from different places in one's life. Second, when these experiences occur, they can persist at varying intensities and durations.

Vocation can be felt as emerging from within us or be prompted by external circumstances and interactions, often spanning between individual and community influences. This continuum illustrates how our personal introspective journeys intersect with communal experiences and expectations. On one end, the individual dimension involves reflecting on our desires, strengths, and passions. On the other end, the communal dimension encompasses how our communities shape and affirm our callings.

The overlapping space in the middle highlights the dynamic interplay where personal and communal elements converge, shaping a holistic understanding of vocation. This interplay of inner convictions and communal expectations mirrors the dynamic nature of our moral lives. The places where beliefs, behaviors, values, and relationships converge shape both our actions and how we come to see and name our sense of call. By exploring this continuum, we can better appreciate how our internal reflections and external engagements together inform and guide our vocational paths.

Internal Call: Rational and Affective Dimensions

I think about internal experiences of call as something that can manifest in two distinct ways: rational and affective. I believe there is more overlap between these two "distinct ways" than many like to claim, but I think (and feel) it is worth distinguishing between them on an experiential basis. Understanding these dimensions helps individuals navigate their vocational journeys with an adaptive approach, incorporating both thoughtful analysis and emotional resonance. Here, we explore how each type of experience uniquely contributes to vocational discernment and how they can be integrated for a fuller understanding of one's calling.

Rational experiences involve a logical and thoughtful process of discernment. These can take the form of persistent thoughts that linger longer than expected, nudging us toward a particular direction. For example, someone might consistently think about pursuing a career in counseling after repeatedly finding themselves as the go-to person for friends seeking advice. These thoughts often arise unexpectedly but stay with us, subtly influencing our decisions and actions. Over time, this growing sense of rightness about a particular choice or trajectory solidifies, providing a sense of clarity and purpose that feels true and deeply rooted in one's inner life.

This dimension also involves deep introspective reflection, where individuals consider their personal stories, life experiences, and significant moments that have shaped their identity. By listening attentively to their own life story, individuals can uncover commitments and values that are central to their sense of vocation, aligning their future actions with these foundational elements. When we think about a choice, we can ask ourselves what decisions best fit the story we want our life to tell.

Affective experiences, in contrast, are characterized by strong emotional responses and visceral reactions. Engaging with specific media, such as a book or film, might evoke a profound sense of "more-ness" or heightened awareness that transcends ordinary experiences. For instance, someone might watch a documentary about social justice and feel an overwhelming sense of urgency and passion to join advocacy work. Imagining oneself on a specific path can elicit visceral reactions, such as joy or dread. These gut feelings serve as emotional signposts that guide us toward or away from particular vocational paths based on how they resonate with our core values and desires.

It's crucial to recognize, too, how our experiences of callings are often filtered through the lenses of social location. For some, particularly those whose identities align with societal norms of leadership or authority, an emerging sense of call might find ready affirmation from their communities. The path may appear, if not easy, then at least validated. However, for those whose identities have been historically marginalized, the experience of call can be fraught with additional layers of struggle.

A call experienced by a woman in a patriarchal tradition, a queer person in a heteronormative institution, a person of color in a predominantly white space, or a person with a disability in a world not built for them, might be met with skepticism, outright dismissal, or attempts to reshape it into something more "acceptable" to the dominant culture. Thus, the very way we experience a call, and how it is (or is not) recognized by others, is profoundly shaped by the social and political realities of our lives.

Tending our call, then, often involves critically discerning the power dynamics at play both within us and around us as well as listening to the inner voice or the communal affirmation. In navigating these complex social and political realities, individuals may find that their most reliable compass lies within their own affective and embodied ways of knowing.

More than feeling good, this reliance on affective and embodied knowing can be a profound resource for navigating difficult or even traumatic experiences related to one's calling. Theologian Lakisha Lockhart shares a powerful account of a degrading, racist, and sexist encounter during a theological seminar. In the aftermath, overwhelmed by aggression, sadness, and self-doubt, she found herself instinctively dancing in her room. This embodied act became a space for processing the pain, questioning assumptions, and rediscovering her sense of self and purpose in relation to God. "I had danced before, but this was the first time I danced out of anger and frustration," she writes. "It was what my body knew how to do, so I did it. I danced until my body felt like mine again."[29] Lockhart's experience vividly illustrates how the wisdom of the body can surface, offering clarity, resilience, and a path back to vocational integrity even when rational thought feels blocked or overwhelmed. Lockhart's experience underscores that, while discerning call sometimes happens through quiet contemplation, discernment also occurs through movement, tears, and the body's innate capacity for processing and meaning-making. In another recounting of that same experience, Lockhart notes that the experience of the dance didn't just reground her physically; it also opened a profound space for cognitive and spiritual reorientation. Her body's instinctive movement created an opening for her mind to follow, allowing her to process the encounter and its implications through embodied exploration rather than linear thought:

> I danced with the thought that my voice, my ideas and I still mattered to God, if no one else. Once I stopped moving I noticed that two and a half hours had gone by. I immediately began to write these new revelations in my journal, including how much I needed to dance and how much I found out about myself, the professor, God and this work through my embodying it in dance form. In that moment I felt the presence of God and it was transformative.[30]

Here, the physical act of dancing became inseparable from theological insight and vocational clarification. The movement wasn't just stress relief: It was a form of embodied prayer and reflection that yielded insight about herself, God, and her calling, culminating in a clarifying encounter with the divine.

Lockhart's experience, where embodied movement led to a felt sense of God's presence and transformation, resonates with the understanding within Christian tradition of an internal call. This often involves a deeply personal sense that God is speaking directly to one's heart or mind. This call is experienced, as Lockhart illustrates, through affective responses, embodied wisdom, and intuition. These intuitive understandings, felt more than logically deduced, can provide critical

---

29 Lakisha R. Lockhart-Rusch, *Doing Theological Double Dutch: A Womanist Pedagogy of Play* (Grand Rapids, MI: William B. Eerdmans, 2025), chap. 1, loc. 334 of 2743, kindle.

30 Lakisha Renee Lockhart, "Doing Double-Dutch: Womanish Modes of Play as a Pedagogical Resource for Theological Education" (PhD diss., Boston College, 2018), 2.

insights into what might be a life-giving direction versus one that could be draining or unfulfilling. By paying close attention to these varied cues (emotional, physical, and spiritual) individuals can better understand what paths may align with their callings.

While both types of experiences are integral to vocational discernment, they differ in how they manifest and influence our decision-making processes. Rational experiences are more cerebral and structured, involving logical analysis and reflection, whereas affective experiences are more intuitive and emotional, involving gut feelings and visceral reactions. Rational discernment often involves a step-by-step process of evaluating and reflecting, while affective discernment relies on emotional cues and intuitive insights. Rational experiences lead to a sense of clarity and purpose derived from thoughtful consideration. In contrast, affective experiences lead to a sense of alignment and resonance based on embodied insight that is less understandable by logic.

By recognizing and integrating both rational and affective dimensions, individuals can develop a more complete understanding of their vocation. Rational analysis provides clarity and direction, while affective insights offer emotional validation and resonance. Together, these dimensions help individuals navigate their vocational journeys with an adaptive approach, ensuring that their decisions are both intellectually sound and emotionally fulfilling.

Not every type of experience is necessary to confirm a call. However, recognizing the diverse ways vocation can manifest is profoundly beneficial. God's call may appear differently in various seasons of our lives, and understanding these variations equips us both to discern our own paths and to accompany others on theirs. Some individuals may naturally experience their calling through rational reflection, while others might feel it more strongly through emotional resonance. Appreciating these differences fosters empathy and helps us support those whose vocational journeys differ from our own, especially as we explore how internal experiences connect with external dimensions of call.

External Call: Being Drawn Outward and Affirmed Inwardly

External experiences of call can manifest in two distinct ways: being drawn outward or affirmed inwardly. Understanding these dimensions helps individuals navigate their vocational journeys with a balanced approach, incorporating both external feedback and situational cues. Here, we explore how each type of experience uniquely contributes to vocational discernment and how they can be integrated for a fuller understanding of one's calling.

Being "drawn outward" is the experience where vocation emerges from your interactions with the broader world. This drawing out can include resonating deeply with the work of a mentor and thinking, "That is what I need to be doing, too." For example, someone might admire a teacher who dedicates their life to working with children and feel compelled to pursue a similar path in education or social work. Additionally, being drawn outward can manifest as a strong sense of belonging or commitment to serve a particular people or community in certain circumstances. For instance, someone might volunteer at a local shelter and feel a profound sense of purpose and connection, leading them to a career in community service or nonprofit work. This sense of dedication can guide us toward specific vocational paths based on our desire to contribute to the well-being of those communities. We are being drawn outward when we feel pulled toward something external to ourselves.

Being "affirmed inwardly" involves experiences where vocation emerges from recognition and validation by your community or context. This inward affirmation can include having one's gifts and talents named and affirmed by the community. For example, a church congregation might recognize a member's exceptional ability to connect with and support others, encouraging them to pursue pastoral ministry or counseling. Another example of being affirmed inwardly is finding yourself in "the right place at the right time to help." These serendipitous moments often feel like divine appointments. For instance, a person might be present at an emergency and instinctively take charge to help, leading them to realize their calling in emergency response or healthcare. Such situational affirmations offer spontaneous and immediate feedback, guiding individuals toward specific vocational paths based on how their actions align with the needs and opportunities present in their environment.

While both types of experiences are integral to vocational discernment, they differ in how they manifest and influence our decision-making processes. Being drawn outward is more about the ongoing relational interactions and the continuous feedback, encouragement, and support from others. In contrast, being affirmed inwardly involves confirmations that one is on the right path through situational cues and communal validation. Outward experiences lead to a sense of purpose and belonging derived from consistent external affirmation. In contrast, inward experiences lead to a sense of alignment and readiness that we experience as arising from our own felt sense of the world and God's movement in our lives.

Individuals can develop a more complete understanding of their vocation by recognizing and integrating the dimensions of being drawn outward and affirmed inwardly. Together, these dimensions help individuals navigate their vocational journeys with an adaptive approach, ensuring that their decisions are both externally supported and situationally relevant. Importantly and as noted above, some people are more inclined to experience their calling through being drawn outward, while others may resonate more with being affirmed inwardly. No matter how one experiences their vocational call, there is no guarantee or perfect test to confirm a call with absolute certainty. This is true whether the experience of call is internal or external, rational or affective, drawn outward or affirmed inwardly. This is especially the case when a call comes to us suddenly or with great intensity.

> **A Practice to Consider:**
> # Tracing the Call
>
> *Our callings unfold at the intersection of our inner convictions and the affirmations of others. Tracing these threads helps us recognize how they weave together to guide our next steps.*
>
> 1. Draw a simple chart with two columns labeled "Internal" and "External."
> 2. Under "Internal," list any recurring thoughts or emotions that guide your sense of purpose that fit with the internal frame of the affective and rational.
> 3. Under "External," list moments when others have recognized your gifts, as you were drawn outward or affirmed inwardly.
> 4. Look for patterns or themes across both columns to clarify your next steps.

Integration and Duration of Call

The journey of vocational discernment is deeply personal yet inherently communal, unfolding through the dynamic interplay of internal and external dimensions. Whether through rational reflection, emotional resonance, being drawn outward, or receiving affirmation inwardly, these experiences rarely exist in isolation. Instead, they interact and inform one another, creating a richer, more nuanced understanding of our callings. Recognizing this interplay allows us to see how God's call is not confined to a single method or moment but weaves through our relationships, contexts, and inner lives.

This interconnectedness also reminds us that discernment is a lifelong process. Just as our internal reflections and external engagements evolve, so, too, does our experience of vocation. What feels like a moment of clarity in one season may transform into doubt or expansion in another. Similarly, calls affirmed by others may deepen through personal introspection, while internal nudges can gain clarity and purpose when shared in community. Embracing this dynamic process helps us remain open to the continuing revelation that is the movement of Spirit in the world, something that can often surprise or challenge us.

In addition to the internal and external dimensions of calling, it is also important to consider the varying intensities and durations of vocational experiences. These aspects can significantly affect how we perceive and respond to our sense of call, shaping our paths and decisions. As I have seen it, the experience of call can be felt (1) in the short term, (2) across an extended period, (3) in a fluctuating way, or (4) with episodic return. It is helpful to know this not only because how you experience being called may change over time but also because it can help you to connect and collaborate with others who have a different experience of God's call.

Some vocational experiences are marked by intense, short-term revelations or epiphanies. These moments can feel like sudden bursts of clarity or inspiration, compelling us to take immediate action. For example, a person might attend a conference or retreat and experience a profound sense of calling to a particular cause or career. This type of experience can be transformative, providing a clear sense of direction that propels us forward. However, the intensity of these experiences can also fade over time, leading to doubts or second-guessing. Finding ways to sustain the initial inspiration through regular reflection, community support, or ongoing education is beneficial. By nurturing the initial spark, we can contribute to the likelihood that it continues to guide us even after the beginning intensity has diminished some. At times, the feeling of a retreat or conference can be a bit of a "mountain top" experience, and we chase that feeling, mistaking desire for God's call. That isn't to say that an intense and sudden feeling can never help deepen into vocation, but as usual, discernment is critical.

In contrast, other vocational experiences may unfold more gradually, characterized by a steady, enduring sense of call. These long-term experiences often develop over years or even decades, allowing for deep reflection and gradual alignment with our life's work. For instance, I once was meeting with someone as a spiritual director when I asked him if he had ever been told that what he seemed called to was a ministry of pastoral care. I was just getting to know this person more deeply, so I was asking as a kind of check-in: It appeared to me as if he was stewarding gifts of care and healing, but I wasn't sure, so I wanted to see if that idea resonated with him. At the time, this man was in his late seventies, and I was pleasantly surprised to discover that while no one had ever named this for him before, he felt it was not only true but was also something that had been true for a very long time even though he hadn't recognized it. Having had it named for him opened the way for some significant changes in his life as he tried to begin to prioritize and order his life so that he could most faithfully exercise the gifts of pastoral care he had long been carrying.

Long-term vocational experiences offer the benefit of stability and sustained commitment. They allow for a deeper integration of our calling into various aspects of our lives. However, they also require patience and perseverance, as the gradual nature of these experiences may lack the immediate clarity of short-term intense calls. It is also the case that, as creatures of habit, people can assume that what they've done for a decade is what they should be doing by default, thereby missing new ways in which their ministry may grow. We should remain attentive to subtle cues and ongoing developments that affirm or refine our sense of vocation over time.

There are also experiences of vocation that fluctuate in intensity over different periods. These vocational calls may come and go, surging at certain times and receding at others. For example, a person might feel a strong calling to social justice work during a particular political movement, only to find that intensity wanes in quieter times. These fluctuations can be challenging, as they may lead to feelings of inconsistency or uncertainty about one's "true calling." This is part of the reason why I am dubious about "true calling" as a concept.

A more helpful framing might be to view vocation as a series of interconnected callings that shift in prominence over time, like a constellation of purpose with different stars shining brighter at different moments. This conceptualization invites us to engage in an ongoing dialogue between our inner selves, our communities, and the divine. Navigating fluctuating vocational experiences requires flexibility and adaptability. It's helpful to recognize that such variations are natural and do not necessarily diminish the validity of the calling.

These shifts don't necessarily mark failure or indecision; they can be signs of our moral framework adapting to new realities, recalibrating to hold what is newly seen or felt as true. By remaining open to the ebb and flow of intensity, we can find ways to engage with our vocation during peak moments while also sustaining our commitment during quieter times.

Some vocational experiences are episodic, emerging in distinct phases or episodes throughout life. These experiences may not follow a linear progression but rather appear at critical junctures, often influenced by significant life events such as career changes, personal crises, or spiritual awakenings. For example, a person might feel called to a particular ministry during a period of life transition, only to later shift their focus to another area of service as circumstances change. Episodic vocational experiences highlight the dynamic and evolving nature of calling. They remind us that our vocation can adapt and transform in response to new insights and life stages. Embracing the episodic nature of vocation allows us to remain responsive to God's ongoing call, recognizing that each phase of our journey offers unique opportunities for growth and service.

By acknowledging the varying intensities and durations of vocational experiences, we can approach our discernment with greater awareness and compassion.

Understanding that our sense of call can manifest in diverse ways helps us remain open to the many forms and phases our vocation might take, ultimately leading us to a more integrated and fulfilling life's work. Embracing the episodic nature of vocation allows us to remain responsive to God's ongoing call, recognizing that each phase of our journey offers unique opportunities for growth and service. However, not everything that "calls" us is right to respond to. We may well have some time when we attempt to be faithful and only learn after the fact that we were deluding ourselves. That's ok. We're called to follow Christ and model ourselves after his life and witness, not to be perfect.

This is a hard thing to accept, especially when you read texts like Matthew 5:48, which says pretty explicitly we ought to "be perfect, therefore, as your heavenly Father is perfect." The Greek word τέλειος (*teleios*) often translated as "perfect," can also mean "complete" or "mature." Many commentators argue that in this context, τέλειος does not mean sinless perfection, but rather maturity or completeness in character, especially in love.[31] This nuance invites us to view our vocational journey as a process of ongoing growth and development, mirroring our spiritual journey.

Just as our faith deepens and evolves over time, so, too, can our understanding and living out of our vocation. This approach encourages a grace-filled attitude toward discernment, acknowledging that missteps and uncertainties are part of the journey. It reminds us that our goal is to continually strive toward Christ-likeness, learning and growing through each experience. By embracing this dynamic view of vocation, we open ourselves to God's ongoing work in our lives, fostering the kind of spiritual maturity and completeness that Scripture encourages. This view of completeness invites us to see vocational discernment not as arriving at a single, perfect answer, but as the ongoing pursuit of coherence among our deepest convictions, our daily practices, and the communities that help us remember who we are.

This scriptural framework provides a helpful lens through which to view the often challenging process of discerning our vocation. Indeed, feeling called to something is inherently complex and personal, often requiring a leap of faith. Recognizing this complexity helps us approach our vocational journeys with humility and openness. The way we understand and interpret these experiences can have significant consequences. Narrowing our sense of vocation may lead to a focused and deeply committed path, whereas broadening our understanding can open up diverse opportunities and ways

---

31 W. D. Davies and Dale C. Allison Jr., *A Critical and Exegetical Commentary on the Gospel According to Saint Matthew, Volume 1: Introduction and Commentary on Matthew I–VII*, International Critical Commentary (Edinburgh: T&T Clark, 1988), 563.

to serve. As we move forward, we ought to consider how these varying interpretations of vocation shape our lives and the lives of those around us. This leads us to examine the broader implications and responsibilities that come with embracing our vocation.

Consequences of Call

The process of discerning a call can be complex, often requiring a mix of various approaches and perspectives. While there are benefits to both narrowing and broadening our sense of vocation, listening both internally and externally, and feeling called in different time spans, each approach has its own potential pitfalls and limitations. I'll talk more about discernment next chapter, but, for now, I want to emphasize that the decisions you make about how you think about vocation (its size, shape, scale, and orientation) have a direct impact on your discernment process.

Narrowing our sense of what counts as "vocation" can provide clarity and focus, helping us to channel our energies and resources into specific tasks or roles. In practical terms, this might involve dedicating time and effort to mastering a particular discipline, deepening relationships within a specific community, or committing to a singular mission that reflects one's values and passions, understanding it to be your call. For instance, someone who feels called to pastoral ministry in a congregation might benefit from developing the particular skills and knowledge required for that vocation. This focused approach can lead to deep expertise and a strong sense of identity within that calling. This kind of focused vocational pursuit can lead to profound personal, professional, and spiritual fulfillment.

However, an overly narrow focus can also be limiting. This narrowing of perspective can lead to a kind of vocational tunnel vision, where we become so focused on one aspect of our calling that we neglect other vital parts of who we are and what we're meant to do. For example, someone who almost entirely identifies with their congregational duties may not be able to be as attentive to their other roles as a parent, community member, artist, or advocate for social justice. They might find themselves struggling to manage the demands of their ministerial work with family responsibilities, missing opportunities to engage in community events outside the church, neglecting creative pursuits that could enrich their spiritual life and ministry, or overlooking social issues that demand attention beyond the walls of their congregation.

This narrow perspective on vocation can lead to burnout, as the individual may feel confined by the singular identity and miss out on the richness of a different kind of emphasis in their life. The pressure to excel in this one area of vocation can become overwhelming, leading to stress, exhaustion, and a sense of incompleteness. Moreover, by focusing too narrowly on one aspect of their calling, individuals may inadvertently limit their effectiveness in that very role. A pastor who neglects their role as a community member, for instance, may find themselves out of touch with the broader needs and concerns of the people they serve. Similarly, neglecting personal growth in areas outside of their primary vocation can lead to a lack of fresh perspectives and insights that could otherwise enrich their work and ministry.

Conversely, a broad understanding of vocation can encompass various roles and activities, offering flexibility and adaptability. In practical terms, this might look like weaving together professional work, volunteer efforts, creative pursuits, and personal relationships, all oriented around a unifying sense of purpose. This perspective is especially useful in today's interconnected world, where many individuals juggle multiple responsibilities, interests, and connections around the globe. A broad sense of vocation allows for the integration of diverse experiences and can lead to a more holistic sense of purpose. For example, imagine someone who feels called toward raising awareness about environmental and ecological concerns. This vocation might be expressed through their work as a teacher, their involvement in community organizing, and the time spent bringing groups out into the wilderness. This broader view can enable them to find connections and synergies between these various activities, enriching each aspect of their life.

Yet this broadness can also be overwhelming. Without sufficient focus, individuals may struggle to find a clear direction or to feel a sense of purpose. The lack of specificity can lead to indecision and a diffuse sense of identity, making it challenging to articulate one's calling or make concrete decisions about how to live it out. This ambiguity can be particularly distressing in a culture that often demands clear career paths and measurable outcomes. We should be mindful that the breadth of our vocational understanding does not dilute our sense of purpose or lead to a lack of commitment. There's a risk of becoming a "jack of all trades, master of none," where the individual has a surface-level engagement with many areas but lacks depth in any particular domain. For some, this can result in a sense of rootlessness or a feeling of not making a significant impact in any area.

An individual laboring under too abstract of a sense of call may find themselves managing too many roles and feeling stretched thin, unable to give their full attention to any single pursuit, leading to a sense of frustration and inefficacy. This constant juggling act can be exhausting, both mentally and emotionally. It may lead to a sense of never fully meeting expectations in any area, whether those expectations are self-imposed, come from others, or are divinely inspired. For some, the stress of trying to maintain multiple vocational expressions can lead to burnout, much like an overly narrow focus, but for different reasons. Instead of feeling confined by a singular identity, the individual may feel overwhelmed by the multiplicity of ways they're trying to embody a call. This can result in a paradoxical situation where, in attempting to honor all aspects of their calling, they struggle to fully live out any of them.

Given these challenges of both narrow and broad understandings of vocation, it's beneficial to cultivate a deep awareness of our inward landscape. Our inner world (our desires, passions, hopes, imagination, commitments, and intuitions) forms the spinning core of who we are and the place from which we're called. Through inner cultivation, we create a better basis for decision-making, enabling us to discern paths that align with our best sense of ourselves rather than external pressures, societal expectations, or personal wish fulfillment.

Attuning ourselves to these internal stirrings helps us recognize patterns and themes that point toward our vocation, offering clarity amid life's complexities. This self-awareness also nurtures a deeper connection with the divine or our understanding of what is sacred, grounding our discernment in something larger than ourselves. Intentionally focusing inward equips us to make choices that are personally fulfilling and meaningfully contribute to the world around us. Howard Thurman has some beautiful writing about seeking a sense of call in this way.

Thurman encourages us to turn inward and listen deeply to the still, small voice that calls us to purpose. In a world filled with distractions and external demands, Thurman reminds us that our most meaningful call often emerges from this place of inner stillness and self-discovery.

> There is in you something that waits and listens for the sound of the genuine in yourself and sometimes there is so much traffic going on in your minds, so many different kinds of signals, so many vast impulses floating through your organism that go back thousands of generations, long before you were even a thought in the mind of creation, and you are buffeted by these, and in the midst of all of this you have got to find out what your name is. Who are you? How does the sound of the genuine come through to you?[32]

Thurman's words highlight the challenge of naming call amid the cacophony of life's demands and influences. While his concept of the "sound of the genuine" is often interpreted to suggest an essence or core to our vocation, I think it can be seen otherwise.

The sound of the genuine might refer to vocation as an ongoing dialogue between our inner stirrings and the world around us, rather than a fixed, unchanging

---

[32] Howard Thurman, "The Sound of the Genuine," Baccalaureate Speech, Spelman College, May 4, 1980. https://thurman.pitts.emory.edu/items/show/838.

"genuine" self. The sound of the genuine isn't a single tone or song but a persistent call-and-response, a dynamic dialogue between our evolving sense of self, the changing needs of our communities, and our sense of Spirit's work in our midst. This perspective allows for growth, adaptation, and responsiveness to new insights and experiences. It acknowledges that what feels deeply true or "genuine" to us at one stage of life might shift as we encounter new challenges and opportunities. Furthermore, there are "dynamic dialogues" that are more genuine than others: conversations and discourses that lead us toward who we are called to be, while others lead us down other paths.

From my perspective, the value in Thurman's approach lies not in finding an immutable core self, but in cultivating a practice of deep listening and reflection. This practice can help us navigate the competing demands on our attention and energy, allowing us to make choices that feel aligned with our evolving sense of purpose. It invites us to regularly check in with ourselves, our values, and our understanding of how we're called to serve, recognizing that these may change over time. Yet, as Thurman suggests, accessing this wisdom is not always easy. We are constantly bombarded by a multitude of influences, both internal and external, that can drown out the sound of the genuine.

In our vocational discernment, we must cultivate stillness and attentiveness practices that allow us to cut through the mental chatter and tune into our deepest selves. This cultivation might involve practices of contemplation, meditation, or simply carving out quiet moments in our day to reflect on our experiences and longings. At the same time, Thurman's insight reminds us that our vocational journeys are not solely individual endeavors. The "vast impulses" that buffet us are collective, shaped by the histories and communities that have formed us.

This cultivation might also be seeking out community, activity, and experimentation. Relying solely on internal listening can be limiting, as it may cause us to become insulated from external realities and feedback. Without external input, we risk becoming self-referential and missing out on valuable perspectives and insights others can offer. In addition to carved-out "quiet moments," listening might also involve gathering friends, eating a good meal together, and hearing what they think about what God has been doing with you.

On the flip side, external listening grounds us in the realities of our communities and the world around us. It provides us with an opportunity to pay attention to the feedback, needs, and expectations of others. It helps ensure that our vocations are responsive to the needs of those we serve and that we remain connected to the larger context of our work. For instance, a community organizer might regularly seek feedback from the people they serve to ensure their efforts address the most pressing issues. This external listening can enhance the relevance and effectiveness of their work. Yet excessive focus on external input as the place to locate vocation can also be problematic. It can lead to over-dependence on others' opinions and expectations, potentially causing us to lose sight of our own values and desires. This dynamic can be especially harmful for those navigating life within institutions shaped by dominant cultural norms, places where affirmation is often contingent on maintaining the status quo, and places where one's experiences of difference may not be recognized or welcomed. Calls that challenge dominant norms are often met with resistance or dismissal. Consider, for example, the discomfort that might arise when giving voice to the ecological dangers of late-stage capitalism in the United States or a disabled person's call to leadership. This isn't about individual prejudice alone. It's about how power circulates in our religious institutions, validating some voices while silencing others. People feeling such calls might be encouraged to conform to behaviors and standards that don't align with their identity or cultural background, leading to disconnection and dissatisfaction.

Reflection on vocation influences how individuals understand their present and shapes their future trajectory. As they discern their calling, they begin to envision how their unique gifts and passions can be used in the service of others and the greater good. This forward-looking perspective helps set meaningful goals and pursue paths that lead to personal and communal flourishing. This vocational journey is not merely about acquiring skills and credentials but about growing into the person they are called to be. It involves continual learning, self-discovery, and adaptation, responding to new insights and challenges along the way.

As we consider these various forms of call, we must reflect on how our understanding of vocation shapes both our own lives and the communities we serve. Narrowing our sense of vocation may lead to focused and deeply committed paths, while broadening it can open us to new opportunities for growth and service. In either case, responding faithfully to God's call carries profound implications for our shared journey of faith. My encouragement to you is that you consider the size, scope, scale, and orientation of discernment that is right for you given the moment you are in. Because this process is not static but adaptive, invite ongoing reflection and adjustment as your circumstances and insights evolve.

Reaching an Equilibrium

My own understanding of vocation occupies a space between Thurman's idea of the "sound of the genuine" and an approach that more explicitly acknowledges the importance of community. Personal reflection and communal belonging work together in shaping our understanding of calling. The quiet moments of listening to our lives that Palmer describes become more meaningful when we recognize, as Tutu suggests, that our very capacity for self-understanding emerges through relationship with others. Or perhaps more accurately, it's a perspective that oscillates between these two poles, in constant motion yet still maintaining a kind of stability. The dynamic interplay between individual calling and communal context leads me to think about vocation in terms of equilibrium rather than "balance" or "integration."

Equilibrium, as a concept, offers a more nuanced and flexible framework for understanding the complexities of vocation in our ever-changing world. It allows us to consider how we might maintain a sense of purpose and direction while also adapting to new circumstances and evolving understandings of ourselves and our communities. The concept of equilibrium in vocation is particularly valuable because it acknowledges the ongoing nature of our calling, the need for continual adjustment, and the interplay between our inner stirrings and external realities. To better understand why equilibrium is such a useful metaphor for vocation, it's helpful to contrast it with other commonly used concepts.

Unlike the concept of "balance," which implies a static state where opposing forces cancel each other out, equilibrium in biological systems is a dynamic process of continual adjustment and response to changing conditions. There is no single perfectly balanced point where we can find everything "just right." For example, our bodies do not achieve balance like a perfectly centered seesaw; instead, they maintain equilibrium through processes like sweating to cool down when hot and shivering to warm up when cold. In other words, equilibrium isn't about everything being perfectly still or balanced at all times. It's about being able to adjust and adapt to changes as they happen, keeping things stable overall.

Just as our bodies constantly make small changes to maintain a healthy state, our vocational equilibrium means we're always fine-tuning our path, responding to new challenges, opportunities, and shifts in our inner and outer worlds. It's a state of dynamic stability where we keep moving forward, even if the terrain changes along the way. This constant state of flux and adjustment ensures that we remain alive and functional, even though we are never in a fixed state of balance. We are in motion. This is something I've had to learn the hard way.

During the long, disorienting stretch of the COVID pandemic, I began to notice changes in myself I couldn't quite make sense of. There were sudden spikes of anxiety. My memory started slipping. My speech, once fluid and quick, became halting at times. Teaching and writing took more energy. I found myself staring at a blank screen, not because I didn't have thoughts, but because getting them out felt ... blocked.

Eventually, a neuropsychology assessment ruled out degenerative disease but couldn't pinpoint exactly why these changes were happening. Maybe my ADHD was getting worse. Generalized Anxiety Disorder? Good candidate for Assessment for

Autism Spectrum Disorders. Long COVID? Maybe just burnout? There were lots of trails to pursue, but no clear "solution." Even now, I don't fully know what's happening in my mind. I just know that it's different than it used to be.

What I do know is this: I couldn't keep living the way I had been. I couldn't track as many conversations, respond to as many needs, or remain constantly attuned to the movements of my professional and ministerial networks. One of the most draining roles I had unknowingly taken on was that of the connector: the person who always knew what good work was happening, who was publishing what, who needed to meet whom. I loved that role. But it had become a constant hum in the back of my mind, and I no longer had the bandwidth to sustain it.

And in a book about calling, that matters. Not because vocation disappears in these moments, but because its shape starts to shift. After a period of real mental and emotional strain, I made some significant changes. I stepped back from boards. I laid down volunteer roles. I stopped saying "yes" to side projects that used to feel energizing but had become exhausting. I had reached the limit of what I could carry, and I was starting to realize that the cost of pretending I was fine was too high. Ultimately, the cost of a thing is part of making it; discerning at what cost we proceed becomes essential not just for strategy, but for the sake of flourishing. So I chose to make my life smaller on purpose. More contained. More focused. And it helped. I had more capacity to be present at home. I had less anxiety when I opened my laptop. I wasn't cured or fixed, but I felt like I could breathe again. I remember telling a friend, "I think I've finally found balance."

But, of course, life doesn't stay balanced. My daughter grew older, and her world grew wider: capoeira practice, theater rehearsals, new social needs. At church, too, things changed. People began needing different forms of pastoral care. And in my professional life, just by showing up and being open, I found myself drawn into new conversations and communities, some of which stirred real longing in me. But I kept brushing those nudges aside with the same phrase: This is a season of "no." I'd said "no" before, and it had helped. So I kept saying it, even when the conditions that made it necessary had shifted.

Eventually, I realized I wasn't actually discerning anymore: I was defaulting. What had started as a healthy decision had calcified into a habit. Saying "no" had once been an act of fidelity. But, over time, it became a shield, a way to avoid the uncomfortable work of listening again. Because listening might mean realizing I had to say "yes" to something new. Or risk being stretched again. Or revisit hard conversations about limits and energy and call. And I wasn't sure I was ready for that.

That's when the metaphor of balance started to fail me. I wasn't trying to preserve some sacred and unchanging center. It was a snapshot, a still frame of a moment that had already passed. And the longer I clung to it, the more brittle it became.

What I needed wasn't balance. I needed equilibrium, something alive and responsive, something that could shift as the terrain shifted beneath me. Equilibrium, I've come to believe, isn't about arriving at a perfect configuration of commitments. It's about staying honest. Honest about what's changed. Honest about what's possible. Honest about where the Spirit might be nudging me, even if it's inconvenient, even if it disrupts the story I've been telling myself.

And we must acknowledge that wrestling with the stories we tell ourselves feels vastly different depending on our social location. For those navigating systemic barriers—racism that questions your competence, sexism that limits your opportunities, ableism that restricts your access, or economic injustice that demands constant preoccupation with survival—finding equilibrium is not merely an internal adjustment. It is an ongoing act of resistance and resilience. The "mundane" aspects of a call can be compounded by the daily exhaustion of fighting for dignity and recognition. The "messy" can involve confronting oppressive structures that actively seek to throw you off center. Therefore, reaching what feels like a sustainable equilibrium often requires both personal spiritual practices and communal support systems with a commitment to transforming the very conditions that create such profound disequilibrium for so many.

This isn't graceful work. I don't have a formula for it. Or, maybe, it's profoundly full of Grace, but I'm not graceful doing it. What I do have is a growing capacity to pause. To check in. To ask, again and again, What is mine to do now? Not six months ago. Not when I was operating at full cognitive bandwidth. Not when I had fewer responsibilities or more energy. Now.

And the answers, as they come, are helping me stay faithful, not in spite of the shifting terrain, but through it. Equilibrium asks of us attentiveness, not constancy. Responsiveness, not balance.

In the pages ahead, we'll explore how that kind of spiritual agility is sustained, not just through private reflection, but through community, practice, and a willingness to reorient again and again. Scholars like Kathleen Cahalan echo this insight in their own way, showing how the very language we use to talk about vocation can open (or constrain) our capacity to respond with agility.

Cahalan's approach to vocation further illuminates the concept of equilibrium by examining how our language shapes our understanding of calling. She similarly critiques a static nature of thinking about vocation as a noun ("I'm searching for my vocation"), which can imply a fixed, predetermined state, as if vocation is something handed to us fully formed.[33] Instead, Cahalan argues for framing vocation dynamically,

---

[33] Kathleen A. Cahalan, *The Stories We Live: Finding God's Calling All around Us* (Grand Rapids, MI: Wm. B. Eerdmans, 2017), xi.

using prepositions to describe vocation relationally and contextually: called *by* God, *to* follow, *for* service, *through* others, and *within* God.[34] These prepositions articulate the directional and relational aspects of calling, capturing the interplay between divine invitation, personal identity, and communal context.

Kathleen Cahalan's relational understanding of vocation resonates deeply with the idea of vocational equilibrium. Equilibrium, much like the body maintaining its balance through constant micro-adjustments, is a dynamic process. Cahalan's use of prepositions reveals vocation as a continuous navigation of relationships and circumstances rather than a singular, unchanging destination. When we see ourselves as called through others, for instance, we acknowledge the essential communal dimensions of our calling. Her prepositional framework underscores that our callings are inherently in motion, constantly formed and reformed by our evolving connections with God, with community, and with the world itself. Adopting this relational lens helps us shift our focus from achieving a perfect, static balance to engaging faithfully with the dynamic interplay of life, faith, and our ever-unfolding call.

Similarly, "integration" as a goal suggests a seamless blending of elements into a harmonious whole, which can be an appealing idea when thinking about vocation. It implies a smooth fusion of our various roles, passions, and responsibilities into a single cohesive life purpose. I think it is possible that some folks do get to this level of distillation. However, for everyone else, this concept of integration can sometimes overlook the natural tensions and fluctuations that are inherent in our vocational journeys. Equilibrium, on the other hand, recognizes and accommodates these inherent tensions and fluctuations within a system. It acknowledges that our vocational path isn't always smooth, singular, or perfectly harmonious but rather a mix of different, sometimes competing, elements in motion.

In the context of vocation, seeking equilibrium means continuously engaging with our inner callings and external circumstances, adjusting and realigning as necessary to maintain a dynamic harmony that supports our growth and flourishing. This approach allows for the coexistence of different aspects of our calling, even when they seem at odds with each other. For instance, a person might feel called both to demanding professional work and to deep family involvement. Rather than trying to seamlessly integrate these potentially conflicting calls, an equilibrium approach would involve finding a dynamic balance, allowing for shifts in focus and energy as circumstances change.

Equilibrium in vocation also means being responsive to the ebbs and flows of life. Just as our bodies adjust to maintain homeostasis in changing environments, our vocational equilibrium involves adapting to new life stages, unexpected challenges, or shifts in our understanding of our purpose. This might mean leaning more heavily

---

34 Ibid., xii.

into one aspect of our calling during certain periods, while allowing others to take a back seat, always with the understanding that this arrangement is fluid and subject to change. By embracing this equilibrium model, we can navigate the complexities of our callings with greater flexibility and resilience, honoring the complex nature of our vocations while maintaining a sense of overall purpose and direction.

Bonnie Miller-McLemore powerfully articulates this understanding of vocation as a lifelong journey in her recent book, wonderfully named, *Follow Your Bliss and Other Lies about Calling*. There, she offers valuable insights into the complex, evolving nature of vocational discernment. Miller-McLemore challenges simplistic notions of calling, noting that "we lie about calling when we don't mention that everyone has multiple desires and faces an ongoing clash of commitments as diverse callings demand our time, attention, care, and energy."[35] This clash of commitments can lead to feelings of being overwhelmed, exhausted, and unable to fulfill any one calling as well as we might wish. Recognizing these tensions is necessary for a more grounded understanding of vocation.

Furthermore, Miller-McLemore emphasizes that our sense of calling continues to develop throughout life, contrary to the idea that vocation is settled early in adulthood. She writes, "Calling is more about constantly readjusting to life's shifting boundaries than arriving at some permanent pinnacle."[36] This perspective aligns with our understanding of vocation as a dynamic equilibrium, inviting us to see vocation as a lifelong process of discernment and adaptation rather than a one-time decision.

This evolving nature of vocation becomes particularly apparent in later adulthood, when individuals often face the challenge of relinquishing long-held callings. Miller-McLemore observes that "relinquishing callings requires review and retelling of our lives, a going backward over life to go forward, a reversal and renewal of calling in a different form and direction."[37] Learning to tell new stories about yourself can be challenging and often involves grief and lament. It can also lead to new forms of service and a deeper understanding of one's life journey. I'll spend more time thinking about vocation and storytelling later in this book, but, for now, it is enough to say that, by recognizing the value in both holding on to *and* letting go of callings, we can develop a more mature and flexible approach to vocation that adapts to the changing seasons of life.

This perspective on the evolving nature of vocation resonates with Thurman's insights about listening for the "sound of the genuine." Like Thurman, I do think

---

35 Bonnie J. Miller-McLemore, *Follow Your Bliss and Other Lies about Calling* (New York: Oxford University Press, 2024), 66–67.
36 Ibid., 121.
37 Ibid., 145.

that "there is in you something that waits and listens for the sound of the genuine in yourself" and that "sometimes there is so much traffic going on in your minds" that it is hard to hear the sound you are searching for. However, I think that, functionally, we benefit from affirming that the solution to filtering out the noise of that traffic is neither found solely by turning inward to your own deepest longings nor by appealing externally to God for guidance. Instead, I think we ought to appeal to both of those things, testing our sense of both in community and then again through practice. Sometimes, the road is made by walking, and the fullness of the sound of the genuine will never be heard until you make it for the first time in your pursuit of life abundant for you and yours.

All of the above being noted, I find it important to affirm that there exists what the womanist ethicist and theologian Emilie Townes refers to as "The Fantastic Hegemonic Imagination."[38]

Although I return to Townes in the seventh chapter's discussion of accompaniment, it is worth saying that systems and structures of social exclusion and injustice not only function to diminish and demean people materially but also to shape the hopes, dreams, and imagined futures of people's interior lives. Systems of power and privilege press on flesh and set up shop in our souls. Resistance to injustice and marginalization is both internal and spiritual, as well as external and material. Acting justly and loving mercy mean doing work in the world and in our souls.

Because of this, we need to name that the "traffic" distracting folks from call is often not just random noise but the death-dealing siren's drone of the "Fantastic Hegemonic Imagination." Put succinctly, vocation is about faithfully finding the things in your life that can yield more life for you and your community, whatever shape it takes. This finding work is done with intention, self-reflection, prayer, and in community. Sometimes, this means finding the "sound of the genuine," saying "yes" to it, and following it where it leads. Other times, it will mean recognizing that some of the voices and weights that we carry are deadening and ought to be set down: There are things we need to say "no" to and walk away from to move our lives toward greater life. Learning how to "pick things up" and "put things down" is part of every vocational journey.

I believe vocation is a co-creative process with God, where we actively participate in discerning and shaping our callings. This process involves both deep introspection and active engagement with the world as we seek to align our lives with God's purposes. It is not a passive waiting for divine revelation. It is an active, ongoing dialogue with God, ourselves, our communities, and our traditions. Through prayer, reflection, and

---

[38] Emilie Maureen Townes, *Womanist Ethics and the Cultural Production of Evil* (New York: Palgrave Macmillan, 2006), 21.

action, we co-create our vocational paths, constantly adjusting and refining our sense of call in response to new insights and circumstances. This collaborative approach to vocation allows us to embrace the fullness of our humanity and our divine potential.

For me, vocation involves a dual and reciprocal process of liberation: (1) freeing ourselves from internal and external obstacles that hinder our ability to live fully into our callings and (2) exercising the freedom to pursue faithful lives of meaning and purpose for the benefit of others and creation. This liberation is about personal fulfillment and about contributing to the flourishing of our communities.

In Jesus's time, the conquests of empire were declared as "good news" (*euangelion*.) Each time Caesar achieved a military victory or was hailed as divine, it was declared to be "gospel." To use the term "gospel" and proclaim the "kingdom of God" in that same language as Rome was a deliberate act of subversion on Jesus's part.[39] Jesus's vocation, and the one he called others into, was not neutral or apolitical; it announced a radically different kind of reign, one that healed rather than conquered, restored rather than punished. His public ministry became a counternarrative to imperial logic, offering a vision of life rooted in justice, mercy, and mutual care. To follow that call was (and is) to participate in a movement that challenges the dominant order by embodying another way of being in the world.

By addressing both the internal barriers (such as fear, doubt, and disordered attachments) and the external challenges (such as social injustices and systemic oppressions), we can move toward a more holistic and transformative understanding of vocation. This is not simply about choosing the right career or role. It is about discerning how our lives can resist the logic of domination and instead bear witness to a different kind of order. Just as Jesus proclaimed good news that contradicted the violent "peace" of Rome, we are invited to embody vocations that challenge the status quo and participate in the slow, faithful work of repair and renewal. Justice, compassion, and community are not ancillary to this process; they are its heart. Discernment, then, becomes a question of what kind of world we are helping to build and whose reign we are proclaiming in the process.

I see vocation as a call to human flourishing for ourselves, for those around us, and for creation itself. It's about discovering and nurturing our unique gifts and passions and finding ways to use them to serve the common good and the broader ecosystem of which we are a part. This perspective invites us to think expansively about our callings, recognizing that they may manifest in various forms and contexts throughout our lives. By focusing on flourishing, we can approach vocational discernment with a sense of hope and possibility, trusting that each step we take, no

---

39 N. T. Wright, "Paul's Gospel and Caesar's Empire," *Reflections* 2 (Spring 1999: Public Lecture Series 1998): 40–65. Princeton, NJ: Center for Theological Inquiry, 1999.

matter how small, contributes to a larger story of meaning and purpose. This vision of vocation encourages us to remain open to growth, transformation, and the abundant life God desires for all creation.

Ultimately, vocation is about becoming more fully who we are meant to be in service to others, creation, and God. Understanding that different emphases within vocation are appropriate for different people in different contexts is profoundly beneficial. What works for one person might not be suitable for another, and what is helpful in one context might be detrimental in another. Finding the proper equilibrium between narrow and broad, internal and external, is the work of discernment. The next chapter will guide us through this process, inviting us to see discernment as the companion to vocation, a vital tool for navigating the path toward our calling amid life's complexities.

Questions for Reflection

1. Do you currently, or have you ever, had a sense of vocation? A gentle (or insistent) pull toward something particular that is larger than yourself? If so, how would you describe the feeling or direction of that orientation? What images, metaphors, or even scripture stories, if any, come to mind when you try to name it?

2. Reflecting on your journey, can you identify pivotal moments when your sense of vocation evolved, deepened, or perhaps even felt disrupted? What relationships, experiences, or even societal shifts triggered these changes? How did you navigate your response? What practices, communities, or inner resources helped you (or might have helped you)?

3. In this chapter, a "Moral Orienting System" was described as the evolving set of values, relationships, beliefs, and practices that help us make meaning, navigate responsibility, and seek call in our lives. What are some of the things that most help you orient yourself in times of confusion or change?

4. Many of us wrestle with balancing the wisdom of our "inner voice" (those deep convictions or callings) with the important external feedback and needs of our communities and the world. How do you personally navigate this delicate dance? What specific practices, rhythms, or forms of discernment help you create a life-giving equilibrium between these internal and external currents, especially when they seem to be in tension?

5. Thinking about your relationships, have you ever had the privilege (or challenge) of accompanying another person as they sought clarity about their vocation? What did that experience feel like for you? What did you learn about vocation, discernment, or even your own calling through the process of walking alongside them?

6. This chapter suggests that vocation is something actively "co-authored" with the Divine. It highlights that God's invitations are often found within the possibilities, constraints, and choices of our lived realities, especially for those navigating systemic injustices. When you think about your own path, where have you felt that tension or collaboration between divine invitation and your active choices, particularly in the face of life's unchosen circumstances or systemic pressures? How has this "co-authoring" shaped your understanding of what a "faithful" response to call might look like, especially when the path isn't clear or easy?

2

Discernment

Anxiety is the dizziness of freedom.

—Søren Kierkegaard

Your problem is how you are going to spend this one odd and precious life you have been issued. Whether you're going to live it trying to look good and creating the illusion that you have power over people and circumstances, or whether you are going to taste it, enjoy it, and find out the truth about who you are.

—Anne Lamott

For many, pursuing a sense of vocation often involves envisioning a clear, singular goal. We are on the lookout for a specific job, achievement, or status that promises fulfillment. Yet this quest often leads to a frantic chase, much like Harry Potter's pursuit of the golden snitch. Or someone trying to herd cats. The chase can be exhilarating but ultimately leaves us feeling scattered and exhausted, driven by the need to prove or sustain an image of control. This, I believe, is what Kierkegaard refers to as the "dizziness of freedom," the anxiety that arises when we face the vast possibilities before us and consider them alongside the weight of choosing.[1]

But discerning a call is not always about relentless striving. Vocational discernment, rather than an act of acquisition, can be a process of release. It may call us to ask: What

---

[1] Søren Kierkegaard, *The Concept of Anxiety: A Simple Psychologically Oriented Deliberation in View of the Dogmatic Problem of Hereditary Sin*, trans. Alastair Hannay (New York: Liveright, 2014), 61.

can we let go of? What parts of our lives should we allow to fall away so that we can live more intentionally, investing our time and energy in ways that resonate with who we truly are? Into who we might become?

In this, we move closer to tasting life's fullness, as Anne Lamott describes,[2] finding ourselves not in what we accumulate, but in what we courageously choose to set free. The task of finding out what needs to be set free can be challenging, especially when it is something that has been meaningful to us for some time. Bonnie Miller-McLemore is great on this:

> We underestimate the turmoil of relinquishing a calling, and then we are surprised by it. Letting go of some of our most demanding callings—of paid work, for example, or of children as they go off to college—is wonderful. In a way. But to extol the freedom too quickly bypasses intermediary steps of relinquishment and lament.[3]

This perspective invites a shift in understanding vocation from a pursuit to a process of sifting and letting go. The very etymology of discernment highlights this process of sorting through our lives to determine what is nourishing and what can be set aside. Our English word comes from the Latin "*discernere*," which is made up of "*dis-*" which means "off, away," added to "*cernere*," which means "to separate." So, linguistically, discernment is the active work of distinguishing what is to be kept close from what is to be released or moved away from. It isn't that the things we relinquish are inherently bad or a mistake. But all things have their season, and, sometimes, recognizing that entails some grief.[4]

When I think of discernment, I think of how I use colanders when I cook. Boiling is essential to prepare noodles, but, once they are ready, we need to drain away the hot water. This doesn't mean the water was bad; it served its purpose. To get at the now-cooked noodles, we need to remove the water. In the same way, discernment helps us identify which aspects of our lives, our goals, or our ambitions have served their purpose and can now be released to allow us to embrace what will be nourishing and life-giving in the next phase of our life. Discernment is about determining what season we are in, what new growth is possible, and what needs to be pruned back.

One of the most meaningful experiences I've had in accompanying someone through vocational discernment involved a friend who had achieved significant success

---

[2] Anne Lamott, *Plan B: Further Thoughts on Faith* (New York: Riverhead Books, 2005).

[3] Bonnie J. Miller-McLemore, *Follow Your Bliss and Other Lies about Calling* (New York: Oxford University Press, 2024), 142.

[4] Ecclesiastes 3:1.

in his creative work. Originally, he had gone to college to study art and philosophy but ended up dropping out due to personal struggles. However, over the years he built up his art practice so that today he is one of the few people who can actually say he is a professional artist and makes his living from that. His projects, which involve creating intricate metal pieces sometimes 20 feet tall, require both artistic vision and collaboration with a team. Over time, he began to feel a growing disconnection from his identity as a creative professional. Much of his energy was consumed by managing people and logistics, leaving him questioning whether he was truly fulfilling his calling.

Through months of reflection and conversation together, it became clear that what energized him wasn't just the act of creation itself but the process of building teams and cultivating environments where people felt safe, connected, and free to explore new ideas. This realization revealed a dimension of his work and life that he hadn't fully appreciated before. In fact, this collaborative and relational work was deeply fulfilling, even though it wasn't the vision he had imagined years earlier.

This insight required reframing his understanding of vocation. The vision he had held for years, shaped by early ideals, no longer fully aligned with the joy he found in his work today. Instead of viewing this as a departure from his calling, he began to see it as an evolution, an expansion of what it meant to live into his vocation. He realized that, while his calling encompassed the creation of physical works, it also included the fostering of creativity and collaboration in others. This reframing allowed him to reconnect with his vocation as a dynamic and living expression, shaped by both past ideals and present realities. Things had changed. They will likely change again.

By focusing on release in addition to pursuit, individuals and communities may begin to recognize when goals and visions of vocation no longer serve them. From there, they can explore letting them go, where possible, to prioritize what remains nourishing. As I see it, discernment about vocation is primarily a function of four connected questions:

- What size, scale, sense, and orientation of vocation is right for the current season of life I am in?
- What things do I need more of to better move in the direction my vocation calls me toward?
- What things do I need less of to better move?
- What priority should be assigned to the work of getting what I need more of and letting go of what is an obstacle?

As we explored in the first chapter, I see vocation as a dynamic and unfolding journey, deeply rooted in our unique gifts, experiences, and social contexts. We reflected on how our sense of calling is shaped by both internal desires and external influences, and how navigating these often complex dynamics requires a deliberate and thoughtful approach. I argued that one of the ways to understand vocation is the process of finding a way to live in the freedom that comes when our liberation is bound up with the liberation of others.

Following this vision means recognizing that discernment is not a solitary act. As we'll explore further in the sixth chapter, our communities play a crucial role in guiding us, helping to shape and refine our understanding of who we are and who we are called to become. Sometimes, listening to the perspectives of community inspires and emboldens us to step into something new or challenging. Other times, these voices may sow doubt, challenging our capacity to lead or serve. Discernment, then, becomes the sacred work of sorting through these voices, of holding them alongside our inner convictions and the divine wisdom that comes to us in surprising ways.

This process is about opening ourselves to the ongoing interplay between God's call and our responses to it rather than fitting into a rigid, predetermined plan. It's about asking, again and again, how we might live more fully into the freedom and responsibility that come with vocation. Here, in the tension between the already and the not yet, discernment becomes a spiritual practice. It is a way of being in the world that requires both courage and humility, as we seek to align our lives with the deeper purposes of God.

Discernment: Definitions and Perspectives

Discernment is often associated with "finding the will of God." I sometimes see and hear people talking about this "finding" as if they thought they were looking for a specific set of divine assembly instructions, like our lives were complicated kits from Ikea. This "assembly instructions" model constricts our freedom, reducing our choices to fitting into a preordained plan. Of the several reasons why I think this "instructions" model is unsatisfactory, the principal one is that it constricts our freedom so much. The range of our freedom is reduced to choosing to "fit in," whether we like it or not, with what God has "planned" for us. First, we just have to figure out what that plan is.

The idea that God's will is a rigid, predetermined set of assembly instructions, akin to a manufacturer dictating every detail of our lives, can be limiting and anxiety-inducing. This assembly-model vision constrains our freedom and creativity, reducing our role to merely fitting into a preordained structure. Instead, we can envision God's will as a dynamic, relational process that invites our active participation and co-creation. This approach emphasizes a partnership with God, in which we are called to discern and respond to divine guidance in a way that is both responsive and responsible. This perspective does not negate the existence of the "will of God." Instead, it challenges us to rethink how we understand and relate to it.

Biblical texts like Genesis 1:26–28, Exodus 3:1–12, John 15:1–8, and 1 Corinthians 3:9 highlight themes of freedom, discernment, and co-creation with God, emphasizing an active, participatory role in God's work. How this role looks differs between Christian traditions. The Reformed tradition, usually emphasizing God's sovereignty and divine providence, might seem at odds with open-ended discernment, but it acknowledges common grace, aligning daily decisions with divine activity. This perspective allows for the unfolding of vocation to be seen as part of God's sovereign plan, where human actions, though limited, are a means by which divine purposes are progressively revealed in ordinary life.

Catholicism's Ignatian spirituality focuses on "finding God in all things," integrating prayer, reflection, and action, viewing discernment as a dynamic interaction between human freedom and divine guidance. This approach embraces adaptability by encouraging believers to engage in regular discernment practices, such as the Examen, which foster a deep awareness of God's ongoing call in the ever-changing circumstances of life.

Traditions emphasizing the Holy Spirit highlight a relational process of continuous listening and responding to God's promptings, enriching the understanding of discernment with the active role of spiritual gifts in everyday life. This framework sees the Spirit's guidance as dynamic and evolving, affirming that an unfolding sense of vocation aligns with the Spirit's work to equip and direct believers as they grow in faith and respond to changing needs around them.

The thing to take away is that there is room for discernment in all of these traditions. Whether it's through acknowledging God's grace in the Reformed tradition, integrating reflective practices in Catholicism, or continuously listening to the Spirit in charismatic traditions, discernment is a valuable and adaptable practice. For me, it is important to make sure to develop an understanding of the will of God that recognizes the reality and value of human freedom.

In my view, God's will for us is that we should learn to respond in freedom to God's love for us and to freely shape our lives by the choices that we make. God has given us instructions to assist us in the responsible exercise of our freedom: a conscience and the powers of judgment, scripture, tradition, the church, friends, spiritual directors, and wisdom developed from experience. What, then, can we say about "God's will"? David Lonsdale, involved for many years in adult Christian formation, provides this succinct summary:

> God's will is that we should exercise our freedom responsibly and well by choosing what honestly seems the best course of action in a given set of circumstances, using all the relevant aids that we have been given for that

purpose. There is a sense in which we create, in terms of concrete action in given circumstances, the will of God in this exercise of freedom. There is no blueprint in God's mind with which we have to comply.[5]

This exercise aims not for perfect compliance with an unknown plan, but for choices made with integrity, reflecting a coherence among our values, beliefs, and relationships.

Lonsdale's understanding resonates with the idea that living a "vocational life" is also a practice of listening and adaptation. This shift allows us to see discernment as an ongoing, adaptive process of engaging deeply with both our inner selves and the circumstances around us. It calls us to cultivate a heightened awareness of God's presence and to respond faithfully to the evolving callings that emerge in our lives.

Historically, discernment has been an integral practice within many religious traditions, offering a way to navigate the complexities of life with wisdom and grace. In Christianity, discernment is often associated with the practice of "listening with the ear of the heart" and involves an ongoing process of prayerful reflection and attentive listening to the movements of the Spirit.[6] In other words, developing an awareness that goes beyond logic, noticing subtle shifts in intuition, resonance, ethical clarity, or relational dynamics; those inner and outer "movements" that can signal the ways in which a potential path forward might help to ground (or disorient!) us.

Discernment is not confined to moments of crisis or major decisions but is a daily exercise in noticing the subtle ways in which God communicates through our experiences, emotions, and relationships. I know a man who only owns one style of socks, but, nonetheless, prays every morning to see if God has some particular pair he is supposed to wear that day. He doesn't think that socks are a particularly important thing to pray about, but it does mean he starts every day with the assumption that God might have something to say about how he is living his life. It gets him into the habit of listening.

The practice is the thing in which the formation takes place, not the outcome. The act and process of discernment itself is as (or more) important than the decision(s) discernment helps us to reach. Seen this way, discernment calls us to a deeper level of self-awareness and an attentive openness to the divine, recognizing that discernment is an ongoing journey rather than a single, definitive moment

---

5 David Lonsdale, "Discernment of Spirits," in *An Ignatian Spirituality Reader: Contemporary Writings on Ignatius of Loyola, the Spiritual Exercises, Discernment, and More*, ed. George W. Traub (Chicago: Loyola Press, 2008), 174.

6 Benedict's Rule begins "Listen carefully, my Son, to the master's instructions, and attend to them with the ear of your heart." *The Rule of St. Benedict in Latin and English* (Collegeville, MN: Liturgical Press, 1981), Prologue, 1.

of clarity. Through this lens, discernment becomes a way of living that integrates our spiritual, emotional, and intellectual dimensions, guiding us toward a more meaningful and fulfilling response to our vocation. Specific decisions may indeed require active discernment, but it is also the case that living a discerning life in general helps to yield situations in which decisions and discernment can be done with greater familiarity and ease.

To deepen our understanding of discernment, I've found it helpful to explore its scriptural foundations. The biblical language of discernment offers rich insights, highlighting the importance of understanding, listening, and distinguishing between different spirits and truths. By examining the original Hebrew and Greek words often translated as "discernment," we can gain a deeper appreciation for how this practice has been understood and valued within Jewish and Christian traditions. When we read the word "discernment" in English in scripture, it can be a translation of a number of different words from Hebrew or Greek.

A Word Study of Discernment

In the Hebrew scriptures, several terms convey the concept of discernment. The word בִּין (*bin* or *biyn*) signifies understanding, perceiving, and discerning, as seen in Proverbs 2:3: "Indeed, if you call out for insight and cry aloud for *biyn*." Another term, שָׁמַע (*shama*), means to hear, listen, understand, and obey. This is evident in Deuteronomy 6:4: "*shama*, O Israel: The LORD our God, the LORD is one," which emphasizes listening and understanding God's commandments. Finally, בִּינָה (*binah*) refers to understanding, insight, and discernment, as highlighted in Proverbs 8:14: "Counsel and sound judgment are mine; I have *binah*, I have power."

In the New Testament, Greek words further elaborate on the nuances of discernment. διακρίνω (*diakrino*) means to distinguish, judge, and discern, as found in 1 Corinthians 12:10: "to another miraculous powers, to another prophecy, to another *diakrino* between spirits." Another term, δοκιμάζω (*dokimazo*), signifies testing, proving, examining, and discerning, as seen in Romans 12:2: "Do not conform to the pattern of this world, but be transformed by the renewing of your mind. Then you will be able to test and *dokimazo* what God's will is, his good, pleasing and perfect will." Last, ἀνακρίνω (*anakrino*) involves examining, investigating, questioning, and discerning, as illustrated in 1 Corinthians 2:14–15: "The person without the Spirit does not accept the things that come from the Spirit of God but considers them foolishness, and cannot understand them because they are *anakrino* only through the Spirit." From these scriptural insights, we learn that discernment is deeply rooted in understanding, listening, and distinguishing.

In the Hebrew scriptures, terms like *biyn*, *shama*, and *binah* emphasize the necessity of perceiving and understanding God's will, listening attentively to divine guidance, and applying insight to our lives. In the New Testament, *diakrino, dokimazo,* and *anakrino* highlight the importance of distinguishing between spirits, testing and proving what is good, and examining truths with an attentive mind. I take from the biblical perspective that discernment involves a comprehensive engagement of our intellectual, emotional, and spiritual faculties. It is a holistic process that calls us to integrate heart and mind, to listen deeply, and to thoughtfully navigate the complexities of our vocation with divine guidance. This integration of feeling and thinking may be unusual today, but it was more normative in ages past.

In the Hebrew tradition, the word לֵב (*lev*) encompasses both "heart" and "mind," underscoring the holistic nature of discernment, integrating emotions and intellect as the center of being.[7] Feeling and thinking were both seated in the heart. This holistic view challenges the modern dichotomy between heart and mind, inviting us to consider how our intellectual and emotional lives are deeply intertwined. This understanding calls us to a deeper form of self-awareness and reflection. It asks us to recognize that our emotions are not separate from our reasoning processes. They are integral to how we perceive and interpret the world around us.

In the context of discernment, this means that insight often comes from engaging with our entire being, not just our rational thoughts or emotional responses in isolation. By embracing this integrated understanding of heart and mind, we open ourselves to a richer and more profound practice of discernment. It encourages us both to cultivate a deeper awareness of how our thoughts and emotions interact and to seek a harmonious alignment with our deepest values and divine guidance. When I invite my students to practice theological reflection, I find it is useful to encourage them to emphasize this holistic vision.

For example, when I ask students to describe a personal encounter they want to think about theologically, I start by asking them to highlight not "just the facts," but also the emotions evoked by the experience. I'll talk about this more in the next chapter, but I'll note here that, when doing theological reflection, I encourage people to consider their background and personal history, which can help them recognize the interplay between emotions and thoughts. By analyzing the social dynamics at play, we can explore how power and social location can influence a situation. I suggest that we ought to move on to find a connection to scripture or theological principles only once there is some sense of the broader context of an experience. These connections

---

7 For example, Proverbs 3:3, 6:21, and 7:3 all refer to the heart as the center of thinking and reason, and Proverbs 15:15 and 30 have emotions there as well.

further encourage us to see how our embedded theology and context shape both our emotional and intellectual reactions. This helps make visible some of the factors that influence us but are not always evident. I find this is also part of discernment.

In the *Encyclopedia of Psychology and Religion,* discernment is defined from a psychological and secular perspective as "an intentional process that seeks to render unconscious material available to consciousness for the sake of making healthful and appropriate decisions."[8] For a religious person, this definition can serve as a bridge, highlighting how practices like prayer, meditation, or spiritual reflection might also function as tools for bringing hidden insights to light and aligning life choices with deeper values or divine guidance. The need to make healthful and meaningful decisions is a common human concern, and religious and philosophical traditions throughout the world offer nuanced perspectives on it.

Hindu and Yoga traditions both use a Sanskrit term—विवेक (*viveka*)—that broadly translates to "discernment." *Viveka* emphasizes the cultivation of a keen ability to prioritize and detach from obstacles that hinder spiritual progress. In Vedanta, *viveka* is the ability to distinguish between the real (the eternal self, *atman*) and the unreal (the impermanent material world, *maya*). This discernment guides ethical living, mindfulness, and the alignment of actions with one's higher spiritual aspirations. Developing *viveka* involves study, reflection, meditation, self-inquiry, and cultivating detachment from material distractions.[9]

What I find fascinating is that the word *viveka* has precisely the same etymology as *discern*: It is the prefix *vi-* attached to the root *-vich*. The root *-vich* means to sift or to separate, and *vi-* is used to mean away from.[10] Similarly, the Arabic فُرْقَان (*furqān*) is a term used in the Qur'an to refer to the criterion or standard by which to discern right from wrong, truth from falsehood, and guidance from misguidance. It is often used as an attribute of the Qur'an itself, emphasizing its role as a decisive factor and a clear proof. The word is derived from the f-r-q root (ف-ر-ق), which carries the meaning of separation, distinction, and differentiation.[11] The same root gives rise to other words like *farq* (difference) and *faraqa* (to separate or distinguish). What are we to make of this shared linguistic and philosophical heritage?

---

8 Harold G. Koenig, "Discernment," in *Encyclopedia of Psychology and Religion*, 3rd ed., ed. David A. Leeming (New York: Springer, 2020), 505.

9 W. J. Johnson. "Viveka," in *A Dictionary of Hinduism*, 1st ed. (New York: Oxford University Press, 2010), 353.

10 Monier Monier-Williams, *A Sanskrit-English Dictionary*, ed. Carl Cappeller, Ernst Leumann, and Montagu Sneade Faithfull Monier-Williams (1872; Oxford: Clarendon Press, 1899).

11 John Bowker, "Furqān," in *The Concise Oxford Dictionary of World Religions* online (New York: Oxford University Press, 2003).

For me, this connection highlights the common human concern with separating the life-giving from the life-denying, the true from the false, and the permanent from the transient. It suggests that the act of discernment is less about acquiring or chasing after things and more about the deliberate, often difficult, work of sifting things away to reveal what truly matters. This process manifests differently across contexts and forms, shaped by cultural, spiritual, and individual understandings of what is worth holding onto. As I see it, discernment invites us into a thoughtful and evolving process of aligning our lives with what fosters meaning, connection, and flourishing.

To fully appreciate the depth and richness of discernment, we need to examine how it operates on both an individual and communal level. Each dimension brings its own unique insights and challenges, contributing to a comprehensive understanding of how we can navigate our vocational journeys with intention and grace. Individual discernment is an intimate process of self-reflection and inner listening, where we seek to align our actions with our deepest values and divine guidance. It involves creating space for solitude, recognizing and interpreting the signs within us, and making decisions that resonate with our fullest sense of ourselves.

On the other hand, communal discernment emphasizes the collective wisdom and support that comes from engaging with others. It involves listening to and integrating the voices and insights of our communities, which can provide broader perspectives and help us see beyond our individual limitations. Dalit theology, as articulated by Arvind P. Nirmal and other theologians from oppressed caste contexts in India, offers a profound model of such communal discernment.[12] Grounded in the lived experiences of Dalit Christians, this theological framework begins with the realities of marginalization and exclusion. In this context, discernment is not an individualistic process but a deeply communal act, shaped by the collective struggle for justice and equality.

A compelling example of this communal discernment is found in the practice of *satsangs,* gatherings for spiritual reflection, song, and dialogue. In these spaces, particularly as demonstrated in movements like *Sachchai,* individuals from marginalized communities are encouraged to share testimonies, interpret scripture collectively, and use symbolic acts such as speaking into a microphone as a reclaiming of voice and dignity.[13] For Dalit women, this act is especially significant in challenging

---

12 See, for example, Arvind P. Nirmal, "Towards a Christian Dalit Theology," in *Indigenous People: Dalits: Dalit Issues in Today's Theological Debate*, ed. James Massey (Delhi, India: Indian Society for Promoting Christian Knowledge, 1994), 214–30.

13 Amar Bahadur BK, "Speaking Is Healing: Dalit Women Gain a Voice through a Charismatic Healing Movement in Nepal," *CASTE: A Global Journal on Social Exclusion* 1, no. 2 (October 2020): 73–90, https://doi.org/10.26812/caste.v1i2.171.

both caste and patriarchal structures that have historically silenced them.[14] Rooted in the belief that God stands with the marginalized, these practices affirm the agency of the marginalized and create sacred spaces where discernment becomes a communal and liberative act, centered on the experiences of those on the margins. When people make meaning together, they are making power together.

This approach challenges communities to ask: How are our discernment practices amplifying the voices of the marginalized? How do they incorporate symbols, stories, and rituals that ground theology in the lived experiences of the oppressed? By embracing these practices, discernment becomes not just a spiritual act but also a revolutionary commitment to justice and solidarity, calling communities into deeper engagement with both the divine and the realities of the world's brokenness.

Through shared experiences and collective reflection, communal discernment enriches our understanding and ensures that our personal decisions resonate with a broader, shared vision of purpose and vocation. By exploring both individual and communal discernment, we can develop a more holistic and integrated approach to vocational discernment. This dual focus allows us to balance personal introspection with communal engagement, helping us navigate our vocational paths with greater clarity, intention, and awareness of grace.

Individual Discernment

As a Christian, I think that one of the tools I have for helping me to discern is to ask if the thing I am considering seems likely to yield a "fruit of the Spirit," which Paul offers as love, joy, peace, patience, kindness, generosity, faithfulness, gentleness, and self-control.[15] As I see it, these virtues are not only markers of spiritual alignment to consider after the fact, but also indicators of a life lived in harmony with God's call while discernment is ongoing. To discern well, I must consider whether a choice reflects these qualities, not just in outcomes but in the process itself. Does the decision invite greater peace or love into my life and the lives of others? Does it require patience and self-control? Does considering this nurture generosity and kindness in my life?

Such questions help me sift through the motivations and desires shaping my decisions, guiding me toward paths that are life-giving rather than self-serving. They can also help me realize when it *is* life-giving to be self-serving. That is, when prioritizing my own needs, boundaries, or well-being ultimately enables me to better

---

14 Ibid.
15 Galatians 5:22–23.

serve others and participate in God's call. Discernment also brings us into contact with the deeper framework that helps us recognize what feels morally sound, a sense of inner integrity, relational trust, and clarity of purpose. More than just the right decision, discernment is about alignment with what we most value and are called to embody. Recognizing that self-care and self-preservation can be acts of faithfulness allows discernment to move beyond rigid selflessness, embracing a holistic view of what it means to live in alignment with God's purposes. While these spiritual markers offer valuable guidance, they are not automatic; their cultivation requires intentionality, patience, and openness to God's shaping presence. This deeper work of discernment invites us to create space for reflection and growth, nurturing the conditions in which these fruits can flourish.

I believe that deepening the capacity for individual discernment is largely about cultivating the habit of making room in our lives to be able to experience and name the presence of the divine. It's a practice that invites us to create space to sit with our thoughts and feelings, and to sift through the various influences that shape our decisions. This process aligns with what many traditions describe as developing a more refined capacity for listening to the Spirit. The United Methodist Church has a good definition that helps to clarify this point:

> Discernment is a gift of deep intuition and insight. Discerning people can separate truth from fiction and know at a visceral level when people are being honest. Deeply sensitive and "tuned in," those with the gift of discernment are open to feelings, new ideas, and intuition as valid and credible information. Discernment is not irrational, but trans-rational—beyond empirical—knowledge.[16]

Both Methodist and Ignatian perspectives view discernment as a perspective that transcends rational knowledge. They emphasize being attuned to feelings, new ideas, and intuition as valid sources of information, inviting a deep engagement with the interior life. Ignatian spirituality offers a structured and accessible framework for cultivating the kind of sensitivity and attentiveness to the divine that the United Methodist definition describes. By focusing on the "motions of the soul" and the interior movements of thoughts, emotions, and desires, Ignatian discernment provides practical tools for developing the gift of discernment in one's daily life.

---

16 The United Methodist Church, "Spiritual Gifts: Discernment." https://www.umc.org/en/content/spiritual-gifts-discernment.

Ignatian Perspectives

In the landscape of individual discernment practices, Catholic Ignatian spirituality stands out prominently, and for good reason. The Ignatian approach offers a structured, time-tested method that has been refined over centuries. Its prevalence in discussions of discernment stems from several key factors. First, despite its depth, Ignatian discernment is remarkably accessible, providing practical tools that individuals can apply in their daily lives. This approach demonstrates a nuanced understanding of human psychology, particularly in its attention to the "movements of the soul," making it insightful and relevant. Second, while rooted in Christian tradition, many of the Ignatian principles can be adapted to various spiritual contexts, showcasing its flexibility. Finally, Ignatian discernment emphasizes finding the sacred in the ordinary, encouraging an everyday spirituality that is particularly pertinent for vocational discernment.

As the term is used in Jesuit and Ignatian circles, discernment encompasses both a general approach to making decisions in the presence of God and a more structured method derived from the rules set forth in *The Spiritual Exercises* of Ignatius Loyola.[17] At its core, Ignatian discernment is the process of prayerfully reflecting on one's interior experiences to determine God's will and make good decisions. The "Discernment of Spirits" is central to Ignatian discernment and involves interpreting internal movements of thoughts and emotions to distinguish between what is motivated by the Holy Spirit and what is driven by impulse or habit.[18]

Although Ignatius did not provide a single concise definition of discernment in his Spiritual Exercises, his understanding of discernment can be pieced together from various passages. As I see it, Ignatian discernment is functionally about three key elements. First, it involves reflecting on one's ultimate purpose, which is to love and serve God. Second, it requires examining one's desires, thoughts, and feelings to see if they align with this purpose. And third, it entails choosing a course of action that helps fulfill this purpose. The "First Principle and Foundation" of the Spiritual Exercises encapsulates this perspective:

---

[17] The Spiritual Exercises of Ignatius Loyola are a set of Christian meditations, prayers, and mental exercises developed by Saint Ignatius of Loyola, the founder of the Jesuits. Originally intended as a thirty-day retreat, they are designed to deepen one's relationship with God, enhance spiritual growth, and help individuals discern God's will in their lives. The exercises are structured to facilitate a profound spiritual journey, encompassing themes such as sin, repentance, the life of Christ, and the resurrection. They can be adapted for use over different periods, including the "19th Annotation" version which integrates the exercises into daily life over several months.

[18] A fairly accessible book on this is Timothy M. Gallagher, OMV, *The Discernment of Spirits: An Ignatian Guide for Everyday Living* (New York: Crossroad, 2005).

> The goal of our life is to live with God forever. God, who loves us, gave us life. Our own response of love allows God's life to flow into us without limit.[19]

For Ignatius, discernment is a continuous, prayer-infused process of seeking God's will in the concrete circumstances of life, combining spiritual practices with sound reasoning and judgment.

It's important to note that loving and praising God isn't just a one-way street of adoration but is part of more deeply appreciating the presence of grace. Jesus said he came so that we may have life, and have it abundantly.[20] I think that a full and abundant life partly entails a sense of purpose, meaning, and connection to others and creation. Ignatian spirituality is particularly resonant with this as it emphasizes the dailiness of connecting with the divine. It encourages us to find God in all things, to seek the sacred in the ordinary moments of our lives, and to cultivate a deep sense of gratitude for the many gifts we receive each day. This approach to spirituality fosters a profound awareness of God's presence and activity in every aspect of our lives, guiding us toward a more intentional and spiritually rich existence.

Jesuit priest and writer James Martin, in his book *The Jesuit Guide to (Almost) Everything*, highlights four key principles that are integral to the Ignatian approach to discernment. First, Ignatian spirituality is about finding God in all things, recognizing that every aspect of life, including work, relationships, and suffering, is within the realm of the spiritual. Second, it involves being a contemplative in action, balancing an active life with a meditative stance and seeing the world as one's monastery. Third, it embraces an incarnational spirituality, believing that God is present in the everyday events of our lives. Finally, it seeks freedom and detachment, avoiding "disordered affections" that prevent us from making free and life-giving decisions.[21]

These principles underscore the Ignatian understanding of discernment as a dynamic process, requiring ongoing attentiveness to God's presence and guidance in all aspects of life. It involves honesty, humility, and openness to God's leading, helping individuals make choices that align with their deepest desires and fullest sense of themselves in God. This holistic approach integrates emotions, thoughts, spiritual insights, and bodily sensations, fostering a profound engagement with one's inner life and the divine, ultimately leading to a more abundant and purposeful life.

---

19 David L. Fleming, *Modern Spiritual Exercises: A Contemporary Reading of the Spiritual Exercises of St. Ignatius* (Garden City, NY: Image Books, 1983).

20 John 10:10.

21 James Martin, *The Jesuit Guide to (Almost) Everything: A Spirituality for Real Life* (New York: HarperOne, 2010), 11–12.

> **A Practice to Consider:**
> ## Condensed Examen
>
> *Reflection at the end of each day opens a sacred space to notice where we align with our purpose and where we drift. In these small moments, we invite clarity and direction for our ongoing journey.*
>
> The full Examen has more to it than this, but sometimes even a small moment for reflection can be beneficial. At day's end, reflect on when you felt most in tune with your purpose, and when you felt farthest from it. Keep a record of your answers each day and monthly reflect on them and see if they suggest some direction to consider.

The Ignatian tradition offers several specific practices that can inform individual discernment. One such practice is the Daily Examen, a reflective prayer practice that involves reviewing the day in the presence of God. The Examen typically includes five steps: giving thanks, asking for grace to know one's sins, reviewing the day, asking for forgiveness, and making a resolution for the future. This daily habit helps individuals become more aware of God's presence in their everyday lives and discern how they are responding to God's call.

The Ignatian Spiritual Exercises—a retreat-based program of meditations, prayers, and contemplations—help deepen one's relationship with God. They can be done in a thirty-day retreat or over several months, a format called "the 19th Annotation." Even without a retreat, some prayer practices can be integrated into personal discernment. For example, one of the imaginative techniques within the Spiritual Exercises is the "Meditation on the Two Standards (or Two Flags)."[22] This exercise presents a powerful and vivid imagery of two opposing forces: the standard of Christ and the standard of Satan. Participants are invited to envision a great battlefield with Christ's standard on one side and Satan's on the other. This meditation helps individuals to reflect deeply on their allegiances, choices, and values. It compels them to consider which side they align with in their daily actions and decisions. By contemplating the characteristics and consequences of each standard, individuals can gain clarity on the values they wish to uphold and the spiritual battles they face. This exercise is not merely about choosing sides but about committing to live out the values of Christ, such as love,

---

22 There are many books on the Exercises, but I tend to go to Kevin O'Brien, SJ, *The Ignatian Adventure: Experiencing the Spiritual Exercises of St. Ignatius in Daily Life* (Chicago: Loyola Press, 2011). O'Brien also has a short, useful video about this exercise here: https://www.youtube.com/watch?v=ODnPP9U12Jo.

humility, and service, more fully in their lives, thereby fostering a deeper commitment to their faith.

For those who feel that Ignatius's former life as a military man is too present in the Two Standards, another Ignatian practice is Gospel Contemplation or Gospel Imagination.[23] This method involves placing oneself imaginatively within a Gospel story, engaging all the senses and emotions to experience the events of Jesus's life more vividly and personally. For example, if meditating on the Nativity scene, one would imagine the sights, sounds, smells, and emotions of that holy night.

Perhaps you might feel the chill of the air in the stable, the texture of the straw, the expressions of awe on the faces of Mary and Joseph, or the piercing cries of the newborn Jesus rising above the songs of the angels. This deep, sensory engagement allows individuals to encounter the Gospel narrative in a profoundly personal way, making it easier to discern God's call. By immersing oneself in the life and teachings of Jesus, individuals can draw insights and guidance that are directly applicable to their own lives, leading to greater clarity and commitment in their spiritual journey.

Ignatian spirituality also emphasizes the importance of spiritual direction, a practice in which an individual meets regularly with a spiritual director to reflect on their spiritual journey. The spiritual director acts as a companion, offering guidance and support as the individual seeks to understand and follow God's will. Through this relationship, individuals can explore their experiences, discern the movements of the Spirit in their lives, and receive personalized guidance on their path of discernment.

For those who may not have (or want) access to a formal spiritual director, it is still valuable to seek out a trusted pastor, faithful friend, or someone with a listening ear. Relationships are important in the discernment process, as they provide a space for honest conversation and reflection. I'll talk about it more in the seventh chapter's discussion of accompaniment, but here I'll note that asking someone to truly listen and help discern can foster a deeper understanding of one's spiritual journey. These conversations can be immensely supportive, providing insight and encouragement, and helping individuals stay attuned to God's presence and guidance in their lives. It is important, though, to clarify if you are looking for advice, feedback, reflection, critique, or just a listening and supportive presence. People don't always know how best to be with each other, so providing some insight into what you're looking for can be very helpful, both to them and you.

However you proceed, it's useful to recognize that Ignatian discernment, while valuable, is not the only tool kit available. In fact, I believe that discernment often transcends any single method or tradition. It's a deeply personal process that requires us to develop our own unique "discernment muscles." This may involve integrating

---

23 O'Brien has another useful video here: https://www.youtube.com/watch?v=gwgtGO_Cju0.

insights from various spiritual practices and traditions, and being open to the diverse ways in which the divine might be speaking to us. As we grow in our discernment, we become more adept at navigating the complexities of our spiritual journeys, finding the path that resonates most deeply with our own experiences and callings.

Additional Practices

While traditional methods such as prayer, meditation, and spiritual direction are invaluable, there are numerous additional practices that can enrich and deepen the discernment process. These practices, which may draw from different traditions and areas of life, offer fresh perspectives and tools for tuning into divine guidance. They invite us to explore discernment in a more holistic way, integrating mind, body, and spirit. However, it is important to approach this diversity of practices with a word of caution. The breadth of available options can expand our sense of what is possible, but it can also lead to a tendency to jump from one practice to another without fully committing to any. This "spiritual salad bar" approach can sometimes be an excuse to avoid deepening into a practice when the going gets tough. Discernment often requires perseverance and dedication to a chosen path, even when challenges arise.

For example, embodied wisdom is one often overlooked aspect of individual discernment. This concept recognizes that our bodies often hold insights that our conscious minds haven't yet processed. Pay attention to physical sensations when contemplating different paths. Do you feel a sense of expansion or contraction in your chest? Does a particular option make you feel grounded or unsteady? These bodily cues can provide important information about how we are being guided and can complement more traditional discernment practices. However, sometimes paying attention to your body may raise concerning feelings, prompting you to bail on that type of reflection. This could be as simple as indigestion from too much garlic or as complex as unresolved trauma that might require exploration with a therapist. Just because a practice is tough doesn't mean that it should be abandoned. Sometimes, pushing through the discomfort can lead to deeper understanding and growth, highlighting areas that need healing and attention.

Embodied wisdom is just one of the many practices that can enrich your discernment journey. By tuning in to the physical responses of our bodies, we can gain insights that might otherwise remain hidden. Yet there are other valuable practices that can also offer profound guidance and clarity. "Future self-dialogue" is another practice that folks have often found helpful. This involves imaginatively conversing with your future self about the decision at hand. How does your future self, looking back, view the choice you're considering? What wisdom or perspective does this older, more experienced version of you offer? This exercise can provide a unique vantage point, helping to clarify long-term implications that might not be immediately apparent.

Another practice that can be deeply enriching is what I call a "Visio Divina Gallery Walk."[24] This involves using curated images to connect with inner reflections and perceptions. To set up a Visio Divina Gallery, I curate a diverse collection of images that evoke a range of emotions, themes, and stories, including nature, people, abstract art, and everyday scenes. I then place these images with ample space between them, allowing participants to move freely and engage with each image without feeling crowded. I invite participants to slowly wander around the room, holding a question in mind and taking their time to look at each image and pay attention to their initial reactions and feelings. They should select an image that evokes a strong reaction, whether positive or negative. Once they have chosen an image, they should sit quietly with it, observe it closely, and reflect on questions such as: What emotions or thoughts arise when you look at this image? What details stand out the most? If this image is a message from God, what might God be trying to say to you through it? This practice allows for deep personal insights and can be enhanced through optional group sharing, either in small groups or with the larger group, fostering a sense of community and shared spiritual journey.

Whatever practice is used, regardless of its origin, I've observed that effective individual discernment often involves a dance between structure and spontaneity. While very detailed processes like the Spiritual Exercises can be incredibly valuable, it's equally important to remain open to unexpected moments of clarity. These might come during a walk in nature, in the middle of a conversation, or even while doing mundane tasks. Cultivating an attitude of openness to these spontaneous insights can enrich our discernment process. As we engage in individual discernment, it's important to approach the process with both intention and grace: intention in the sense of committing to regular practices of reflection and self-examination, and grace in allowing ourselves the space to grow, change, and sometimes make mistakes in our discernment journey.

It's also worth noting that individual discernment, while personal, doesn't happen in a vacuum. Our discernment is always influenced by our cultural context, personal history, and relationships. Recognizing these influences is important. For instance, someone raised in a culture that highly values financial success might need to consciously examine whether their decisions are aligned with their vocational call or are more reflective of internalized cultural expectations.

---

24 If you're interested in seeing some of the images I have used in the past, you can check them out at https://tiny.cc/VDGW.

Ultimately, individual discernment is about developing a deep attunement to how our actions can be best put to use to deepen the divine presence in our lives and serve ever more deeply. It's a lifelong practice of listening, reflecting, and responding to the call of vocation as it unfolds uniquely for each of us. As we cultivate this personal practice, we lay the groundwork for engaging more fully in communal discernment, which we'll explore in the next section. The insights gained through individual discernment become the threads we bring to the communal tapestry of shared wisdom and collective discernment.

Communal Discernment

The early years of the Jesuits offer a compelling example of the importance of communal discernment. Ignatius of Loyola emphasized the role of community in discerning God's will, leading to the emergence of the *deliberatio* process. This method of group discernment and decision-making significantly influenced the formation and development of the Society of Jesus. Rooted in the need to make important decisions about their collective future, the *deliberatio* process involved several key elements: group discernment through days of prayer and discussions, a structured approach to analyzing arguments, a goal of reaching decisions without dissent, and an extended duration for reflection. This process, first used in the spring of 1539, shaped the future of the Jesuit order.[25] The 1539 deliberations continued for almost three months.

These deliberations provide an invaluable record of the considerations that gave rise to the Jesuit order. The process was thorough and deeply spiritual, reflecting the Jesuits' commitment to finding and following God's will. It included prayer, meditation, and personal reflection, followed by proposing and analyzing arguments concerning the vow of obedience. The final decision, reached without dissent, established the practice of obedience to one member to better fulfill divine will and preserve the Society.[26] The impact of the *deliberatio* process was profound, leading to the formal establishment of the Society of Jesus and laying the groundwork for its hierarchical structure. It provided a framework for decision-making that balanced individual reflection, group discussion, and spiritual discernment, becoming a hallmark of Jesuit practice. This process fostered unity among the diverse early Jesuits, emphasized spiritual preparation, and allowed for adaptability in their methods, reinforcing the order's spiritual foundation.

---

25 "The Deliberation of Our First Fathers," trans. Dominic Maruca, *Woodstock Letters* 95, no. 3 (Summer 1966): 325–33, https://jesuits-eum.org/readings/the-deliberations-of-our-first-fathers/.

26 Ibid.

The *deliberatio* process became an integral part of the Jesuit tradition, influencing not only the early years of the Society but also its future development. It embodied key Jesuit principles such as finding God's will, maintaining unity in diversity, and balancing action with contemplation. The process continues to be valued in Jesuit decision-making, serving as a link to the order's founding spirit and a tool for addressing contemporary challenges. It is intriguing to note that, during the initial deliberation, one of the key decisions made was to establish a Jesuit superior. Consequently, in Jesuit governance, the *deliberatio* transitioned from its original role as a decision-making body to a consultative one, assisting the superior, who ultimately makes the final decisions. It proceeded this way for centuries, until after Vatican II, when Father General Pedro Arrupe reemphasized the role of communal discernment as an aid to the decision-making of the superior. Jesuit provincials are now required to have a commission for the choice of ministries to help carry out this type of discernment.[27]

Following Arrupe's decision to reemphasize communal discernment, it was a Jesuit scholar who decided to undertake one of the largest research projects about Quaker practices.[28] When it was released in 1973, Michael J. Sheeran, SJ's work *Beyond Majority Rule* was intended to serve as a means for Jesuits to "rediscover for themselves their own birthright of communal discernment."[29] The Jesuit tradition of communal discernment, with its structured and spiritually grounded approach, provides a valuable model for understanding how power dynamics can be navigated in collective decision-making. However, it is not the only tradition that offers insights into communal discernment. Just as the Jesuits developed methods to balance individual and collective input, the Quaker tradition also evolved its own distinctive approach to communal discernment, emerging from a very different context and resulting in the near-total elimination of formal hierarchy.

Whereas the Jesuits' structured approach provided a clear framework for decision-making that resulted in the decision to have superiors, the Quakers sought to emphasize the primacy of a personal spiritual experience that eliminated hierarchy. This divergence in approach highlights the diversity in methods of communal

---

[27] Thomas Worcester, SJ, ed., "Jesuits and Vatican II," in *The Cambridge Encyclopedia of the Jesuits* (Cambridge: Cambridge University Press, 2017), 818–19.

[28] As a small matter of personal connection, I should note that it is because of that very book, *Beyond Majority Rule*, by Michael J. Sheeran (Philadelphia: Philadelphia Yearly Meeting of the Religious Society of Friends, 1996), that I first realized that I was interested in learning more about the Jesuits, Ignatian spirituality, and the way that other traditions thought about discernment and vocation.

[29] Michael J. Sheeran, "A Tradition In Common," *Saint Joseph's Magazine* (1987): 30.

discernment and the potential challenges each can face. The early Quakers emphasized the direct experience of God as the source of authority. This could lead to a sense of individual infallibility, and this emphasis on individual experience soon proved problematic, as separate insights could vary and even contradict one another, leaving the nascent Quaker community adrift.

An incident with James Nayler, a prominent early British Quaker minister, highlighted the risks of unchecked individual leadings. In 1656, feeling led by God to do so, Nayler and his followers staged a provocative reenactment of Christ's entry into Jerusalem in the city of Bristol, which was perceived as blasphemous by the authorities.[30] Nayler faced severe punishment, and the event brought increased persecution upon Quakers. In response, other early Quaker leaders began to establish structures and processes for communal discernment and accountability. These developments were controversial and met with resistance from some who felt they infringed on individual freedom. However, they also marked a recognition of the need to balance individual leadings with communal wisdom.

The Quaker decision-making process emerged as a way to seek unity and the "sense of the meeting" through worshipful listening and collective discernment. Central to this process is the belief that each person has access to divine guidance, but that discernment is enriched and tested through the gathered wisdom of the community. Today, the Quaker notion of discernment is much more inclined to recognize the fallibility of those practicing it.

> Spiritual Discernment is ... the faculty we use to distinguish the true movement of the Spirit ... from the wholly human urge to share, to instruct, or to straighten people out.... It is the ability to see into people, situations and possibilities to identify what is of God in them and what is of the numerous other sources in ourselves—and what may be both.[31]

This "both" highlights the complex interplay between the divine and the human within discernment. It suggests that our motivations, actions, and insights can simultaneously carry elements of God's presence and our personal biases or limitations.

Recognizing this duality is important because it encourages humility and vigilance, reminding us to remain open to correction and growth as we discern the path forward

---

[30] A good book on James Nayler is Leo Damrosch, *The Sorrows of the Quaker Jesus: James Nayler and the Puritan Crackdown on the Free Spirit* (Cambridge, MA: Harvard University Press, 1996).

[31] Patricia Loring, *Spiritual Discernment: The Context and Goal of Clearness Committees*, Pendle Hill Pamphlet #305 (Wallingford, PA: Pendle Hill Publications, 1992), 3.

in faith and community. Early Quakers used the phrase "keeping watch" to describe the practice of maintaining spiritual attentiveness, both to divine guidance and to the human impulses that might cloud it.[32] This vigilance was not limited to moments of worship, extending into daily life and fostering a continual awareness of the movements of the Spirit and a commitment to align one's actions with the Light within. This discipline undergirds the Quaker approach to discernment, urging practitioners to stay grounded in both personal introspection and communal accountability.

While communal discernment can serve as a valuable check on individual excess and provide a broader perspective, it is important to acknowledge that it can also be used to suppress valid leadings and maintain unjust power structures. Throughout Quaker history, there have been instances when the corporate discernment of the community has been slow to recognize prophetic calls for change, such as in the case of slavery or women's equality.

Friends are often quick to recognize our early calls for abolition, which is true: The Quaker Benjamin Lay was publicly writing and preaching about the evils of slavery as early as 1737. But it wasn't until twenty-one years later that Quakers finally took an abolition position as a group.[33] Similarly, we are often proud to note that both Lucretia Mott and Susan B. Anthony were early Quaker voices for women's equality in the United States, but we fail to remember that both women were chastised for their radical vision, and Anthony left The Religious Society of Friends to pursue her social reform efforts more freely and to find a more supportive environment for her activism.

This kind of tension isn't new, nor is it found in just my Quaker tradition. It's a familiar struggle: one person has a bold, forward-looking vision, but the wider community moves slowly or even pushes back against the new idea. I think this same pattern appears today in many groups working for social change, including progressive movements, organizations, and churches. Sometimes, these groups rightly want to avoid mistakes of the past. They remember times when rigid thinking or exclusion silenced important new ideas or marginalized those with prophetic voices. So a new approach emerges that strongly emphasizes individual freedom and personal expression. This comes from a good place, valuing each person's experience and viewpoint.

However, if this focus on the individual doesn't come into some equilibrium with the community and with tradition, it can unintentionally weaken the group's ability to

---

[32] William Penn, *Some Fruits of Solitude: In Reflections and Maxims Relating to the Conduct of Human Life* (New York: H. M. Caldwell, 1903).

[33] Nathaniel Smith Kogan, "Aberrations in the Body and in the Body Politic: The Eighteenth-Century Life of Benjamin Lay, Disabled Abolitionist," *Disability Studies Quarterly* 36, no. 3 (2016), https://doi.org/10.18061/dsq.v36i3.5135.

work together. Groups need clear ways for people to support and challenge each other in mutual accountability. They also need shared ways to decide on common goals. Without that kind of engagement, even with the best intentions, a group can become fragmented, losing its shared direction.

When this happens, it gets really hard for the group to agree on priorities. It's tough to commit to and sustain the difficult, often messy, work of building collective power and making deep, lasting change. So the problem today isn't always that new ideas are openly shut down. Instead, there can be a subtle drift. The vital work of building a strong, united "we" can fade into the background, leaving a diminished capacity for a community that can act together. What takes its place? Often, it's just many individual "I's" sharing their own perspectives. These individual insights might be valuable, but they don't automatically create the collective strength needed to make a difference or to collaborate enough to produce sufficient leverage to push systems to change. Learning how to braid these individual threads into a stronger communal fabric is essential, and, here, the long histories of communities wrestling with discernment can offer vital lessons.

By my analysis, the historical experiences of the Jesuits and Quakers highlight at least eight key lessons: They balance structure with flexibility, value individual and collective wisdom, prioritize spiritual preparation, seek unity, allow ample time, integrate action and contemplation, remain open to correction, and foster a culture of discernment. Practically speaking, these lessons encourage us to view discernment as an ongoing process woven into daily life, rather than a one-time event. This involves cultivating habits of reflection and prayerful consideration in both major decisions and small moments. When facing important choices, resist the urge to rush, allowing time for individual reflection and seeking diverse perspectives. Remember that discernment is about aligning (and realigning) your life with your deepest values and sense of purpose, not just making decisions.

In addition to these takeaways, it's useful to consider how power dynamics interact with discernment. Both the Jesuit and Quaker traditions evolved in their understanding of this interplay. For instance, the Jesuit tradition initially established a hierarchical structure with the superior making final decisions after consultation. However, following Vatican II, there was a shift toward emphasizing communal discernment as an aid to the superior's decision-making, recognizing the value of diverse voices in the process. Similarly, early Quakers grappled with the tension between individual leadings and community wisdom, as exemplified in the James Nayler incident. This led to the development of more structured processes for communal discernment and accountability, balancing the belief in individual divine guidance with the need for collective wisdom and safeguards against potential misuse of spiritual authority.

These historical examples highlight the inherent challenges and possibilities in communal discernment. Building on this wisdom, a liberation theology of vocation suggests the telos or ultimate goal of such discernment must be oriented toward transformation. This means moving beyond solely internal matters to collectively discern: How are we, as a faith community, called to confront the external systems (economic, political, social) that hinder the flourishing of diverse vocations in our midst? And equally important, how must we transform our own internal culture and practices to foster genuine intercultural belonging, ensuring our communal life truly supports and empowers all whom God calls, rather than merely making space for them within existing structures?

Behind these questions is a reminder to be attentive to how power dynamics shape our discernment processes, regardless of our social location. If you find yourself in a position of privilege, this attentiveness means actively seeking out voices and perspectives that challenge your assumptions, especially from those who may be marginalized or underrepresented in your usual circles of influence. It involves a willingness to listen deeply and to critically examine how your privilege might be shaping your understanding of divine guidance.

Conversely, if you come from a marginalized or underrepresented group, this awareness of power dynamics in discernment is equally relevant, albeit in different ways. It might involve recognizing the inherent value of your own voice and experiences, even when they diverge from dominant narratives. It could mean finding ways to amplify your perspective in communal discernment processes, perhaps by building coalitions with others who share similar experiences. It may also involve discerning when to challenge existing power structures and when to create alternative spaces for discernment that honor your community's wisdom and experiences.

For those whose identities encompass both privileged and marginalized aspects, discernment takes on an added layer of complexity. You may find yourself shifting between different social locations depending on the context, requiring a highly adaptable approach to discernment. This intersectional experience calls for developing a keen awareness of how various aspects of your identity interact and influence your perceptions and those of others. In some settings, you may need to amplify marginalized voices, including your own, while in others, you might leverage your privilege to create space for diverse perspectives. This approach to discernment can be demanding, but it also offers a unique vantage point, allowing you to facilitate understanding across different social boundaries and contribute to more expansive discernment processes.

Regardless of your social location, engaging consciously with these power dynamics can lead you toward a more inclusive and equitable approach to discernment. We'll get into the specifics more in the sixth chapter's discussion of identity and belonging, but, here, it is worth noting that this approach both provides potential guidance for your individual choices and contributes to the collective wisdom and flourishing of your community, helping to create spaces where all voices are valued in the pursuit of divine guidance. By embracing these practices and awareness, you can develop a more holistic, spiritually grounded approach to discernment that honors both individual insight and collective wisdom, while remaining attentive to the complex interplay of power and privilege in our discernment processes.

When this kind of layered discernment has shown up in my own life, it has usually been a powerful experience. The times when personal call, communal responsibility, and identity have all come together have been some of the most significant moments of clarity and vocational change. One of the clearest examples was when my wife and I sought clearness around our marriage.

In the tradition of the Religious Society of Friends (Quakers), marriage isn't simply a private agreement or romantic milestone. It can be understood as a ministry, a shared spiritual vocation that, if rightly led, is held "under the care" of a local worshiping community, known as a Meeting. That phrase isn't meant to be metaphorical. When a marriage is taken "under the care" of a Meeting, it implies a real and ongoing commitment: that the community will support, accompany, and hold the couple accountable as they live out their shared call.

In Quaker practice, "clearness" refers to a communal process of spiritual discernment. When a person or couple is considering a significant decision, they may ask the Meeting to appoint a clearness committee. We see this most often when people are discerning about marriage, congregational membership, or a change in ministry. The clearness committee is made up by a small group of trusted members who meet with them to listen deeply, ask searching questions, and help test whether what is felt inwardly is spiritually grounded and rightly ordered.

When Kristina and I felt led toward marriage, we didn't approach the Meeting for permission or logistical support. We wrote to Rochester Monthly Meeting asking them to form a clearness committee. We weren't asking them to approve a wedding but to help us discern whether we were, in fact, already joined in Spirit as spouses. We wanted to know if what we felt was true, and whether it was something the Meeting could faithfully hold as ministry.

The committee met with us, and, at the end of that first session, they said they were clear to recommend to the Meeting that it was right for us to be married and that the Meeting should take the marriage under its care. Instead of feeling affirmed, one of us (I don't remember who) asked, "What does that mean? Practically speaking, what does it mean for a marriage to be under the care of a Meeting? What practices are attached to that phrase? What would it ask of us? What of you?" That's not verbatim, but it was something like that.

That question stopped the process. The committee, for all their goodwill, didn't have an answer. They couldn't respond with any specificity. And I was annoyed. Not at them personally, but at the way religious language, language meant to carry weight and consequence, was being used as if it were self-evident. "Under the care" of the Meeting sounded lovely. But without shared practices or accountability, it felt like spiritual sophistry. The committee couldn't articulate what they were saying "yes" to. So we and the committee members all agreed to pause. Functionally, we undid the decision that was supposed to have affirmed and approved the next step in our marriage.

Months later, we tried again. In the time between, the clearness committee and members of the Meeting had continued to meet, reflect, and wrestle with what it truly meant to take a marriage under their care. They, too, had been changed by the process. When we reconvened, there was a shared readiness, a mutual understanding that what we were seeking was not simply approval to wed, but a way to name and nurture our union as a form of ministry, grounded in Spirit and upheld by community.

The same Friends who had first walked with us became our long-term support committee. They continued to meet with us, not just before the wedding for logistics, but after, for ongoing pastoral care. Sometimes individually, sometimes together. Their accompaniment wasn't symbolic; it was ongoing and real. Our process didn't just clarify our own call; it helped reshape the Meeting's understanding of what marriage could be. We all emerged with a stronger sense of it not just as a private commitment between two people, but a public act of ministry, held in accountability and nurtured by community.

That process changed me. It taught me how often we mistake spiritual consensus for spiritual depth. Sometimes, we don't need forward motion; we need a halt, a moment to ask whether the words we're using are still anchored in practice, still connected to actionable commitments grounded in material circumstances. It was never about seeking clarity for its own sake. It was about refusing to pretend we had clarity when we didn't.

Ultimately, the practice of discernment (both individual and communal) is about cultivating a deeper attunement to the divine presence in our lives and in our world. It's about learning to listen deeply, to both our own inner stirrings and the collective wisdom of our communities and voices on the margins asking questions that usually aren't asked. As we navigate the complexities of vocation in a world marked by inequality and injustice, may we approach discernment with humility, courage, and a commitment to transformation, both personal and systemic. In doing so, we open ourselves to the possibility of a more meaningful and liberating understanding of our callings, one that resonates with our deepest values and contributes to the flourishing of all.

Constant Attunement and Calibration

At the end of the last chapter, I wrote that I saw vocation as a dynamic process of seeking equilibrium rather than a static balance or seamless integration. I described it as a co-creative process with God, involving both deep introspection and active engagement with the world. I emphasized that vocation is about liberation, about freeing ourselves from internal and external obstacles while embracing the freedom to pursue lives of meaning and purpose. I framed vocation as a call to human flourishing, not just for ourselves but for those around us and for creation itself. It's about discovering and nurturing the gifts we steward and the passions we possess, finding ways to use them in service to the common good and the broader relational ecosystem we are part of. This understanding of vocation invites us to think expansively about our callings, recognizing that they may manifest in various forms and contexts throughout our lives.

Given this understanding of vocation, discernment emerges as an equally dynamic and adaptive practice. It becomes a continual process of attunement and adjustment, always with an eye toward power dynamics and the pursuit of justice. Discernment, in this light, is not merely about making decisions, but about cultivating a posture of ongoing engagement with the complexities of our inner lives, our communities, and the broader systems that shape our world.

This approach to discernment involves a constant oscillation between introspection and action, between individual reflection and communal wisdom. It's about learning to navigate the tension between our inner callings and the external realities that surround us. We're called to listen deeply to the "sound of the genuine" within ourselves, as Thurman describes, while simultaneously engaging critically with the voices and needs of our communities. This dual attention allows us to recognize and resist what Emilie Townes calls the "Fantastic Hegemonic Imagination": those internalized systems of injustice that can distort our sense of what's possible.[34]

If vocation is about liberation and flourishing, then discernment must be practiced with an acute awareness of power. We must continually ask ourselves: Whose voices are we listening to? Whose interests are being served by our choices? How might our discernment process be influenced by privilege or marginalization? By keeping these questions at the forefront, we can work toward a more just and inclusive approach to discernment that aligns with our understanding of vocation as a call to collective flourishing.

This expansive view of vocation challenges us to approach discernment not just as a tool for personal fulfillment, but as a practice that contributes to the flourishing of all creation. It calls us to consider how our vocational choices affect our communities, our spiritual ecosystems, and future generations. This expanded view of discernment

---

34 Emilie M. Townes, *Womanist Ethics and the Cultural Production of Evil* (New York: Palgrave Macmillan, 2006), 21.

Discernment

pushes us to think beyond individual career paths or personal callings and to consider our role in broader movements for social justice and spiritual growth. This understanding of discernment as an ongoing process aligns with the various understandings of ministry that we'll explore in the ninth chapter, where we'll see how different expressions of ministry require different types of discernment and responsiveness to God's leading.

As we continue our exploration of vocation and ministry, let us embrace discernment as a dynamic, critical, and communal practice. This journey calls for humility, as we acknowledge the limits of our own perspectives and the necessity of drawing on the wisdom of others. It also demands courage to confront unjust systems and imagine bold new possibilities. Above all, it invites hope, a trust that God accompanies us in the ongoing process of seeking, listening, and releasing what no longer serves.

Discernment thrives when rooted in intentional reflection and spiritual formation. By reflecting on our choices and desires and allowing that reflection to be shaped by practices of formation, we create fertile ground for our calling to grow and mature. In the next chapter, I consider the relationship between formation and discernment, exploring how this integration anchors our vocational journey in the rhythm of action and contemplation.

Questions for Reflection

1. Thinking about your own spiritual journey, have you encountered discernment as a formal practice? Perhaps through a structured program or spiritual tradition? Or has your experience been more informal? What did that process feel like for you, whether formal or informal? What helped, what hindered?

2. This chapter highlights the dance between individual listening and communal wisdom in discernment. When you face a significant vocational or spiritual question, who are the trusted individuals or communities you instinctively turn to for clarity or support? What qualities draw you to them? Is it their grounding, their questions, their ability to listen without judgment? Reflecting on your own needs, how might you intentionally cultivate or contribute to spaces where such mutual listening and shared wisdom can flourish?

3. Identify someone in your life whom you perceive as grounded, reflective, and faithful. If you feel comfortable, consider inviting them to share a story about a time they experienced a strong sense of calling or had to make a difficult discernment. As you listen, pay attention to: What did it feel like in their body, mind, and spirit? How did they navigate the process, especially

any "dizziness of freedom" or moments of letting go? What in their story most resonates with, challenges, or perhaps even clarifies something in your own journey?

4. This chapter introduces discernment not as a grasping for answers, but as a process of sifting and letting go, like using a colander to drain away what is no longer needed to reveal what is nourishing. What aspects of your current life might you feel invited to release in this season? What "hot water" needs draining so that you can more fully embrace what is truly vital and life-giving for your vocational path right now, even if that release involves some grief or uncertainty?

5. The chapter explores the idea of God's will as a dynamic, relational process that invites our active participation and co-creation. How does this perspective resonate with or challenge your understanding of discernment and vocation? How does this vision resonate with your own experiences of discernment? Does it feel liberating, perhaps unsettling, or does it affirm something you've already sensed about your vocational journey? Something else?

6. The chapter invites us to embrace a posture of being "rooted and flexible," honoring the wisdom of our communities while remaining responsive to the evolving needs of our world. What are the traditions or foundations that anchor your sense of calling? How might you cultivate a spirit of openness and innovation in response to the changing contexts of ministry and service?

3

Formation and Reflection

The spiritual life does not remove us from the world but leads us deeper into it.

—Henri Nouwen

Tell me, what is it you plan to do with your one wild and precious life?

—Mary Oliver

As we live, seeking to understand our vocation, we often feel the pull between our own untamed, "wild and precious"[1] potential and the call to immerse ourselves ever more deeply[2] in the world around us. This duality, between the boundless possibilities within us and the grounding, sometimes weighty, reality of our interconnected lives, shapes our journey. The ways we immerse ourselves in the world are shaped by our unique contexts. For some, this may involve navigating systemic barriers, caring for others, or responding to urgent communal needs. For others, it may mean exploring opportunities for personal growth and connection. For all of us, what we are called toward can change and grow over time.

Two processes, spiritual formation and theological reflection, play vital roles in guiding us through this growth and change. Formation involves cultivating individual

---

1 Mary Oliver, "The Summer Day," in *New and Selected Poems*, 94 (Boston: Beacon Press, 1992). See also epigraph.

2 As Henri Nouwen says in the epigraph. H. J. M. Nouwen, *Making All Things New: An Invitation to the Spiritual Life* (San Francisco: HarperOne, 1981).

and communal capacities, while reflection invites us to examine how our experiences align with our values, beliefs, and context. Together, these practices shape our understanding of ourselves, our relationship with the divine, and our place in the world. In this chapter, we'll explore how spiritual formation and theological reflection work in tandem to guide our ongoing vocational development, helping us to live a spiritual life that is both intentional and deeply engaged with the complexities of our shared existence.

More than just personal growth, spiritual formation is the lifelong process of being shaped into the fullness of who we are called to be. It's about developing our capacity to live with greater awareness, compassion, and purpose, more deeply living into our vocational calling, whatever it may be. Our formation takes place through our experiences, relationships, and the communities we engage with. It's a journey that involves both active engagement and receptive openness to the divine working in our lives.

In parallel, theological reflection is the practice of making meaning from our experiences and connecting them to our deepest values and beliefs. It's a way of pausing in our busy lives to consider the deeper significance of what we encounter and to intentionally shape our future actions based on what we learn. This commitment to linking lived reality with critical understanding echoes Paulo Freire's insistence that true learning involves a "reading of the world" that precedes and informs our "reading of the word," always pushing us toward transformative praxis.[3] For Freire, understanding our lived context (the world) is essential before engaging with sacred narratives (the word) because this dialogue fuels praxis: that continuous cycle of informed action and critical reflection aimed at changing our reality.

In this way, theological reflection supports the integrity of our interior moral life, helping us notice where our beliefs, values, behaviors, and relationships are aligned as well as where they may be in tension. When theological reflection is practiced well, it becomes one of the key tools by which we tend to our mental and spiritual well-being. It allows us to recognize when something no longer fits: when our actions are misaligned with our convictions or when inherited beliefs begin to chafe against lived experience. Reflection, then, becomes not just an academic or spiritual exercise, but a moral one: a way of discerning where we are, what is being asked of us, and how we might live with greater integrity in the face of disorientation or change.

Both reflection and formation are profoundly influenced by the traditions we inherit and engage with. These traditions offer us frameworks for understanding,

---

[3] Paulo Feire, "Reading the World and Reading the Word: An Interview with Paulo Freire," *Language Arts* 62, no. 1 (1985): 15–21.

languages for articulating our experiences, and practices for deepening our spiritual lives. However, our relationship with tradition is complex and dynamic. As we'll explore, tradition can be both a source of guidance and a site of tension, inviting us to engage critically and creatively with inherited wisdom while remaining open to new insights and interpretations.

These elements interact within a living spiritual ecosystem, much like a forest. In this model, tradition provides the foundational elements (the soil, climate, and existing plant life) within which formation and reflection grow, adapt, and contribute to the ongoing development of our inward spiritual landscape. Yet, just as not all soil is equally fertile, some may find their inherited traditions to be rocky ground, requiring reworking, enrichment, or entirely new cultivation to sustain spiritual growth. Sometimes there are weeds and invasive species that need to be pulled out for native species to thrive. In some cases, careful tending is required to discern which elements of tradition support growth and which may need to be pruned or cleared to create space for new life to emerge. This dynamic interplay helps us navigate the complexities of our vocational journeys with greater intentionality and depth. As we explore this relationship, we'll consider how our individual journeys connect to larger traditions and communities and how we can engage with these traditions in ways that are both respectful and transformative.

The Practice of Theological Reflection

Theological reflection helps us interpret our experiences, integrate them into our spiritual formation, and discern how they inform our vocational path. By reflecting on our daily encounters and decisions, we align our actions with our faith and values, leading to more coherent and intentional spiritual growth. It's a practice that helps us see the connections between our daily lives and spiritual beliefs, between the ordinary and the sacred. Through theological reflection, we bring our lived experiences into dialogue with our faith traditions, allowing each to inform and challenge the other.

For those who identify as "spiritual but not religious" or find themselves distant from the tradition(s) of their upbringing, theological reflection can still be a powerful tool to reassess and/or develop new frameworks for understanding their experiences and values. In these cases, the "theology" in theological reflection might be understood more broadly as one's personal philosophy, ethical principles, or spiritual intuitions. This approach to reflection can involve asking questions like: How does this experience align with my understanding of what is good or meaningful? What does it reveal about my connection to something greater than myself? How does it challenge or affirm my current beliefs and values? What insights does it offer about the nature of existence or my place in the universe? Even without a formal religious framework, individuals can draw many types of sources for this reflective process. These might include philosophical texts, nature, art, literature, personal experiences, or insights from various wisdom traditions.

The theologian Edward Foley suggests that, for this kind of work, it is better to use "reflective believing" rather than "theological reflection."[4] While terminology and details may vary, the shared purpose of these practices is to invite deeper engagement with life's complexities, fostering a way of thinking that is transformative, actionable, and aligned with something larger than oneself. As I mentioned in the preceding chapter, the thing to be on the lookout for is a "spiritual salad bar" approach where we jump from one tradition to another without going deep into any. The key is to engage in a thoughtful dialogue between one's lived experiences and one's evolving understanding of life's deeper questions. This kind of engagement aligns closely with what Ada María Isasi-Díaz refers to as *lo cotidiano*, the everyday realities and struggles of life that form the foundation for theological reflection.[5]

Influenced by other Latin American liberation theologies but centered on the struggles of Latina women, Isasi-Díaz became a founder of the movement known as *mujerista* theology. This movement advocated for the importance of affirming how the daily experience of Latinas shapes their lives in faith. The validation of *lo cotidiano* as a source of wisdom and knowledge is vital to the work of theologizing in a *mujerista* way.[6] *Lo cotidiano* is Spanish (like the English word "quotidian") and refers to the multiple layers of daily life experience for Latinas. It is an intersectional category that considers race, class, gender, faith, and society's various privileges and marginalizations. As she puts it, it is the "stuff" of Latina women's reality.[7] In this theological tradition, reflection begins with an experience of the everyday, and imagination's role is important because it is often how the hope of a better day tomorrow is sustained: the hope for a better world for our children and their children.

The insistence on particularity and dailiness of *lo cotidiano* is part of its power. As Isasi-Díaz frames it, focusing on the particular resists the tendency toward abstract, disembodied universalization, such as the idea that life's hardships are justified

---

4 Edward Foley, *Theological Reflection across Religious Traditions: The Turn to Reflective Believing* (Lanham, MD: Rowman & Littlefield, 2015).

5 The ideas in the passages below first appeared in L. Callid Keefe-Perry, *Sense of the Possible: An Introduction to Theology and Imagination* (Eugene, OR: Cascade Books, 2023), 90–91.

6 Ada María Isasi-Díaz, "Lo Cotidiano: A Key Element of Mujerista Theology," *Journal of Hispanic/Latino Theology* 10, no. 1 (2002): 5–17.

7 Ada María Isasi-Díaz, *Mujerista Theology: Theology for the Twenty-First Century* (Maryknoll, NY: Orbis Books, 1996), 66–67.

because faithfulness will be rewarded in heaven. Instead, grounding theology in the regular experience of living as a Latina woman fosters a spirit of change and liberation. This approach invites Latina women to reflect on God and the future through the language of daily life and shared experiences, clearing away the clutter of technical academic jargon.

> Taking seriously the descriptive function of *lo cotidiano* makes it possible for new narratives to emerge, narratives created by the poor and oppressed who take charge of reality. In these narratives they find themselves and see themselves as moral subjects who exercise their right and power of self-definition.... New narratives help us to see and to value parts of ourselves that we have ignored or that we do not know well, and they help us to know ourselves differently from the way oppressors define us.[8]

Lo cotidiano emphasizes the sacredness of ordinary experiences and the ways these daily encounters can reveal deeper truths about justice, community, and vocation.

For *mujerista* theologians, reflection is not an abstract intellectual exercise but a grounded, communal practice that is deeply connected to the lived experiences of marginalized communities. Profound theological insights emerge through the details of cooking meals, caregiving, and navigating systems of injustice. This approach challenges us to see God's presence and transformative work not only in grand or overtly spiritual moments but also in the rhythms of our daily lives, pushing us to discern how these experiences call us to act with compassion, justice, and solidarity. By centering *lo cotidiano*, theological reflection becomes inherently justice-seeking, as it draws from the real struggles and joys of life to envision a world where those on the margins are lifted up and empowered.

I distinctly remember the first time I met Isasi-Díaz in person. I was at a conference at Drew Theological School, where she taught for years. Midway through the second day of papers and panel discussions, there was a break for some extended questions and comments from the audience. Isasi-Díaz, who appeared to have been listening intently to all the sessions, approached the microphone.

"I've found this all very fascinating," she said, "and I'm hoping it might be something I'll think about more. To help me with that, could one of you on the panel try to explain to me what we've all been doing here and why it matters? Oh ... and imagine I never finished high school and need to work more than a full-time job to feed my kids."

And she meant it. She wasn't being glib or mocking in any serious way. She wanted one of us to try and take the talk out of abstraction and see if we could ground it

---

8 Isasi-Díaz, "*Lo Cotidiano*," 11.

in something material. She stood at the mic for some time before someone tried. Sometimes abstraction distracts.

The commitment to grounding theological reflection in everyday realities, as Isasi-Díaz modeled, challenges us to move beyond overly intellectualized frameworks that have no clear roots in the stuff of life. Her insistence on making theology accessible and relevant, even for those without formal education or spare time, underscores the importance of starting from concrete, lived experiences. This resonates deeply with the goals of vocational discernment, where the questions we ask about meaning and purpose must be rooted in the realities of our daily lives. Whether reflecting on the challenges of navigating work, caregiving, or community responsibilities, the process of engaging with *lo cotidiano* reminds us that theology does not reside solely in lofty ideas but in the transformative power of examining how our lived experiences intersect with the divine. This grounded approach prepares us to ask deeper questions central to theological reflection.

As I see it, theological reflection involves thoroughly examining our experiences, exploring relevant spiritual or philosophical resources, and considering their interactions. It challenges us to move beyond surface-level interpretations, confronting the complexities and ambiguities that arise when our real-world experiences meet our ideals and beliefs. Effective theological reflection challenges us to move beyond simplistic or comfortable interpretations. It pushes us to confront the tensions between our experiences and beliefs, question our assumptions, and be open to new insights that might emerge from this dialogue. This confrontation can sometimes be uncomfortable or unsettling, but the most profound growth and understanding occur in these moments of discomfort. There are many versions of what constitutes "theological reflection," but the way that I teach it has six steps.[9]

First, I begin by identifying a specific *experience* or situation that has significantly affected me. This experience could be an event that "grabs" me emotionally, intellectually, or spiritually. It can be anything that lingers in my thoughts, raises questions, or challenges my usual ways of thinking or behaving. The key is to choose an experience that feels meaningful and worthy of deeper exploration. "Theological reflection" isn't "reflection on theology," but a practice of deepening our capacity to use perspectives from our faith traditions to reflect on various aspects of life. I am of the opinion that nearly anything can be reflected on theologically, from news stories to pop culture, personal stories, and historical events.

Second, once some experience or event is selected for reflection, it is important to *contextualize* it in relation to my life. Are there any personal experiences or background

---

9 If you're interested, see "Theological Reflection in Practice" in the appendix.

influences that made this event striking for me? Am I "grabbed" by this event because of something out of my own history and something it brings up internally? Are there any bodily sensations that arise when focusing on the selected experience? As I teach it, theological reflection isn't just a cognitive activity; paying attention to our bodies, feelings, and intuition is part of the practice. Contextualizing this way is important for several reasons. It helps me recognize my biases and preconceptions, uncovering deeper personal or spiritual issues, including those that may be exciting and good but underexamined. I need to know where I am before I know where I can go. After all, maps work better when you know where you are.

Reflecting this way also serves to distinguish between my reaction to immediate circumstances and internal responses, revealing patterns I may have in the way I tend to interpret experiences. By explicitly acknowledging these influences, I can better understand why I'm reacting the way I am, potentially identify distortions in my perception, and uncover opportunities for growth. This step turns the mirror inward, making the process not just about understanding the event but also about understanding myself more deeply as an active participant whose personal history and inner life play an important role in how I perceive and make meaning of the world around me.

Third, I examine the *social dynamics* at play in the experience, considering how structural systems of power, privilege, and marginalization influenced the event. This step matters to me because, as a Christian, being Christ-like means serving the "least of these," which requires developing the ability to see who has been marginalized, a skill that often needs intentional practice. By analyzing who is centered and who is peripheral in a situation, I'm training myself to see the world more as Christ did, with particular attention to the overlooked or marginalized.

Even for non-Christians, this awareness fosters empathy, a nuanced understanding of social interactions, and recognizing systemic inequities. It moves us beyond a purely individual understanding of experiences to see how they're shaped by broader social forces, challenging us to grow beyond our own perspectives and actively engage with the complex realities of our diverse world. Whether motivated by religious conviction or secular ethics, this step is integral to developing a more just and compassionate worldview.

Fourth, I look for *connections* between this experience and my faith tradition, spiritual beliefs, or value system. As a person of faith, this might involve relating the experience to scripture, theology, church history, or personal experiences from my faith community. If I were spiritual but not religious, this might involve drawing on personal philosophies, ethical frameworks, or insights from various wisdom traditions. The goal is to identify a "lens" through which to view and interpret the experience.

When choosing what to connect to, I find it helpful to let my intuition guide me initially. What scriptures, teachings, or philosophical ideas come to mind when I reflect on this experience? Sometimes, a particular story, concept, or teaching will resonate naturally with the situation at hand.

However, I also make a conscious effort to consider less obvious connections. What aspects of my tradition or belief system challenge or complicate my initial interpretation of this experience? Are there teachings or principles that I overlook that are relevant here? It's also valuable to consider multiple potential connections rather than settling on the first one that comes to mind. This can involve exploring different aspects of your tradition or drawing on diverse sources within it. For example, consider how your experience relates to a scriptural narrative, a theological concept, and a historical event or figure from your tradition. This approach can lead to richer insights and a more nuanced understanding of both your experience and your faith or value system.

Fifth, I engage in a process of *reconsideration*. After bringing my experience into conversation with my faith tradition or value system, I reflect on what new insights this connection provides for understanding the experience in a new or changed way. I ask myself what new understandings or perspectives have emerged from this dialogue. This step is key to the process as a whole because it's where the real transformative power of theological reflection often occurs. I consider how the "lens" I've used offers new or more nuanced interpretations of how I understand divinity or ultimate meaning to be at work in the world.

When I explain this step to students, I often encourage them to imagine a parallel universe with another version of themselves. This alternate self is essentially the same person as me, but with a key difference. They are equally good, intelligent, kind, and committed, but the same spiritual or religious tradition hasn't formed them. They lack the reference points to the religious symbols, stories, teachings, or practices that have shaped our perspective. The "reconsideration" part of theological reflection, then, becomes a way of asking, "How do I see things differently because of my tradition compared to a version of me who hasn't been influenced by it?" This thought experiment can be powerfully illuminating. It helps us recognize the unique ways our faith or philosophical framework shapes our worldview, ethical considerations, and responses to life events.

It also challenges us to articulate the value and impact of our beliefs more clearly as we consider how they've transformed our understanding in ways that might not be obvious to someone outside our tradition. This process often leads to a deeper appreciation of our spiritual heritage while also opening us to critical reflection on aspects of our tradition we might have taken for granted. Ultimately, this reconsideration step invites us to engage more consciously and intentionally with our faith or value system, recognizing its profound influence on how we interpret and respond to the world around us.

Sixth, and finally, I focus on *integrating these new insights into practice*. What does this reconsideration suggest for changes in my future actions, attitudes, or understandings? How might I do things differently when faced with a similar situation in the future? What new attitudes or perspectives might I bring to my daily life or ministry? This step is about moving from reflection to action, ensuring that the insights gained through this process don't remain abstract but become embodied in my life and work. Here, theological reflection moves beyond an intellectual exercise to become a tool for genuine transformation and growth, helping me live out my faith or values more fully and intentionally in the world. Theological reflection isn't about finding easy answers or neatly resolving every question. Often, it leads us to deeper questions and a greater appreciation for the complexity of life and faith. The outcome is usually a new perspective on truth and meaning for living that becomes part of our ongoing formation, shaping how we engage with future experiences and deepening our spiritual lives.

For students in theological education programs, theological reflection often becomes a regular academic exercise. You may be asked to write reflection papers or engage in group reflections on your experiences. When I assign things like this, I tell students that I am far more interested in them developing the habit of theological reflection as a part of their life in faith than I am in them just doing an assignment well. At its core, theological reflection is about meaningfully connecting our experiences to our deepest values and beliefs. It's about developing a more intentional and examined way of living. I've often wished I could invite congregations to practice theological reflection together as individuals and as a church. I think that practice has the potential to deepen many people's sense of connections among their lives, their community, and their faith tradition.

Even for those who don't consider themselves connected to a particular religious tradition or aren't in formal theological education, the practice of reflecting deeply on experiences and connecting them to personal values can lead to greater self-awareness, more intentional decision-making, and a richer, more meaningful life. It's a way of pausing in our often busy lives to consider the deeper significance of our experiences and to intentionally shape our future actions based on what we learn. For those in secular professions, a similar process of reflection can help in ethical decision-making and personal growth. Teachers might reflect on classroom experiences in education in light of their educational philosophy. In healthcare, practitioners might reflect on patient interactions in light of their understanding of healing and care. Artists might ask themselves if the pieces they make represent or resonate with their hopes and dreams.

> ### A Practice to Consider:
> ## Theological Reflection
>
> *Theological reflection invites us to bring our lived experiences into dialogue with our faith and values, uncovering deeper meanings and guiding our steps toward intentional and transformative living.*
>
> Reflect on a recent experience using the six-step theological reflection process described here. Take time with each step, moving through the process slowly and thoughtfully. Really write it out. For full guidelines on each step, see the appendix.

The key is to approach this practice with openness and curiosity. Whether you're drawing on religious teachings, philosophical ideas, personal values, or all three, the goal is to engage in a dialogue among your lived experiences, your beliefs and principles, and something broader than yourself. Reflecting together with others, whether in a religious community, a study group, or among friends, can often lead to deeper insights. Don't hesitate to engage in reflection with peers, mentors, or others whose perspectives you value. Their insights can enrich your own reflections and help you see your experiences in new ways. This dialogue can lead to new insights, challenge assumptions, and ultimately guide you toward living in greater alignment with what you believe to be true and good. Over time, you'll likely find that this practice deepens your understanding of your faith or philosophy and enriches your personal life and engagement with the world around you. This deepening is a vital part of how I see spiritual formation.

Considering Spiritual Formation

Spiritual formation unfolds gradually as we grow into the fullness of who we are called to be, requiring both patient attention and timely response to signs of change. It's a journey of becoming more fully human, more deeply attuned to the divine presence in our lives and in the world around us. This process isn't about achieving perfection or reaching a fixed endpoint. Rather, it's about developing our capacity to live with greater awareness, compassion, and purpose, more deeply living into our vocational calling, whatever it may be.

American Methodist Bible scholar M. Robert Mulholland describes Christian spiritual formation as "the process of being conformed to the image of Christ for the sake of others," highlighting it as a transformative, ongoing process oriented toward serving others.[10] Mulholland challenges us to recognize that spiritual formation is not something we choose to engage in but rather an ongoing reality of our human experience.

> Human life is, by its very nature, spiritual formation. The question is not whether to undertake spiritual formation. The question is, what kind of spiritual formation are we already engaged in? Are we being increasingly conformed to the brokenness and disintegration of the world, or are we being increasingly conformed to the wholeness and integration of the image of Christ?[11]

This framing invites us to view spiritual formation not as an isolated "religious activity" but as an integral part of our daily lives and choices. But not all formation is liberating.

Racism, sexism, and capitalism also form us. A liberative theology of formation requires that we ask: Who or what is shaping me? And toward what ends? Practices are pathways for imagined futures to find home in the flesh; our repeated actions carry theological weight, making envisioned futures real through embodied habit. This is part of why I like how Mulholland's definition implicitly underscores the importance of reflection in formation.

By regularly reflecting on our experiences and actions, Christians can better understand how we are being conformed to the image of Christ and identify areas where we can further grow and serve others. This challenges us to be intentional about how we're being shaped, recognizing that every experience and interaction has the potential to either move us toward greater wholeness or further fragmentation. In reflecting on this "movement," I find that the idea of "theosis," or "deification," is helpful to consider.

Theosis refers to the process by which human beings become partakers of the divine nature.[12] This concept is deeply rooted in Eastern Orthodox theology and has seen renewed interest in various Christian traditions, including Catholicism and some streams of Protestantism, especially Mulholland's own Wesleyan-Methodist tradition. The idea is encapsulated by the belief that, through grace, humans can achieve union with God, not by becoming divine in essence, but by participating in the divine energies. In simpler terms, theosis is about drawing closer to God's presence and embodying God's love and goodness in our lives, while still remaining fully human.

---

10 M. Robert Mulholland Jr., *Shaped by the Word: The Power of Scripture in Spiritual Formation* (Nashville, TN: Upper Room Books, 2000), 25.

11 Ibid., 25–26.

12 Scripturally, we see resonant ideas in 2 Peter 1:4, 2 Corinthians 3:18, and Ephesians 4:13, among other places.

Kenosis, or self-emptying, is central to theosis, reflecting Christ's humility and love by shedding ego and selfish desires to make room for God's presence. The call to kenosis is integral to spiritual formation as it fosters humility, surrender, and a transformation of self into the image of Christ.

I've found this idea helpful to remember because it offers a vision of spiritual growth not just as a surface-level moral improvement but as a deep part of our being. We are constantly being shaped by the world around us; that is unavoidable. So the question is, "How will I use my time and energy to shape this process in a way that aligns with my vocation?" I'm not doing it all alone, but I do have agency. The concept of theosis reminds me that spiritual formation is a cooperative process between divine grace and human effort. Like the conversation about vocation in the first chapter, there is a similar danger in thinking that a "pull yourself up by your bootstraps" approach to spiritual formation is appropriate. In life, that orientation will lead you to isolation and the disconnective tendencies of presumed self-sufficiency. In matters of spirituality, it will lead you to bad theology.

I can't make myself holy by force of will. What I *can* do is try to increasingly order my life so that I am prioritizing the commitments that orient me toward a growing awareness of God and the exercise of the gifts of the Spirit that I steward. Reflecting on theosis encourages me to actively participate in my spiritual growth while also recognizing my dependence on God's transformative power. Last, the emphasis on kenosis within theosis provides a practical focus for my spiritual practices, encouraging me to cultivate humility, self-giving love, and Christ-likeness in my daily life. I'm not great at this, but having it as a goal helps keep me attentive to the dailiness of what it means to try and be faithful.

Sanctification is another useful concept to consider when thinking about spiritual formation. While theosis emphasizes the ultimate goal of union with God with my very being, sanctification focuses on the ongoing process of becoming holy or set apart for God's purposes through conforming to God's will.[13] The concept of sanctification has deep roots in both the Hebrew Bible and the Christian scriptures, evolving from primarily ritual understandings to more ethical and socially transformative ones. In the Christian tradition, sanctification is often understood as both an event and a process. Pauline literature, in particular, expands the ethical dimension of sanctification. It's seen as a ritual cleansing and a moral transformation empowered by the Holy Spirit. This transformation involves both putting off the old self and putting on the new self, which is being renewed in the image of its Creator.[14] I think here of passages like

---

13 Brenda B. Colijn, "Sanctification," in *The Oxford Encyclopedia of the Bible and Ethics*, online edition (New York: Oxford University Press, 2015).

14 Colossians 3:9–10.

Romans 12:2, "Do not be conformed to this age, but be transformed by the renewing of the mind, so that you may discern what is the will of God." This aligns closely with our understanding of spiritual formation as a process of being shaped into the image of Christ.

Importantly, sanctification in the Christian scriptures is both individual and communal. Believers are sanctified individually and as part of the body of Christ. This communal aspect of sanctification reminds us that spiritual formation is not a solitary journey but one that takes place within and for the benefit of the community of faith. The concept of sanctification also highlights the tension between the "already" and the "not yet" in spiritual formation. Believers are already declared holy in Christ and are also called to pursue holiness.[15] This paradox reminds us that spiritual formation involves both resting in God's grace and actively participating in our growth. Understanding sanctification can enrich our approach to spiritual formation.

First, sanctification emphasizes the holistic nature of transformation, encompassing not just our actions but our very being, while highlighting the role of the Holy Spirit in empowering and guiding our growth. It reminds us of the communal context of our formation, as we are sanctified not just for our own sake but for the sake of others. Importantly, it helps us hold in tension the reality of our current state and the vision of what we are becoming. For Christians, integrating these aspects of sanctification into our understanding of spiritual formation gives us a more comprehensive view of the journey of becoming more like Christ, recognizing it as a process that involves individual transformation and communal growth, empowered by divine grace and requiring active participation.

Theosis and sanctification share a vision of transformation but differ in emphasis and scope. Both involve the believer's growth in God's likeness, yet theosis focuses on participation in the divine nature, rooted in the mystical union described by 2 Peter 1:4, while sanctification emphasizes moral and spiritual purification, aligning with commands such as "Be holy, for I am holy" from 1 Peter 1:16. Despite these theological distinctions, their practical significance converges: They call believers to an integrated life of worship, prayer, and ethical action. Theologically, this convergence invites reflection on how our relationship with God reshapes every aspect of our lives. Practically, it challenges us to view ordinary acts not merely as duties but as ways to embody divine love and holiness. Showing kindness, practicing humility, and pursuing justice are ways of embodied love. By rooting spiritual practices in this dual vision, Christians can better navigate the tension between aspirational transformation and the realities of daily life.

---

15 Hebrews 12:14.

While these concepts of theosis and sanctification provide a rich theological foundation for understanding spiritual formation, having a more practical framework for visualizing and assessing this complex process can be helpful. I imagine practices of spiritual formation as a musician's mixing board with various volume sliders, each representing different dimensions contributing to our overall spiritual growth.[16] As we consider these dimensions, it's also worth reflecting on how access to, and societal validation of, these different avenues of formation can be shaped by factors like economic resources, educational background, cultural context, or social location.

This approach also helps us recognize that formation involves both inputs (sources of growth) and outputs (evidence of growth) across various areas of our spiritual lives. Each of the various sliders represents a different dimension of formation. These sliders represent both the sources from which formation arises and the evidence by which we can assess spiritual growth:

1. *Intellectual Engagement:* This slider encompasses the study of doctrine, scripture, and theological concepts as a means of formation. It also represents the evidence of this formation through growing doctrinal understanding, theological insight, and the ability to articulate and apply faith concepts.
2. *Community Connection:* This dimension involves participation in communal practices and engagement with historical traditions as formative processes. It also includes the evidence of formation through deepening community involvement, embodiment of traditional wisdom, and the ability to contribute meaningfully to one's faith community.
3. *Mystical and Personal Experience:* This slider reflects both the role of personal, emotional, and mystical experiences in shaping faith and the evidence of formation through emotional maturity, personal transformation, and the depth of one's experiential connection with the divine.
4. *Spiritual Practices:* This encompasses engagement in various spiritual disciplines, such as prayer, meditation, fasting, or contemplative practices, as sources of formation. It also represents evidence of growth through the deepening and maturing of these practices and their impact on one's daily life and character.
5. *The Exercise of Spiritual Gifts:* This dimension involves cultivating and using one's spiritual gifts as a means of formation. It also includes evidence of spiritual growth through the effective and loving use of these gifts in service to others and the broader community.

---

16 The full "sliders" exercise can be found in the appendix.

Taken together, these dimensions speak to the underlying structure that helps us make meaning. When one area shifts dramatically, we often feel it ripple across our whole sense of integrity and call. Formation recalibrates the inner scaffolding that holds up how we live and love. When we speak of sources and evidence of spiritual formation, we acknowledge these dimensions' dual nature. Each slider is connected to both an input and an output in the formation process.

As sources, these dimensions are the wellsprings from which spiritual growth emerges. They are the practices, experiences, and engagements that shape us. As evidence, they are the visible or discernible signs of that growth. They are the ways in which we can observe or measure spiritual development. This dual nature reminds us that spiritual formation is not a linear process but a cyclical one, where our growth in each area stems from, and leads to, further engagement in that dimension. For example, intellectual engagement with scripture might lead to deeper understanding, motivating more study, and creating a positive growth feedback loop. It also might push me to the edge of an encounter with Divine Mystery, where my intellect is insufficient to comprehend the fullness of God, leading me to a mystical experience.

Different faith traditions and individual journeys may adjust these sliders differently, emphasizing certain aspects while downplaying others, both in terms of how formation happens and where they look for evidence of it. By considering various dimensions of formation, individuals and communities can explore spiritual growth in ways that reflect their unique contexts and capacities. Being "more formed" spiritually doesn't suggest a hierarchy of spiritual achievement. Instead, it points to the development of certain capacities across these various dimensions. As we grow spiritually, we become more attuned to our experiences of God in our inner life: our thoughts, emotions, motivations, and patterns of behavior. Formation also helps us bring together our beliefs, actions, relationships, and work into a more coherent whole. This deepening self-awareness allows us to recognize both our gifts and our growing edges, enabling more intentional growth.

That being said, it's good to note that none of these dimensions represent foolproof indicators of genuine spiritual formation. In fact, there is a danger in overemphasizing any one aspect to the exclusion of others, or in creating environments where individuals feel pressured to "perform" certain behaviors to fit in. This pressure can lead to primarily performative expressions of spirituality that actually hinder genuine growth and community. For example, I still remember a conversation I had when I was in seminary as a classmate shared a poignant story about his brother.

In a Pentecostal worship service, my classmate's brother felt compelled to fake speaking in tongues because others expected him to have this experience of the Holy Spirit. Despite being a faithful believer, he had never genuinely experienced speaking in tongues. Feeling the need to conform, he faked this act to fit in with the community and conform to their expectations. However, such performances, born out of pressure rather than meaningful experience, can be detrimental to effective community-building and the deepening of faith. They create a facade that prevents genuine vulnerability and growth, functionally working against the very spiritual formation they're meant to evidence. Spiritual formation should be a holistic process that draws upon various aspects of our being and experience, not a checklist of external behaviors or experiences to be achieved.

Formation involves both active and receptive elements. We engage in practices that foster growth, but we also open ourselves to the work of the divine in our lives. As the American psychiatrist and spiritual director Gerald May put it, this involves standing "undefended and opened" before God.[17] This dual nature of formation reminds us that, while we have a role to play in our growth, ultimately, we respond to and cooperate with grace beyond our own making.

A Practice to Consider:
Set Your Sliders

Spiritual formation, like a soundboard, balances multiple dimensions of our growth. Reflecting on these levels allows us to fine-tune our journey in alignment with both personal and communal faith experiences.

1. Imagine your spiritual formation as a soundboard with sliders for each of the dimensions mentioned.
2. Your Community: Write down a level (1–10) for each slider that represents the mix of emphases you feel in your current faith community or tradition.
3. Yourself: Now, adjust each slider to represent the mix you feel best fits your own orientation currently.
4. After setting these levels, compare the two. Where do they align? Where do they differ? For a full description of this exercise, see the appendix.

The process of formation is deeply contextual. It's shaped by our personal experiences, our cultural background, our social location, and the communities we're part of. This contextual nature means that formation looks different for each person, even as we share common elements in our journeys. If it helps, you can turn back to the ecosystem metaphor again. Our unique circumstances and experiences become

---

17 Gerald G. May, *Addiction and Grace: Love and Spirituality in the Healing of Addictions* (New York: HarperSanFrancisco, 1988), 107.

the raw material through which we can see Spirit leading us forward, making each person's journey of formation uniquely their own.

In reflection and discernment processes, it can be beneficial to be mindful of the various dimensions of formation while remaining open to the unique ways in which the divine may be working in our lives and the lives of others. That is to say that different levels of emphasis exist even if your community's "levels" are different. This understanding of spiritual formation reminds us that it is a complex process that resists one-size-fits-all approaches, inviting us to engage with and assess our spiritual growth in diverse and interconnected ways. However, navigating this rich landscape of spiritual formation requires a tool for integration and discernment. This navigation is where the practice of theological reflection becomes invaluable, for it helps us navigate the complexities of spiritual formation and guides us toward more intentional and meaningful spiritual growth.

The Living Ecosystem of Tradition

Though they can each be considered separately, I believe that spiritual formation and theological reflection happen in parallel, each part of the other. I visualize this relationship as a double helix or a spiral, where each process feeds into and enhances the other in a continuous cycle of growth and transformation.

In this model, formation provides the substance for reflection. As we grow spiritually, we develop new understandings and experiences that become the material for our reflection. This reflection, in turn, allows us to adapt and change, informing our ongoing formation. By examining our experiences through a theological lens, we generate insights that deepen our understanding of ourselves, others, and the divine. These insights then guide our future growth, helping us make intentional changes that align more closely with our evolving understanding and values.

I've found that, without taking tradition into account, this reciprocal way of thinking about formation and reflection still paints a picture that is too individualized and disconnected. When we consider the role of tradition in these processes, we need to expand our metaphor. While the double helix effectively illustrates the intertwined nature of formation and reflection, it doesn't fully capture how these processes are situated within and influenced by tradition.

To address this, I've eventually come to a different metaphor. I find it useful to consider tradition as a vast, living ecosystem within which the paired practices of formation and reflection both grow and thrive. I usually think of a forest, but, if thinking about a desert or plain works better for you, I imagine it will work well, too. Much like how a tree's growth is influenced by its specific location in the forest, our formation is shaped by our personal experiences (like local soil conditions), our cultural background (the broader climate), our social location (proximity to other trees), and the communities we're part of (the surrounding ecosystem).

In this expanded model, tradition provides the foundational elements of the ecosystem, the soil, climate, water sources, and existing plant life. These elements represent the stories, symbols, practices, and teachings that have been cultivated over time. They create the conditions in which our formation and reflection occur. Formation, in this context, is like the growth of a tree, drawing nutrients from the rich soil of tradition, reaching toward the light of divine guidance, and being shaped by the climate of our cultural and historical context. Reflection, then, is akin to the tree's processes of adaptation and interaction: how it responds to changes in its environment, interacts with other organisms, and contributes back to the ecosystem. This is much like how we engage critically with our tradition, learn from others, and offer our own insights back to our faith community.

Formation, like the growth of trees in our ecosystem, is a continuous process of development and adaptation. As we grow, we develop deep roots in the soil of our tradition, drawing nourishment from the wisdom, practices, and stories that have sustained our faith community for generations. Our trunk grows stronger as we internalize core beliefs and values, providing stability and support for our expanding branches of knowledge and experience. These branches reach out in various directions, exploring new ideas, encountering different perspectives, and seeking the light of understanding.

Just as a tree's growth is influenced by its environment, our formation is shaped by the particular conditions of our spiritual ecosystem. We might grow tall and straight in an area of abundant light and resources, or we might develop a more gnarled and resilient form in challenging conditions. But growth is not always smooth or expansive. Sometimes, spiritual formation involves pruning, dormancy, or the painful shedding of what no longer serves. If the soil has become toxic, there may be times we will need to do some uprooting. The seasons of our life feature times of abundance and scarcity, joy and sorrow. All contribute to the unique shape of our spiritual growth. Throughout this process, we grow individually and become part of the larger canopy of our faith community, providing shelter and support for others.

Reflection, in this ecosystem model, is akin to the tree's adaptive processes and interactions with its environment. It's how we make sense of our growth, consider our connections to other "trees," and respond to changes in our spiritual climate. Through reflection, we might shed old beliefs like a tree sheds leaves, redirect our growth like a tree bending toward light, or deepen our understanding like roots growing further into rich soil. This process allows us to integrate new experiences and insights, ensuring our growth remains vital and responsive.

Formation and Reflection

Seen this way, reflection extends beyond individual introspection to active engagement with our surroundings. As we reflect, we release oxygen into our spiritual ecosystem through sharing insights, asking questions, and offering critiques. Discarded ideas or outgrown practices are fallen leaves that decompose to enrich the soil for others. New ideas, fresh interpretations, or innovative practices are the fruit of our reflection, providing nourishment for other members of our faith community. In this way, our personal reflections contribute to our spiritual forest's overall health and evolution.

As the ecosystem itself, tradition provides the vital context for formation and reflection. It's the forest in which we grow, offering a rich diversity of resources and influences. The soil of tradition is layered with the decomposed wisdom of countless generations, providing nutrients for our growth. The climate of tradition shapes the overall environment in which we develop, its overarching narratives, core beliefs, and ethical frameworks grounding our growth. Established institutions, practices, and interpretations are the existing plant life, creating a complex network of relationships that we must navigate as we grow.

Yet tradition is not static. Like any living ecosystem, it's in a constant state of subtle change and renewal. New ideas take root and grow, sometimes reshaping the landscape. Old growth might fall, creating space for new life. What influence has industrialization, colonization, and capitalism had on our spirituality? What about realizing the importance of pluralism, diversity, and our impact on the environment and global climate health? Outside influences or new interpretations are like the introduction of a new species: Both can challenge the ecosystem, sometimes threatening its balance, other times enriching its diversity. Our individual processes of formation and reflection, therefore, don't just occur *within* tradition but actively contribute to tradition's ongoing evolution. We are not merely inhabitants of this spiritual forest. We are co-creators, responsible for its cultivation and care. As we grow and reflect, we draw sustenance from our tradition and contribute to its ongoing renewal. Our personal insights, questions, and experiences become part of the ecosystem's diversity, enriching the soil for future generations and helping the tradition respond to new challenges and opportunities. This interplay between tradition, formation, and reflection is also a core dynamic of our moral orienting systems, as discussed in the first chapter. Taken collectively, they help us interpret our experiences and discern vocation amid both rootedness and disruption.

While I've gone on at length with this "ecosystem" metaphor, I want to note that, even without the particulars of the ecology comparisons, this understanding of tradition as a living, evolving being aligns with contemporary perspectives on the nature of religious communities. It recognizes that healthy traditions require both stability and adaptability. They must maintain their core identity while also remaining open to new growth and change. This kind of thinking has been particularly prevalent in the Catholic context in recent years. Pope Francis was especially sensitive to recognizing that the "signs of the time" point toward the need for reflection and change.

> Christian doctrine is not a closed system, incapable of raising questions, doubts, inquiries, but is living, is able to unsettle, is able to enliven.... The reform of the Church ... is *semper reformanda* [always reforming]. She is not exhausted in the countless plans to change her structures. It instead means being implanted and rooted in Christ, allowing herself to be led by the Spirit. Thus everything will be possible with genius and creativity. The Church of Italy lets herself be carried by His powerful—and thus, at times, restless—breath.... May she be a free Church, open to the challenges of the present, never on the defensive out of fear of losing something.[18]

In this spirit, since 2021, the Catholic Church has been in a "Synodal Process" that emphasizes communal listening, discernment, and participation.[19] This process invites all 1.3 billion members of the global Catholic Church to engage in a collective journey of reflection and formation, recognizing that the Church is always in need of renewal and adaptation to better respond to the needs of its time.

Pope Francis has articulated this as a dynamic and living engagement with the signs of the times, encouraging a Church that is open, adaptive, and responsive to the movements of the Holy Spirit. The synodal process is not merely about structural changes but about fostering deeper communion, participation, and mission within the Church. It involves gathering input from diverse voices within the Church community, ensuring that the process of reflection and formation is inclusive and representative of the whole body of Christ. This communal approach to discernment underscores the interconnectedness of individual and communal growth. As the Church collectively reflects and discerns its path forward, individual members find their own spiritual journeys enriched and supported by the broader community. Through this ongoing

---

18 Pope Francis, "Meeting with the Participants in the Fifth Convention of the Italian Church: Address of the Holy Father," Pastoral Visit of His Holiness Pope Francis to Prato and Florence (10 November 2015), Cathedral of Santa Maria del Fiore, Florence, Tuesday, 10 November 2015, https://www.vatican.va/content/francesco/en/speeches/2015/november/documents/papa-francesco_20151110_firenze-convegno-chiesa-italiana.html.

19 Catholics reading this are likely already familiar with "The Synod." For everyone else interested, I've found some good, accessible information about the process in "For a Synodal Church: Communion, Participation, and Mission," https://www.synod.va/content/dam/synod/document/common/vademecum/Vademecum-EN-A4.pdf.

dialogue and collective discernment, the Church becomes a living, breathing body that grows and adapts. This process strengthens the faith community and equips it to engage more effectively with the world, embodying the Gospel's transformative power in contemporary society.

By engaging in this ongoing cycle of formation and reflection within the living ecosystem of tradition, we open ourselves to profound transformation. We become more fully who we are called to be, more deeply attuned to the divine presence in our lives and in the world around us, and more capable of responding to that presence with wisdom, compassion, and grace. However, like any complex ecosystem, our spiritual forest presents both opportunities for growth and challenges to navigate. As we continue to explore this living tradition, we must consider how to find a healthy equilibrium between preservation and adaptation, how to nurture diversity while maintaining unity, and how to address the potential conflicts that arise when new forms of thought and practice interact. In the next section, we'll examine these opportunities and challenges in greater depth, exploring how we can cultivate a healthy, vibrant spiritual ecosystem that supports both individual flourishing and collective renewal.

The Challenges and Opportunities of Tradition

Like languages, traditions are living systems that evolve. Because of their importance within the processes of formation and reflection, several points about traditions are worth making. First, tradition profoundly shapes our spiritual identity and provides a sense of belonging to a larger narrative. We'll talk more about this in the next chapter. Still, for now, it is enough to note that engaging with tradition connects us to a larger narrative, offering a framework for understanding our place in the world, our relationship to the divine, and the context in which we discern our unique vocational calling. This engagement can be compelling in our formation process, as it provides us with language, symbols, and practices that can deepen our spiritual experiences and help us make meaning in our lives. We're connecting ourselves to generations of believers who have wrestled with similar questions and experiences. This connection can provide a sense of rootedness and continuity that can be profoundly formative, especially in times of uncertainty or change. Because of the potential consequences of formation, we are presented with both a challenge and an opportunity.

Seen one way, the more depth there is to a tradition, the more resources we have to do the work of meaning-making by reflecting through that tradition and looking at our own experiences. Seen another way, the weight of centuries of interpretation and practice can sometimes feel constraining, limiting our ability to engage with contemporary issues or personal experiences that fall outside traditional frameworks. What would Jesus say about the global use of fossil fuels and climate change? There is no clear-cut answer to that question. That is partly why it's important to recognize that our engagement with tradition should not merely be a passive reception of inherited wisdom but an active and dynamic process of interpretation and reinterpretation.

I find it helpful to think of tradition as offering both tools and rules. The tools are the inherited practices that help us do the work of faith: methods of prayer and theological reflection, forms of communal discernment, stories that illuminate our path, and songs that give voice to our joy and lament. These are the resources we pick up and use. The rules are the structures that give a tradition its shape: its doctrines, ethical boundaries, polity, and the often unspoken norms that govern belonging. These rules can provide stability and coherence, a container in which the tools can be used faithfully. But the two can also come into conflict. Sometimes the rules can feel so rigid they prevent us from using the tools effectively. Other times, we can become so attached to a particular tool that we turn it into a rule, losing its life-giving flexibility. Discerning the difference means knowing when to use a tool, when to abide by a rule, and when to challenge a rule that has become a cage. This kind of discernment is a central task of living in a tradition with integrity.

As we bring our own lived experiences into dialogue with traditional teachings and practices, we participate in the ongoing evolution of our faith tradition. Active engagement with tradition can lead to a deepening of faith that is both rooted in historical continuity and responsive to present realities. It challenges us to hold in creative tension the wisdom of the past and the pressing questions of our time, fostering a spiritual formation that is both grounded and responsive.

Second, we must recognize that traditions are not static entities but dynamic processes that evolve over time. While we often think of traditions as fixed and unchanging, they are shaped by the ongoing reflections and experiences of the communities that hold them. This dynamic nature of tradition means it can adapt to new contexts and insights while maintaining a connection to its roots. The British Anglican theologian David Brown provides a compelling perspective on this idea.[20] He suggests that "tradition, so far from being something secondary or reactionary, is the motor that sustains revelation both within Scripture and beyond."[21] He argues that rather than viewing tradition as a human interpretation layered onto an initial and "pure" divine revelation, it should be seen as an ongoing part of revelation itself.

---

20 See chapter 5 of my book *Sense of the Possible* for a fuller reflection on Brown's argument.

21 David Brown, *Tradition and Imagination: Revelation and Change* (New York: Oxford University Press, 1999), 1.

> Instead of thinking of tradition as purely human reflection added on to an original and unchanging divine disclosure, or even of it as small, but significant, divinely added supplements, we need to see that continuing human reflection is itself an indispensable part of the process of divine disclosure. Revelation is mediated to the community of faith through a continuous stream of developing tradition.[22]

As Brown sees it, our ongoing reflections and experiences are essential parts of how God reveals truth to us. Tradition is alive and constantly unfolding, helping us grow and understand our faith in deeper and more relevant ways. This perspective allows us to see tradition not as a constraint but as a living conversation with our past and present. The American Methodist practical theologian Mary Elizabeth Moore has written similarly, especially as it pertains to religious education. Moore talks about the importance of an active process of "tradition-ing" in religious education. She suggests that there are two foundations for those committed to traditioning: the community and the individual.[23]

The community is responsible for interpreting and transforming itself lest it slip into irrelevance. As an interpreting body, it explores the tradition's past, present, and future in view of its knowledge of the world, the church, and relationships with other communities and peoples. It is because the community is a transforming one that it has continuity. Without change, it first ceases to be vibrant and then ceases to be at all. But change for change's sake is as damning as traditionalism. Change must be grounded in faithfulness, with attention toward the inbreaking of the reign of God.[24]

At the individual level, the person is also always in process, linked in their very being to God, other people, and creation. The person both shapes and is shaped by community. As such, traditioning education emphasizes the importance of knowledge of what has come before for the sake of interpretation and transformation. Knowledge of the past and present should be held in dialogue with hopes for the future of what may come. And all of this, what has been, what is, and what may yet be, is to be the content of religious education. Moore wants those who inherit the faith tradition to

---

22 Ibid., 169.

23 Mary Elizabeth Moore, *Education for Continuity and Change: A New Model for Christian Religious Education* (Nashville, TN: Abingdon Press, 1983).

24 I use the term "God's Reign" intentionally to emphasize the active, liberative movement of God rather than a static place or political structure. The Greek term often translated as "kingdom" in the New Testament is *basileia* (βασιλεία), which can refer to both the reign or rule of a sovereign and their domain. I follow those interpreters who stress its dynamic sense: as God's *reigning*, not God's *realm*. While "kingdom of God" is scripturally familiar and "kindom" offers a relational corrective to patriarchal imagery, "Reign" better names the unfolding action of divine justice and mercy in the world.

be able to both pass on the practices and stories that came before and to be able to use them to interpret their own experiences and guide them in their own changes as they seek to be responsive to God's call and the needs of the church and world.

Moore understands the task of religious education to be about "educating for continuity and change."[25] For her, continuity is about maintaining connective links between Christ and the early church until the present day. Affirming change means recognizing that continuity and connection can be maintained while still inviting conversion, transformation, and renewal.[26] She acknowledges that considering new interpretations and/or changes in practice can feel uncomfortable. She also accepts that, as far as innovation goes, there *is* such a thing as "going too far." But, despite this, Moore argues that healthy growth often requires the risk of destabilization. This innovation is worth pursuing because "the closing of imagination and the failure to risk new ventures will likely destroy a community over time."[27] In the absence of change, continuity becomes untenable, diminishing the community's ability to adapt and survive. When a community ignores the ever-changing realities of the world around it, it risks becoming increasingly isolated and disconnected from other communities and individuals who embrace transformation.

Third, and related to the previous, we must recognize the diversity that exists within traditions. Even within a single religious tradition, there can be multiple interpretations and expressions of faith. There is no monolithic "tradition" that is timeless, solid, and unassailable. This diversity reflects the richness of human experience and the many ways people have encountered and responded to the divine throughout history. Understanding this internal diversity can be liberating in our formation and reflection processes. It reminds us that there isn't always a single "correct" way to live out our faith and discernment of vocation. Instead, we're invited to engage in a process of discernment, drawing on the wisdom of various streams within our tradition to find the expressions that most deeply resonate with our experiences, calling, and the record of God's work in the world.

When we recognize the multiplicity within traditions, we are also invited to consider the role of power dynamics in shaping how traditions are interpreted and expressed. Throughout history, certain voices and perspectives within traditions have been privileged over others, frequently reflecting broader societal inequities related to race, gender, class, ability, sexuality, and other factors. As we engage with our traditions, it's faithful to ask whose voices have been centered and whose have been

---

25 Moore, *Education for Continuity and Change*.
26 Ibid., 21–23.
27 Mary Elizabeth Moore, "Imagination at the Center: Identity on the Margins," *Process Studies* 34, no. 2 (2005): 199.

marginalized. This critical engagement can lead us to seek out and amplify historically overlooked or silenced perspectives within our traditions. By intentionally broadening the range of voices we listen to within our traditions, we enrich our spiritual formation and contribute to a more inclusive and just expression of faith.

The British Quaker theologian Grace Jantzen offers a compelling example in her analysis of how classical Greek war literature, particularly Homer's works, became foundational to Western thought. While Sappho was similarly prolific in terms of her output of poetry, its impact was significantly overshadowed due to her gender. We only have scraps of Sappho's writing, while we have volumes from Homer. Jantzen's reflection on this historical privileging of voices provides a powerful framework for engaging with our own spiritual traditions:

> Fragments remain. And in their very fragmentary and jagged nature they disrupt the smooth narrative of Western self-constitution.... We cannot undo the history of the West. But by challenging its alleged inevitability, by looking as far as we can down the roads not taken, we can become clearer about the ways power and knowledge have forged a violent and deathly narrative that could have been otherwise.[28]

This perspective invites us to approach our traditions with a critical eye, seeking out the "fragments" that disrupt dominant narratives. We'll talk more about how such seeking can affect call in the sixth chapter. For now, it is enough to say that, in the context of spiritual formation and vocational discernment, "seeking fragments" might mean exploring interpretations of scripture or theological concepts that have been marginalized or overlooked. It could also encourage questioning the "alleged inevitability" of how we've understood our traditions and imagining alternative possibilities for living out our faith.

By engaging with these often-fragmented voices from the margins of our traditions, we open ourselves to new insights that can profoundly shape our spiritual formation and understanding of vocation. This approach doesn't seek to discard tradition but rather to enrich it by recovering lost or suppressed wisdom. It encourages us to remain humble in our interpretations, recognizing that our understanding of our faith tradition is always partial and open to new revelations. In doing so, we deepen our own spiritual lives while also contributing to the ongoing evolution of our traditions in more inclusive, just, and life-giving ways. That leads me to my next point.

Fourth, just because traditions play a marked role in our formation and reflection doesn't mean that we must uncritically accept everything we've inherited. I think about

---

28 Grace M. Jantzen, *Foundations of Violence* (London: Routledge, 2004), 67.

the possible orientations of how to relate to tradition as existing along a continuum. On one side, there is a kind of "traditionalism," or the maintenance of tradition as "doing something because it has always been done." On this extreme, traditional religious practices are passed on in a kind of rote way. They are done, as it were, as bodies without souls. Innovation and adaptability are viewed as enemies or obstacles to faithfulness, with the only true way forward being framed as a replication of the past. On the other extreme, there is discontent with the past and inherited patterns, systems, and power structures. Here, tradition is rejected with an often unspoken assumption that all tradition is traditionalism and ought to be left behind. Continuity and traditional values are viewed as enemies or obstacles to faithfulness, with the best way to proceed being framed as something that must be new.

It should be acknowledged that both of these extremes are outlandish, but they point to tendencies that can emerge and the resulting challenges. The further folks are to either side, the more likely they are to claim that those they disagree with are all the way out at the extreme opposite edge. Accepting a tradition just because it is the tradition is *traditionalism* and often doesn't serve as a means to deepen in faithfulness. Similarly, a total rejection of something simply because it is traditional can be equally problematic. This approach, what I sometimes call *novelty worship*, assumes that newer ideas are inherently better or more valid than older ones. It risks discarding valuable wisdom and practices that have stood the test of time and have shaped countless lives in meaningful, positive ways.

Instead, a more fruitful approach involves critically engaging with tradition. This means approaching our inherited wisdom with both respect and discernment. We can appreciate tradition's depth and richness while recognizing that human interpretations and historical contexts have shaped it. The Vietnamese American Catholic theologian Peter Phan has written about this exact tension in an insightful and gorgeous way:

> Memory anchors the theologian in the ocean of history and tradition, the Church's and one's own; but the stability and security it affords is impermanent and illusory. Remembering is not re-producing reality exactly as it happened ... but re-creating it imaginatively; it is re-membering disparate fragments of the past together and forming them into a new pattern under the pressure of present experiences, with a view to shaping a possible future.... Like a pair of wings, memory and imagination carry the theologian aloft in the work of linking past and future, east and west, north and south, earth and heaven.[29]

---

[29] Peter Phan, "Betwixt and Between: Doing Theology with Memory and Imagination," in *Journeys at the Margin: Toward an Autobiographical Theology in American-Asian Perspective*, ed, Peter Phan and Jung Young Lee (Collegeville, MN: Liturgical Press, 1999), 114.

This resonates with Moore's sense of continuity and change. In fact, Francis, Brown, Phan, and Moore all see tradition as dynamic, not just a static collection of truths but something that evolves as we engage with it.

This perspective invites us to approach our traditions with reverence and creativity, recognizing that our reflections and experiences become part of an ongoing story of our faith and the faith tradition itself. We each are a living part of the communities that shape us. As we change, they change, even if only incrementally. We are challenged to hold in tension the wisdom of the past and the pressing questions of the present, allowing both to inform and shape our spiritual formation and vocational discernment. This dynamic understanding of tradition sets the stage for approaching the inevitable tensions and struggles we encounter within our faith traditions.

Many people today find themselves grappling with "traditional teachings" on gender roles, sexuality, or the relationship between faith and science. These tensions can be incredibly challenging for those exploring their vocation, particularly if they feel called to roles that don't fit traditional expectations. Or when someone's very identity is marginalized or theologically labeled as "disordered." Consider, for example, a woman feeling called to ministry in a tradition that has historically limited leadership roles to men, or a scientist trying to reconcile their faith with evolutionary theory. Depending on their context, different people will experience this tension more acutely than others.

Yet in wrestling with these challenges, we often experience the most profound growth. This struggle can lead us to deeper theological reflection, pushing us to examine the surface-level teachings of our tradition and the underlying principles that inform them. It can prompt us to engage more deeply with our sacred texts, explore our traditions' historical context, and seek out diverse perspectives within our faith communities. In the language of the first chapter, this is the experience of our Moral Orienting System being disrupted. When our inherited tradition (a key part of our MOS) clashes with our lived experience or evolving convictions, the resulting disorientation is not an inherent sign of failure but an invitation to reconsider and reintegrate.

This tension often calls us to a more intentional and grounded faith. Rather than simply inheriting beliefs uncritically, we're challenged to actively engage with our tradition, question, doubt, and ultimately claim its articulations of faith as our own. This process of wrestling with tradition can lead to a more mature and nuanced faith that acknowledges complexity, embraces mystery, and informs a deeper understanding of our vocational calling amid challenging cultural and theological contexts.

That being said, it's important to acknowledge that, for some individuals, engaging with their tradition may feel more consistently life-sapping than life-giving. If you find yourself in this situation, please sit with that feeling. Don't ignore your pain; it is a part of you trying to tell you something. It's important to recognize that, while tradition can be a source of great wisdom and spiritual nourishment, it should not come at the cost of your fundamental well-being or sense of self. If you've made sincere efforts to engage critically and openly with your tradition, sought out diverse perspectives within it, and still find that it consistently feels only oppressive or alienating, it may be time to consider other paths. This doesn't necessarily mean abandoning faith altogether. Still, it might involve exploring different expressions of your faith tradition or even other spiritual traditions that resonate more deeply with your experiences and values. Remember, the ultimate goal of spiritual formation is to foster growth, intentionality, faithfulness, and a deeper connection with the divine, others, and creation. If your current tradition hinders rather than facilitates this growth, it's valid to question whether it's the right spiritual home for you.

However, if this kind of questioning *always* leads you to the conclusion that the issue is someone or something other than you, you probably want to reconsider. While it's right to recognize the very real ways marginalized people can feel excluded due to their identities, it's equally important to engage in honest self-reflection. Sometimes, the discomfort or alienation we feel within a tradition isn't solely due to systemic issues. It may stem from unresolved personal conflicts, misunderstandings, or mistakes we've made. This doesn't negate the reality of exclusion that many face, but it reminds us that growth often requires looking inward as well as outward. Acknowledging that "it might be you" doesn't mean dismissing valid concerns about exclusion or injustice. Instead, it's about cultivating a nuanced perspective that recognizes both personal responsibility and systemic challenges. This approach can empower us to address issues within ourselves and our communities effectively, fostering genuine growth and positive change.

This process of discernment can be challenging and even painful, but it can also lead to profound spiritual growth and a more grounded expression of your faith. You might go through "wilderness" periods, when you're between traditions or unsure of your path. However, you might also join Jacob in learning that wrestling with the sacred sometimes leads to unexpected blessings, even if they come with some bumps and bruises.[30] These wilderness moments are not to be rushed through or avoided; they are integral to your journey. In these times, you might find clarity in the very struggle itself, discovering new aspects of yourself and your relationship with the divine that you had not previously recognized.

Your spiritual journey is your own. Although tradition can provide valuable guidance and community, it should serve to enhance your relationship with the divine and your sense of purpose, not diminish it. Trust in your own experiences and insights, seek wisdom from diverse sources, and be open to where your spiritual

---

30 Genesis 32:22–32.

journey might lead you. The divine, in its infinite wisdom and love, is not confined to any single tradition and can meet you wherever you are on your path. In fact, these periods of rough growth can also be times of great discovery and renewal for yourself *and* the community.

As individuals engage critically with tradition and bring their lived experiences into dialogue with inherited wisdom, they contribute to the ongoing development of the tradition itself. This is how traditions remain living and relevant, adapting to new contexts while maintaining their core attributes. In the context of vocational discernment, this engagement with challenging aspects of tradition can be particularly significant. It can help us discern between cultural accretions and core spiritual truths, guiding us toward a vocation that aligns not just with the surface elements of our tradition, but with its deepest values and principles. It can also equip us to be bridge-builders, helping others navigate similar tensions and contributing to the ongoing renewal of our faith communities. By engaging in intentional practices of formation and reflection, we open ourselves to deeper insights and a greater capacity to respond to our callings. This process helps us discern our unique vocation and align our actions with our deepest values and sense of purpose.

Questions for Reflection

1. This chapter describes theological reflection as a way to make meaning from our experiences by bringing them into dialogue with our deepest values and beliefs. Even if you haven't followed the six specific steps outlined, can you recall a time, perhaps informally, when a similar kind of reflective practice was an important part of your faith life or spiritual journey? What did that process involve for you, and what fruit did it bear? Anything?

2. Consider the metaphor of spiritual formation as a soundboard with various "sliders" representing dimensions like Intellectual Engagement, Community Connection, Mystical and Personal Experience, Spiritual Practices, and the Exercise of Spiritual Gifts. Thinking about the faith community or tradition that has most shaped you, which of these dimensions feel most "turned up" or emphasized? Are there any dimensions you sense are underutilized or perhaps even quiet? What might be gained if they were given more attention?

3. The chapter touches on theological concepts like sanctification (being conformed to God's will) and theosis (partaking in the divine nature). How do these ideas resonate with or perhaps challenge your own understanding of spiritual growth? In what concrete ways might these concepts shape your view of what it means to become more faithful?

4. Think about the traditions that have shaped your understanding of faith and spirituality. How do these traditions provide a framework for interpreting your experiences? Are there times when your experiences have challenged or enriched your understanding of these traditions? Vice versa?

5. The "living ecosystem of tradition" metaphor suggests we need to find a healthy equilibrium between stability (our roots) and adaptability (our growth). Reflect on an instance in your faith journey where you've felt a tension between honoring and preserving a cherished tradition, and the need to adapt or respond to new realities or understandings. How did you navigate this tension, and what did you learn about yourself or your tradition in the process?

6. Think about Grace Jantzen's concept of "looking down the roads not taken" in our traditions. Are there aspects of your spiritual tradition that you feel have been overlooked or marginalized? How might exploring these neglected areas enrich your spiritual formation?

PART II

GROWTH

Growth is rarely tidy. Like a plant reaching both down and out—roots deepening into unseen soil even as branches stretch toward light—these middle chapters explore how vocation unfolds in relationship with our wider ecosystems. We are not isolated organisms. We are shaped by weather and wind, by the soil we inherit, by what grows alongside us. Sometimes, we thrive. Sometimes, we wither. Sometimes, we must be broken open before anything new can take root.

Here, we tend to the ways that systems shape us, how identity and belonging are negotiated, and how joy and lament intermingle in the vocational journey. This is the slow, sometimes uncomfortable work of becoming. Growth involves pressure as well as nourishment—tension as well as tenderness. There are seasons of pruning, dormancy, and even rot. Some growth is not visible. Some must be undone. To develop with integrity, we must be willing to remain rooted while responding to changing conditions. Vocation matures in the interplay between inner conviction and outer complexity, between stability and change.

To grow is to be vulnerable—to stretch, to risk, to adapt. These chapters invite you to notice where growth is already happening, even if it's quiet or uneven. They ask what sustains you, what challenges you, and what kinds of environments allow you to flourish. Like any living thing, your calling evolves in relationship. And sometimes, it must break free from what once nourished it in the past to survive for what comes next.

What We Do Not See

In 2018, scientists notified us they had discovered something: a new organ in the human body. The eightieth. This "interstitium," they said, accounted for 20 percent of the total body of an adult. It is roughly equivalent to 10 liters of fluid. How does something like that go unnoticed? What does it do?

If your body is a city with sewers so everything stays clean, then the interstitium is a system of pipes, running to our lymph nodes, the water treatment center of our soft insides. Too much fluid somewhere? A flood or rain burst near the northern lakes of the heart? The interstitium is a water tank, storing fluid when there's too much and releasing it in drought. It also is your body's highway system, how nutrients and immune cells commute. Vital roles. How did it manage to hide for so long? Because it can't be seen outside of a living body.

Before, when we wanted to study body tissues, we would prepare them as pressing a flower in a book. When we did this, the liquid inside the interstitium drained out and the structure collapsed, making it hard to see. It lasts a long time, but we get only the shape and experience of a dried flower, not what it looked like in the field. Nothing of salt breezes. No smell of heather or touch of sun. The interstitium only became visible when pathologists started using a technique called a "confocal laser endomicroscopy"—a way of seeing that allowed them to observe microscopic tissues in living people *without* removing anything. Now we can look and study without slivers or segmentation. When we could finally observe without needing to slice it from the body, we saw the body was more than we had thought.

In 2019, another group discovered something else. People had been poking around under the soil with questions since 1885, but it wasn't cracked until a group from Zurich and Stanford studied it. What we've learned is that there's an underground internet made of fungi and plant roots all connected by tiny threads. Very tiny. Not visible to the naked eye. Microscopic filaments. We call them "mycorrhizal networks."

Through these things, a big tree can send extra water or nutrients to a smaller tree, or the fungi can help plants find nutrients in the soil. In return, the plants give the fungi sugar, which they make from sunlight. Scientists think trees might send chemical messages to warn each other about dangers, like pests or diseases. Trees receiving warning signals preemptively begin to produce defensive compounds to protect themselves from potential threats: plant hormones that repel bugs, those that make leaves bitter, those that attract wasps, a small forest air force that deters intruders.

❦

Today, hanging in the National Gallery of Art, there is a painting called *The Peaceable Kingdom*. In the foreground are two chubby white children dressed in white surrounded serenely by a lion, lamb, ox, leopard, bear, and wolf. The animals mostly lie peacefully, their expressions calm. The background features a scene with a group of white people meeting with a group of Native Americans. The image has simplified forms, warm, earthy tones, and a flattened perspective. It is the Quaker Edward Hicks's interpretation of Isaiah 11, a prophetic vision of a future harmony. On that day, the spirit of the Lord will allow the wolf to lie with the lamb and the calf with the lion. No one will hurt or destroy, for the earth will be as full of the knowledge of God as the waters that cover the sea.

Years ago, I taught Sunday School in my Meeting in Rochester. I recall talking once to our youngest ones about this painting. How this is a way of thinking about life on earth as it is in heaven. Not just something to wait for, but something to work toward while we still draw breath. I remember a child. Blue dress. Blonde hair. *But what does the Lion eat in Heaven?* Isaiah tells us that the lion shall eat straw like the ox. And that is what I said that day, but I wonder. Is that the plan? Would the lion still dream of the hunt and chase?

The folks in the background of that image are meant to be the Lenape Unami Turtle Clan meeting with Quakers at the Treaty of Shackamaxon. There, Chief Tamanend and William Penn set terms and agreed to live in peace as long as the waters run in the rivers and creeks and as long as the stars and moon endure. And so the land was purchased rather than stolen. All good. But Penn's own sons attempted to break the terms of the agreement. And Penn himself, this peaceful man who refused to colonize without paying coin, this Quaker minister after which a state is named, also enslaved people. That is not in the painting.

The thing is, when we speak of human "predators," we know that anything and everything predatory about them is wrong. There's no good excuse for exploitation.

But is it so wrong that the lion would like the tender flesh of the lamb? Surely, from the lamb's perspective, but what of mine? Of yours? Is our idea of heaven just that all the things that make us uncomfortable have gone away? Something more *is* promised, but lions do not eat straw. What are *our* hungers? Which ones can be laid down? Which are in us for good?

I once heard the wise Lynne Westwood talk about how she almost got in trouble. A professor of religious education, she used to invite students to say what their communities were and who they were learning for. And some people had a hard time with that. They didn't want to do the assignment. Some folks liked learning for the sake of learning. *I'm doing this just for me.* Not for anyone and without any named roots in the soil of home. And there's something in that. Sure. A freedom to explore without any tether. But I want my ministers to be thinking of who they come from and to whom they'll return. Promises. Full flowers. Filaments.

4

Systems Thinking

In the sublime area of man against Reality humanity has but one weapon, the imagination.
—Benjamin de Casseres

What we practice at the small scale sets the patterns for the whole system.
—adrienne maree brown

Building on our exploration of formation and reflection in the preceding chapter, we now turn to how these processes operate within larger systems. You'll see systems thinking themes throughout the whole of this book, but I think it's worth explicitly naming the foundational ideas to increase the likelihood that you'll notice them as you come across them. Readers attentive to the earlier chapters may already have noticed how systems shape our understanding of tradition, vocation, and discernment. From the institutional dynamics that shape ministry to the cultural patterns that inform our belonging, systems thinking has been humming in the background. This chapter brings it into the foreground not to flatten complexity, but to offer a lens that helps us attend more clearly to the patterns, pressures, and possibilities at play in our vocational lives.

For years, I've been teaching Bowen Family Systems theory as a practical tool to help students understand organizational life, especially within faith communities. I would present the content, demonstrate its utility, and encourage students to apply this lens to group dynamics, observing how these patterns influenced both individuals and the collective. Students often found this approach useful, and, as we wrapped up our discussions, I'd broaden the conversation to emphasize the value of systems thinking beyond just one theory.

It wasn't until I wrote a book exploring imagination that I began to rethink the role of systems thinking itself, beginning to consider it not merely as a tool for interpreting social patterns but also as a way of "seeing" the whole, a lens that helps illuminate not only what is but what could be. Why did my research on imagination reshape this conversation?[1] Systems thinking invites us to "zoom out," broadening our awareness of dynamics and interconnections that might otherwise remain hidden. Yet this clarity of vision is only one side of the journey. When we pair it with imagination, our view expands to include the potential woven into these connections, the chance to reimagine how we relate, create, and lead. What might our systems and society look like in the future? How might I be part of positive change?

Systems thinking provides the structure within which our understanding can develop and take hold, while imagination helps these insights flourish into something vital and living, allowing us to envision transformative possibilities within those systems. With an expanded systemic awareness, our vocational journeys, and the systems we inhabit, can become canvases for new possibilities, where innovation arises from an awareness of interconnectedness and what more might be possible.

For example, a student might initially imagine their calling as leading a traditional congregation. However, by applying systems thinking and expanding their imagination, they might begin to envision new forms of spiritual community that respond to changing societal needs. They might consider how their ministry could address systemic issues in their community or how they could leverage technology to create new forms of spiritual connection. Integrating systems thinking with imagination in our approach to vocation invites us to consider both the forest and the trees. For some, this involves engaging with structures that have historically supported their calling, while others may need to navigate systems that restrict or obscure these possibilities, requiring reimagination, resilience, and the work of naming and dismantling the barriers that deny new life. In such cases, we often have to navigate deep moral disorientation in addition to whatever logistical barriers might exist. Stories, relationships, and dreams that once made sense of their vocation may no longer hold, and discernment becomes a process of reorientation: reconnecting to what is good and possible in the midst of systems that can obscure both.

Having already written about imagination, I thought it seemed like the time to think through the role that systems thinking might play in ministry. While the term

---

[1] See the epigraph on imagination by Benjamin de Casseres, "Shelley," *The Poetry Journal* 6, no. 1 (July 1916): 19–20.

"systems thinking" itself might sound academic, it's something many people already practice intuitively. Think of the church volunteer who understands how changes in the neighborhood affect their food pantry ministry, or the workplace chaplain who recognizes how company policies affect their ability to provide spiritual care. These ministers often have unique insights into how different parts of their communities interconnect, even if they don't use formal systems terminology to describe it.

A systems-informed approach to thinking about vocation invites us to view our calls not as isolated pursuits but as part of a larger, interconnected ecosystem of purpose and meaning. As we cultivate a systems perspective, we are reminded that discernment, discussed in the second chapter, involves both personal journey and awareness of how the system called "community" affects diverse paths, enabling some and constraining others. This awareness calls us to discern with attention to systemic inequities and possibilities for transformation.

Consider the story of a student of mine who had served faithfully as a pastor in a United Methodist congregation in rural Pennsylvania. Over the course of several years, he witnessed a significant shift in his county's cultural and moral orientation, as much of the community increasingly aligned with the Make America Great Again movement and its political and theological overtones. The congregation he had known and loved was being reshaped. This was happening not only in terms of voting patterns or civic engagement, but in terms of what they now named as good, true, and holy.

The moral world of the church was being resocialized, and this resocialization came with new pressures: the expectation that he would preach a gospel of nationalism, exclusion, and power. He could not. Not only did the new moral landscape violate his conscience, it rendered him increasingly invisible to the congregation. They stopped hearing him. They no longer trusted him. Eventually, he stepped down. Not because he had lost his sense of call, but because the community had been so thoroughly reoriented that his presence no longer registered as pastoral.

As we explored in the first chapter, a Moral Orienting System is "a complex multidimensional system of one's values, beliefs, behaviors, and meaningful relationships as informed and affected by one's lived experiences."[2] That definition helps us name what was happening here for the pastor and for the congregation, too. This story reveals that systems do more than shape opportunity: They shape moral possibility. They form the boundaries of what is sayable, believable, and livable. When a system undergoes moral reorientation, as this congregation did, it not only redefines what is good; it reshapes the very conditions under which vocation can be discerned and lived.

---

2 Zachary Moon, *Warriors between Worlds: Moral Injury and Identities in Crisis* (Lanham, MD: Lexington Books, 2019), 25.

To engage vocation seriously in such contexts, we need more than psychological insight or interpersonal care. We need a systemic lens. Vocation is never only personal. It is always entangled in what a community or institution is willing to recognize as faithful or just. And when those recognitions shift, it is often those most rooted in love and integrity who find themselves disoriented, trying to live with fidelity in a system that no longer knows what to do with them.

And yet that very disorientation may be a sign of spiritual health. The pastor's refusal to preach what he understood as a false gospel was not a sign of failure, but of fidelity. His sorrow, his frustration, and his sense of not belonging were each a mark that something was working *right*. His moral orienting system was still functioning. It was telling the truth. To feel ill-fit in a deformed moral ecology is not a pathology. It is a form of witness.

This is why liberative vocational discernment must be alert to both interior clarity and systemic deformation. It is not enough to ask whether one feels called. We must ask: What kind of world is this call being lived within? And what does fidelity look like when the systems around us no longer recognize the good?

The Power of Systems

Systems thinking emphasizes understanding complex situations by considering the whole, focusing on relationships, patterns, and contexts rather than isolated components. This perspective stands in contrast to more traditional, linear ways of thinking that often dominate our problem-solving approaches. In our day-to-day lives, we often default to what we might call "usual" thinking. This approach tends to be linear, focusing on direct cause-and-effect relationships. We see a problem, we identify what we believe to be its immediate cause, and we try to address that cause directly. While this can be effective for simple issues, it often falls short when dealing with complex, interconnected problems.[3]

In her book *Follow Your Bliss and Other Lies about Calling*, Bonnie Miller-McLemore writes that "callings are not purely individual matters of knowing and choosing what we alone want or should do but are deeply relational and communal. They are shaped within and controlled by our intimate relationships and social contexts."[4] I agree, and I think that the systemic forces that create those contexts are important to consider.

---

3 I'm influenced here by the Cynefin Framework, a good summary of which can be found in David J. Snowden and Mary E. Boone, "A Leader's Framework for Decision Making," *Harvard Business Review* 85, no. 11 (2007): 68–76.

4 Bonnie Miller-McLemore, *Follow Your Bliss and Other Lies about Calling* (New York: Oxford University Press, 2024), 5.

Miller-McLemore emphasizes the relational and contextual factors that shape vocation, such as family expectations, social norms, and community influence. I suggest that such factors cannot be fully understood without also addressing systemic structures that perpetuate injustice and affect each of these contexts. Liberation theology challenges us to see vocation as a call to resist these structures and work toward justice, making systemic transformation a core dimension of a vocation-centered life.

Systems thinking, on the other hand, encourages us to step back and consider the broader context. It asks us to look at how different elements within a system interact with one another, how changes in one area might ripple out to affect others, and how feedback loops might amplify or dampen effects over time. As Paulo Freire reminds us, without understanding these conditioning structures, we risk remaining objects of our reality rather than subjects capable of transforming it.[5] When we grasp these underlying dynamics and our own potential to influence them, we move from being passively shaped by our circumstances to actively co-creating new responses and possibilities. This approach can reveal insights and solutions that might not be apparent when we're focused solely on individual parts or immediate causes. A powerful illustration of systems thinking is the reintroduction of wolves to Yellowstone National Park in 1995.[6]

Wolves were eliminated there in the 1920s, killed because cattle ranchers were afraid they would lose their stock animals. The consequences were unexpected. Elk populations exploded, leading to overgrazing and subsequent changes in vegetation, river behavior, and various species populations. When wolves were reintroduced in 1995, the effects were far-reaching and often surprising. Their presence not only reduced elk numbers but also changed elk behavior, allowing willow trees and other vegetation to recover in certain areas. This led to a cascade of effects: increased bird populations, the return of beavers, creation of new habitats, and even changes in river structures. This "trophic cascade" beautifully illustrates the interconnected nature of ecosystems and the power of systems thinking. A traditional approach might have focused on directly managing elk numbers or replanting vegetation. Instead, by reintroducing a key element of the system (wolves) the entire ecosystem began to rebalance itself in ways that would have been hard to predict or engineer directly.[7]

---

5 Paulo Freire, *Pedagogy of the Oppressed: 50th Anniversary Edition*, 4th ed., foreword by Donaldo Macedo (New York: Bloomsbury Academic, 2018), 71–86.

6 See, for example, Rafaela Graça Scheiffer, "Wolves, Systems Thinking and Trophic Cascades," *The Ecologist* (October 17, 2018).

7 William J. Ripple, Robert L. Beschta, Jennifer K. Fortin, and Charles T. Robbins, "Trophic Cascades from Wolves to Grizzly Bears in Yellowstone," *Journal of Animal Ecology* 83, no. 1 (2014): 223–33.

Writer, activist, and facilitator adrienne maree brown's concept of emergent strategy, drawn from her work on complexity and social justice, offers a dynamic and adaptive approach to systems thinking. brown defines emergent strategy as "a way of describing how complex systems and patterns arise out of a multiplicity of relatively simple interactions."[8] Her work outlines several core principles that can enrich our understanding of systems and their application to vocational discernment. Among these principles, three stand out as particularly relevant to our exploration of vocation and systems thinking.

The first is "small is good, small is all," which emphasizes that large-scale change emerges from small actions and interactions. brown posits that "the large is a reflection of the small," encouraging us to pay attention to micro-level dynamics that can ripple out to create macro-level shifts.[9] Rather than always seeking grand gestures or sweeping transformations, she encourages us to value and cultivate the small, everyday actions that align with our sense of calling. For instance, a teacher might find that a brief, encouraging conversation with a struggling student has ripple effects that transform not only that student's life but also the classroom dynamics and even the broader school community. By attending to these small-scale interactions and choices, we can more intentionally shape the larger systems we inhabit and embody our vocations in profound ways. The large is composed of an interlocking connection of small items whose connections to one another are not apparent at first.

The second principle, "move at the speed of trust," advises focusing on "critical connections more than critical mass" to build resilience through relationships.[10] This suggests that when it comes to creating meaningful change and pursuing our callings effectively, the quality and depth of our connections are more important than the quantity. For a community organizer, this might mean prioritizing deep, ongoing engagement with a core group of committed individuals rather than always striving for the largest possible audience. By moving at the speed of trust, we create resilient networks that can weather challenges and adapt to changing circumstances, providing a stable foundation for living out our vocations even in turbulent times.

A third principle, "never a failure, always a lesson," reframes setbacks as opportunities for growth and learning.[11] Embracing this requires a deep shift in how we perceive and respond to difficulties in our vocational journeys. Instead of becom-

---

8 adrienne maree brown, *Emergent Strategy: Shaping Change, Changing Worlds* (Chico, CA: AK Press, 2017), 3. See also the epigraph, which is from page 59.

9 Ibid., 41.

10 Ibid., 70.

11 Ibid., 41.

ing discouraged when a particular path doesn't unfold as expected, we're invited to approach these experiences with curiosity and openness. For example, a nonprofit leader might view a failed fundraising campaign not as a personal or organizational shortcoming, but as an opportunity to gain insights into donor preferences, refine communication strategies, or even reassess the organization's approach to resource mobilization. By cultivating this learning mind-set, we remain open to the evolving nature of our callings and the systems within which they unfold, allowing for greater flexibility and innovation.

In addition to providing practical guidance for navigating complex systems, these principles of emergent strategy also invite us to engage our imagination more fully in the process of vocational discernment. By embracing the idea that small actions can lead to large-scale change, we're encouraged to imagine new possibilities for how our seemingly minor choices might ripple out to create significant impact. The emphasis on moving at the speed of trust invites us to imagine more collaborative and relationally rich ways of pursuing our callings. By reframing setbacks as lessons, we're challenged to imagine alternative narratives for our vocational journeys, seeing potential for growth and transformation where we might previously have seen only failure.

Miller-McLemore discusses the complex and often painful realities when callings can fail or falter. She writes, "Fractured callings are delicate, morally ambiguous matters whose causes are multiple and whose consequences are ambiguous."[12] She emphasizes the inevitability of failure in life, stressing the importance of naming these moments with humility and grace rather than judgment. She focuses on the inevitability of human limitations and the necessity of compassionate self-understanding in vocational discernment. Her work highlights the importance of humility and grace in naming these moments, and I want to affirm that. I also want to make sure that, when appropriate, we have the courage to see and name that sometimes, a pattern of consistent fracture may be exposing systemic injustices. Fractured callings are not only personal struggles. They are also opportunities to challenge the societal and institutional forces that constrain vocation and flourishing.

Fractured callings are not just about burnout or confusion. They reflect a breakdown in moral coherence. When systemic injustices strain the beliefs, relationships, or behaviors that once felt vocationally aligned, disorientation may be the most honest response. In such moments, the work of vocation is not just to endure, but to discern anew what integrity now requires.

The capacity for narrative to reframe and transform our perceptions and plans will be discussed in more detail with the eighth chapter's focus on storytelling, but, for

---

12 Miller-McLemore, *Follow Your Bliss*, 90.

now, it is enough to acknowledge that a systems-aware approach allows us to envision our vocations not as isolated pursuits, but as integral parts of larger, interconnected wholes. It encourages us to imagine how our individual callings might contribute to the flourishing of our communities, social ecosystems, and society at large. By expanding our imaginative capacity in this way, we open ourselves to more creative and interconnected approaches to vocational discernment and action. This kind of openness can also help to reveal some of the ways that more narrow perspectives can obscure problematic dynamics.

When we speak of sinful systems or structures of oppression, our analysis must be intersectional and encompassing. While race, gender, and culture are undeniable and critical lenses through which we understand how power marginalizes and harms, we must also critically examine the devastating role of class and economic exploitation. Systems that concentrate wealth and power in the hands of a few create widespread precarity and suffering across diverse communities. Indeed, part of the insidious genius of these systems is their ability to pit marginalized groups against each other, obscuring the shared interest in dismantling the larger structures that exploit an overwhelming majority for the benefit of a tiny elite. A truly liberative approach helps us see how different forms of oppression are often interconnected and mutually reinforcing, even while acknowledging that individuals may experience varying degrees of privilege and penalty within those systems.

The call to engage with "sinful systems and structures of oppression," as we've just discussed, can feel overwhelming. These vast networks of power are formidable. Yet if our vocations are to be part of the future we long for, we need ways to understand how these systems actually function, not just in the abstract, but in the very fabric of our lives, our families, and our communities. This is where particular theories of systems can become vital conversation partners.

I have consistently found Bowen Family Systems Theory to be a valuable framework. Developed by psychiatrist Murray Bowen, this theory offers a compelling lens on the emotional currents and relational patterns that flow through families and, by extension, other human groups. While no single theory can capture the whole of systemic reality, especially the macro-level injustices we've named, Bowen's insights provide useful tools for discerning how we are personally entangled in and shaped by systemic dynamics and where we might find leverage for healthier, more liberated ways of being and acting. It helps me see that the "system" isn't just "out there," but also "in here," in my own habits and ways of seeing. Let's turn to some of Bowen's core ideas and consider how they might illuminate our vocational journeys within these intricate human systems.

Systems Thinking

> **A Practice to Consider:**
> # Systems Mapping Me
>
> *Our lives are part of intricate systems where relationships, roles, and resources intersect. Mapping these connections reveals patterns that shape our calling and highlight areas needing attention or care.*
>
> 1. Create a map to visualize the networks influencing your calling. Start with a central circle labeled "Me."
> 2. Map Key Systems: Draw surrounding circles for important systems in your life, like family, work, community, finances, etc.
> 3. Connect Influences: Draw lines between systems where you notice interconnections. For example, family might intersect with finances, or work might intersect with community. Use solid lines for strong connections and dotted lines for weaker ones.
> 4. Get Details: Inside each circle, list people or factors affecting you. Use different colors for support (green), challenges (red), and resources (blue).
> 5. Notice: What patterns or insights emerge as you look at your map? Are there areas with more green (support) or red (challenges)? Which systems or connections seem most influential in your current sense of calling? Which ones might need more attention or care?
>
> Full guidelines are in the appendix.

Bowen Family Systems Theory

Bowen Family Systems Theory (BFST), developed by psychiatrist Murray Bowen in the mid-twentieth century to understand the hidden emotional currents within families, revolutionized understanding of human behavior by proposing that some psychological issues stem from larger family systems rather than residing solely within individuals.[13] This approach, which views families as emotional units, has since influenced fields beyond psychology, including organizational management and spiritual care. The first time someone explained Bowen Theory to me, I felt like a light had turned on. Suddenly, my reactions during family holidays made a lot more sense.

While systems thinking offers a broad and often abstract framework for understanding complex interactions, Bowen's theory zooms in with a kind of compassionate precision. It offers specific insights that are surprisingly resonant in

---

[13] One of the most significant texts about Bowen's theory is Michael E. Kerr and Murray Bowen, *Family Evaluation: An Approach Based on Bowen Theory* (New York: W. W. Norton, 1988).

organizational life and faith communities, places where people often bring the full weight of their family dynamics, whether they realize it or not. We'll focus here on three core concepts from BFST: System Equilibrium, System Boundaries, and Triangles. Each of these illuminates common patterns in the groups we lead and love. My hope is that these are patterns that, once seen, can't be unseen. And more importantly, once named, they can begin to shift. These aren't just theories for therapists; they're tools for people who care about how groups live, grow, and stay stuck.

Organizations, like families, develop their own cultures, norms, and patterns of interaction over time. They face similar challenges in managing anxiety, adapting to change, and maintaining stability. The principles that govern family dynamics can often be observed in organizational settings as well. The three we'll look at in detail are the tendency toward equilibrium, the formation of triangles, and the transmission of anxiety. This makes BFST a valuable tool for understanding and addressing dynamics in a wide range of social systems.

For instance, a church congregation, much like a family, has its own history, traditions, and ways of managing conflict. A nonprofit organization, similar to a family unit, must balance individual needs with collective goals. Community groups, like extended families, often grapple with issues of belonging, boundary-setting, and shared responsibility. By applying BFST concepts to these contexts, leaders can gain deeper insights into group dynamics and more effectively guide their organizations through challenges and changes. With this understanding, let's explore how system equilibrium, a key concept in BFST, manifests in organizations.

System Equilibrium

System equilibrium, in the context of organizational dynamics, refers to the tendency of a system to maintain a state of dynamic balance or stability, even in the face of internal or external pressures for change. This concept, borrowed from biology and physics, suggests that organizations, like living organisms, naturally resist disruptions to their established patterns and seek to return to a familiar state of functioning. System equilibrium describes how organizations strive to maintain this stability and dynamic balance in the face of what seem like good reasons to change. This homeostatic tendency influences organizational dynamics and behaviors in several important ways.

Organizations naturally resist disruptions to their established patterns of interaction, often reacting to pull the system back to its familiar state when change is attempted. This resistance can make lasting change difficult without addressing the whole system. Organizations also develop habitual ways of managing anxiety and emotional tension, aiming to keep anxiety at tolerable levels, even if the methods are ultimately dysfunctional.[14] Think of it like a thermostat in a house: When things get too hot or too cold, the system kicks in to bring the temperature back to its familiar setting. Organizations often have similar "thermostats" for managing anxiety or change, even if returning to the familiar setting isn't always healthy in the long run. For instance, an organization may scapegoat one department to deflect tension away from leadership issues.

Imagine a mid-sized nonprofit organization dedicated to youth education. The organization has been experiencing financial difficulties and declining program enrollment for the past year. The leadership team, consisting of the executive director and department heads, is under pressure from the board to improve results. Unfortunately, instead of addressing systemic issues like outdated programming or ineffective outreach strategies, the leadership team begins to focus criticism on the marketing department. They claim that poor marketing is the root cause of their enrollment and funding challenges. In team meetings, the marketing director and their staff are repeatedly singled out for criticism. Other departments start to distance themselves from marketing, refusing to collaborate on projects.

As I see it, this scapegoating serves at least four functions, none of them beneficial in the long run, but all useful in the moment to halt potentially useful change. First, it provides an overly simple explanation for complex problems. Second, it deflects attention from leadership's role in the organization's struggles. Third, it creates a false sense of unity among other departments. Last, it temporarily reduces anxiety by giving everyone a common "enemy" to focus on. While this might "help" in the short run, this approach is ultimately dysfunctional. It fails to address the real, systemic issues facing the organization, damages morale, hinders interdepartmental cooperation, and may lead to the loss of talented marketing staff. The scapegoating allows the organization to maintain its familiar patterns without making necessary changes, even though this stability comes at a significant cost to its long-term health and effectiveness.

This pattern of scapegoating illustrates how organizations often manage anxiety in ways that maintain the status quo, even at the expense of long-term health and growth. Such dynamics are part of a broader tendency in systems to seek equilibrium, even if that equilibrium is unhealthy. The level of functioning of individual members within a system tends to rise and fall reciprocally to maintain overall system stability, with regression in one area often balancing out progress in another. When anxiety in the system becomes too high, "symptoms" often develop in the most vulnerable parts of the organization as a way of absorbing and binding that anxiety, temporarily restoring

---

14 Stephen M. Gavazzi and Ji-Young Lim, "Family Systems Theory," in *Encyclopedia of Adolescence*, ed. Roger J. Levesque (Cham, Switzerland: Springer, 2023), https://doi.org/10.1007/978-3-319-32132-5_455-3.

equilibrium without resolving underlying issues. In long-standing organizations, the drive for equilibrium can perpetuate dysfunctional patterns across different "generations" of leadership, as members unconsciously take on familiar roles and relationship positions.

Crucially, the anxieties that ripple through a system are often not neutral. They are frequently ignited and amplified by societal power dynamics. When a system is confronted with challenges to its established norms around race, gender, sexuality, class, or ability, anxiety predictably rises. For example, a person of color rising to leadership in a predominantly white institution may trigger anxiety in those unaccustomed to sharing or ceding power. A woman challenging patriarchal theological interpretations may become the lightning rod for a system's fear of change.

The anxious responses in such cases often manifest as attempts to silence, discredit, or push out the individual or group perceived as the source of anxiety, rather than the system examining its own complicity in injustice. This is a form of systemic sabotage, often happening beneath the level of conscious thought, but nevertheless rooted in the preservation of existing privilege. Such instances of systemic sabotage, fueled by anxiety around power and privilege, highlight why a mere focus on individual actions falls short. Instead, understanding the drive toward system equilibrium offers leaders a more effective lens.

Understanding system equilibrium helps leaders recognize how problematic patterns are maintained and why change can be so challenging in their organizations. Effective interventions often focus on gradually shifting the system's equilibrium to a healthier state rather than targeting individual "problem" behaviors or departments in isolation. For congregational leaders applying BFST concepts, recognizing the pull toward equilibrium can provide insight into resistance to spiritual growth or organizational change within church communities. Consider a congregation where a long-standing, but toxic, power dynamic exists.

When a new leader attempts to shift this dynamic, they might encounter strong resistance. This resistance isn't necessarily because people prefer the unhealthy situation, but because the system is striving to maintain its familiar equilibrium. For leaders seeking to manage a community's resistance to change and foster healthier equilibrium, I recommend five interrelated strategies to students. I think these ideas are all good ideas in general, but they are particularly useful when a system is stuck in the rut of an unhealthy equilibrium that needs to be disrupted.

First, I encourage people to introduce changes gradually rather than all at once. This incremental method allows the system to adjust slowly, reducing the shock of destabilization. By breaking down large changes into smaller, more manageable steps, leaders can help their organizations adapt more smoothly. Destabilization still occurs, but it doesn't cause as much whiplash.[15] Approaching things gradually might involve piloting new initiatives in specific departments before rolling them out organization-wide or phasing in new processes over an extended period. Such an approach not only minimizes disruption, it also allows for learning and adjustment along the way. Furthermore, it permits more time in which people can voice concerns and hopes. This leads me to the next strategy: clear communication.

Leaders should articulate the reasons for change and the vision for the future with transparency and consistency. This involves not just explaining what changes are happening, but *why* they are happening and how they align with the organization's mission, vision, and values. By helping people imagine a positive future state, leaders can inspire hope and motivation rather than fear and resistance. This might involve storytelling, visual aids, or collaborative visioning exercises to make the abstract concrete and relatable. Regular updates and open forums for discussion can also help maintain clarity and trust throughout the change process. This interactivity is life-giving and is at the heart of my next suggestion.

Involving stakeholders in the change process is vital for creating buy-in and distributing the responsibility for change throughout the system. This goes beyond simply informing people about changes; it means actively engaging them in the planning and implementation process. Leaders might form cross-functional teams to spearhead initiatives, seek input from various levels of the organization, or create feedback mechanisms to ensure that diverse perspectives are heard and incorporated. By giving people a sense of ownership and agency in the change process, leaders can transform potential resisters into champions of change.

Especially in congregational settings where there is a history of clergy having enormous unilateral institutional authority, a willingness to accept feedback can be met with suspicion. It is therefore of the utmost importance that if you say you want to hear people, that you make good on that offer and show concretely the ways in which their input mattered to the final decision. With gradual change, clear communication, and stakeholder involvement, it becomes extremely important for leaders to continually monitor and adjust their approach as change unfolds. So much so, in fact, that I think it is its own strategy.

A plan for ongoing processes of evaluation and adaptation is integral to ensuring the effectiveness of the previously implemented strategies. Paying close attention to how the system responds to changes allows leaders to identify unintended consequences or areas where the approach isn't working as expected. Thinking back to the Yellowstone

---

15 This connects to Moore's concept of "tradition-ing" as discussed in the third chapter, "Formation and Reflection."

example, what are the "beavers" and "willow trees" of your system? This might involve regular check-ins with team members, surveys to gauge organizational climate, or analysis of key performance indicators. By maintaining this vigilant stance, leaders can quickly identify when the pace of change needs adjusting, when communication needs clarifying, or when stakeholder involvement needs to be broadened or deepened. Leaders should be prepared to adjust their strategies if they notice negative impacts or if the organization isn't progressing as hoped.

The flexibility and willingness to course-correct both demonstrates a commitment to the organization's well-being and reinforces the trust built through transparent communication and stakeholder engagement. One of the neat things about planning internal assessments in an organization in which there is clear communication, willingness to listen to feedback, and a commitment to gradual change is that the whole community can be part of noticing change and self-evaluating themselves! This collective awareness and participation in the change process can be particularly valuable when addressing sensitive issues or in seasons when it is time to confront long-standing issues of inequity or oppression.

In a closely related point, I think it is vital to do ongoing work to develop and maintain a trauma-informed culture in the organization even while managing organizational change.[16] I'll talk more about trauma-informed culture in the fifth chapter, "Joy and Lament," but, here, I'll note that, even with gradual changes, clear communications, stakeholder involvement, and ongoing adjustments, the disequilibrium often needed to begin a culture shift may still be profoundly unsettling, potentially triggering past traumas or creating new ones for some individuals. Implementing trauma-informed practices that prioritize emotional safety and provide appropriate support during transitions should be woven into each step of the change process.

This might involve offering counseling services alongside stakeholder engagement initiatives, creating spaces for "courageous risk-taking" during communication sessions,[17] or providing training on stress management and resilience as part of the gradual change rollout. By acknowledging and addressing the emotional impact of change at every stage, leaders can create a more supportive environment that helps individuals navigate transitions more effectively. This trauma-sensitive approach supports the well-being of individuals while also enhancing the organization's capacity to adapt and thrive through change, making it a critical capstone to the entire change management process.

---

16 You can find one of the tools I use to help organizations think about the extent to which they are trauma-informed in the appendix.

17 L. Callid Keefe-Perry and Zachary Moon, "Courage in Chaos: The Importance of Trauma-Informed Adult Religious Education," *Religious Education* 114, no. 1 (2019): 30–41.

Remember, under stress, a system often reverts to habitual patterns of functioning, even if those methods are not healthy. As leaders, our role is to guide the system toward a new, healthier equilibrium while managing the inevitable anxiety that comes with change. This process requires us to imagine new possibilities for our organizations and to help others envision these possibilities as well. Part of doing this means being good about setting healthy boundaries for ourselves and our community.

System Boundaries

System boundaries in organizational contexts refer to the invisible demarcations that define the organization's structure, regulate the flow of information and resources, and manage relationships both within the organization and with external entities.[18] These boundaries play a role in maintaining organizational health, efficiency, and identity. They aren't all life-giving *or* life-limiting, but can stretch in either direction.

Consider an organization with "hidden rules" about decorum, where what it means to be "part of the group" is based on dominant and unexamined patterns of dress, communication, and cultural reference. For example, in a faith community where leadership discussions favor quick, assertive speaking styles common in the dominant culture, individuals whose cultural backgrounds emphasize more reflective, slower-paced, or indirect communication might find their contributions consistently overlooked or interrupted. They may learn that their way of engaging isn't seen as "leadership material," not because their ideas lack value, but because their communication style doesn't match the unspoken norm. This implicit boundary around communication becomes exclusionary, silencing valuable perspectives and reinforcing a narrow cultural standard. Such boundaries, though often subtle, can stifle diversity and impose conformity, making individuals feel that their contributions are not welcome unless they adapt to the dominant style.

Boundaries are not inherently bad, however. For instance, a Native American tribal organization might have specific protocols for decision-making that involve elder consultation and consensus-building. These boundaries, rooted in long-standing cultural practices, are not exclusionary but rather serve to maintain the tribe's cultural integrity and ensure that decisions are made in a manner consistent with their values and traditions. The key difference is that the first type of boundary enforces conformity and suppresses diversity, while the second type upholds cultural identity and fosters a sense of belonging within a shared value system.

---

[18] Susan C. Schneider, "Managing Boundaries in Organizations," *Political Psychology* 8, no. 3 (1987): 379–93, https://doi.org/10.2307/3791041.

Within BFST, boundaries in organizational systems can be conceptualized as clear, diffuse, or rigid. In organizations with clear boundaries, there's a healthy balance between collaboration and individual autonomy. Information flows effectively, roles and norms are well-defined, and there's a strong sense of organizational identity without stifling innovation or external input. These organizations tend to be adaptable yet stable, maintaining their core mission while responding to changing environments. Clear boundaries foster a sense of security among members, enabling them to take calculated risks and innovate within a supportive framework.

Diffuse boundaries occur when there's little independence between different parts of the organization and/or external sources of influence. In systems with diffuse boundaries, there may be a lack of clear roles, inappropriate oversharing (or over-requesting) of information, and difficulty in making independent decisions. There may be little sense of a clear organizational culture, with shifts primarily happening as a result of outside factors rather than commitments or decisions internal to the organization. This can lead to a loss of organizational focus and identity. Members in such systems often feel overwhelmed and uncertain, struggling to prioritize tasks or make decisions without constant input from others. The organization may appear chaotic, with frequent changes in direction and a lack of consistent policies or procedures.

Rigid boundaries create isolation or disengagement between different parts of the organization. In systems with rigid boundaries, communication is limited, departments or individuals may work in silos, and there's resistance to external ideas or collaboration. This can lead to inefficiency, lack of innovation, and difficulty adapting to change. Organizations with rigid boundaries might appear stable on the surface, but they often struggle with internal power struggles, resource hoarding, and an inability to respond effectively to social changes or the shifting needs of community members. People in these systems may feel constrained, with little opportunity for growth or creative expression.

The permeability of boundaries can vary across different organizational subsystems and change over time. For example, boundaries may need to adjust as an organization grows, begins new ministries, or faces crisis situations. Healthy boundaries serve several important functions in organizational systems. They clarify the organization's mission, values, and unique characteristics. They allow different departments or individuals to develop specialized skills while remaining connected to the larger organizational purpose. In vocational terms, healthy boundaries allow us to remain attentive to our sense of calling while still engaging meaningfully with our communities and contexts. They help us navigate the tension between individual purpose, collective needs, and the capacities of the spiritual gifts that we steward.

Leaders can help their organizations recognize and adjust dysfunctional boundary patterns, encouraging a balance between connectedness and appropriate differentiation. Boundary issues often arise during times of organizational stress, growth, or transition. Common boundary problems in organizations include role confusion, when job responsibilities are unclear or overlapping; triangulation, when conflicts between two parties consistently involve a third party, weakening existing boundaries; overinvolvement, when leaders or departments become too enmeshed in others' responsibilities; and disengagement, when rigid boundaries lead to departmental isolation and lack of collaboration.[19] Addressing boundary issues in organizations often involves helping members recognize unhealthy patterns, improve communication, and establish clearer, more functional boundaries. This process can be challenging, as it may disrupt the organization's established equilibrium. Recognizing this challenge, I have several strategies I usually recommend when I teach this in organizations and for my students.

I often suggest that leaders seeking to foster healthy boundaries in their organizations can begin with a comprehensive boundary audit.[20] One of the ways I talk about this is to say "maps are more useful when you know where you are." Beginning with an audit of internal assessment helps to let you know where you are. By starting with this overarching assessment, leaders can gain a clearer picture of where their organization stands and what specific areas need attention. This process involves systematically examining how information flows, decisions are made, and relationships are managed both within the organization and with external entities. A boundary audit might include surveys of staff and stakeholders, analysis of communication patterns, and review of organizational policies.

For example, leaders might track how often departments collaborate, examine the clarity of reporting structures, or assess the frequency and nature of interactions with external partners. A church community might reflect on the larger culture of its denomination or regional authority, considering the ways in which that body might have influence on them. This approach aligns closely with the strategy of gradual change discussed earlier, as it provides a foundation for incremental improvements based on a thorough understanding of the current system.

Building on the insights gained from the boundary audit, the next step is to clarify roles and responsibilities within the organization. When I teach this, I usually

---

19 Leslie Ann Fox, Jean Clark, Rita Bowen, and Susan Postal, "Using Systems-based Leadership to Advance the Future State of Health Integrated Management," *AHIMA's National Convention and Exhibit Proceedings*, October 2007.

20 In appendix.

frame it in the context of the Confucian concept of the "rectification of names" 正名 (*zhèngmíng*), which emphasizes the importance of ensuring that things in material reality correspond to what they are called. In *The Analects*, Confucius is asked what the first thing a good leader should do, and he responds, "the rectification of names." He goes on:

> If names be not correct, language is not in accordance with the truth of things. If language be not in accordance with the truth of things, affairs cannot be carried on to success. When names are not correct, what is said will not sound reasonable; when what is said does not sound reasonable, affairs will not culminate in success.[21]

In organizational terms, this means ensuring that everyone understands their role and the boundaries of their authority and that these roles accurately reflect the actual responsibilities and functions within the organization. This clarity not only improves efficiency but also contributes to a sense of security and purpose among community members.

An illustrative example of what can happen when names are not "rectified" in a nonprofit context might involve a social justice organization that prides itself on being "inclusive" and "community-driven." Let's imagine this organization has a staff member, Alex, with the title "Community Outreach Coordinator." The organization's mission statement emphasizes amplifying marginalized voices and promoting grassroots activism. However, when Alex begins to raise concerns about the organization's own lack of diversity in leadership positions, they are labeled as "unruly" and "disruptive." Leadership claims that Alex is causing "organizational damage" by voicing these concerns, particularly to community members and on social media platforms. The organization's board decides to silence Alex, removing them from key meetings and community events. Eventually, they are asked to step down from their role, with the official reason being "failure to align with organizational values."

The repercussions of this misalignment are far-reaching. Other staff members, seeing how Alex was treated, become hesitant to voice concerns or challenge the status quo. Community members who were engaged by Alex feel betrayed and lose trust in the organization. Donors and partners who believe in the organization's inclusive mission may question their support when they learn of these internal dynamics. Organizational events begin to be skipped by key community members. By silencing Alex, the organization loses a valuable opportunity for self-reflection and growth.

---

21 Confucius, *The Analects of Confucius*, trans. Arthur Waley (New York: Vintage Books, 1989), 13.3.

The very issues Alex raised may continue unaddressed, potentially widening the gap between the organization's stated mission and its actual impact. This example underscores the importance of "rectifying names" not just in terms of individual roles, but in an organization's overall identity and practices. When an organization claims to be inclusive and community-driven, it must be prepared to engage with challenging feedback and diverse perspectives, even when they are uncomfortable or disruptive to the status quo.

By ensuring that an organization's stated values and identity align with its actual practices, we can build genuine trust with our communities and create space for meaningful growth and change. "Rectification of names" is not just about job titles, but about the deep alignment between what a group of people *say* they are committed to and how they actually operate. For example, if an organization claims to welcome nonbinary individuals but fails to undertake the necessary cultural work to prevent misgendering, the depth of their "welcome" deserves some scrutiny. This misalignment not only undermines trust but also signals a lack of genuine commitment, potentially alienating those the organization seeks to include and serve.

It's important to revisit and refine these role definitions regularly, especially as the organization evolves or faces new challenges. This step directly supports the clear communication strategy outlined earlier, as it provides a framework for transparent and consistent messaging about organizational structure and individual responsibilities. Just as Confucius believed that social order begins with the correct use of names, organizational health can be significantly enhanced when roles and titles accurately reflect the realities of the work being done.

With roles and responsibilities clarified, leaders can then focus on implementing transparent decision-making processes. This step involves clearly articulating how decisions are made and who is involved in various types of decisions. Transparency in decision-making helps maintain appropriate boundaries while fostering a sense of inclusion and engagement among team members. It can prevent feelings of exclusion or resentment that might arise when decision-making processes are opaque or seemingly arbitrary. This transparency also supports the overall goal of maintaining clear and healthy boundaries by ensuring that everyone understands their place in the decision-making hierarchy. This approach directly builds on the stakeholder involvement strategy, creating clear pathways for participation and input in organizational processes.

As the internal structure becomes more defined, it's important to turn attention to the organization's external boundaries. Encouraging healthy external engagement creates opportunities for the organization to interact with outside ideas and influences in a structured way. This might involve bringing in guest speakers, attending conferences, or partnering with other organizations. These experiences can spark imagination and innovation, preventing the organization from becoming too insular. However, it's important to manage these external engagements thoughtfully to ensure they enrich rather than dilute the organization's identity and focus, leading to "mission drift." This strategy connects with the earlier emphasis on gradual change and stakeholder involvement, as it provides a structured way to introduce new ideas and perspectives into the organization.

Finally, leaders should commit to regular review and adjustment of boundary practices. As organizations grow and evolve, and as their contexts change, boundaries that were once appropriate may need to be reconsidered. Periodic reviews allow leaders to assess the effectiveness of current boundaries and make necessary adjustments. This ongoing process should encourage creative thinking about how boundaries might evolve to better serve the organization's mission. By maintaining this flexible and adaptive approach, leaders can ensure that their organization's boundaries remain healthy and supportive of its goals over time. This strategy directly mirrors the earlier emphasis on monitoring and adjusting, creating a continuous feedback loop for organizational improvement and adaptation.

Maintaining clear and appropriate boundaries is an important part of organizational health and effectiveness. However, even in systems with well-defined boundaries, complex relational dynamics emerge that challenge these structures. One such dynamic is triangulation, a concept that intersects with and often complicates boundary management. As we turn our attention to this concept, we'll see how it can both reinforce and undermine organizational boundaries, influencing communication patterns, decision-making processes, and overall system health.

Emotional Triangles

Triangulation, a key concept in BFST, is equally applicable and significant in organizational contexts. This process occurs when the relationship between two parties becomes unstable, and one or both parties involve a third party to reduce tension.[22] Essentially, instead of two people dealing directly with their tension, they pull in a third person (or sometimes even an issue or object) to stabilize the relationship, shifting the focus and lowering the immediate anxiety between the original pair. If you've ever been caught in the middle of two coworkers' unspoken tension or watched a child become the peacekeeper between fighting parents, you've seen a triangle in action. These are the quiet traps we get stuck in when we're trying to stay safe or keep things calm, even when they're not working. These patterns, while sometimes helping win an argument in the moment, often create more complex problems in the long run.

---

22 Kerr and Bowen, *Family Evaluation*, 151–83.

In organizations, triangulation can complicate communication and conflict resolution. For example, a program manager might complain to the executive director about a colleague rather than addressing the issue directly. This creates a triangle that may temporarily reduce tension between the program manager and their colleague, but it ultimately fails to resolve the underlying issue and can create new problems within the organizational system. This is especially true because the points of a triangle in a system are not limited to interpersonal dynamics. Triangles can manifest in various forms, involving elements such as policies, resources, or even abstract concepts.

For instance, a triangle might form between a leader, a staff member, and a contentious policy that is repeatedly brought up, or between two departments competing for a limited resource. Systems often manage anxiety through triangulation in ways that can be detrimental to overall health. This might involve "fusion," where individual autonomy is sacrificed in an attempt to achieve harmony, or "cut-off," where distance is created from the source of anxiety.[23] Alternatively, systems might respond by strengthening subgroups or factions, creating internal divisions.

Triangulation often follows the grooves of systemic power. In anxiety-ridden organizational systems, BIPOC leaders are disproportionately likely to be scapegoated or silenced when addressing systemic issues. When BIPOC professionals raise concerns about structural inequities, organizational leadership often responds by remaining silent, suggesting that the individual is overly sensitive, or worse, gaslighting them by framing the person who speaks out as the problem.[24] Systemic anxiety is managed by redirecting tension onto marginalized individuals, leading many BIPOC leaders to exit institutions while feeling their full capabilities were never recognized or valued. Gendered expectations also play out here: Women or femme-presenting folks may be positioned as emotional shock absorbers, while others are excused from accountability. These responses, while temporarily reducing tension, often lead to more complex issues within the organizational system, highlighting the importance of recognizing and addressing triangulation patterns in a constructive manner. I've been part of these problems myself.

Early in my career, I was a middle school teacher. I remember that time as an ongoing example of triangulation that later helped me understand how these dynamics play out in institutional settings. As a relatively new teacher, I found myself drawn into a triangle between experienced faculty members and the administration. A group of veteran teachers had growing concerns about how the school was being run and so

---

23 Ibid., 300–305.

24 Altha J. Stewart, "Dismantling Structural Racism in Academic Psychiatry to Achieve Workforce Diversity," *American Journal of Psychiatry* 178, no. 3 (2021): 207–22, https://doi.org/10.1176/appi.ajp.2020.21010025.

did I. However, rather than addressing this directly with the administration, we would frequently complain to each other and other new teachers about how leadership "just doesn't get what it's like in the classroom." We'd share stories of the current principal's missteps, recall how excellent the former principal was, and express frustration about current policies that seemed disconnected from classroom realities.

Being new and wanting to be collegial, I initially participated in these conversations, effectively becoming part of a triangle where teacher frustrations were voiced to other teachers rather than addressed with administration. It took me a while to recognize that by engaging in these conversations, I was helping to maintain a pattern that prevented direct dialogue about real concerns. The breakthrough came when I realized that these hallway conversations, while providing temporary emotional relief through shared complaints, weren't actually improving our school culture or addressing student needs. I didn't know about "triangles" at the time, but, looking back at it now, I realize that, once I began encouraging direct communication and focusing conversations on specific situations rather than general complaints about administration, I saw how triangulation had been preventing meaningful change. It is easy to fall into triangulation patterns, which means it is important to recognize and address them directly.

Understanding these patterns helps leaders nurture healthier organizational dynamics, tending to both immediate needs and long-term flourishing. Recognizing triangulation patterns is the first step in addressing them. Leaders should be aware of signs such as frequent complaints about third parties, staff members consistently relaying messages through intermediaries, or the formation of alliances against individuals or departments. As with how I teach the concept of boundaries building off of system equilibrium, I recommend the following set of interconnected strategies that also build upon my understanding of system equilibrium and boundaries.

First and foremost, leaders must cultivate mindfulness about triangulation. This awareness aligns closely with the boundary audit process discussed earlier. Just as leaders examine how information flows and decisions are made in a boundary audit, they should also be attentive to how triangles form in organizational relationships. This involves recognizing signs of triangulation, such as when staff members consistently complain about others to them or when they find themselves being drawn into conflicts that don't directly involve them. This awareness supports healthy boundaries and contributes to the overall equilibrium of the system by identifying potential sources of instability.

Building on this awareness, leaders should work to identify different types of conflict within their organization. This step echoes the process of clarifying roles and responsibilities in boundary management. By understanding the nature of conflicts, leaders can better navigate the underlying issues and avoid being inadvertently drawn into triangles. This nuanced understanding allows leaders to address root causes rather than symptoms, promoting more effective and lasting resolutions. It also supports the "rectification of names" concept discussed in the boundaries section, ensuring that the nature of conflicts is accurately identified and addressed.

Once aware of triangulation and the types of conflict present, leaders should focus on their own role in potential triangles. This involves a commitment to working on one's own side of the triangle, the only side over which one has direct control. By focusing on their own behavior and gradually shifting their responses to potential triangles, leaders can model new patterns of interaction without abruptly destabilizing the entire system. Leaders should strive to maintain emotional contact with others while remaining autonomous in their own emotional functioning. This balance allows leaders to be empathetic and engaged without becoming enmeshed in others' conflicts. Differentiated leadership involves maintaining a non-anxious presence in the face of organizational tension, which can help calm the entire system and maintain a healthy equilibrium. Relatedly, it is a good idea for people who are in the helping professions to be in therapy and/or spiritual direction. The fact that it also helps with the organization is a bonus.

To support this direct communication, leaders should implement and model clear conflict resolution processes. This strategy directly supports the transparent decision-making processes discussed in the boundaries section. By providing structured alternatives to triangulation, leaders create a culture where direct, responsible communication is the norm rather than the exception. This clarity in communication and conflict resolution helps maintain clear organizational boundaries while also contributing to a healthier system equilibrium.

Finally, leaders can commit to ongoing education about triangulation and systems thinking for their entire team. This echoes the emphasis on regular review and adjustment of practices discussed in both the equilibrium and boundaries sections. When all members of an organization understand these dynamics, they're better equipped to recognize and avoid unhealthy patterns. This education supports the maintenance of healthy boundaries and contributes to a more stable and adaptive system equilibrium.

By implementing these strategies in a sequential and interconnected manner, leaders can create an organizational culture that minimizes unhealthy triangulation, maintains clear and appropriate boundaries, and fosters a healthy system equilibrium. This comprehensive approach can both resolve immediate conflicts more effectively and contribute to the long-term health and resilience of the entire organizational system.

Thus, engaging with Bowen's insights equips individuals not merely to understand systems, but to participate more freely and justly within them, opening up more liberative pathways for vocational expression for themselves and others. Does that mean a well-led system won't have disequilibrium? Not at all. In fact, an organization on its way to greater health and flourishing will often have *more* disequilibrium as part of its intentional commitment to change. The difference in this kind of disequilibrium, though, is that it will be planned, communicated about, assessed, and communally processed.

To conclude this section, I think it is useful to name the interconnected nature of the principles we've discussed. It might have felt like the equilibrium, boundaries, and triangulation strategies were folding in on themselves and interweaving. They were. This interconnectedness itself reflects one last insight from adrienne maree brown's work on emergent strategy that I think is worth naming: the concept of fractals, or "the relationship between small and large." brown observes: "How we are at the small scale is how we are at the large scale. The patterns of the universe repeat at scale."[25] This principle beautifully encapsulates systems thinking. The patterns we see in maintaining equilibrium, setting boundaries, and managing triangulation at the individual level are often mirrored in the larger organizational context.

The way a leader manages their own anxiety and maintains healthy personal boundaries can reverberate throughout the entire organization, influencing its overall culture and effectiveness. This fractal nature of systems suggests at least two insights for organizational leaders. First, there are deep patterns and structures that underlie human interactions at all levels. Second, and perhaps more importantly, the practices we cultivate at a small scale can have profound impacts at larger scales. When we work on our own differentiation, for example, we're not just improving our individual functioning; we're potentially shifting the dynamics of our entire organization.

Given the above, it's important to recognize that these principles of systems thinking are not just relevant for established organizational leaders but are equally valuable for students and individuals in the process of vocational discernment. In fact, I say that "leaders-in-training" are almost always already leaders. Whether they're leading a study group, organizing a community service project, or simply navigating relationships within their cohort, school, or church, they're already engaging with systems and practicing leadership.

Given the fractal nature of systems, these "small" decisions about how to act and lead can have significant impacts. How they manage boundaries in their personal relationships, how they navigate triangles in their friend group, or how they contribute to the emotional climate of their classroom—all of these seemingly minor actions are shaping their leadership style and influencing the systems around them. By consciously applying systems thinking to these everyday situations, they're not only preparing

---

25 brown, *Emergent Strategy*, 31.

for future leadership roles but actively shaping the systems they're currently part of. This perspective empowers students to see their current experiences as valuable laboratories for developing systemic awareness and leadership skills that will serve them well in their future service.

This perspective on leadership development and systems thinking naturally leads us to consider broader theological implications. As we transition to exploring biblical and theological perspectives on systems, the fractal principle we've discussed provides a valuable bridge. Many theological traditions recognize the interconnectedness of all creation and the ways in which divine patterns are reflected at various scales of existence. From the microcosm to the macrocosm, from the individual to the community, from the local church to the global Body of Christ, we find recurring themes and structures that speak to the fundamental nature of our relationships with each other and with the divine.

This metaphor invites us to consider our individual vocations as part of a larger, interconnected body. Our calling isn't just about personal fulfillment, but about how we contribute to the overall health and function of the community of faith. As we move forward, let's keep in mind the fractal nature of systems and the profound implications it holds for our leadership and our spiritual lives. Just as our small-scale actions can reverberate at larger scales in our organizations, so, too, can our understanding of divine patterns inform and transform our approach to leadership and community building. This holistic view of vocation and leadership aligns closely with many theological understandings of our role in God's creation, which we will explore next.

Systems in Scripture and Theology

Although the term "systems thinking" is modern, the concept of interconnectedness and holistic understanding is deeply rooted in scripture. The Bible offers several powerful metaphors and teachings that reflect a systemic worldview. One of the places I see this idea in scripture is in the "triangular covenant" between God, Israel, and the land. This relationship is evident in multiple passages throughout the Hebrew scriptures. In Genesis 12:7 and 15:18–21, God establishes a covenant with Abraham that explicitly includes the land as a component. Later, in Deuteronomy 11:29–32 and 28:1–2, Moses reiterates the importance of the land in the covenant and the conditions tied to Israel's possession and prosperity in it. This triangular relationship illustrates a dynamic system where human actions affect not just their relationship with God, but also the ecological realities of the land.

This ecological awareness is further exemplified in prophetic writings like Hosea, which draws explicit connections between human behavior and the health of the creation and all its creatures: "I will make for you a covenant . . . with the wild animals, the birds of the air, and the creeping things of the ground" (Hosea 2:18). Such passages suggest that God's calls have implications beyond human society, extending to our relationship with all of creation. They invite us to consider how our vocational choices might affect not just our immediate communities, but the broader ecosystems we inhabit, and how these choices reflect our relationship with the divine.[26] Jesus's own teachings are often resonant with this kind of interconnected view.

The way that Christ describes the Reign of God often employs organic, systemic metaphors. In the Parable of the Sower, Jesus illustrates how the action of sowing seeds can yield vastly different outcomes depending on the environment in which the seeds fall (Mark 4:1–20). This parable reflects the systems thinking principle that outcomes depend on the interplay of various factors within a system. In vocational terms, it suggests that the impact of our calling isn't solely determined by our efforts or intentions, but also by the broader context in which we operate. It invites us to consider how we might cultivate fertile "soil" in our communities and institutions to allow vocations to flourish and bear fruit.

Similarly, Jesus's metaphor of the Vine and the Branches offers a powerful image of interconnectedness and mutual dependence (John 15:1–8). By describing himself as the vine and his followers as the branches, Jesus emphasizes that our individuality is intimately connected to and draws sustenance from God. This metaphor challenges us to see our lives not as isolated pursuits, but as extensions of Christ's own ministry, deeply rooted in and nourished by our relationship with him. It also highlights the systemic nature of spiritual fruitfulness: the health of each branch affects the overall vitality of the vine.

Other parables, like yeast working through dough or seeds growing into large plants, suggest that our actions, no matter how small they may seem, can have far-reaching effects in regard to aligning ourselves with God's Reign (Mt. 13). These images encourage us to view our callings not just in terms of immediate impact, but as catalysts for broader, systemic change that aligns with God's purposes for the world. They invite us to imagine how our seemingly small contributions might, over time, transform entire systems and communities.

Perhaps the clearest systems metaphor in scripture is Paul's description of the church as the Body of Christ. In Romans 12:4–5, he states that "just as each of us has one body with many members, and these members do not all have the same function, so in Christ we, though many, form one body, and each member belongs to

---

26 An excellent resource for thinking this way comes from the work of the Watershed Discipleship movement; see *Watershed Discipleship: Reinhabiting Bioregional Faith and Practice*, ed. Ched Myers (Eugene, OR: Cascade Books, 2016).

all the others." This imagery emphasizes the interdependence of individuals within the community, reflecting that the whole is greater than the sum of its parts. Seen through this lens, vocational discernment involves more than just understanding our personal talents and desires. It involves understanding how these fit into and serve the broader needs of the body.

In this way, we are "members one of another," where each person's role is vital to the functioning of the whole and we ourselves are who we are because of our relationship with each other (Ephesians 4:25 and Romans 12:5). This understanding of our fundamental interrelatedness is sometimes discussed theologically as "intersubjectivity," the idea that who we are is connected to other people. Theologies of Ubuntu are some of the clearest places where I see this perspective take root.

Ubuntu Theology

The notion of interconnectedness is not limited to theological metaphors or abstract concepts; it is deeply embedded in cultural wisdom and lived experiences. One such perspective that vividly illustrates this truth is the African concept of Ubuntu, which emphasizes the inextricable bond between individuals and their communities. This philosophy aligns seamlessly with systems thinking, offering a profound lens for understanding the relational dynamics that shape our lives. Desmond Tutu eloquently explains:

> In Xhosa, we say, "*Umntu ngumtu ngabantu.*" This expression is very difficult to render in English, but we could translate it by saying, "A person is a person through other persons." We need other human beings for us to learn how to be human, for none of us comes fully formed into the world.... For us, the solitary human being is a contradiction in terms.[27]

This worldview challenges many Western notions of individualism, offering a radically different understanding of human identity and development.

In the Ubuntu perspective, our very humanity is not an inherent, isolated possession. Our humanity emerges through our relationships and interactions with others. This has profound implications for how we understand personal growth, education, and societal development. It invites us to consider how our unique gifts and talents have been nurtured and revealed through our relationships, and how our sense

---

27 Desmond Tutu, "Ubuntu: On the Nature of Human Community," in *God Is Not a Christian: And Other Provocations*, ed. John Allen (New York: HarperOne, 2011), 21–26.

of purpose is intrinsically tied to our connections with others. If we are fundamentally relational beings, then our accomplishments cannot be solely attributed to individual effort or merit. Instead, they are the fruit of a complex web of support, influence, and collective effort. Tutu continues:

> Ubuntu is the essence of being human. It speaks of how my humanity is caught up and bound up inextricably with yours. It says, not as Descartes did, "I think, therefore I am," but rather, "I am because I belong." I need other human beings in order to be human. The completely self-sufficient human being is subhuman. I can be me only if you are fully you.[28]

This shift from "I think, therefore I am" to "I am because I belong" represents a deep reorientation of how we understand human existence and consciousness. It suggests that our very sense of self is relational and communal rather than primarily cognitive or individualistic. This has far-reaching implications for how we approach vocational discernment and personal development.

In the context of vocation, this perspective invites us to consider our callings in terms of how they contribute to and are sustained by our communities in addition to terms of personal fulfillment or individual impact. It suggests that the most meaningful and fulfilling vocations are those that not only utilize the spiritual gifts we steward, but also those that strengthen the bonds of community and contribute to collective flourishing. Tutu's assertion that "I can be me only if you are fully you" challenges us to see the flourishing of others as part of our own fullest expression of self rather than in competition with our own success. In vocational terms, this might mean seeking out roles and callings that allow us to thrive while creating space and opportunities for others to fully express their gifts and potential.

The idea that "the completely self-sufficient human being is subhuman" is particularly provocative in any culture that valorizes independence and self-reliance. Contrary to celebrated individual achievement or self-sufficiency, it suggests that our fullest humanity is realized through interdependence and mutual support. Tutu's explanation of Ubuntu extends beyond mere interdependence to a profound understanding of interconnectedness. In significant resonance with the biblical frame of the Church as the Body of Christ, Tutu writes that "I have gifts that you don't have, and you have gifts that I don't have. We are different in order to know our need of each other. To be human is to be dependent."[29] This understanding of interdependence offers a powerful framework for reimagining how we approach diversity and difference in our communities and workplaces.

---

28 Ibid.
29 Ibid.

The recognition that "to be human is to be dependent" challenges many prevailing narratives about strength, vulnerability, and success. It suggests that acknowledging and embracing our interdependence is a source of resilience and creativity. In vocational terms, this might mean seeking out mentorship, fostering collaborative relationships, and recognizing how our work is supported by and supports the efforts of countless others. This perspective also has important implications for how we understand leadership and authority. Rather than seeing leadership as a position of independent power or control, Ubuntu invites us to conceptualize it as a role of facilitating connection, nurturing gifts, and fostering collective flourishing. It challenges us to develop models of leadership and organizational structure that honor the interdependence and complementarity of all members.

The theologian Puleng LenkaBula pushes the concept of Ubuntu further, particularly in relation to ecological justice. LenkaBula uses the term "*botho*," from her Sesotho-speaking background, recognizing that it has similar contours to the Bantu language term, Ubuntu.[30]

> *Botho* can also be understood as a resource in the care and nurture of the wellbeing of creation in order that humanity may live in fullness and that the integrity of creation is preserved.... Its emphasis on harmonious relationships between humanity and the earth articulates an ethic of self-respect, respect for other humanity, and for the earth, which entrenches attitudes that are non-exploitative, and not extractive of others and of creation. This is helpful in that *botho* encourages people to value creation and other human beings not only as means to ends, but also as ends in themselves.[31]

LenkaBula's extension of *botho* to include ecological relationships builds on Tutu's Ubuntu emphasis on human interconnectedness, challenging us to expand our understanding of "community" beyond human society to encompass the entire web of life.

This perspective invites us to consider how we humans are yoked to communities beyond our human kin. Together, I read Tutu and LenkaBula as inviting us to critically examine the systemic contexts in which we live and serve. This may lead to difficult questions: How can we pursue our callings in ways that challenge exploitative economic models and foster ecological justice? The Ubuntu vision suggests that a deeper fulfillment comes from contributing to the flourishing of all life. This might

---

[30] Puleng LenkaBula, "Beyond Anthropocentricity: Botho/Ubuntu and the Quest for Economic and Ecological Justice in Africa," *Religion and Theology* 15, no. 3–4 (2008): 375–94, doi: https://doi.org/10.1163/157430108X376591 378.

[31] Ibid., 387.

mean redefining "productivity" or "success" in our work to include strengthening human communities, as Tutu emphasizes, and ecological regeneration, as LenkaBula advocates.

As we integrate these insights into our understanding of vocation, we begin to see our callings as deeply embedded within complex webs of human, ecological, and spiritual relationship. This holistic perspective challenges us to view our vocations not as isolated pursuits, but as integral parts of a larger, interconnected system. This understanding invites us to consider how our vocational choices might ripple out to affect the broader ecosystems in which we live in our immediate communities. It encourages us to reflect on how our work aligns with and contributes to the flourishing of all life. This includes life that is human and other-than-human as well as even the planet itself. Moreover, this interconnected view of vocation calls us to a deeper spiritual awareness, recognizing that our individual purpose is intimately tied to larger spiritual realities and the ongoing work of the divine in the world. In reflecting on this spiritual dimension, I find a great resource in the work of Walter Wink.

Walter Wink and "The Powers"

Another powerful way to understand the spiritual dimension of systems comes from the work of biblical scholar Walter Wink. Wink undertook a deep study of the New Testament terms often translated as "principalities and powers" (like angels, demons, or spiritual rulers). He argued that these weren't just supernatural beings, but also represented the invisible spiritual reality or dimension of earthly institutions and social structures.

These institutions and structures are things like governments, economic systems, or even cultural forces. For Wink, "The Powers" have both an outer form (like a corporation's building and policies) and an inner spirit or ethos (like the difference between a government genuinely serving its people versus one serving its own power, or a religious institution focused on compassion versus one driven by self-preservation). Understanding the inner dimensions of social structures helps us see how systems themselves can be forces for good or ill, carrying their own kind of spiritual weight and influence.

Throughout his lifelong study of the Powers, Wink set out to show means by which we can begin to discern the interior spirituality of organizations and the ways that individual human lives are profoundly affected by them. Our personal spiritual condition is intricately connected to the institutions of which we are part. Wink roots his proposal in an interpretation of scripture.

> The New Testament's "principalities and powers" is a generic category referring to the determining forces of physical, social, and psychic existence. These powers usually consist of an outer manifestation and an inner spirituality or interiority. Power must become incarnate, institutionalized or systemic in order to be effective.[32]

Put simply, institutions have both logistical and spiritual dimensions, and understanding these dual aspects enables us to see how systems shape, and are shaped by, the spiritual and ethical lives of those within them.

Wink suggests that Christians in the earliest years of the Jesus movement believed that social systems that go against the purpose for which they were created are capable of significant violence. For many twenty-first-century Americans across the political spectrum, this is not such a difficult proposition to agree with. What is somewhat more novel is Wink's claim that, lacking the terminology from fields like sociology and psychology, early Christians named and described these corrupted systems as best they could, using terminology related to the Powers. It was only later that the powers (such as Satan, Elements, and Angels) were reinterpreted as physically embodied figures unrelated to social/spiritual institutions. In fact, he suggests that the Powers are very much organizationally real, and it is partially because of their later interpretation as winged and horned creatures that their true nature is often misunderstood.

Wink argues that understanding biblical language through this lens can reveal the roots of current spiritual maladies in people and systems, potentially offering ways forward. On the other hand, if we continue to regard the notion of the Devil as a trivial, outmoded, medieval idea because we associate the idea with horns and a forked tail, we will miss the opportunity to see more deeply into a reality that is not as easily apprehended as the physical one. In a sense, this is a call for a "rectification of names" as we discussed earlier, where we realign our understanding of these concepts with their true nature and function in our spiritual and social realities. If we do not at least attempt to discern the nature of the Powers, and the ways in which we are affected by Them, the spiritual reality of our condition will remain unknown because it is unnamed.

In Wink's view, every outward, visible human organization in society has an inner spiritual reality. This idea resonates with the metaphor of tradition as a living ecosystem explored in the third chapter, suggesting that our institutions are not just structures but dynamic spiritual environments. Wink argues that "the powers" include institutions (governments, corporations, schools, religious organizations, etc.), social

---

[32] Walter Wink, *Unmasking the Powers: The Invisible Forces That Determine Human Existence* (Philadelphia: Fortress Press, 1986), 4.

structures (political and economic systems), and ideologies (belief systems that shape how people understand and interact with the world). This means that a corporation, for example, is not just its buildings, employees, and products, but also its corporate culture, values, and the collective ethos that drives its decisions.

Biblically, we can use Wink's work to interpret the Book of Revelation, among others. In Revelation, the letters in chapters 2 and 3 are addressed not to the churches themselves, but to the "angels" of the churches. For example, Revelation 2:1 begins, "To the angel of the church in Ephesus write." This pattern continues for all seven churches addressed. From Wink's perspective, these "angels" represent the churches' spiritual identities: They embody each church's collective vocation, its collective ethos, and its spiritual orientation. By writing to the angel rather than individual members, the text recognizes that the church is more than just a collection of individuals. It is a system with its own identity and spiritual reality. By addressing the angels, the letters in Revelation suggest that change in the church involves more than just altering external behaviors. It requires engaging with and transforming the inner, spiritual dimension of the community. The letters call for repentance and change, implying that the church as an entity has the capacity to respond and transform. The capacity for the transformation of the Powers is an important part of Wink's proposal. He has three points in this regard.[33]

First, the Powers are good. They were created to serve God's purposes and contribute to human flourishing. Originally, institutions and systems were meant to organize society for the common good. Second, most Powers are fallen. They have become corrupted and often serve their own interests rather than their divine purpose. This is why we see institutions that exploit rather than serve, ideologies that oppress rather than liberate. Third, the Powers can be redeemed. Despite their fallen nature, they can be transformed and realigned with their divine vocation. This is not about destroying the powers, but about recalling them to their original purpose. Wink writes, "The demons projected onto the screen of the cosmos really are demonic, and play havoc with humanity. Only they are not 'up there' but over there, in the socio-spiritual structures that make up the one and only real world."[34] This framework challenges simplistic views of good and evil, inviting us to engage critically and compassionately with the systems and institutions that shape our world.

Wink argues that addressing social issues requires engaging with both the outer, physical manifestations of the powers and their inner, spiritual realities.

---

[33] Walter Wink, *The Powers That Be: Theology for a New Millennium* (New York: Doubleday, 1998), 25.

[34] Ibid., 26.

> When a particular Power becomes idolatrous—that is, when it pursues a vocation other than the one for which God created it and makes its own interests the highest good—then that Power becomes demonic. The spiritual task is to unmask this idolatry and recall the Powers to their created purposes in the world. But this can scarcely be accomplished by individuals. A group is needed—what the New Testament calls an *ekklesia* (assembly)—one that exists specifically for the task of recalling these Powers to their divine vocation. That was to be the task of the church, "so that through the church, the wisdom of God in its rich variety might now be made known to the rulers and authorities in the heavenly places" (Eph. 3:10). And the church must perform this task despite its being as fallen and idolatrous as any other institution in society.[35]

For those discerning a call to leadership, Wink's ideas suggest that part of their vocation might involve not just individual actions but engagement with and transformation of larger systems or "powers."

This could mean working to redeem unjust institutions, challenge oppressive ideologies, or heal broken social structures. Wink contends that the task of the church is to "unmask this idolatry and recall the Powers to their created purposes in the world."[36] I find that this perspective encourages us to view organizations and institutions holistically, recognizing both their visible structures and invisible spiritual realities. This approach invites us to consider the unseen dynamics at play in our contexts, much like how we might discern the unspoken rules or emotional undercurrents in a family system. This holistic view challenges us to discern our personal gifts and passions as well as how we might contribute to the healing and alignment of the "Powers" that shape our world. It's not just that a corporation or a police department does harm: It's how that harm takes on a life of its own, becoming justified by "the way things are done," even by people who don't mean to cause harm.

This critique of how systems can lose their way extends to the very models of leadership we often adopt within them. For instance, Kristina Lizardy-Hajbi offers a pointed decolonial critique of widely accepted leadership styles, such as servant leadership, arguing that they can sometimes mask underlying power dynamics or reinscribe colonial realities if not critically examined.[37] Such analyses urge us to look beyond the surface appeal of popular leadership frameworks and ask whose interests they truly serve within our systems.

---

35 Ibid., 7.
36 Ibid., 29.
37 Kristina Lizardy-Hajbi, *Unraveling Religious Leadership: Power, Authority, and Decoloniality* (Minneapolis: Fortress Press, 2024), 120–22.

I think we're wise to consider Lizardy-Hajbi's concern. Sometimes, leadership models that claim to champion humility and service can, if unexamined, inadvertently perpetuate the very power imbalances they claim to subvert. A "servant leader," for instance, might operate from a position of unacknowledged privilege, setting the agenda for who is served and how, without fundamentally altering the systemic conditions that create marginalization. In such cases, the "service" risks becoming a way of managing inequity rather than dismantling it, subtly reinforcing colonial dynamics where the supposed servant still holds the power to define the terms. This critique resonates deeply with Wink's understanding of the Powers.

A seemingly benevolent outer form of a leadership style can conceal an inner spirit, or ethos, that remains tethered to fallen systems that prioritize their own preservation or the interests of the dominant group over true justice and collective flourishing. The masking that Lizardy-Hajbi identifies is one of the ways that the Powers can operate, their problematic spiritual realities obscured by laudable language while material practices and norms remain and continue to do harm. Recognizing these hidden architectures of power, both in their institutional expression and their spiritual ethos, becomes an important task not only for effective leadership, but for anyone attempting to discern their vocation faithfully within these complex systems.

For those in vocational discernment, Wink's ideas offer a powerful framework for understanding the broader implications of calling. It suggests that our vocations are not just about finding personal fulfillment or even serving others on an individual level. Our vocations are about participating in the redemption and transformation of larger systems. This might mean choosing career paths that allow us to engage with systemic issues, developing leadership styles that challenge unjust power structures, or cultivating spiritual practices that help us discern and respond to the "spiritual realities" of the institutions we're part of. This expanded view of vocation can be both daunting and inspiring, calling us to a level of engagement and responsibility that goes beyond personal success to encompass societal transformation.

How the Stars Are Named

My hope is that this chapter successfully makes the case that we're called to a more expansive understanding of vocation: one that recognizes our individual callings as part of a larger ecosystem of relationships, institutions, and spiritual realities. The Frederick Buechner quote routinely referenced in much of the vocation literature ("the place God calls you to is the place where your deep gladness and the world's deep hunger meet"[38]) isn't wrong, but it doesn't tell the whole story.

---

38 Frederick Buechner, *Wishful Thinking: A Theological ABC* (New York: Harper & Row, 1973).

> **A Practice to Consider:**
> # Seeing Angels
>
> *Communities, like individuals, have their own spiritual identities and callings. Imagining these as "angels" invites us to see both their aspirations and imperfections, fostering a deeper connection to their collective purpose and our role within it.*
>
> 1. Consider Your Community: Consider the values, strengths, and challenges that define your community. What qualities or ideals does it strive toward? What unique tensions or purposes shape its identity?
> 2. Create a Visual Representation: Using drawing, collage, or mixed media, bring this "angel" of your community to life. Experiment with symbols, colors, and forms that embody its spiritual character, whether in a literal, abstract, or symbolic way. Focus on representing both the aspirations and the imperfections that give your community its complexity and uniqueness.
> 3. Reflect on Your Creation: Step back and observe your artwork. What part of the angel's "work" or purpose aligns with your own calling? Where do you see yourself contributing to its strengths or addressing its challenges? What might this "angel" need from you to flourish? How might it, in turn, support you in living out your vocation?

What if an individual's "deep gladness" has been systematically suppressed or deemed illegitimate by the very structures that also generate the world's deepest hungers? Who gets to define that "hunger," and whose hunger is deemed worthy of a response? Furthermore, how do we account for the pervasive spiritual and structural realities of our institutions that often dictate who has the agency to act on their gladness or even to name the world's needs? The quote, while inspiring, doesn't inherently equip us to navigate a world where our personal passions and the world's needs are so thoroughly mediated by systems, some of which are profoundly unjust or idolatrous. To truly understand our place and calling, we need a lens that brings these systemic forces into view.

A systems-aware approach to vocation considers the complex web of relationships, power dynamics, and institutional realities that shape both our joy and the world's needs, challenging us to discern our callings within larger contexts. A systems approach to thinking about vocation doesn't diminish the importance of personal passion or societal needs. Rather, it enriches our understanding of both, situating them within a more comprehensive framework of interconnection and mutual influence. It challenges us to pursue vocations that bring personal fulfillment and meet immediate needs while contributing to the flourishing of the entire web of life, all its dimensions of human, ecological, and spiritual context.

The way we perceive and engage with our vocations is profoundly influenced by the systems within which we have been raised, including the collective stories, symbols, practices, and understandings we share with our communities. For some, these systems may nurture vocation; for others, they may require resistance, reclamation, or reimagining before they are able to support flourishing and growth. Not all plants thrive in all soil. We are profoundly influenced by patterns much larger than it is easy to see. Recognizing influential systems is like an unlabeled connect-the-dot game, a social exercise of articulating shared understandings grounded in lived experiences. It is important to recognize that what we think we feel and see is at least partially influenced by what we've been told we will see.

For example, the connection of stars often seen as a ladle and called "the big dipper" in the United States is also the same set of stars named "the plough" in Ireland. And zooming out, those same stars can be seen as part of Ursa Major, "The Bear." Likewise, for the First Nations Gwich'in people, this same grouping of stars is just the tail of the much larger figure of Yahdii, The Tailed Man, who walks across the sky from east to west every night. Same stars. Different stories. Just as different cultures see different constellations in the same night sky, our understanding of vocation is shaped by the narratives and patterns we've inherited and the experiences we've lived.

A systems-aware approach to vocation invites us to recognize these shared stories and how they influence our discernment process. It challenges us to look beyond our immediate perspective, to consider how others might "connect the dots" differently, and to remain open to new patterns and possibilities we might not have seen before. Our individual vocational journeys are part of broader, overlapping stories, some collective and celebrated, others hidden or fractured. Some both. Recognizing this complexity invites us to consider whose stories are included, whose are missing, and how our vocations can contribute to a more inclusive and just narrative. It would be a profound act of hubris to try to understand the whole thing. The goal is, instead, to cultivate an awareness of the broader context in which our vocations unfold. This systems-aware approach encourages us to remain humble and curious, recognizing that our perspective is always limited and shaped by our particular place within the larger web of relationships and institutions.

An expanded view of vocation opens new possibilities for transformative change, allowing our callings to address immediate needs while reshaping the systems that create them. This might involve challenging unjust structures, nurturing more life-affirming institutions, or fostering new ways of relating to one another and to the earth. This approach invites us to engage in ongoing discernment, recognizing that our vocations may evolve as we gain deeper insights into the systems we're part of. It calls us to remain attentive to the ripple effects of our choices, considering how our actions might influence not just our immediate sphere but the broader ecological and social systems we inhabit. As you continue in your work to live into your calling, I hope that you can do it with both boldness and humility, trusting that even small actions, when aligned with the deeper patterns of life and justice, can contribute to significant transformation.

Questions for Reflection

1. This chapter discusses "system equilibrium," the tendency for organizations or communities to resist disruption and maintain familiar patterns, even if they aren't entirely healthy. Can you recall a time in a community or organization you were part of where you experienced this kind of resistance to change? A time when a change started but then old habits reemerged? How did you navigate it, or how might you approach such resistance differently now, knowing about these systemic pulls toward stability?

2. Consider the idea of system boundaries, those invisible lines that define how a group functions. Reflecting on a community or organization you know well, would you describe its boundaries as generally clear (fostering healthy autonomy and connection), diffuse (leading to enmeshment or lack of focus), or rigid (creating isolation and hindering collaboration)? What are the tangible effects of these boundary types on the people within that system and its overall mission?

3. Think about a time when you've been part of an "emotional triangle" in an organization or community, where tension between two parties was managed by bringing in a third person or issue. What role did you play in that dynamic? Knowing what you now know about triangulation from this chapter, how might you approach a similar situation differently to foster more direct communication and healthier relationships?

4. This chapter explores how power dynamics related to social location, authority, or unspoken norms can influence how systems operate and who thrives within them. In an organizational or community system you're familiar with, how do you see power operating, perhaps in both visible and subtle ways? How might a deeper awareness of these power dynamics inform your approach to leadership, participation, or advocacy within that system?

5. Walter Wink's concept of "The Powers" suggests that institutions and social structures have a spiritual reality or ethos that can be either life-giving or life-denying. Thinking about an institution or system you're part of (like a workplace, church, or club), does this framework help you understand its deeper spiritual character? If so, how? What implications might this have for how you ethically engage with, resist, or seek to redeem that system?

6. After exploring systems thinking in this chapter, from the idea that "small is good, small is all" to understanding concepts like feedback loops and interconnectedness, how might this broader perspective influence your personal approach to vocational discernment? What new questions, considerations, or even possibilities does it raise for you as you think about your calling and the impact you hope to make?

5

Joy and Lament

Lament is honesty before God and each other.
—Soong-Chan Rah

I look at joy as an act of resistance against despair and its forces.
—Willie James Jennings

The preceding chapter explored how systems shape our vocational journeys. We now turn to the emotional landscape of that journey. Too often, when people write or teach about vocation, they focus primarily on the beginning: What am I to do with my one wild and precious life? What kind of service am I called to? The beginning is a good place to start, but there is much more to the story. After someone has intentionally chosen to devote their energy, attention, and time to vocational discernment, there comes a moment when the realities of the world rudely assert themselves. This often comes sooner than we expect it. "Saying yes" to the call of service doesn't magically make everything easy. Go figure. This chapter is about what happens after the honeymoon of ministry is over.

When I think about the role of joy and lament in vocational discernment, I routinely go to William James Jennings's view that joy is "an act of resistance."[1] Joy is not merely a burst of happiness; it is an intentional defiance of despair, a choice to claim life and possibility even in the face of struggle. For Jennings, joy actively resists

---

[1] Willie Jennings and Miroslav Volf, "Joy and the Act of Resistance Against Despair," *For the Life of the World* (podcast), episode 57 (February 28, 2021). See also the epigraph.

the forces that press down on us, the currents that might pull us into hopelessness. Joy is a way of saying, "Despite it all, there is still beauty, still goodness, still a reason to continue." In this sense, joy becomes a courageous act, one that grounds us when challenges arise, and it fuels our resilience as we continue to pursue our calling.

Yet this joyful resistance does not mean turning away from the realities of suffering and struggle. Here, Soong-Chan Rah's words call me back to earth: "Lament is honesty before God and each other."[2] As Rah describes it, lament is essential to discernment because it demands that we face what is broken within ourselves, within our communities, and within the world around us. Lament is a voice of truth, the recognition of pain and injustice that we cannot ignore. If joy is a stance of resistance, then lament is the grounding truth of our experience, the acknowledgment of what is and the courage to name it. Together, joy and lament act as balancing forces in the discernment process, helping us hold both hope and truth in tension. These two emotions are not opposites but partners in our journey, each shaping and deepening our vocational path.

I have found that many people feel called to ministry long before any official recognition, especially as lay ministry becomes more common. Whether in graduate school, a church training program, or a denominational licensing gathering, there is a kind of exhilaration in being with others who feel called to service. I think about the bands of prophets we read about in scripture and what it would have been like to encounter a group of folks with stringed instruments, a tambourine, a flute, and a harp, all making music and prophesying on their way down a mountain (1 Samuel 10). Being with people who have chosen to dedicate their lives to service can sometimes feel like that.

So, yes, this chapter is about that initial joy, about the excitement of agreeing that there might be something more in store for you in service. But it's also about the inevitable moments when that joy is tempered by frustration, when the path forward becomes less clear. The "highs and lows" of discernment are not obstacles to a clearer sense of calling; rather, they are the means through which growth happens and a deeper understanding of service can emerge.

What comes next for me? I know I am ordained, but now what? I know it was right to have a family, but I still feel called to serve. How is that supposed to work? Or perhaps you feel alive in service, but you find yourself surrounded by people who don't "get it" in school, in training programs, or at denominational meetings. Is this the right place for you? There are vocations within vocations, and even those of us who long ago said "yes" to service will encounter questions that demand ongoing discernment.

---

2 Soong-Chan Rah, *Prophetic Lament: A Call for Justice in Troubled Times* (Downers Grove, IL: InterVarsity Press, 2015). For the epigraph see page 47.

As we navigate these ongoing questions and challenges, we may oscillate between profound joy and deep lament. These emotions aren't just reactions; they are integral to the vocational journey itself. They refine our purpose, deepen our resilience, and, most importantly, connect us honestly with ourselves, with God, and with others. By learning to navigate the landscape of joy and lament, we cultivate a sustainable approach to our calling, one that is deeply personal yet communal, resilient yet truthful. Joy and lament, held together, create a more holistic understanding of our vocation, one that acknowledges both the heights and depths of this shared journey.

Bumps on the Road

Especially for people that "caught the spark" during an event or a program, deciding to do something with your feeling of calling can be joyous. I see this particularly with people who spent years in campus ministry as a student and felt connected in a way they hadn't when at their home congregation. I also see it with people who did a retreat or intensive and, as a result, felt like they were clamoring for more. Sometimes, an encounter with someone held in high esteem happens, and, as a result of a transformative conversation, you decide there needs to be something more in your life. This joy may manifest as a growing awareness of one's gifts, a passion for service, or a sense of purpose in following Christ. It is a powerful motivator that draws individuals toward a deeper exploration of their call.

Whatever the reason, the early stages of vocational discernment often begin with a sense of joy, a deep resonance with God's calling that energizes and excites. However, I think it is healthy to recognize that this initial period of excitement and clarity is often short-lived. One of the most significant markers of moving beyond the very early stages of vocational discernment is the jarring realization that not everything is unfolding as imagined. This transition can be particularly disorienting for those experiencing vocational discernment for the first time. For instance, we might find joy in the overall arc of our ministry even when faced with daily frustrations. Likewise, we might experience deep lament over systemic injustices while still taking pleasure in small victories.

Randy Woodley, a Cherokee theologian, emphasizes that lament is deeply tied to land justice and the ongoing effects of colonization. He writes that "to be human is to care for creation," highlighting the sacred relationship between people and the earth.[3] For Indigenous traditions, lament is not only an emotional response but also a call to action for ecological restoration and communal healing. This perspective reframes

---

3 Randy Woodley, "The Fullness Thereof," *Sojourners Magazine* online (May 2019).

lament as a way to confront the brokenness of the world, including our disconnection from the land, and to envision a path toward renewal. Incorporating this understanding into our vocational journeys challenges us to see lament not just as personal sorrow but as a broader engagement with the healing of the earth and its people.

Given the vastness of the ecological crisis, Woodley's understanding of lament as a call to restoration reminds us that even the smallest acts of healing can carry profound significance. Whether planting a garden, advocating for policy change, or building community, the seed of what comes next is within them. These small victories, though seemingly modest in the face of systemic injustice, become seeds of hope and resistance, grounding us in the larger work of justice while affirming our capacity to act meaningfully in the present.

Woodley's powerful articulation of lament rooted in land justice and the wounds of colonization opens our eyes to how deeply intertwined our sorrows can be with systemic realities. This is not unique to the experience of Indigenous communities. Economic systems that perpetuate precarity for millions, racialized violence that targets bodies and spirits, and patriarchal or heteronormative structures that seek to diminish the full humanity of those they marginalize: These are all potent generators of communal lament. In the face of such pervasive forces, the cultivation of collective joy within these same communities becomes more than mere happiness or a fleeting emotion. It emerges as a profound act of spiritual and political resistance, a conscious choice to affirm life, dignity, and hope when dominant systems attempt to dictate despair. This resistant joy, often nurtured in shared cultural expression, sacred ritual, or acts of mutual care, becomes a vital spiritual resource, sustaining communities and individuals as they navigate vocations that call them to challenge these very systems and to imagine a world more aligned with divine justice.

By developing this nuanced emotional awareness, we can cultivate greater resilience and depth in our vocational pursuits, allowing both our celebrations and our sorrows to inform and enrich our service. For mentors and those accompanying others in their vocational journeys, naming the fact that these processes often contain a range of experiences can be deeply supportive. There are things to learn, and not just from the positive moments. Recognizing this diversity of experience can also encourage mutual learning, whether one is a mentor or still discerning their own call. While that might seem obvious to you now, it is important to remember you might not always have known that.

I remember distinctly trying to name how I felt called to public ministry when I was very early in my own journey of discernment. At that time, a much-loved member of our congregation invited me to lunch. After some pleasantries, he shared what I think is one of the best pieces of advice I've ever received.

> I know that right now you're very excited about us and loving how we do things and how you can be of service here. And that's great. But I need you to know that one day we [Quakers] will, for one reason or another, disappoint you deeply. And that's okay, that doesn't mean the work isn't worth doing. Faith is bigger than any person.

Those weren't his exact words, but that's the gist of what he said. I know that because I was profoundly annoyed by them and him that day. Why was he talking about disappointment when I was looking for accompaniment and mentoring? Where was his trust that we could find faithful ways forward?

Today, I recognize the profound wisdom in this advice. His words were not a pessimistic prediction but a realistic and compassionate preparation for the complex emotional landscape of ministry. He was acknowledging that vocational journeys, especially in religious contexts, often involve deep emotional investments and high expectations, which can make disappointments particularly painful when they inevitably occur. By forewarning me about potential disappointments, he was helping me develop a more nuanced and mature understanding of what it means to be part of a faith community and to serve in ministry. He was encouraging me to see beyond the initial enthusiasm and idealism to recognize that real, meaningful ministry involves navigating both joys and sorrows, successes and failures. And boy have I been disappointed over the years.... And that is all right.

In retrospect, I see that my mentor was modeling the very vulnerability and honesty that help create spaces for both joy and lament in vocational discernment. He really was excited for me and wanted to encourage my deepening engagement with our tradition. He also wanted to make sure I wasn't heading into the next phase of my journey wearing rose-colored glasses. By sharing this potentially unwelcome truth, he was demonstrating the importance of addressing both the highs and lows of ministry, even when it might be uncomfortable. This wisdom from my mentor has shaped my own approach to accompanying others on their vocational journeys. I've come to understand that creating space for both joy and lament is not just about allowing for emotional expression, but about fostering a deeper, more resilient engagement with one's calling. It's about helping individuals develop the capacity to hold both the excitement of new possibilities and the disappointment of unmet expectations.

This balanced perspective becomes particularly important when individuals encounter challenges that go beyond personal disappointments to reveal systemic issues within the very institutions meant to nurture their growth. As I've walked alongside others in their vocational discernment, I've seen how this ability to navigate both joy and lament can be especially important when confronting deeper, more pervasive problems in our faith communities and educational institutions. I'm not happy for the challenging times, and I'm not suggesting you should be either: We ought not celebrate pain or suffering. At the same time, I think it is important to recognize that sometimes growth can come after periods of intense change. In the growing season after a forest fire, all kinds of plants and animals thrive that were not there when things were the way they were before.

I often have conversations with people who love the idea of learning more about ministry and theology but find that the context they have to do it in is less than compelling. Not everyone has the privilege of bringing their full self into a seminary community or any other space of formation without fear of rejection or harm. For many, the act of sharing personal passions, identities, or struggles can come with risks of being misunderstood, judged, or excluded. Sometimes, that is because they encounter unintentional but still painful systemic racism in a Christian institution of theological education. This kind of institutional betrayal can deeply disrupt one's Moral Orienting System (the framework of values, beliefs, and relationships we explored in the first chapter), leaving individuals feeling spiritually and ethically unmoored. They feel frustrated that an environment meant to nurture their calling instead becomes a source of disillusionment.

This situation highlights the difference between frustration and lament. The immediate feelings of anger or disappointment when encountering bias or exclusion might be classified as frustration. However, as these experiences accumulate and reveal deeper systemic issues, they can evolve into a profound lament, a sorrow not just for personal experiences, but for the ways in which institutions meant to foster spiritual growth can perpetuate harm. And it doesn't just happen around issues of race, of course.

Encounters with systemic issues can occur across various dimensions of identity and experience. LGBTQ+ individuals may find themselves grappling with institutional policies or theological stances that conflict with their sense of self and calling. Women in traditionally male-dominated religious spaces might encounter subtle or overt sexism that challenges their sense of belonging and purpose. Beyond identity-based challenges, individuals may also struggle with institutional rigidity or outdated practices that seem at odds with their vision of ministry.

For instance, someone called to innovative forms of community outreach might feel stifled by a church's insistence on traditional programs and structures. Especially in the context of theological education in graduate school, I also know many folks who wished that the program they were part of had been more spiritual or faith-based. Sometimes, even programs in theology and religion can get caught up in being an excellent school and forget to be an excellent place of worship and formation.

These kinds of experiences often lead to a complex interplay of emotions. There's the initial joy of pursuing one's calling, followed by the shock and frustration of encountering barriers. As understanding deepens, this can evolve into a profound lament for the gap between the ideal of inclusive, nurturing spiritual communities and the often-flawed reality of the present. However, these challenges, while painful, can also be transformative. They often push individuals to engage more deeply with their faith, to question long-held assumptions, and to envision new ways of embodying their calling. Many find that navigating these difficulties actually clarifies and strengthens their sense of vocation.

For example, a woman facing resistance to her leadership in a religious setting might initially feel frustrated and discouraged. Over time, this experience could evolve into a lament for the ways gender bias limits the full expression of diverse gifts within the church. Yet this very lament might fuel a renewed commitment to her calling, perhaps leading her to advocate for change or to seek out more inclusive spaces where her gifts can flourish. In this way, both joy and lament become integral parts of the vocational journey, each informing and deepening the other. The joy of answering a call provides the strength to face challenges, while the capacity for lament allows for a more nuanced, empathetic engagement with the complexities of religious institutions, communities, and society writ large.

The joy of learning and deepening one's understanding of theology and ministry can coexist with lament over the imperfections and injustices within systems of formation and education. This coexistence isn't about diminishing either emotion but about holding them in tension, allowing both to shape and inform one's vocational journey. For those navigating these challenges, finding communities of support can be vital, whether they are formal or not. These might include affinity groups within institutions, mentorship relationships, or connections with others who share similar experiences. Such communities create spaces where both joy and lament are honored, frustrations can be voiced and processed, and strategies for change can emerge. In addition to being healthy, having a place to express the full range of your emotions and experiences is deeply formative.

For some, vocational spaces are shaped by systemic barriers, cultural norms, or theological positions that stifle rather than celebrate diverse expressions of identity and calling. For example, an LGBTQ+ student in a seminary that upholds traditionalist theology may feel compelled to hide their identity to avoid rejection, or a person of color might find that their experiences of systemic racism are dismissed or minimized in predominantly white spaces. Similarly, women in male-dominated theological contexts might encounter subtle or overt sexism that undermines their contributions or questions their leadership capabilities.

These dynamics both hinder individuals from bringing their full selves into these spaces and impoverish the community as a whole by silencing valuable perspectives and gifts. When we seek to foster these spaces for greater exploration of joy and lament, we must ask: Whose joy is uplifted here? Whose lament is given voice and legitimacy? Power and privilege profoundly shape these questions. Often, communities unconsciously replicate societal hierarchies. Times for "joy" might center the celebrations of the dominant group, while the unique joys of those on the margins (joys found in resistance, in cultural specificity not universalism, in survival) go unacknowledged or are even subtly discouraged if they don't fit the prevailing mood.

Even more starkly, the capacity for lament can be policed by power. The laments of those experiencing systemic injustice (grief over racial violence, anger at economic exploitation, sorrow over homophobic or transphobic exclusion) may be dismissed as "divisive," "too angry," or "making people uncomfortable." Healing spaces for lament must actively dismantle these barriers, creating environments where the prophetic cry against injustice is not only permitted but received as sacred and necessary. This requires those with privilege to decenter our own comfort and learn to sit with the painful truths that marginalized communities have long carried, recognizing that what feels like disruption to some is, for others, the painful normal of their everyday lives.

This reality underscores the critical importance of creating environments where the expression of one's identity, gifts, and struggles is met with both respect and genuine affirmation. Such spaces are not merely idealistic aspirations but vital for the kind of deep formation that vocational discernment requires. This will be explored in greater detail in the seventh chapter's consideration of accompaniment, but here I'll note that when individuals are free to share their joys and laments without fear, the community itself is enriched, gaining the insight and resilience that come from holding the full spectrum of human experience. This kind of inclusivity is not only about justice but also about cultivating the trust, openness, and emotional depth necessary for meaningful discernment and spiritual growth.

The interplay between joy and lament provides a framework for understanding how these emotions contribute to resilience and clarity in vocational journeys. Far from being opposites, they are complementary and coexisting forces that enrich our capacity to navigate the complexities of life and ministry. Joy celebrates the beauty and goodness in our calling, offering strength and hope, while lament names the pain and brokenness we encounter, grounding us in truth and compassion. Together, they invite a more profound engagement with God, self, community, and creation, fostering the emotional depth and spiritual maturity vital for meaningful discernment and sustained service.

What Psychology Says

Psychological research offers nuanced insights into the experiences of joy and lament. These findings can deepen our understanding of how these emotions shape our spiritual journeys and influence our sense of calling, providing a more comprehensive framework for those engaged in ministry, theological education, or personal vocational exploration.

Joy, from a psychological perspective, is far more than a fleeting feeling of happiness. It's a complex emotional state with profound effects on our cognitive abilities and overall well-being. The broaden-and-build theory, developed by psychologist Barbara Fredrickson, suggests that positive emotions like joy expand our "thought-action repertoires," enhancing our ability to think creatively and adapt to new situations.[4] This expanded mental capacity can be particularly valuable in ministry contexts, where adaptability and creative problem-solving are often vital. Having plans for joy can help to expand our capacity to see new possibilities, to recognize the nature of the new thing that God is doing in our midst.

Research has shown that individuals experiencing joy perform better on tasks requiring flexible thinking. For example, a study by Fredrickson and Christine Branigan found that participants induced to feel positive emotions showed more global (big picture) processing on a global-local visual processing task compared to those in neutral or negative emotional states.[5] This suggests that joy can broaden attention and cognitive processing styles. Similarly, Hwajin Yang and Sujin Yang demonstrated that inducing a positive mood led to improved performance on the Dimensional Change Card Sort task, a measure of cognitive flexibility, compared to neutral mood conditions.[6]

These findings support the notion that joy enhances our ability to adapt our thinking and see connections between ideas. This can be particularly valuable in vocational discernment and ministry, contexts where creative problem-solving is often required. Relatedly, joy has been linked to increased activity in the left prefrontal cortex, an area associated with positive emotions and approach behaviors. Neuroscientist Richard Davidson's research has shown that individuals with higher levels of left prefrontal activity report feeling more enthusiastic, alert, and engaged, qualities that can significantly enhance one's capacity for ministry and service.[7]

---

[4] Barbara L. Fredrickson, "What Good Are Positive Emotions?" *Review of General Psychology* 2, no. 3 (September 1998): 300–319.

[5] Barbara L. Fredrickson and Christine Branigan, "Positive Emotions Broaden the Scope of Attention and Thought-Action Repertoires," *Cognition & Emotion* 19, no. 3 (2005): 313–32.

[6] Hwajin Yang and Sujin Yang, "Positive Affect Facilitates Task Switching in the Dimensional Change Card Sort Task: Implications for the Shifting Aspect of Executive Function," *Cognition & Emotion* 28, no. 7 (2014): 1242–54.

[7] Richard J. Davidson, Daren C. Jackson, and Ned H. Kalin, "Emotion, Plasticity, Context, and Regulation: Perspectives from Affective Neuroscience," *Psychological Bulletin* 126, no. 6 (2000): 890–909.

For our purposes, these insights suggest that cultivating joy isn't just about feeling good. It's also about developing a mind-set that's more open to recognizing and responding to God's call in diverse and sometimes unexpected ways. For those of us (myself included) who sometimes struggle to make time for joy, it might help to know that experiencing joy isn't just about relaxation and self-care. While it can be that, when we experience joy in our service or studies, we may find ourselves more capable of imagining new possibilities for ministry or finding innovative solutions to challenges in our communities. There is a similar positive implication to making space for lamentation as well.

Lament, while often viewed as a negative experience, also plays a beneficial role in psychological health and spiritual growth. Psychologists have found that the act of lamentation can serve as a powerful emotional release mechanism. In particular, there is a benefit from openly expressing grief, disappointment, or frustration. This process of acknowledging and expressing difficult emotions can prevent emotional numbness and contribute to long-term resilience. The cathartic nature of lament has been well-documented in psychological literature. Research by James W. Pennebaker and Sandra K. Beall demonstrated that expressive writing about traumatic experiences led to improved physical health outcomes, including fewer physician visits and improved immune function.[8] This important study laid the groundwork for understanding how expressing negative emotions, akin to lamentation, can have tangible health benefits.

In the context of spiritual growth, Kenneth Pargament and colleagues explored religious coping methods, including spiritual expressions of grief and anger toward God.[9] Their findings indicated that individuals who engaged in these forms of religious coping, which share similarities with lamentation, often experienced post-traumatic growth and deeper spiritual connection. This aligns with more recent work by Julie Exline and colleagues, who found that expressing anger toward God, when done in the context of an overall positive relationship with the divine, was associated with greater religious commitment and spiritual growth over time.[10]

A meta-analysis by Gene Ano and Erin Vasconcelles examined the effects of religious/spiritual struggles on psychological well-being.[11] The authors found that,

---

8 James W. Pennebaker and Sandra K. Beall, "Confronting a Traumatic Event: Toward an Understanding of Inhibition and Disease," *Journal of Abnormal Psychology* 95, no. 3 (1986): 274–81.

9 Kenneth I. Pargament et al., "Patterns of Positive and Negative Religious Coping with Major Life Stressors," *Journal for the Scientific Study of Religion* 37, no. 4 (1998): 710–24.

10 Julie J. Exline et al. "Anger toward God: Social-Cognitive Predictors, Prevalence, and Links with Adjustment to Bereavement and Cancer," *Journal of Personality and Social Psychology* 100, no. 1 (2011): 129–48.

11 Gene G. Ano and Erin B. Vasconcelles, "Religious Coping and Psychological Adjustment to Stress: A Meta-Analysis," *Journal of Clinical Psychology* 61, no. 4 (2005): 461–80.

while these struggles can initially lead to distress, they often result in post-traumatic growth and deeper faith when processed in a supportive context. In fact, neuroimaging studies have shown that the act of naming and expressing negative emotions can reduce activity in the amygdala, the brain's fear center.[12] This suggests that lament may help regulate our emotional responses to challenges, allowing us to approach difficulties with greater clarity and composure. This engagement, rather than diminishing our sense of calling, often leads to a more mature and nuanced understanding of our vocation.

Taken as a whole, these studies suggest that lamentation, far from being detrimental to faith, can actually deepen one's spiritual journey and contribute to a more mature religious understanding. Lament allows individuals to process and integrate painful experiences, rather than suppressing or avoiding them. In the context of vocational discernment, the ability to lament can be a valuable tool for processing the inevitable disappointments and setbacks that come with any spiritual journey. When we encounter systemic injustices in our ministry contexts or face personal doubts about our calling, the practice of lament allows us to engage with these difficulties honestly and deeply. This engagement is all the more important given the realization that both joy and lament have a role to play in expanding our capacity to serve and discern how we are being called.

Psychological research also suggests that joy and lament are not opposing forces, but complementary experiences that can enhance each other. The capacity to fully experience joy is often linked to the ability to engage deeply with sorrow. The natural rhythm between joy and lament enriches our understanding of vocation, each season bringing its own gifts, leading to greater emotional depth and meaning in our vocational pursuits. The concept of emotional dialectics, introduced by Nico Frijda, proposes that opposing emotions can coexist and even enhance each other.[13] This idea has been further developed in the field of positive psychology. Recent empirical studies have provided support for this perspective. Jonathan Adler and Hal Hershfield found that individuals who expressed both positive and negative emotions when recalling significant life events had greater psychological well-being compared to those who expressed only positive or only negative emotions.[14] This suggests that the ability to engage with both joy and sorrow may contribute to a more balanced and resilient emotional life.

---

12 Matthew D. Lieberman et al., "Putting Feelings into Words: Affect Labeling Disrupts Amygdala Activity in Response to Affective Stimuli," *Psychological Science* 18, no. 5 (May 2007): 421–28, https://doi.org/10.1111/j.1467-9280.2007.01916.x.

13 Nico H. Frijda, *The Emotions* (Cambridge: Cambridge University Press, 1986).

14 Jonathan M. Adler and Hal E. Hershfield, "Mixed Emotional Experience Is Associated with and Precedes Improvements in Psychological Well-Being," *PLoS ONE* 7, no. 4 (2012): e35633.

Many of these "negative" emotions are not only emotional responses but moral signals. We see this in shame, guilt, disgust, and even humiliation. As Zachary Moon puts it, they arise from our moral orienting systems: the internalized, relationally shaped frameworks that tell us what is right, who we belong to, and what matters most.[15] When our vocational lives lead us into spaces where those systems are disrupted, these emotions emerge as evidence that something sacred has been violated by betrayal, by powerlessness, or by failure. Recognizing this can shift our posture from avoidance to attentive moral discernment. In this sense, moral emotions are not just reactions but invitations to name with greater precision what we are feeling and why that feeling matters.

This dynamic interplay is reflected in the concept of "emotional granularity," developed by psychologist Lisa Feldman Barrett.[16] Emotional granularity refers to the ability to differentiate between and articulate a wide range of emotional experiences. Individuals with high emotional granularity tend to be more resilient and better equipped to navigate complex emotional landscapes, a valuable skill in vocational contexts, where one might encounter both profound joys and deep sorrows. Understanding these psychological dynamics can help us approach our vocational journey with greater wisdom and self-awareness. It encourages us to create space for both joyful celebration and honest lament in our spiritual communities, recognizing that both play meaningful roles in shaping our service and discovery.

For those leading ministry training programs or theological education, these insights highlight the importance of fostering environments that allow for both joy and lament. This is just as true in churches as it is in graduate schools, community groups, and friend groups. Part of the work of forming ministers is giving them space to celebrate and cry. In formal spaces, this might involve creating rituals that celebrate milestones while also providing opportunities for students to express doubts, fears, or disappointments. In educational settings, it could also mean integrating practices of lament into curricula, helping future ministers develop an emotional granularity that can support long-term service.

For those of you who are, yourselves, actively discerning vocational call, I encourage you to include questions about space to express a range of emotional experiences as part of your reflection on both your ministerial identity and the place you are called to serve. Not all communities and cultures have the same norms

---

15 Zachary Moon, "Mapping Moral Emotions and Sense of Responsibility with Those Suffering with Moral Injury," *International Journal of Narrative Therapy and Community Work* 4 (2021): 74–78.

16 Lisa Feldman Barrett, "Feelings or Words? Understanding the Content in Self-Report Ratings of Experienced Emotion," *Journal of Personality and Social Psychology* 87, no. 2 (2004): 266–81.

Joy and Lament

regarding how emotions are expressed, so I can't claim to know exactly how you ought to interpret this in your specific context, but I do know that emotional awareness and expression are vital components of a healthy vocational journey.

Consider how your potential ministry settings approach joy and lament. Are there opportunities for genuine celebration? Is there space for honest expressions of grief, doubt, or frustration? These questions can provide valuable insights into the emotional and spiritual health of a community and how well it might align with your own needs and values. Reflect on your own emotional patterns and needs. Are you someone who requires regular outlets for exuberant joy? Do you value environments that allow for open expression of lament? Understanding your own emotional landscape can help you discern which vocational paths and communities might be most nurturing and sustainable for you in the long term.

It's also worth considering how different cultural contexts might shape the expression of joy and lament. Some cultures may have more overt expressions of emotion, while others may value more restrained or ritualized forms of emotional expression. As you discern your calling, think about how these cultural norms align with your own emotional needs and ministerial style. Remember, too, that your capacity for emotional granularity and expression is not fixed. Like any skill, it can be developed and refined over time. As you progress in your vocational journey, seek out opportunities to expand your emotional vocabulary and deepen your comfort with a wide range of emotional experiences.

When my mother's father was nearing the end of his life, my parents decided that they would move in with him so that he could pass away in his own home. They became his primary caregivers as he slowly slipped away. As might be expected, this period was a painful one for my mother. Not only because losing a parent is often hard, but particularly because my grandfather was a fairly typical male member of his generation and wasn't always very communicative about his care and love. But he was grateful that he could die comfortably in his home and didn't have to be somewhere else to end his journey. And he appreciated that my parents were helping him do that.

One of the unexpected things that emerged from that time is that my father had a revelation of sorts. While caring for his father-in-law, he realized that, unlike my grandfather, who faced death with peace and courage, he himself was far from feeling the same sense of ease. As he tells it, there was one day when he was helping move my grandfather's frail body and something clicked. He suddenly realized that someday he wanted to be able to die without anxiety and that, to do that, he would have to change his life. That day marked a turning point after which he began to bike again, get fit, got into therapy, and began a reconnection to his siblings and children no one had anticipated. When I later preached my grandfather's funeral, it wasn't just a sermon of lament, but also one in which I had already begun to see the impact of his life in joyful ways.

At the end of the day, creating space for both joy and lament in your vocational discernment process can lead to a more meaningful and sustainable ministry. It allows you to bring a broader sense of self to your calling, honoring both the heights of joy and the depths of sorrow that are present in many meaningful works of service. In the next section, I explore some of the ways theological traditions have conceptualized these emotions, examining biblical narratives, theological writings, and spiritual practices that engage with joy and lament.

Theological Insights

The interplay of joy and lament in vocational discernment and ministerial formation is deeply rooted in scriptural, theological, and spiritual traditions. This rich tapestry of insights can profoundly inform our approach to vocation, offering a nuanced understanding of how these emotional experiences are valued and interpreted within various religious contexts.

A Practice to Consider:
Double Journal

Life's journey is marked by both moments of joy and times of lament. Honoring both allows us to engage the fullness of our experiences and discern more about our calling and growth.

1. Set Up Your Journal: Use a single, small journal with two entry points. Start joys from the front cover. Start laments from the back cover.
2. Write in Balance: Each time you write a joy, match it with a lament, and vice versa. The entries don't need be the same length, but try to make sure for each joy entry there is one of lamentation.
3. Meet in the Middle: When your entries eventually meet in the middle of the journal, pause and read through: First, all the laments (starting from the back). Then, all the joys (starting from the front).
4. Reflect: As you review both, look for themes, patterns, or insights. How do the joys and laments speak to or inform each other? What do they reveal about your calling, growth, or current season of life?

Scriptural foundations provide numerous examples of both joy and lament, often interwoven in the lives of faithful individuals and communities. The Book of Psalms, in particular, offers a powerful illustration of this dynamic. Old Testament scholar Walter Brueggemann's work on the Psalms highlights what he terms the "plea-to-praise movement," where expressions of deep sorrow often transition unexpectedly into declarations of joy and trust in God's faithfulness. Brueggemann writes that the move from petition to praise, from lament to doxology, is not a simple shift of mood. It is rather a deep theological assertion that God can always "respond to transform the situation of need."[17] This pattern reflects the complex nature of spiritual life and the transformative power of honest engagement with God.

Brueggemann further elucidates this dynamic through his influential framework of orientation, disorientation, and new orientation in the Psalms. He suggests that the Psalms reflect the cyclical nature of faith experiences. Psalms of orientation express a sense of well-being and gratitude in times of stability and order. Psalms of disorientation voice the anguish and confusion that arise when life's circumstances shatter our sense of security and meaning. These are the laments that cry out to God in times of crisis. Finally, Psalms of new orientation articulate the joy and wonder of experiencing God's transformative power, leading to a renewed, often deeper faith.

This framework provides a valuable lens for understanding the role of joy and lament in vocational discernment. It suggests that periods of disorientation are not only normal but potentially generative parts of the faith journey. Doubt, struggle, and lament often cannot be skipped. We cannot force it. As Brueggemann notes, "The new situation is not an achievement or a working out of the dislocation but a newness that comes to us."[18] In the context of vocational discernment, this perspective encourages individuals to embrace both joyful certainty and painful questioning as integral to the process of discovering and living out one's calling. It reminds us that vocational clarity often emerges not despite our struggles, but through them, as we wrestle honestly with God and our circumstances.

Theologically, the interrelated effects of joy and lament reflect several key concepts. First, the interrelation speaks to a deep trust in God's presence. Lament, far from indicating a lack of faith, is understood as a profound expression of trust in God's ability to hear and respond to human suffering. Brueggemann argues that lament is "a bold form of faith" that "insists that the relationship with God is vigorous enough

---

[17] Walter Brueggemann, *The Message of the Psalms: A Theological Commentary* (Minneapolis: Augsburg, 1984), 138.

[18] Walter Brueggemann, "The Psalms and the Life of Faith: A Suggested Typology of Function," in *Soundings in the Theology of Psalms: Perspectives and Methods in Contemporary Scholarship*, ed. Rolf A. Jacobson (Minneapolis: Fortress Press, 2010), 5.

to bear the weight of candor."[19] This perspective challenges simplistic notions of faith that equate belief with constant positivity.

The embrace of both joy and lament fosters faith. As Brueggemann asserts in his essay "The Costly Loss of Lament," the absence of lament can lead to the development of a "false self" that suppresses real emotions and concerns. He warns that "a community of faith which negates laments soon concludes that the hard issues of justice are improper questions to pose at the throne, because the throne seems to be only a place of praise."[20] As a result, the practice of making space for both praise and lament can be seen as a pathway to spiritual growth. Brueggemann notes, "The lament-to-praise movement is not only a literary pattern, but also a movement in the life of faith and in the life of the community."[21] In this way, lament is not just an outlet for sorrow but a profound act of faith, holding open a space where truth, justice, and hope are given voice alongside gratitude and praise.

Consider the prophet Jeremiah, often called the "weeping prophet." His ministry was marked by profound lament over the state of his people and the coming judgment. Yet this very lament was an integral part of his prophetic voice and his faithfulness to his calling. I'll talk about this at length in the eighth chapter, "Storytelling," but I'm convinced that in our own vocational journeys, lament can be a form of truth-telling, a way of naming injustices and acknowledging pain that ultimately leads to deeper engagement with our work. By engaging with both joy and lament, individuals can develop a more profound sense of compassion and justice.

In this journey, vocational discernment also involves navigating the risks of failure, but, within this process, lies what Paulo Freire calls the "*inedito viavel*," or the "untested feasibility."[22] Freire uses this concept to describe the vision of something conceivably possible yet untried. It is a horizon of potential that can be reached only through courage, creativity, and attempts at something new. While the world often prioritizes clear, conventional success, reclaiming failure as a part of vocational discernment allows us to embrace these untested pathways, pushing beyond established norms and boundaries. Trying something untested will inherently lead to some failures, and that's okay! In fact, attempts at change and innovation that never fail are likely not really innovation, just adoption of something else someone already figured out.

---

19 Walter Brueggemann, "The Costly Loss of Lament," *Journal for the Study of the Old Testament* 11, no. 36 (1986): 57–71.

20 Ibid., 64.

21 Ibid.

22 Paulo Freire first discusses this in a *Pedagogy of Hope*, but a great secondary source on this is José Beltrán-Llavador, "A Praxis of Hope: Lessons from the 'Untested Feasibility' for Twenty-First-Century Education," *Globalisation, Societies and Education* (2023), https://doi.org/10.1080/14767724.2023.2209520.

Joy and Lament

Many prophetic and justice-oriented callings (like Jeremiah's) inherently challenge dominant systems, which brings a risk of perceived failure. Yet Freire's *inedito viavel* reminds us that the unexplored paths we dare to imagine and attempt are vital for transforming the world and living out our deepest callings. As we step into this unknown, we face potential setbacks and failures, but these experiences will sometimes lead to more liberating ways of being. And when they don't, they are opportunities for learning lessons of humility and perseverance. By viewing failure as a teacher, we deepen our trust in the unfolding of our vocation, learning that each step, even the difficult ones, is part of engaging the uncharted and viable possibilities of our lives.

Pursuing such uncharted possibilities often draws its energy from a profound, embodied yearning that I first talked about way back in the introduction: the Portuguese concept of *saudade*. If you recall, the Brazilian theologian Rubem Alves wrote often about *saudade* as more than simple wishfulness; it is that deep, sometimes melancholic ache for what is absent, for a future that has not yet been born but which the heart insists is possible. Failures encountered in the pursuit of such a longed-for *inedito viavel* are therefore not just setbacks; they often bring us face to face with a particular kind of lament. It is a lamentation born from the frustration of that insistent hope, an ache for the deferred arrival of a more whole and just future when our efforts to realize this vision meet resistance, rejection, or setbacks.

This lament isn't merely disappointment; it's a necessary part of the journey. It lets us acknowledge the gap between the world as it is and as it could be. Some of my greatest sorrows connect to projects I poured myself into that showed no obvious lasting results, or efforts I later realized I could have supported better. In this way, lament becomes a powerful response to failure, helping us witness the pain of unrealized possibilities while fueling our determination to continue forward.

In this light, *saudade* returns as a kind of holy discontent, a longing for a future not yet born, yet deeply sensed. It is the ache that keeps us reaching, even when the path is obscured. Not despair, but fidelity to the dream. The heart's insistent reminder that something more is possible, and must be. In the face of lament, *saudade* does not promise resolution; it promises refusal. Refusal to give up on joy, on justice, on the not-yet-visible *more* that still calls to us. But faithful longing is not the same as valorizing pain. *Saudade* may keep us tender and open, but vocation rooted in liberation demands that we name and challenge the sources of suffering, not spiritualize them.

In her recent book on vocation, Bonnie Miller-McLemore eloquently describes the burdens of vocation, noting that callings often involve "a burden or yoke that others help us bear."[23] While I affirm her insight that vocation entails struggle, I want to be

---

[23] Bonnie J. Miller-McLemore, *Follow Your Bliss and Other Lies about Calling* (New York: Oxford University Press, 2024), 14.

sure to challenge the tendency to romanticize suffering. Liberation theology calls us to resist suffering caused by injustice, focusing on dismantling unjust systems rather than merely enduring their effects. Vocation, in this sense, is a call to alleviate suffering. I think Miller-McLemore would agree, but I feel like it is important enough to say directly: While we've discussed the transformative potential of engaging with both joy and lament, this should not be misconstrued as a glorification of suffering itself.

The notion that suffering is inherently good because it leads to growth or is somehow "God's will" can be deeply problematic and potentially harmful. It is important to resist interpretations that legitimize or passively accept suffering as part of "God's plan." Such views can lead to dangerous complacency in the face of injustice and may discourage active efforts to alleviate suffering. This misinterpretation of redemptive suffering has historically been used to justify injustice and abuse, particularly against marginalized groups. Instead, we should understand that, although growth *can* occur through suffering, this does not make suffering itself good or necessary.

Although suffering can be a catalyst for growth and compassion, it is not good in itself. Suffering, especially that caused by injustice or oppression, should be confronted and alleviated, not celebrated or passively accepted. The goal of engaging with lament is not to seek out or prolong suffering, but to honestly acknowledge pain and injustice as part of the human experience and to work toward healing and transformation. Our theological framework should empower us to confront and challenge unjust systems, to actively work toward the alleviation of suffering, and to create conditions where all people can flourish. This means we should not romanticize struggle or hardship as essential to finding one's calling. Nor should we unduly celebrate "resilience" without interrogating the systems and structures that require certain people to be resilient just to survive while others can more-or-less successfully wander through life in a cloud of delicate mediocrity.

Rather, we should seek to create supportive environments that nurture growth and discovery while actively working to remove unnecessary obstacles and injustices that hinder people's ability to fully explore and live out their call. In the context of vocational discernment, this includes recognizing that, while struggles and doubts can be part of the journey, they are not prerequisites. Our goal should be to cultivate adaptability and compassion in the face of inevitable challenges, not to seek out or glorify challenge. This balanced perspective allows us to engage fully with both the joys and sorrows of our vocational paths while maintaining a commitment to justice, healing, and the alleviation of unnecessary suffering.

Theological perspectives on joy and lament offer a rich framework for understanding these emotions as integral parts of vocational discernment and ministerial formation. By embracing both, individuals and communities can engage more fully and meaningfully with their sense of calling. As Brueggemann reminds us, "The point is to emphasize that a theological understanding of lament is concerned with all aspects of life and refuses to limit faith to praise."[24] This approach fosters a deeper and more resilient faith, one that is equipped to navigate the complexities of ministry in a changing world, finding meaning and purpose in both moments of exultation and periods of struggle. The question then becomes how do we make room for those moments? How do we carve out the time for ourselves and those we accompany to make sure there are opportunities to express praise and the sharp edge of sorrow?

Fostering Space for Rejoicing and Lamentation

As we navigate the complex presence of joy and lament in our vocational journeys, it becomes evident that creating intentional spaces for both experiences is vital. This task falls not only to individuals discerning their call but also to the leaders and educators shaping ministry training programs. By fostering environments that welcome both celebration and sorrow, we can cultivate a more holistic and resilient approach to vocational discernment and ministerial formation.

Central to how I think about this endeavor is the concept of a "holding environment," a term coined by psychoanalyst D. W. Winnicott in the mid-twentieth century.[25] Winnicott developed this concept through his work with mothers and infants, observing how a nurturing, attentive caregiver creates a safe space for a child to develop and explore. In this context, a holding environment refers to the physical and emotional space provided by the mother (or primary caregiver) that allows the infant to feel secure enough to engage with the world around them. This environment is characterized by reliability, empathy, and non-intrusive support.

In the context of vocational discernment, we can extend Winnicott's concept to understand a holding environment as a space where individuals feel safe to express the full range of their experiences without fear of judgment or rejection. It is open for physical, emotional, or spiritual expression. Just as a parent provides a secure base for a child to explore the world, our communities can offer a supportive framework for exploring the joys and challenges of our calling. This environment is not about coddling or protecting individuals from all discomfort, but rather about creating a space where vulnerability is welcomed and growth is supported.

---

24 Brueggemann, "The Costly Loss of Lament," 66.

25 Winnicott talks about this in a number of places, but I'd recommend D. W. Winnicott, *The Child, the Family, and the Outside World* (Middlesex: Penguin, 1973), 86–87.

Practically speaking, creating a holding environment in vocational discernment settings involves several key elements. First, it requires consistency and reliability in relationships and structures, mirroring the dependable presence of a nurturing caregiver. This might mean regular check-ins, clear expectations, and follow-through on commitments. Second, it involves empathetic listening and validation of experiences, allowing individuals to feel truly heard and understood. Third, it necessitates a non-judgmental stance, where doubts, fears, and struggles are met with compassion rather than criticism. Finally, it requires a balance between support and challenge, providing encouragement while also gently pushing individuals toward growth and new insights. By consciously cultivating these elements, leaders in vocational formation can create spaces where individuals feel secure enough to engage deeply and honestly with their sense of calling, even when that process involves uncertainty or difficulty.

Creating such environments requires intentionality, awareness, and a commitment to holistic formation. Leaders in ministry training programs and educational institutions must critically examine how their structures and practices either encourage or inhibit the expression of joy and lament. This examination often reveals the need for a fundamental shift in approach, moving beyond traditional academic models that prioritize intellectual engagement to embrace a more integrated vision of formation. Such a shift might involve restructuring curricula to include regular reflection sessions, incorporating spiritual practices into daily routines, or reimagining assessment methods to value emotional and spiritual growth alongside academic achievement. Ideally this doesn't just happen in one "special place" where feelings are welcome but becomes a presence throughout the curriculum and culture of the organization.

The creation of holding environments in vocational discernment spaces necessitates an approach that addresses both the structural and interpersonal aspects of these communities. It's not enough to provide occasional opportunities for emotional expression if the rest of the time it is clear that those feelings are "supposed" to be kept under wraps; rather, the entire educational or formational experience must be infused with an awareness of the emotional and spiritual journey of discernment. This means training faculty and staff to recognize and respond to the subtle cues that indicate a student may be struggling or experiencing a significant breakthrough. It also involves fostering a culture that sees vulnerability as a strength, welcomes questions and doubts as part of the discernment process, and honors joy and sorrow both as valid responses to God's call.

One of the things that I think can greatly assist in this kind of environment-building is the work of establishing a trauma-sensitive culture in organizations that want to support vocational exploration. Many individuals carry experiences of trauma that can profoundly affect their relationship with their calling and with God. A trauma-sensitive approach recognizes this reality and seeks to create an environment where healing and growth can occur alongside vocational exploration. This goes beyond merely offering mental health resources; it involves a comprehensive reevaluation of institutional practices through a trauma-informed lens. This might include adapting teaching methods to accommodate diverse learning needs, creating flexible policies that recognize the nonlinear nature of healing and growth, and ensuring that all aspects of the program are designed with an awareness of the potential impact of trauma, from admissions to graduation.

By prioritizing safety, trustworthiness, choice, collaboration, and empowerment, institutions can create spaces where all individuals, regardless of their past experiences, can engage fully and meaningfully in the process of vocational discernment.[26] However, fostering spaces for joy and lament isn't without its challenges. Cultural norms and expectations can often create barriers to meaningful expression.

In some communities, there may be an unspoken pressure to maintain a facade of constant joy or spiritual strength, making it difficult for individuals to voice their doubts or sorrows. I'm thinking here of rose j. percy's work and her insistence that real damage is done when people are constantly told they need to be strong and can't miss a step. percy, instead, encourages people to find a "gentle landing," a space where vulnerability and authenticity are welcomed as essential components of healing and growth.[27] This landing is not simply about emotional release; it is about cultivating a rhythm of life that honors both resilience and rest, strength and fragility. It's about giving people permission to pause, grieve, or celebrate without judgment, creating room for wholeness rather than perfection.

Conversely, in spaces focused on social justice or addressing systemic oppression, there might be an implicit expectation of constant critique or lament, leaving little room for expressions of joy or hope. This dynamic can create an environment where celebration feels misplaced or even disloyal to the seriousness and weight of the work, fostering a culture that undervalues the sustaining power of wonder and collective rejoicing. To address these challenges, leaders can take several practical steps that create space for both joy and lament in the vocational journey. There are many that might be considered, but, here, I'll provide four.

---

26 This isn't the place to go into the details of what might constitute a "trauma-sensitive" culture, but one resource I'd recommend is Roger D. Fallot, PhD, and Maxine Harris, PhD, especially in "Creating Cultures of Trauma-Informed Care (CCTIC): A Self-Assessment and Planning Protocol," https://children.wi.gov/Documents/CCTICSelf-AssessmentandPlanningProtocol0709.pdf. In the appendix, I've also included a worksheet I offer schools to help them begin to think about "auditing" themselves in regards to their trauma-awareness.

27 This is a recurring theme in rose j. percy's work, much of which you can find at https://agentlelanding.substack.com/

> **A Practice to Consider:**
> ## Failure Fridays
>
> *Failure is not the end but a teacher, offering lessons if we're willing to receive them. When shared in community, it can transform struggle into collective wisdom and hope.*
>
> Consider starting a "Failure Friday" gathering with a small group. Each person shares a recent struggle or failure and reflects on what it revealed about their journey or calling. It would likely work best with people who value growth, honesty, and mutual support. Appreciating humor would help too! Are there people you could imagine inviting to this practice? Is there a community where this would work? Are there individuals you could bring together?
>
> At the end of each gathering, ask: "What is one thing this failure might make possible?" Consider recording key takeaways or insights over time. Patterns may emerge worth noticing.

First, leaders can model vulnerability by sharing their own experiences of celebration and sorrow in their ministerial path. This helps normalize the full range of emotions that come with discernment and ministry. Something related that I've dreamed of starting for years is what I've come to call "Failure Fridays." As I envision it, this monthly lunchtime gathering could provide a dedicated space for leaders, educators, or community members to share stories of setbacks, mistakes, and learning experiences in their vocational journeys, embracing the lament that often accompanies perceived failure while also celebrating the joy of growth and resilience. The format would be simple: one or two individuals volunteer to share a 10- or 15-minute story about a failure or challenge they've faced, followed by open discussion and reflection. The key is to create an atmosphere of openness and vulnerability, where "failure" is reframed as an opportunity for growth and learning, allowing for both sorrow and hope. Probably also laughter as we learn from mistakes and low points. This practice would serve multiple purposes: It helps destigmatize failure and doubt, provides practical lessons and insights for others, and fosters a sense of community and shared experience in both struggle and triumph. For students or those early in their vocational journey, hearing respected leaders openly discuss their struggles and joys can be incredibly validating and encouraging.

Second, leaders can create diverse opportunities for expression that honor different cultural backgrounds and personal comfort levels, allowing for both joyful proclamation and honest lamentation. This might include discrete events explicitly organized to help grow the edges of an organization's cultural norms, but it could also be structural. For example, a seminary might implement a "Vocational Formation" program that runs alongside traditional academic classes throughout the program, intentionally making room for both rejoicing and grieving. This could include weekly small group meetings, regular one-on-one check-ins with mentors, and assignments designed to foster reflection on the emotional and spiritual aspects of vocational discernment, including moments of profound joy and deep lament. By making this a core part of the curriculum, rather than an optional add-on, or a "once and done" requirement, the institution sends a clear message about the importance of holistic formation and creates a structured space for ongoing engagement with both the highs and lows of the vocational journey.

Third, leaders can implement narrative-based practices that encourage individuals to articulate and reflect on their vocational journeys. This approach recognizes the power of storytelling in shaping our understanding of vocation and creates opportunities for both individual reflection and communal sharing. We'll talk more about the power of story in the eighth chapter, but, for now, consider the practice of "vocational storytelling" sessions. In this activity, individuals from diverse backgrounds and stages of their vocational journey share their stories in a structured format.

Unlike "Failure Fridays," these sessions focus on the broader arc of one's calling, including both highs and lows, moments of exultation and periods of doubt. Storytellers might be invited to share for 20–30 minutes, guided by prompts such as "Describe a moment when you first felt called to this work," or "Share about a time when your understanding of your vocation shifted significantly." Following each story, there can be a facilitated Q&A and group reflection, allowing for communal engagement with both the joyful and sorrowful aspects of the narrative. When I do this activity with students, they regularly report it as important to their own growth. Hearing the various twists and turns of those who have gone before them helps to concretize the idea that we all learn our path by walking.

This practice helps build a rich, collective understanding of vocation as a dynamic and ongoing process, encompassing both celebration and struggle. It also provides mirrors and windows for listeners: opportunities to see aspects of their own journey reflected in others' stories and windows into different ways of experiencing and living out one's calling, including diverse expressions of joy and lament. By regularly featuring a variety of voices and calls, this practice can help expand participants' understanding of what vocation can look like in various contexts, honoring the full spectrum of emotional and spiritual experiences. Ideally, those who are exploring their own vocation would eventually be encouraged to share in this space, too, even if it is just to "try on" their sense of how things are unfolding for them. Being given a space to name how it is you experience being called can be powerful, whether that experience is one of joy, lament, or the complex interplay of both.

Fourth and finally, leaders and institutions can take seriously the collective mental and emotional health of their communities as a measure of vocational fidelity. Too often, our systems for formation and ordination treat mental health as a screening hurdle rather than a sustained commitment. Many denominations require psychological evaluations for ordination candidates, not to support their flourishing, but to ensure they won't "burn out" or cause harm. Similarly, theological schools may refer students to care when they're in crisis, but rarely consider whether the rhythms, pressures, and structures of their programs themselves contribute to that crisis. What if we flipped the script?

Imagine if accrediting bodies included the emotional and spiritual health of students, faculty, and staff as part of what earned a school renewed accreditation. Imagine if seminaries were evaluated not just by academic metrics but by the presence of joy, rest, and vitality in their community. What if denominations supported the mental health of their clergy throughout their careers, not just before ordination, seeing this not as optional pastoral care, but as a necessary component of vocational integrity?

Practically, this might mean sustained access to therapy or spiritual direction, sabbath structures built into job expectations and actually practiced when they are built in, or annual well-being reviews alongside traditional performance evaluations. It could look like institutional rituals of lament and rejoicing that acknowledge the emotional costs of ministry, or dedicated funds for healing retreats and sabbaticals. In any case, this shift would require us to rethink what we measure and to treat well-being not as an afterthought, but as a central sign of faithful formation.

As I see it, fostering spaces for rejoicing and lamentation is about creating environments where individuals can bring more of their whole selves to the process of vocational discernment. It's about recognizing that our calling encompasses not just our gifts and passions, but also our wounds and struggles. By making room for the full spectrum of human experience in our discernment processes, we open ourselves to a richer, more meaningful engagement with our vocation and with the communities we are called to serve.

Valleys and Peaks

In concluding this exploration of joy and lament in vocational discernment, I want to make sure to remember the richness that comes from embracing seemingly opposing experiences. When possible, I try to cultivate a "both/and" perspective rather than an "either/or" one. I see reflection and formation as mutually reinforcing practices that ought to be viewed in relation to each other, not split off from one another.

Likewise, my identity is tied up in my sense of communal belonging and vice versa. This interconnectedness extends to our emotional and spiritual lives, where joy and lament intertwine to create a fuller, more meaningful engagement with our calling.

The theologian Willie James Jennings has said that he looks at joy as "an act of resistance against despair and its forces."[28] This powerful perspective invites us to see joy not as a naïve denial of difficulties, but as a deliberate choice to affirm life and possibility in the face of challenges. Similarly, our capacity for lament allows us to honestly engage with pain and injustice, fueling our commitment to transformation and healing. This is important work because, left untended, this brokenness and pain can destabilize not just our sense of purpose but our felt orientation toward what is good and trustworthy. When the ground shifts beneath our commitments, we often find ourselves needing to rebuild not only our motivation but the moral scaffolding that makes purpose possible.

Attending to these emotional currents is not ancillary to vocational life. It is a vital part of staying oriented amid the turbulence of real ministry and real lives. It enables us to navigate the complexities of our calling with greater emotional intelligence and spiritual depth. By embracing a fuller spectrum of human experience, we open ourselves to a richer understanding of our vocation and the communities we serve. That being said, it is important to acknowledge that creating space for these experiences isn't straightforward. While we've discussed the importance of embracing both joy and sorrow, we must recognize that it doesn't always feel safe for people to be open about their emotions and experiences.

I'm reminded of a friend who was assigned to a mandatory "peer group" as part of her ordination process. Ideally, this group would have been a place for her to feel met and accompanied on her journey. However, after just a few required meetings, she realized that the other members weren't truly prepared to handle the depth of hurt and struggle she had experienced. She tested a few times, sharing small bits of things and even this was too much for the group. Rather than remaining grounded and present, they ended up "in their own stuff," triggered, and unable to accompany her because they had too much of their own work to do. She decided in the future she'd refrain from as much disclosure. Despite this, she had to continue attending as part of the ordination requirements. As a result, she went through the motions but never really benefited from the experience because it never felt safe for her to bring her full self to the group.

Creating spaces that truly honor both joy and lament is tricky. It involves fostering an environment where people feel safe enough to be vulnerable, while also challenging them to grow beyond their comfort zones. This is no easy task, but it's key

---

28 Jennings and Volf, "Joy and the Act of Resistance Against Despair."

for meaningful vocational discernment and formation. For those of us who mentor, accompany, and guide, it is vital that we continue to do our own self work. For those of us who are being mentored, accompanied, and guided, assess whether or not the room is ready to handle you in your fullness.

You are never obligated to share more than feels safe or appropriate. I want you to find spaces in which you can push yourself to bring as much of yourself present as possible, but make sure you curate good spaces for yourself. Trust your instincts and remember that protecting yourself is not the same as being inauthentic: You don't owe anyone anything that increases your pain, and your wounds are not something that anyone can demand you share. Your journey, your identity, and your sense of belonging are uniquely yours to share on your terms, and your call is something you should tend with care.

Questions for Reflection

1. This chapter explores psychological insights suggesting that joy can broaden our thinking and lament can build resilience. Reflecting on your own experiences in ministry, work, or personal life, have you noticed moments when either profound joy or deep lament affected your cognitive abilities, your creativity, or your capacity to persevere through challenges?

2. Walter Brueggemann's framework of orientation (stability), disorientation (crisis/lament), and new orientation (renewed hope/joy) is discussed as a cycle in the life of faith. Can you identify a period in your own life or vocational journey that mirrors these stages? What was it like to move through disorientation, and what, if anything, helped you arrive at a new orientation, perhaps with a changed perspective?

3. The chapter cautions against misinterpreting suffering as inherently redemptive, while also acknowledging its potential for transformation. In your spiritual journey or in accompanying others, how do you navigate the delicate tension between validating pain and injustice (lament) and finding pathways toward healing and growth (joy/hope) without glorifying or spiritualizing the suffering in ways that are damaging?

4. Consider the idea of a "holding environment," a space where individuals feel safe enough to express the full spectrum of their experiences, including both joys and laments. Thinking about a community you are part of, or one you might help create, what specific actions could you take or advocate for to make it a more authentic holding environment for everyone, especially those whose joys or laments are often unvoiced?

Joy and Lament 175

5. Have you ever been in a situation where you felt it wasn't safe or appropriate to share your full range of emotions, even if welcome was supposedly extended? What were the subtle (or not-so-subtle) cues that made you hesitate? Conversely, what specific elements help create an environment where you do feel truly free and safe to express both deep joy and honest lament?

    Note for those reflecting in a group: As you consider this question, please be mindful that others in your group may be feeling this way in the present moment. The aim here is shared understanding and learning, not to pressure anyone into disclosure or put them on the spot. Listen with care.

6. This chapter lifts up Willie James Jennings's idea of joy as an "act of resistance against despair" and Soong-Chan Rah's emphasis on lament as "honesty before God and each other," particularly in the face of systemic injustice. Can you think of a time when choosing joy felt like a deliberate act of resistance for you or your community? Additionally, how might the practice of communal lament be a source of power and solidarity in your context?

6

Identity and Belonging

If I didn't define myself for myself, I would be crunched into other people's fantasies for me and eaten alive.

—Audre Lorde

Community cannot for long feed on itself; it can only flourish with the coming of others from beyond, their unknown and undiscovered siblings.

—Howard Thurman

Having explored in the preceding chapter how joy and lament shape our vocational journeys, we now turn to the question of who we understand ourselves to be as we navigate these emotional landscapes. Responses to both celebration and sorrow are shaped by our sense of identity and the communities (or the lack thereof) that surround us. For those with supportive communities, this influence can be affirming. For others, the absence or harm caused by communities can complicate these emotional landscapes. The ways we define ourselves (or allow others to define us) shape how we experience and express both delight and despair in our vocational journeys.

These definitions also shape the interior frameworks through which we interpret those experiences, shaping what feels permissible to express, how we interpret what is right, and whether we feel free to act on what we discern. When our communities align with our inner convictions, we may feel grounded. But when they don't, we may feel fragmented, as if the price of inclusion is ignoring the inner voice that whispers "something isn't right." This tension between a sense of inner truth and external acceptance is not just emotional; it's vocational and moral, shaping how we understand who we are and where we fit.

In this chapter, I use "identity" to mean more than a fixed category. It includes the social locations we occupy, our race, gender, class, ability, sexuality, and more, but also the spiritual commitments that ground us and the vocational roles we inhabit. People develop ministerial identities too, ways of living into the expectations, responsibilities, burdens, joys, and sorrows that come with a life of service. These aspects of identity are not static or easily sorted; they are lived, layered, and always in motion. Our identities are shaped by culture, community, trauma, resistance, and hope. They are formed and re-formed in response to the people we journey with and the pressures we navigate. Holding space for this complexity allows us to see identity not as something to be definitively "discovered," but as something unfolding over time. This way of understanding invites us to attend more closely to the tensions that arise when who we are internally does not align with how we are perceived or permitted to act externally.

The interplay between joy and lament I talked about last chapter finds a parallel in the relationship between identity and belonging in this one. Just as reflection and formation ideally work together to foster growth and understanding, identity and belonging are deeply interconnected, each informing and reshaping the other. Our identity gradually develops into something uniquely ours as it is shaped by time and attention, nourished by experience and belief. Identity shapes the spaces we are drawn to, the roles we assume, and the ways we engage. As Howard Thurman suggests, belonging itself holds a formative power, calling us into a dynamic relationship with others and urging our communities to expand through our presence.

The communities we inhabit, the traditions we inherit, and the relationships we nurture become woven into our evolving sense of self. But, as Thurman warns, communities risk stagnation when they resist the presence of "unknown and undiscovered siblings" and the uncomfortable truths they carry.[1] When belonging demands silence or the preservation of comfort, both individuals and collectives are diminished. Growth, for us and for our communities, depends on our willingness to face what is unfinished, unhealed, and still unfolding.

At the same time, Audre Lorde cautions that the relationship between identity and belonging can become fraught. A strong sense of identity, while grounding, may sometimes hinder our ability to belong, especially when communities expect us to fit within predefined molds. In spaces that don't fully accept or comprehend all facets of who we are, the pressure to conform can risk "crunching us into other people's

---

1 Howard Thurman, *The Search for Common Ground* (Chicago: Henry Regnery, 1971), 104.

fantasies," leading us to obscure or suppress vital aspects of ourselves.[2] Conversely, a deep yearning for belonging can prompt us to alter or diminish parts of our identity to gain acceptance, compromising the integrity and richness of our evolving selfhood. The tension between remaining faithful and growing over time becomes a tortuous journey, one that requires careful discernment and, sometimes, painful decisions.

More than a decade ago, I sat in a room of Quakers discerning whether to approve a "minute" (a kind of public statement) repudiating the "Doctrine of Discovery."[3] The Doctrine, originating in fifteenth-century Catholic proclamations, gave European Christian powers theological and legal justification to claim lands inhabited by non-Christian peoples. Its logic helped fuel colonization and genocide across the globe and continues to shape US property law today. Many Christian denominations, including parts of the Religious Society of Friends, have worked in recent years to publicly reject its legacy.

I was grateful we were addressing it at all. Naming the long-standing theological scaffolding of empire is challenging. But I also felt uneasy. The language in the minute was strong, even beautiful. And yet I worried: Would it amount to little more than words? What does it mean to repudiate a doctrine in theory while still holding its benefits in practice? What does it mean to call for a "just peace" while remaining on stolen land?

I hesitated. The process had been tender, hard-won. Raising a concern might be seen as undermining unity or momentum. I didn't have an alternative proposal. But I couldn't stay silent. I needed to say that this could not be the endpoint, that even as we disavowed the Doctrine on paper, we continued to benefit from the structures it set in motion. Across the nation, there are meetinghouses standing on land taken from Indigenous peoples. Our institutions were still funded by inherited wealth and systems that disproportionately advantage white settlers. We were not actively working to return land, redistribute resources, or repair the theological harm done in the name of Christ. I was concerned that, without naming those realities, and without committing to forms of repair that addressed concrete material conditions, our statement risked becoming more about our own self-congratulation than about justice.

So, I spoke. Gently, but clearly. I named my concern that, without tangible repair, our repudiation could feel hollow, that we might be more invested in appearing just than in acting justly. I was annoyed with myself that I didn't have anything better

---

2 Audre Lorde, "Learning from the '60s," in *Sister Outsider: Essays and Speeches* (Berkeley, CA: Crossing Press, 1984), 137.

3 New York Yearly Meeting, "Minute on the Doctrine of Discovery," approved July 25, 2012, Silver Bay, New York, https://www.nyym.org/sites/default/files/Minute_Doctrine_of_Discovery.pdf.

Identity and Belonging

to offer. I didn't want to stall the conversation or derail the fragile momentum we'd built. But silence wasn't an option either. Some Friends were made uncomfortable. Others voiced their agreement. The conversation grew more layered, more honest. And then, after some silence, we approved the statement. It was not enough, but it was something. A beginning, not a conclusion. And in that moment, I stayed, not because everything had been resolved, but because something had been risked, and something had shifted.

Or, at least, that was the story I wanted to tell myself. I didn't realize until years later, but that moment taught me something vocationally: Integrity sometimes means speaking up not to offer solutions, but simply to name the gap between our values and our lives. It was a moment of tension between identity and belonging, a test of whether I could remain in community without silencing something vital in myself.

Our vocation is intimately tied to both identity and belonging, as it arises not only from our personal relationship with God but also from our interaction with the communities that recognize, nurture, or perhaps misunderstand our calling. In discerning and embodying our vocation, we are often challenged to navigate this tension, to define ourselves as Lorde suggests. And yet, as Thurman envisions, we also need to reach beyond the boundaries of self, allowing both our identity and our communities to grow. This journey may require us to expand our understanding of self, to find new forms of community, or to transform the communities we are already part of, bringing a fuller self into the world and embracing the richness that comes when identities and communities flourish together.

A Fragmented Framework

I have found that my own reflection on identity and belonging has been greatly aided by recognizing the fragmented nature of my human perception and understanding. Even though I feel like I have a good sense of myself and the communities of which I am a part, it is foolish to think I have the whole scenario comprehended. As Paul reminds us in 1 Corinthians 13:12, "For now we see only a reflection, as in a mirror." If all things are possible with God, then it is always the case that my picture of self and society is limited. Partly, this is a function of being human and the fact that we can't hold it all. But it can also be because we resist acknowledging this reality, choosing instead to obscure certain truths from ourselves, truths that, if confronted, might make us uncomfortable.

This is particularly the case for those engaged in lay ministry, where the lines between "ministry" and "everyday life" often blur. A parent leading youth activities, a workplace chaplain, or a community organizer might not always recognize how their seemingly ordinary actions constitute meaningful ministry. Yet these moments of service, while perhaps less formal than traditional ministry roles, are no less significant in God's work. Sometimes, the most profound ministry happens in these interstitial spaces where life and service naturally merge.

A fragmented understanding, as discussed in the fourth chapter, "Systems Thinking," can offer a broader perspective on identity and belonging as part of larger, complex social systems. For some, stepping back to view these forces is a helpful practice. For others directly affected by systemic inequities, this perspective might emerge from lived experience as well as analytical distance. It isn't always a joyful thing, however. There are definitely times when I've gotten an inkling that there might be more to a story but didn't bother learning the details because I had a sense it could complicate my life. That God might be calling me to something more.

For example, I'm thinking of the unsettling reality behind cell phone production. Reports have shown that cobalt mining for smartphone batteries often involves child labor in hazardous conditions, particularly in the Democratic Republic of Congo, where unethical practices disproportionately harm vulnerable populations.[4] Workers in manufacturing plants, often in countries like China and Vietnam, face poor working conditions, long hours, and exposure to harmful chemicals. There are even allegations of forced labor in some parts of the supply chain. Yet despite knowing this, I still use a smartphone daily, benefiting from these inequities down the line in a "sanitized way." It would be easier to ignore this knowledge, to pretend I don't know the true cost of my convenience. But hiding from such truths doesn't align with my own supposed commitment to learning and ethical living.

This tension mirrors a broader challenge in how we navigate identity and belonging in an interconnected world. As much as it might sting, I must acknowledge that my understanding of even this issue is partial. This isn't limited to child labor or smartphone production. It extends to countless ways that I, simply by being a resident of the United States of America, am implicated in global inequities. For instance, my country, with less than 5 percent of the global population, consumes 16 percent of the world's energy.[5] Functionally, this means that I (and most people I know) use far more than our fair share of resources, perpetuating a system where many are left with far less than they need. This stark disparity often prompts conflicting emotions: guilt over complicity, frustration at the scale of systemic inequity, and, for some, a lived urgency born of direct harm to their communities.

---

[4] Amnesty International, "Is My Phone Powered by Child Labour?" Amnesty International online (2016), https://www.amnesty.org/en/latest/campaigns/2016/06/drc-cobalt-child-labour/.

[5] Center for Sustainable Systems, "US Energy System Factsheet," Pub. No. CSS03-11, University of Michigan (2023).

In the context of identity and belonging, these realities reveal how our collective participation in unjust systems shapes our external choices as well as our sense of self and our place in the world. The choices we make, and the systems that constrain those choices, both reflect and influence who we understand ourselves to be. For some, these realizations provoke deep discomfort, a sense of dissonance between their values and their actions. This discomfort, Paulo Freire might suggest, is the beginning of *conscientização*, the awakening of critical consciousness that allows us to see the contradictions in our world and our place within them.[6]

Once this critical awareness takes root, the once-accepted "normality" of these contradictions can become intolerable, compelling individuals to question their own complicity or passivity and to seek ways to act differently. That tension may prompt a reimagining of their role in the world and a deeper commitment to community and justice. Engaging with this discomfort is necessary; it challenges us to critically examine our identities and the systems we belong to while pushing us toward more intentional and ethical ways of being.

At the same time, I've realized that individual guilt and small-scale lifestyle changes alone are insufficient responses to these systemic issues. Instead, addressing such fragmentation requires us to look at the interconnected systems of economics, culture, and policy that perpetuate inequity. It calls for collective action and a rethinking of belonging, not as a passive acceptance of the status quo, but as an active commitment to fostering more equitable communities. By engaging in these collective efforts, I've found a way to reconcile, even partially, the tensions between my actions and my ideals. Whether local groups, professional networks, or global movements, in these communal spaces, I find strength, accountability, and the resources to confront challenging realities.

This fragmented understanding reminds me that identity and belonging are never static. Just as I must wrestle with these systemic inequities and their implications for my life, I must also remain open to the possibility of transformation, both within myself and the communities I inhabit. This work is deeply tied to vocational discernment, as it involves the ongoing negotiation of who I am, where I belong, and how I am called to act in the world. As with many things, I'm looking for a healthy equilibrium.

I know there will be times when I must (uncomfortably) have my understanding of things broadened, realizing that I have been complicit in large systems of inequity. There also have to be moments where I do not fixate on that, for fear of paralysis, instead turning to seek systemic understanding, and finding strength in community, asking for guidance as to how we can all proceed in ways that are more just and

---

6 Regina Cortina and Marcella Winter, "Paulo Freire's Pedagogy of Liberation," *Current Issues in Comparative Education* 23, no. 2 (2021): 8–19.

connected to Earth and others. It is also a good idea to remember that, even if they are dwarfed in scale by other dynamics, there are likely at least *some* positive things that have happened because of my life that I don't have the slightest clue about.

We often have glimpses of uncomfortable realities about ourselves and our place in the world, yet we may choose to look away. Simultaneously, there are likely positive impacts of our existence that we're equally unaware of. As Paul reminds us, we know only in part. The incompleteness of my understanding and the ongoing nature of this struggle have become central to how I approach questions of identity, belonging, and vocation. This isn't just the work of clergy, but of any who want to center spirituality in their lives. And yet even that language ("wanting" to center spirituality) can miss the mark: For many, the spiritual is not a chosen orientation but what is left when everything else is stripped away, or what we hold onto when nothing else makes sense. In seeking to hold the tensions between complicity and creativity, brokenness and belonging, I began looking for theological visions shaped not by dominance but by defiance.

I began thinking more deeply about this after hearing Brazilian theologian Cleusa Caldeira speak.[7] In her lecture, she introduced the framework of "theoquilombism," a theological lens rooted in the history and legacy of *quilombos*, communities formed by those who escaped slavery in Brazil. I had heard of *quilombos* before, but not in the way she described them: as spaces of theological imagination, not just historical resistance. These were not only sites of refuge, but of invention: places where freedom was practiced in ways that defied the logics of colonial empire and made new forms of life possible.

Crucially, *quilombos* were first and foremost places of safety and liberation for formerly enslaved people. They were Black communities rooted in shared struggle and the urgency of survival. Only later did some of these communities extend themselves to others who were also seeking freedom: Indigenous people, poor whites, and those fleeing conscription or debt.[8] This widening was not the erasure of Black leadership or experience, but an extension of Black-led visions of liberation. That distinction matters.

As a white scholar and minister shaped by my own cultural and theological inheritances, I feel the need to approach Caldeira's vision of *theoquilombism* with deep attentiveness and care. It would be a mistake to take up the language of *quilombos* simply as a metaphor for my own vocational or spiritual longings without honoring the Black freedom traditions that gave rise to them. The temptation to romanticize

---

7 Cleusa Caldeira, "Theoquilombism and the Epistemologies of Blackness," Lecture at Boston College's Clough School of Theology and Ministry (March 11, 2025).

8 Stuart B. Schwartz, *Slaves, Peasants, and Rebels: Reconsidering Brazilian Slavery* (Urbana-Champaign: University of Illinois Press, 1992), 125.

or commodify these spaces must be resisted. Caldeira writes, "From the outset of colonialism in the fifteenth century, the quilombo appeared as a form of Afro-Brazilian resistance that was ethical, political, economic, cultural, and spiritual.... The quilombo places a limit on the rhythm of colonial genocide, giving rise to the possibility of a new way of living one's life."[9] Her words are not mine to domesticate, but they do call me to attend: to notice the moral and spiritual tempo of empire, and to wonder what it means to resist that rhythm in how I live, discern, and accompany others.

And yet even from this position I am moved by the invitation that Caldeira offers to see in the *quilombo* a site of theo-political imagination, a lived theology of collective dignity, ancestral wisdom, and resistant joy. Forged in flight and refusal, their foundations were not abstract ideals but the embodied wisdom of Black people choosing one another in defiance of domination. Choosing life and exploring what it means to live as one who has heard the good news that freedom is possible.

I'm reminded that the word gospel (*euangelion*) was not neutral in Jesus's time. It echoed imperial proclamations of Caesar's reign. Jesus's choice to use it for announcing the Kingdom of God was itself an act of subversion, a reappropriation of a term of oppression as one of liberation.[10] This, too, is the work of *quilombo* theology: reclaiming language, space, and life itself as acts of defiance against empire.

As Caldeira has it, "The *quilombo* is an alternative society to the hegemonic, slave, and capitalist society.... The Quilombolas lived in peace, in a kind of radical fraternity."[11] These are the "individuals who, in such problematic situations, take the initiative to transform themselves into a world of life in fullness."[12] In this framing of John 10:10, fullness is not only a theological promise but a historical and communal task, something to be built and enacted, particularly in resistance to systems of injustice. It is not a distant reward, but an embodied possibility grounded in ancestral memory, communal life, and counter-colonial imagination.

As a metaphor, the *quilombo* invites us to consider vocation not merely as a path discerned within dominant culture, but as something that might require a step outside it, a fugitive discernment that refuses to conform to the moral timelines or vocational shapes sanctioned by structures built by unjust uses of power. These communities complicate our ideas of success, identity, and even time itself. They remind us that

---

9 Cleusa Caldeira, "Theology of the Quilombo: Afro-Brazilian Spiritual Resistance," *Concilium* 2020, no. 1 (2020): 72

10 Rowland Onyenali, "The Markan Proskuneo (Mark 5:6; 15:19) as Anti-Roman Motif in Mark's Gospel," *Biblical Theology Bulletin* 52, no. 2 (2022): 77–87, https://doi.org/10.1177/01461079211027703.

11 Caldeira, "Theoquilombism and the Epistemologies of Blackness." Translation mine.

12 Ibid.

belonging can be deliberate, chosen, and resistant, not just inherited, imposed, or presumed. What if discernment sometimes begins in exile, in the edges, in the wild, in the company of others who have also fled? The theology of the *quilombo* is not only one of escape, but of refusal, renewal, and life built into a fullness starting at the edge.

This kind of countercultural, ancestral belonging, forged in resistance and mutual care, resonates deeply with Willie James Jennings's challenge to the ways whiteness has shaped dominant visions of formation and vocation. Jennings invites us to confront how modern theological education and, by extension, much of our vocational imagination, has been structured around a white, self-sufficient ideal: the autonomous man who masters knowledge, exerts control, and possesses clarity of purpose. Against this, he offers a vision of formation grounded not in control but in communion, not in mastery but in shared vulnerability.

Here, the image of the *quilombo* lingers. These communities were fragments: not of what empire cast aside, but of what empire sought to *consume*. Black bodies, Black labor, Black wisdom. Empire wanted to extract these for its own gain, without acknowledging the fullness of life in return. *Quilombos* emerged from that violence as living refusals, made from what was seized and broken. They were not complete systems or polished utopias. They were provisional, stitched together from rupture and memory, pain and persistence. And still, they held. They sang. They made space for dignity when the world refused it.

This vision challenges vocational theology that has been shaped by ideals of coherence and completion. What if vocation is not the path to a singular, integrated self, but the practice of becoming faithful within the fragments? What if discerning one's call is less about discovering a fixed role and more about learning to live well in the wake of dislocation? To create, to convene, to hold space, even when the pieces don't fit neatly together? To find a space with others seeking the fullness of life?

For those of us who have been centered by dominant systems, vocational discernment requires deep listening, accountability, and a refusal to extract. It asks us to let go of the need to master or explain, and instead to be shaped by traditions of resistance that are not ours to own, but from which we can still learn how to live more justly. And for those of us who have been marginalized or silenced by these same systems, vocation often begins not with freedom but with constraint. Not with clarity, but with the work of surviving and remembering. For some, freedom comes only after a successful flight and survival.

For *all* of us, it might mean building a shared, provisional way of life forged in flight and refusal. A way of being where vocation is not about arrival or achievement, but about practicing freedom together, even in the shadow of what was built to use us up and profit from our life and labor. If vocation is to mean anything in the face of all

Identity and Belonging

that seeks to consume us, how might we begin practicing freedom together? Where are the spaces we can find in which life can be practiced in the fullness of freedom?

This is the kind of question that Willie James Jennings helps us hold. His work offers a theological grammar for fragmentation, not as failure, but as a truth-telling condition of life under empire, and as a site for the Spirit's work. He helps us name the brokenness not as something to be hidden or resolved, but as something to be inhabited with care, with courage, and with others.

Jennings offers a way to grapple with the complex, often uncomfortable realities that shape our identities and sense of belonging. By examining three types of "fragments," he says we can begin to piece together a more comprehensive, if still never complete, understanding of ourselves, our world, and how we are called to live in it. This approach invites us to engage with more awareness of our fragmented realities, uncomfortable truths and all, as we seek to discern our place and purpose in the world. In his book *After Whiteness: An Education in Belonging*, Jennings offers a framework that can help us navigate this fragmentary nature of human understanding.

By framing our knowledge and identities as fragments, Jennings invites us to recognize the incompleteness and brokenness that characterize our lives and our world. This perspective acknowledges the complex nature of our identities, highlighting the historical and social forces that shape us. It challenges the illusion of completeness in theological education and vocational discernment, reminding us of the inherent limitations and ongoing nature of our growth. The fragment metaphor also opens up possibilities for reconstruction, suggesting the potential for creative reassembly in our vocational journeys. This is particularly relevant as we piece together various aspects of our experiences and callings.

Jennings identifies three types of fragments: fragments of faith, colonial fragments, and commodity fragments. His framework provides language to discuss how these different forms of power shape our identities, experiences of belonging, and sense of calling. These fragments allow us to see how historical forces, theological traditions, and economic systems have influenced both our personal and collective stories. By naming and examining these fragments, we gain tools to navigate the complexities of our identities and callings, particularly in contexts shaped by histories of colonization, commodification, and fragmented faith traditions. This framework invites us to critically engage with the forces that have shaped our lives while also offering a way to reclaim and reimagine these fragments as part of a meaningful vocation.

Jennings describes fragments of faith as "the words of Jesus, the words of the prophets, the stories of Israel, the lives of so many who have called themselves Christian through the centuries.... Everything is in slices and slivers, pieces and shards."[13] These

---

13 Willie James Jennings, *After Whiteness: An Education in Belonging* (Grand Rapids, MI:

are the elements of our spiritual heritage and religious experiences that inform our understanding of the divine and our place in the world. In the context of vocational discernment, these fragments provide the connective tissue to tradition, the lenses through which we interpret our spiritual growth and understanding of calling. They might include scripture passages that resonate deeply with us, religious practices that ground us, or theological concepts that shape our worldview.

Jennings elaborates on the fragments of faith, emphasizing their incomplete and scattered nature. He writes, "We have no whole here—no whole picture of ancient Israel, or the prophets, or their families, or Jesus, or his family, or early, middle, or late Christians, or the entirety of their thinking, no full uncovering of their desires, angers, frustrations, hopes, and dreams."[14] This incompleteness is not a flaw, but a fundamental reality of our spiritual inheritance. In the context of vocational discernment, this fragmentary nature of our faith tradition invites us into a dynamic engagement with these pieces. We are called not just to receive these fragments passively, but to actively work with them, piecing them together in ways that speak to our present realities and future callings. This process of working with fragments becomes a central part of our spiritual formation, challenging us to remain open to new insights and interpretations as we seek to understand our place in the ongoing story of faith.

This work with fragments of faith, as Jennings suggests, is not merely an intellectual exercise but a deeply spiritual and communal practice. He emphasizes that "God works with these fragments, moving in the spaces between them to form communion with us. The fragments facilitate communion."[15] This perspective invites us to see the gaps and inconsistencies in our understanding as spaces where divine encounter and new insights can occur rather than as obstacles. However, Jennings also warns that our engagement with these faith fragments can be distorted by other forces.

He notes that "too much theological education, however, takes the fragments of faith, aligns them with colonialist aspiration, and invites us to compositions that drain life."[16] This caution leads us to consider how our interpretation and use of faith fragments might be influenced by historical and cultural forces beyond our immediate awareness. It challenges us to examine critically how we piece together our spiritual understandings and how these constructions might be shaped by or serve colonial legacies. This recognition sets the stage for our exploration of what Jennings terms "colonial fragments," which deeply intertwine with and often distort our engagement with fragments of faith.

William B. Eerdmans, 2020), 32.

14 Ibid.
15 Ibid., 34.
16 Ibid., 37.

Jennings describes colonial fragments as "life formed in fragment, in memory of loss and in loss of memory where worlds were shattered into pieces: land and animals taken; practice and rituals, dance and songs, ancient word and inherited dream, thoughts and prayers existing only in slice and sliver, piece and shard."[17] These fragments represent the profound disruption and fragmentation caused by colonialism, affecting not just material realities but the very fabric of cultural and spiritual life. In the context of vocational discernment, these colonial fragments often manifest as unresolved tensions, gaps in cultural knowledge, or internalized narratives of inferiority or superiority that shape our understanding of our place in the world and our potential callings.

Jennings emphasizes the pervasive nature of these colonial fragments, noting that "many of us work in fragments, trying to tie together, hold together, the witness of our peoples."[18] Piecing together a coherent sense of identity and belonging from colonial fragments is a collective work, often spanning generations, that includes yet surpasses any singular personal endeavor. He illustrates this with an example: "I knew an African ethnomusicologist who told me he could identify and match most of the rhythms of African American music with their originating homes among various peoples on the African continent."[19] This process of reclaiming and reconnecting cultural elements is a crucial part of healing from colonial fragmentation and can deeply inform one's sense of vocation, particularly for those from historically colonized communities. However, Jennings also warns of the dangers of oversimplifying this process of reclamation, cautioning against flattening the complexity of cultural recovery into a romanticized or static narrative.

Wrestling with these colonial fragments can be particularly painful for Christians who realize that their ancestors became Christian through processes of colonization or enslavement. It's a hard truth, loving one's faith and also grappling with how it was imposed upon one's ancestors. Yet this reckoning is worth undertaking because the wake of Christian conquest has affected most people, including not just people of color but also my own Irish and northern European ancestors. The difference lies in how those consequences have played out.

While colonization and conquest led to loss, displacement, and violence for many Indigenous and African peoples, the integration of Christianity among my ancestors often involved a transformation of existing traditions without the same scale of systemic dispossession. That is, while it is true that pre-Christian European

---

17 Ibid., 35.
18 Ibid.
19 Ibid.

spiritualities were often suppressed or subsumed, and that this process was coercive at times, Christianity's spread into Europe did not typically entail the wholesale stripping of land, language, and lifeways that characterized colonial Christianization in other parts of the world. Understanding these varied legacies helps illuminate the shared yet uneven impact of Christian expansion, offering a way to reflect deeply on what it means to hold faith alongside histories of coercion and conquest.

In theological education and many colonially influenced faith traditions, colonial fragments often manifest as Eurocentric theological perspectives, the marginalization of non-Western voices, or assumptions about what constitutes "legitimate" forms of ministry or leadership. For instance, a student from a formerly colonized country might struggle to integrate their Indigenous spiritual practices with Western theological education, experiencing a fragmentation of their spiritual identity.

Recognizing and critically engaging with these colonial fragments is crucial for developing a more informed and connected sense of call. A part of that, says Jennings, is recognizing that "the history of modern colonialism made knowing a thing and owning a thing two sides of the same coin, and examining a thing and producing a thing two sides of a related coin."[20] He argues that this "commodity fragmentation" has deeply influenced Western education, making the acquisition and control of knowledge synonymous with ownership and power.

Jennings explains that this commodification extends beyond material goods to encompass ideas, cultures, and even identities.

> To know a thing is to possess a thing ... is to sell a thing ... is to have the power to discard a thing and then find a thing and resell that thing or give that thing away or have that thing stolen (it was stolen from the beginning) that was not a thing to begin with but was my life.[21]

This powerful statement underscores how commodity fragmentation can lead to a fragmented sense of self, where our worth is determined by our productivity or market value rather than our inherent dignity as human beings. In the context of vocational discernment, this can lead to a distorted understanding of calling, where vocation is seen primarily through the lens of economic value, or social power, rather than as a meaningful contribution or personal fulfillment.

Jennings argues that recognizing and resisting these commodity fragments is crucial for meaningful vocational discernment and spiritual formation. He states, "Education is always education in commodities. This is now inescapable. The lives

---

20 Ibid., 41.
21 Ibid.

of peoples have been shattered into pieces and have been shaped for intellectual exchange."[22] However, he also suggests that, while we cannot entirely escape this reality, we can work against its deepest effects, which turn us into "intellectual merchants untouched by the fragments we touch."[23] This resistance involves cultivating a deeper understanding of vocation that goes beyond economic value, recognizing the inherent worth of all people and cultures, and seeking ways to use our skills and knowledge in service of community and justice rather than for mere personal gain or market demands. It also means resisting calls to change ourselves to match systems that do not value us.

This pressure to conform to dominant norms for the sake of "exchange" within academic or institutional systems can lead to profound internal fragmentation, forcing a painful split between one's authentic voice and the demands of assimilation. Theologian Lakisha Lockhart recounts a stark experience from her doctoral work where, after presenting written work grounded in Womanist thought and centering Black and Brown theologians, she was advised by a professor to "just write more 'Anglo-Saxon' so people can understand."[24] This counsel, demanding she adopt a voice and perspective fundamentally not her own, provoked a period of intense self-doubt and paralysis. She describes the aftermath:

> This exchange tore me apart—to pieces.... Internally I was a mess, my body and my mind were literally at odds. My mind knew the literature and what to write, but my body did too. My body wanted me to write in my voice ... but my mind kept telling me that clearly my voice was not good enough because it was not "Anglo-Saxon" enough.[25]

As a survival strategy, prompted by another Black woman scholar, she resorted to writing two versions: one for herself, one for the institution. Lockhart's experience powerfully illustrates how colonial and commodity fragments intersect in educational settings, shaping not only what knowledge is valued but how it must be presented, often at great personal cost to those forced to conform. It challenges me to reimagine our educational and vocational journeys not as processes of acquiring marketable skills, but as opportunities for deeper engagement with the world and our place in it.

---

22 Ibid., 42.
23 Ibid.
24 Lakisha R. Lockhart-Rusch, "Toward a Theopoetic Wholeness," in *Theopoetics in Color: Embodied, Listening, and Liberating Methodologies*, ed. Lakisha R. Lockhart-Rusch and Oluwatomisin Olayinka Oredein (Chicago: William B. Eerdmans, 2024), 45.
25 Ibid.

Jennings's framework of faith, colonial, and commodity fragments offers a powerful lens through which to examine our fragmented identities and experiences. By recognizing these different types of fragments, we can begin to understand the complex interplay of spiritual heritage, historical forces, and economic systems that shape our sense of self and our place in the world. This framework challenges us to engage critically with our inherited traditions, confront the legacies of colonialism, and resist the commodification of our identities and vocations.

We aren't called to deeper formation so that we might become a more impressive specimen of ministry-in-action, nor are we attempting to study and learn for the sake of ultimate mastery. Instead, our journey of formation calls us toward a deeper commitment that shapes us for a life of service and solidarity rather than accolade. Jennings's framework encourages us to recognize that our identities are continually formed in response to forces both spiritual and societal, and that growth emerges not from domination or perfection, but from a willingness to confront and transform the fragments within us. That process must begin with recognizing and naming some of what it is we carry.

Rather than imagining the human person as a neatly contained, fully coherent self, I lean into a more complex view: one that understands us as deeply shaped by relationships, history, and systems. In the fourth chapter, we looked at Ubuntu and its reminder that we become ourselves through others. We also traced how systems thinking and Walter Wink's language of the Powers help us see the invisible forces that shape our lives. Taken together, these threads and Jennings's insights on fragments offer an understanding of humanity that challenges the individualistic assumptions often baked into vocational language. If we are formed in and through our entanglements, then our callings can't just be about uncovering some buried, private self. They arise in the midst of our connection with other people, with power, with memory, with land, in context, and always with an eye toward the forces that bind and break. A liberation theology of vocation, then, must take all this seriously: the beauty and burden of our connections, the ways we're fragmented, and the justice we long for together.

The recognition of our fragmented selves raises important questions: How do we navigate the tensions between different aspects of our identities? How do we build a sense of belonging when our experiences are shaped by disparate and often conflicting forces? And how do we discern our callings in a world where our understanding is always partial and our identities are continually being shaped and reshaped? In the next section, we'll explore the challenges this fragmentation presents, as well as the opportunities it offers for growth, connection, and meaningful discernment. By grappling with the impact of fragmentation, we can begin to piece together a broader understanding of ourselves and our callings, one that honors the complexity of our experiences and the richness of our diverse heritages.

> **A Practice to Consider:**
> ## A Fragment Inventory
>
> *Our identities are composed of fragments that often seem disjointed. Naming and honoring these pieces helps us embrace the complexity of who we are and the stories we carry.*
>
> 1. Reflect on Your Fragments: Consider the spiritual, cultural, and personal elements that feel distinct in your life.
> 2. Write and Pin: Write each fragment on a small, torn piece of paper and pin them on a board or wall, creating a snapshot of your complex identity.
> 3. Add as Needed: Revisit your display over time, adding new fragments as they arise.
> 4. Reflect: These pieces don't need to all add up to some grand vision. Tensions can exist, grow, or lessen. As the pieces are added or removed, what do you notice?

The Impact of Fragmentation on Identity and Belonging

The recognition of our fragmented identities challenges the notion of a singular, cohesive self. This perspective invites us to consider identity as a mosaic rather than a monolith, as composed of diverse experiences, cultural influences, and personal narratives. If you ever think you've found a monolith, rough it up: We all contain multitudes.

Each fragment represents a facet of our being, our religious upbringing, cultural heritage, educational background, and lived experiences. These fragments don't always fit together seamlessly; they may contradict or compete with one another. For instance, the values instilled by one's family might clash with those acquired through education or professional experiences. This complexity reveals the dynamic nature of identity formation, where we are constantly negotiating and renegotiating our sense of self in response to new experiences and changing contexts.

This negotiation is, in essence, the ongoing work of our Moral Orienting System, striving for coherence when its core components (our values, beliefs, behaviors, and relationships) are pulled in different directions by these fragments. The internal tensions arising from this fragmentation can be a source of growth and creativity, pushing us to develop a more nuanced understanding of ourselves and our place in the world.

For those engaged in vocational discernment, this fragmented reality offers both liberation and challenge. Like the adaptive spirit that we will explore in the seventh chapter, on accompaniment, this fragmented reality invites us to approach our vocation with humility and malleability, honoring the diversity within ourselves and our communities. It frees us from the often paralyzing search for a single, perfect calling that encompasses all aspects of our being. Instead, it opens up the possibility of a complex vocation that honors the diversity of our gifts, passions, and experiences. This perspective allows for a more fluid and evolving understanding of calling that can adapt and grow as we navigate different life stages and contexts. For example, a person might find that their vocation includes elements of teaching, advocacy, and artistic expression, rather than fitting neatly into a single professional category. This liberation can be particularly powerful for those who have felt constrained by narrow definitions of success or purpose. However, it also requires a greater tolerance for ambiguity and a willingness to embrace the ongoing process of discernment rather than seeking a once-and-for-all answer.

The fragmentation of identity, while offering richness and complexity, can also lead to feelings of disconnection or rootlessness. When our sense of self is composed of disparate elements, it can be challenging to find a coherent narrative that ties these pieces together. This challenge is particularly acute for individuals who straddle multiple cultural worlds or whose life experiences don't align neatly with dominant social narratives. For instance, second-generation immigrants might struggle to reconcile their parents' cultural values with those of their adopted country, feeling not fully at home in either context. Similarly, individuals whose personal journeys have led them away from their childhood faith traditions might find it difficult to locate spiritual communities that honor both their religious heritage and their evolved beliefs. This sense of being "in-between" can be isolating, making it hard to find spaces of meaningful belonging. However, it also holds the potential for creating new forms of community that embrace complexity and hybridity.

I was first introduced to the Nahuatl word *nepantla* by the Tejana poet Carolina Hinojosa, who describes it as a state of "in-betweenness," a liminal space where identities, worlds, and traditions intersect.[26] In *nepantla*, this intersection isn't a problem to be solved. It is, instead, a creative and generative space where complexity is celebrated. This concept resonates deeply with the challenges of fragmentation and belonging, offering a framework for reimagining identity as an ongoing process of negotiation and creation. Rather than exile, the "in-between" is the fertile ground of our edge spaces that is perfect for forging new paths and relationships. In the context of ministerial formation, recognizing fragmentation and hybridity necessitates a more nuanced and flexible approach to pastoral identity.

Rather than adhering to a one-size-fits-all model of ministry, this perspective encourages the development of diverse and contextually responsive forms of spiritual

---

[26] Carolina Hinojosa-Cisneros, *Becoming Coztōtōtl* (McAllen, TX: FlowerSong Books, 2019).

Identity and Belonging

leadership. It might involve integrating traditional theological training with Indigenous spiritual practices, blending contemplative traditions with social justice activism, or finding ways to honor both religious commitments and secular professional expertise. For example, a minister working in a multicultural urban context might draw on liberation theology, mindfulness practices, and community organizing principles to create a ministry that resonates with their community. This approach to ministerial formation requires greater creativity and adaptability, but it also holds the potential for more meaningful and influential spiritual leadership that speaks to the complexities of contemporary life.

The recognition of colonial fragments in our identities and educational systems calls for a decolonial approach to vocational discernment. This involves a critical examination of the power structures and historical processes that have shaped our understanding of ministry, leadership, and vocation. It requires us to question whose voices and experiences have been centered in our theological education and whose have been marginalized or silenced. A decolonial approach invites us to actively seek out and elevate perspectives from the global South, Indigenous communities, and other marginalized groups. This might involve reimagining theological curricula to include non-Western theologians, incorporating diverse spiritual practices into ministerial training, or developing new models of leadership that challenge hierarchical power structures. The goal is not to reject Western theological traditions wholesale, but to engage them critically and place them in dialogue with other ways of knowing and being. This approach can lead to more inclusive and culturally responsive forms of ministry that are better equipped to address the complexities of our globalized world.

The impact of commodity fragments on our sense of identity and belonging is particularly pronounced in our current economic climate, in which the pressure to commodify our skills and experiences is ever present. This fragmentation can lead to a sense of self that is primarily defined by market value rather than inherent worth or personal values. In the context of vocational discernment, this often manifests as tension between pursuing financially secure career paths and following callings that may be less lucrative but more personally or socially fulfilling.

For instance, a seminary graduate might feel torn between accepting a well-paid congregational position and working with a grassroots community organization. This commodification of vocation can also lead to the "personal branding" phenomenon, where individuals feel pressured to package and market their identities in ways that are easily consumable. Although this can sometimes lead to increased opportunities, it also risks flattening the richness and complexity of human experience. Resisting this commodification requires an intentional effort to ground our sense of worth and purpose in something beyond market value, whether that's faith, community, or personal values. This is especially hard given the need to pay bills, have insurance, and feed yourself and your loved ones.

The fragmentation of our identities, while challenging, ultimately invites us into a humbler and more open stance toward ourselves and others. It reminds us that our understanding is always partial and evolving, shaped by our limited perspectives and experiences. This recognition can foster greater empathy and curiosity toward others, as we come to see that their fragmented identities are as complex as our own. It challenges us to hold our convictions with humility, recognizing that our truths are always contextual and open to revision. In the realm of vocational discernment and ministerial formation, this humble stance can lead to more collaborative and mutually enriching approaches to spiritual leadership. It encourages us to see our vocations not as fixed and isolating identities, but as invitations to ongoing dialogue and shared exploration with our communities.

Navigating this fragmented reality requires a shift from seeking wholeness through uniformity to finding coherence through creative assembly. The challenge is not to eliminate or smooth over the fragments of our identities, but to find ways of bringing them into generative relationship with one another. This might involve developing practices of reflection that help us identify common threads running through diverse experiences or creating spaces of dialogue where different aspects of our identities can be expressed and explored. In vocational discernment, it might mean developing a portfolio approach to calling, where different fragments of our identities find expression through various roles and commitments. This process of assembly is ongoing and dynamic, requiring continual reflection, adaptation, and openness to new possibilities. It invites us to see our vocations not as fixed destinations but as evolving journeys of growth and discovery.

In this light, the call to belong is also a call to reweave the lived fabric of our moral identities: the beliefs we hold, the communities that shape them, and the ways those communities help us decide how to live. Without such reweaving, disorientation lingers beneath the surface of even our most fervent calls to justice. By embracing this fragmented yet interconnected understanding of identity and vocation, we open ourselves to richer, more meaningful forms of belonging and more responsive, powerful forms of ministry.

When Communities Collide

The fragmentation of identity and belonging we explored in the preceding section often manifests in complex ways, both when different communities attempt to come together and when individuals seek to join new groups. These dynamics are particularly pronounced when there are cultural and/or identity differences between the group's norms and the individual or community seeking inclusion. Because the issue can be complex, I want to start with two concrete examples that might help to clarify the issue.

First, consider Iglesia de la Esperanza, a vibrant Spanish-speaking congregation, that has been sharing space with First Presbyterian Church, an older, predominantly white congregation that owns the church building where both groups worship. On the surface, this arrangement seems like a generous act of inclusion. First Presbyterian allows Iglesia de la Esperanza to use the sanctuary on Sunday afternoons and a classroom for Wednesday evening Bible study. However, beneath this veneer of hospitality, tensions simmer. Iglesia de la Esperanza isn't permitted to hang artwork or leave any visible trace of its presence in the shared spaces. Its lively worship music is deemed "too loud" by some First Presbyterian members who are having committee meetings elsewhere in the building, leading to restrictions on the use of instruments. When the building committee meets to discuss renovations or scheduling, no one from Iglesia de la Esperanza is invited to participate.

This dynamic extends beyond just the use of the space. When the two congregations attempt to hold joint services for special occasions like Easter or Christmas, the planning is invariably dominated by First Presbyterian's traditions and preferences. Hymns are sung primarily in English, with perhaps one token Spanish song included. The sermon is delivered in English with a rushed Spanish translation afterward. Members of Iglesia de la Esperanza often feel like guests in their own spiritual home, their rich cultural traditions reduced to colorful but ultimately peripheral additions to the "main" service. This both diminishes their worship experience and sends a clear message about whose practices and traditions are considered normative and whose are seen as exotic or secondary. Seen through the lens of systems thinking, as explored in the fourth chapter, this dynamic illustrates an unhealthy equilibrium, in which the dominant group maintains stability by implicitly reinforcing exclusionary boundaries, preventing genuine integration.

Second, consider the situation when Kel, a transgender person, is hired by a progressive nonprofit organization that works closely with communities on poverty alleviation initiatives. Several of the larger partners are historic African American churches. The organization prides itself on its commitment to diversity and inclusion, and leadership is excited to have Kel on board. However, Kel quickly notices that they're often left out of meetings with community partners. When they inquire about this, their supervisor explains that some of their partners have "traditional values" and might be uncomfortable with Kel's presence. The supervisor assures Kel that this is just to avoid "rocking the boat" and potentially jeopardizing their important work in these communities.

Kel finds themself in an increasingly difficult position. While they were hired for their expertise and unique perspective, they feel their contributions are being limited due to others' prejudices. The organization's approach puts undue strain on Kel, who must constantly navigate which spaces they are "allowed" to occupy within their own workplace. This situation not only affects Kel's job satisfaction and career growth but also reinforces the very biases the organization claims to stand against. Moreover, it raises questions about the nature of the nonprofit's commitment to diversity and inclusion, and whether these values extend beyond surface-level representation to meaningful integration and advocacy.

Each of these scenarios illustrates what the theologian Boyung Lee critiques as the limitations of "multiculturalism" in various contexts.[27] Lee argues that multiculturalism as often practiced maintains the centrality of the dominant culture while offering only superficial inclusion to marginalized groups or individuals. In this framework, diversity is celebrated but only insofar as it doesn't challenge the fundamental power structures and cultural norms of the dominant group.

This insistence on conformity, where difference is only superficially welcomed as long as it doesn't disrupt the dominant center, echoes the earlier discussion of Lockhart and how she was asked to make her Womanist scholarship more "Anglo-Saxon" for the comfort or understanding of others. She was welcomed into an academic program, but only so long as she was playing by the "right rules." Multicultural efforts often result in tokenistic representations of minority cultures (like the occasional Spanish hymn in a predominantly English service) without addressing the deeper issues of power imbalance and cultural hegemony.

In contrast, Lee advocates for "interculturalism," which seeks to create genuine dialogue and mutual transformation between different cultural groups and individuals.[28] Interculturalism goes beyond mere recognition or celebration of diversity. It requires all parties involved to engage in a process of mutual learning, adaptation, and change. In an intercultural framework, the goal isn't just to make space for different cultures to coexist, but to create new, shared cultural spaces and practices that reflect the contributions and values of all groups involved.

This approach recognizes that cultural exchange is not a one-way street where minority cultures adapt to the dominant one, but a dynamic process where all cultures influence and transform each other. In the context of our scenarios, an intercultural approach might involve First Presbyterian and Iglesia de la Esperanza collaboratively

---

27 Boyung Lee, *Transforming Congregations through Community: Faith Formation from the Seminary to the Church* (Louisville, KY: Westminster John Knox Press, 2013), 121–36.

28 Ibid.

reimagining their worship practices, governance structures, and use of space in ways that genuinely reflect both traditions. For the nonprofit, it would mean not just hiring diverse staff like Kel but actively working to transform their organizational culture and their relationships with community partners to fully embrace and advocate for LGBTQ+ inclusion.

Interculturalism, as Lee envisions it, is inherently transformative and often challenging. It requires those in positions of power to be willing to change and sometimes to cede control. It also demands that all parties involved be open to discomfort, misunderstanding, and conflict as part of the process of creating truly inclusive communities. However, Lee argues that this approach is necessary for creating spaces of meaningful belonging and realizing the full potential of diverse communities. Communal support systems both amplify individual contributions and reimagine relationships of power and belonging, shifting focus from isolated achievements to collective flourishing.

In our examples, both First Presbyterian's approach to Iglesia de la Esperanza and the nonprofit's treatment of Kel exemplify multiculturalism at its most limited. They've "welcomed" the newcomers, but on terms that preserve existing power structures and cultural norms. True solidarity requires a different approach, one that recognizes how leadership arises through connection and solidarity as opposed to fierce independence. Interculturalism, as Lee envisions it, aligns with this vision by demanding a rethinking of governance, social practices, and engagement strategies. Such an approach fully incorporates the needs and perspectives of all community members, whether they are part of a larger group or bring their unique identities into the mix. This shift from coexistence to collaboration creates spaces where meaningful belonging and collective thriving can truly take root.

For those engaged in vocational discernment, understanding these dynamics of multiculturalism versus interculturalism is crucial. These collisions and tensions within communities reflect the systemic dynamics we explored in the fourth chapter, particularly how changes in one part of a system can create ripple effects throughout the whole. Understanding these dynamics can help us navigate community conflicts with greater wisdom and compassion. As you consider your calling and the communities or organizations you might join or serve, it's important to critically examine not just their stated values, but how those values are enacted in practice.

Are you being invited to bring your full self to the table, with all your unique experiences and perspectives? Or are you expected to fit into preexisting norms and structures? The idea of a "cultural commute" is useful here.[29] How far must members

---

[29] Patrick Reyes, *The Purpose Gap* (Tantor Media, 2021), 46–51.

of marginalized communities travel, both physically and culturally, to participate in dominant systems? An intercultural approach must work to reduce these distances by genuinely integrating diverse practices and traditions. Otherwise, the result will be that the "commuters" will always have a longer trip to take to get to the table, and they'll often arrive already tired from emotional labor.

> ### A Practice to Consider:
> # Tending the Web
>
> *If our well-being is tied to the well-being of others, then disconnection diminishes not just you but the entire web of relationships around you.*
>
> 1. Name the Disconnection: Consider where you feel a sense of disconnection. Perhaps a family member, friend, colleague, or someone in your community. How might this disconnection ripple outward, affecting not only us but the larger web of relationships around us?
> 2. Take a Small Action: Identify one simple action you could take this week to nurture connection and affirm mutual well-being in that disconnection. It could be offering a kind word or expression of gratitude, reaching out with an invitation for a shared meal, walk, or conversation. Focus on actions that are gentle, intentional, and genuine, not about fixing everything, but about showing up.
> 3. Reflect: How did this small act of tending affect you? Did it reveal any needs, strengths, or deeper opportunities for mutual care? How might tending this single strand help strengthen the whole web of connection in your life? What small but regular practices could help you tend to other strands of connection in your life?
> 4. In the Future: Return to this practice regularly, seeing it not as a "fix" but as an ongoing rhythm of care for yourself, others, and the whole web that holds you.

Vocational discernment isn't just about finding where you *can* fit. It's about envisioning how you might contribute to transforming spaces to be more genuinely inclusive. This may involve challenging comfortable norms, advocating for marginalized voices (including your own), and being willing to engage in the sometimes difficult work of creating truly intercultural communities. Your vocation might include being an agent of change, helping to shift organizations and communities from a multicultural mind-set to an intercultural one. Also, sometimes, it is okay to rest. We shouldn't forget that in the push to be a useful "agent of change." As we consider what it means to belong and create belonging, we must ask: Whose table are we gathering around, and whose voices are shaping its design?

Whose Table?

The concept of intersectionality, as developed by Kimberlé Crenshaw, provides a powerful lens for making this mind-set shift from multiculturalism to interculturalism. Crenshaw describes intersectionality as "an analytic sensibility, a way of thinking about identity and its relationship to power."[30] She emphasizes that intersectionality is not just about identities but about "the institutions that use identity to exclude and privilege."[31] This framework emerged from Crenshaw's work on how the experiences of Black women were often erased or misunderstood in both feminist and anti-racist discourses.

However, as Alex C. Lange points out, there's a common misunderstanding of intersectionality in many fields, including higher education. Lange argues that intersectionality is often incorrectly used as a synonym for "multiple identities" or "intersections of identity."[32] I've seen this exact misunderstanding play out in many academic spaces as well as church organizations. This reductive understanding strips intersectionality of its critical power analysis. Intersectionality isn't just about recognizing that people have multiple identities. Rather, it's about understanding how these identities interact with systems of power and oppression to create unique experiences of marginalization or privilege, and having seen the complexity, then asking what can be done to make things better. In our vocational contexts, this means going beyond simply acknowledging diversity to actively examining and challenging the power structures that shape our communities and institutions in life-limiting ways.

Turning with Crenshaw to interrogate how structures and institutions use identity to exclude or privilege, we must look beyond individual experiences and examine how systems and policies might be reinforcing inequality, even unintentionally. Crenshaw also warns against the misuse of intersectionality as merely a way to acknowledge multiple identities without addressing power structures. She argues that intersectional work requires concrete action to address barriers to equality. This aligns closely with Lee's concept of interculturalism, pushing us beyond mere recognition of diversity to active engagement with and transformation of power dynamics. In the nonprofit scenario with Kel, for example, an intersectional approach would consider not just Kel's gender identity but how organizational policies, societal norms about gender, assumptions about African Americans, and dynamics of religious conservatism all intersect to create a situation of exclusion.

---

30 Kimberlé Crenshaw, "Why Intersectionality Can't Wait," *Washington Post*, September 24, 2015, https://www.washingtonpost.com/news/in-theory/wp/2015/09/24/why-intersectionality-cant-wait.

31 Ibid.

32 Alex C. Lange, "The (Mis)use of Intersectionality in Student Affairs: A (Revised) Call to Practitioners & Researchers," *Medium*, March 31, 2020.

Neither of our examples is just about surface-level differences in language, gender identity, or cultural practices. These examples highlight how these identities intersect with broader systems of power related to race, class, religion, gender, and other factors. The members of Iglesia de la Esperanza and Kel aren't just experiencing cultural barriers; they're navigating complex webs of social, economic, and cultural expectations that shape their ability to fully belong and participate in these spaces. Crenshaw's work reminds us that meaningful inclusion requires more than simply allowing marginalized groups or individuals to be present. It necessitates a deep restructuring of power dynamics and a willingness to challenge deeply ingrained norms and expectations.

In the context of our examples, this might mean not just allowing Iglesia de la Esperanza to use the space but actively involving them in decision-making processes, adapting building use policies to accommodate different cultural practices, and working to create a truly bilingual and bicultural community. For Kel's nonprofit, it might be critically examining their approach to community engagement, finding ways to respectfully challenge partners' biases and ensuring that all staff members, including Kel, have equal opportunities to contribute to the organization's work. This might involve developing strategies to educate community partners about gender diversity or finding ways for Kel to contribute meaningfully to projects without direct contact if that's Kel's preference.

This intersectional approach to belonging aligns closely with what Lee terms "liberating interdependence."[33] This concept recognizes that our identities and communities are inherently interconnected, and that meaningful liberation and belonging can only be achieved when we work to dismantle the systems that privilege some groups or individuals over others. There is a significant resonance here with the ideas of Ubuntu that I discussed in the fourth chapter's exploration of systems thinking. Both perspectives challenge us to see our individual vocations as part of a larger web of relationships and responsibilities. As we discern our callings, we're invited to consider how our work might contribute to creating more just and inclusive communities, where the flourishing of each individual is understood as integral to the flourishing of all. This interconnected view of vocation pushes us beyond personal fulfillment to a deeper engagement with the systemic changes needed in our institutions and societies.

Belonging isn't always about finding a place already perfectly shaped for our identities to "fit." For some, it may involve seeking or co-creating spaces where communities are willing to embrace difference and adapt their commitments to welcome others in their fullness, recognizing that such presence can transform the community itself. The metaphor of "being welcomed to the table" often masks the

---

33 Lee, *Transforming Congregations*, 129.

underlying power dynamics. It implies that the dominant group holds ownership of the space and has the power to extend or withdraw welcome. A more transformative approach, in line with Lee's interculturalism, might involve reimagining or removing the table altogether, creating new spaces where norms, expectations, and leadership are collectively negotiated and shared, whether between communities or between a community and its individual members.

This shift requires deep, often uncomfortable work from those in positions of power. It means moving beyond tokenistic inclusion or surface-level multiculturalism to actively ceding control and reimagining what community can look like. For marginalized communities and individuals, this process can be equally challenging. It requires navigating the tension between gratitude for partial inclusion and the righteous anger that fuels movements for meaningful equity. It means finding ways to advocate for full belonging without burning bridges or jeopardizing vital resources or opportunities.

As Crenshaw notes, "Intersectionality alone cannot bring invisible bodies into view. Mere words won't change the way that some people—the less-visible members of political constituencies—must continue to wait for leaders, decision-makers and others to see their struggles."[34] This reminder is crucial as we strive to create more inclusive communities and institutions. We must continually ask ourselves: Whose table is it really? Who sets the norms for behavior and discourse? How are those who don't fit these norms treated? Are we truly making space for diverse ways of being and knowing, or are we simply expecting others to assimilate into existing structures?

Remember, though, as we discussed previously, Family Systems theory demonstrates that communities can't be entirely open, permissive, and without norms. That kind of environment, paradoxically, can't be truly "welcoming" because it doesn't feel like there's a "there" there. It is too diffuse, lacking the structure and shared understanding that allows for meaningful connection and belonging. The challenge, then, is to find a healthy equilibrium, to create communities with clear identities and norms that provide a sense of stability and belonging, while also remaining flexible enough to evolve and incorporate new perspectives. This requires attentive listening, attention, and a willingness to have conversations about what parts of our traditions are the most important to us and why.

Discernment plays a crucial role in this process. Both individuals and communities must continually discern how to navigate this tension between openness and structure, between welcoming difference and maintaining a coherent identity. For individuals seeking belonging, this means not just finding a community that accepts us as we are but also being willing to engage with and potentially be transformed by the

---

34 Crenshaw, "Why Intersectionality Can't Wait."

community's existing norms and practices. For communities, it means being clear about their values and expectations while also being open to how new members might reshape and enrich those very norms.

Creating spaces of meaningful belonging is not about eliminating all boundaries or norms, nor is it about creating a single, homogenous "table" where everyone must conform to a set of predetermined norms. Instead, it's about fostering communities that are both grounded and adaptive, with clearly articulated values and practices that are nevertheless open to evolution and growth. Lay ministers often excel at creating these spaces precisely because they operate within the everyday rhythms of life. Whether it's gathering for prayer before a shift at work, hosting a discussion group in their home, or offering spiritual support during a lunch break, they demonstrate how belonging can be fostered in ordinary moments. This ability to create sacred space within secular settings is a unique gift that lay ministry brings to the broader church.

A favorite story of mine from the Christian tradition is the Pentecost passage in Acts 2. There, tongues of flame descend upon the disciples, and everyone begins to speak in their own language, yet all can understand each other. Imagine how different the story would be if the gift of the Holy Spirit wasn't understanding but the imposition of a single, enforced language. Instead, the gift was the miraculous ability to hear and comprehend one another across linguistic and cultural divides, fostering unity without erasing individuality. This biblical image offers a profound metaphor for belonging: not a space where we all become the same but one where our unique voices are honored and made mutually comprehensible. It suggests that building inclusive communities is about cultivating the shared capacity to listen, learn, and understand across differences rather than eliminating them.

As we navigate our vocational journeys and seek to create or join communities of belonging, may we strive for this Pentecost-like dynamic. Let us work toward spaces where diverse voices can speak meaningfully and be genuinely heard, where the richness of our varied experiences and perspectives becomes a source of collective strength rather than division. This is the challenging, ongoing work of cultivating meaningful belonging and liberating interdependence in our increasingly diverse and interconnected world.

From Table to Bed

As we conclude this chapter on identity and belonging, let us shift our metaphor from the table to the bed. Specifically, to the quilt that might adorn it. Quilts, in their various forms, offer rich metaphors for the complex interplay of identity, belonging, and vocation we've explored.

A quilt is a multilayered textile that typically consists of three layers: a woven cloth top, a layer of batting or wadding, and a woven back, all held together by lines of stitching. Quilts serve both functional and aesthetic purposes, providing warmth while also often telling stories through their designs and the fabrics used in their creation.

Two particular types of quilts offer especially apt metaphors for our discussion: the Crazy Quilt and the quilts of Gee's Bend. A Crazy Quilt is characterized by its irregular and often asymmetrical pieces of fabric sewn together without a fixed pattern. Unlike traditional quilts, which usually have a repeating design or block structure, Crazy Quilts are more free-form and eclectic. The fabric pieces in a Crazy Quilt can be of various shapes, sizes, colors, and textures, creating a visually complex and vibrant appearance.

Emerging in the late nineteenth century, Crazy Quilts were especially popular among urban, upper-class women during the Victorian era, reflecting the opulence and eclectic tastes of the time.[35] These quilts often utilized luxurious materials such as silks, velvets, and brocades, which were embellished with intricate embroidery, lace, and beads. They served as decorative showpieces rather than practical items, often displayed in parlors as symbols of refinement and artistic skill. The improvisational style of Crazy Quilts mirrored the creativity and individuality of their makers while also showcasing their access to wealth and leisure.

In contrast, the quilts of Gee's Bend, created by generations of women in the isolated African American community of Gee's Bend, Alabama, are celebrated for their bold, improvised geometric patterns and deeply rooted cultural significance.[36] Unlike the Crazy Quilts, which reflected Victorian opulence and were created for decorative purposes, Gee's Bend quilts emerged from a context of survival, community, and artistic resilience. These quilts often repurposed worn clothing, feed sacks, denim, and other everyday materials, transforming items of necessity into striking works of art. The resourcefulness inherent in their creation highlights the ingenuity of the women of Gee's Bend, who used what was available to meet practical needs while also preserving and expressing their heritage.

The improvisational style of Gee's Bend quilts is distinct, characterized by asymmetry, bold color choices, and dynamic compositions that evoke movement and rhythm. This aesthetic draws on African American artistic traditions and cultural

---

35 Patricia Cox Crews, "Fueled by Silk: Victorian Crazy Quilt Mania," *Textile Society of America Symposium Proceedings*, 2010, https://digitalcommons.unl.edu/tsaconf/15.

36 A great film about these works of art is *Quiltmakers of Gee's Bend*, directed by Celia Carey (Montgomery: Alabama Public Television, 2004), DVD. See also https:// www.arts.gov/stories/blog/2015/quilts-gees-bend-slides.

memory, linking the quilts to a broader lineage of African diasporic art forms. These quilts were often made in communal settings, with women gathering to quilt together, strengthening bonds and sharing stories. Far from being merely functional objects, Gee's Bend quilts served as tangible expressions of identity, history, and perseverance, embodying the lived experiences of their makers in the face of systemic marginalization and isolation. Today, these quilts are recognized as masterpieces of American art, celebrated in museums and exhibitions worldwide for their powerful blend of necessity, creativity, and cultural preservation.

Both types of quilts, in their own ways, reflect the themes of fragmentation, creativity, and the assembling of disparate elements into a cohesive whole that we've explored in this chapter. Like the fragments of identity that Jennings describes, each piece of a quilt has its own history, texture, and significance. Some pieces might represent our faith traditions, others our cultural heritage, and still others our lived experiences or acquired knowledge. Just as colonial and commodity fragments shape our identities, we might find in our quilt scraps of fabric that carry complex histories or represent systems of power and value.

Especially in the context of necessity and resilience, the act of quilting becomes a practice of meaning-making. In pulling together what has been discarded or frayed, it echoes the moral work of reorientation, of vocational discernment: stitching together a life of coherence from fragments of experience, tradition, and conviction. Similarly, these quilts remind us that clarity doesn't come from symmetry or sameness. It emerges from faithful assembly, from the courageous act of holding tension, honoring what we've inherited, and sewing together something new.

In this way, the quilt visually represents the vision of the person this chapter puts forth: the self as relational, fragmented, and systemic, rather than autonomous or uniform. Just as the coherence of the quilt emerges from the skillful assembly of disparate pieces, so, too, does a faithful vocation emerge from the ongoing work of connection, repair, and navigating complexity within the fragments of our lives and communities.

The process of creating a quilt mirrors our journey of vocational discernment. It requires careful consideration of each piece, deciding how it fits with others, where it belongs in the larger design. This echoes the work of navigating our fragmented identities, finding coherence not through uniformity but through creative assembly. The quilter, like someone engaged in vocational discernment, must be both intentional and open to serendipity, allowing unexpected combinations to emerge.

The embellishments on a Crazy Quilt can represent the reflective practices and formative experiences that add depth and meaning to our vocational journeys. These embellishments connect disparate pieces, much as our practices of theological reflection and spiritual formation help us integrate various aspects of our identities

Identity and Belonging

and experiences. Meanwhile, the bold, geometric patterns of a Gee's Bend quilt might represent the strength and resilience we develop as we navigate complex social and cultural landscapes, creating beauty and functionality from whatever materials are at hand.

Importantly, neither of these quilting traditions seeks to hide the seams or differences between pieces. Instead, they celebrate these junctions, often highlighting them with decorative stitching or bold color contrasts. This aligns with Lee's concept of interculturalism and Crenshaw's intersectionality, which call us to acknowledge and engage with our differences rather than glossing over them in pursuit of a false unity.

The quilt as a whole represents the communities that we're part of, including faith communities, professional organizations, or chosen families. Like the scenarios we explored with Iglesia de la Esperanza and Kel, belonging isn't about fitting neatly into preexisting patterns. Instead, it's about contributing our unique pieces to the collective design, transforming the community even as we find our place within it. To contribute is to recognize that our pieces, however irregular or imperfect, carry the beauty of our lived experiences, struggles, and dreams. These pieces might be our skills, our perspectives, or even our vulnerabilities, each shaping the shared story of the community. As each thread strengthens the whole, our willingness to engage ensures that the quilt becomes not just a representation of each of us but also a sign of what we might become together.

Just as a quilt is both a practical item for warmth and a work of art, our vocations serve both personal and communal purposes. They provide us with a sense of purpose and direction while contributing to the greater good. The quilt reminds us that our individual callings are part of a larger tapestry of human experience and divine purpose. Finally, the bed that this quilt adorns represents the grounding we need amid the complexity and fragmentation of our identities and communities. It reminds us that while we celebrate diversity and embrace the challenges of intercultural engagement, we also need spaces of rest, reflection, and rootedness. It can also be a place of joy and lament, a place to feel safe and held. The ways that our expression of those feelings can be part of work is what comes in the next chapter.

Questions for Reflection

1. This chapter opens with Howard Thurman's idea that "community cannot for long feed on itself; it can only flourish with the coming of others from beyond." Reflecting on your own experiences, can you recall a time when a community you were part of felt the need for new perspectives, fresh energy, or "undiscovered siblings" to arrive? What challenges or opportunities did this create for the community and for your sense of belonging within it?

2. Willie James Jennings's framework describes our identities as shaped by fragments of faith, of colonial legacies, and of a world that often treats even sacred things as commodities. In what ways do you see these different types of fragments playing out in your primary community or institution? In your experience, which fragments tend to remain unspoken or hidden, and what might be the cost of that silence for collective belonging and individual wholeness?

3. The chapter discusses "context collapse," where the various audiences and expectations from different parts of our lives increasingly merge, especially in digital spaces, but also offline. Have you experienced moments where different aspects of your identity or the expectations of different social contexts have come into uncomfortable conflict? How did you navigate this "collapse," and what did you learn about your own identity, values, or vocational integrity in the process?

4. The chapter explores the dynamics of inclusion and belonging through examples like Iglesia de la Esperanza and First Presbyterian Church. Have you witnessed or experienced similar situations? What insights did these experiences offer about meaningful inclusion?

5. Consider the distinction that Boyung Lee made between multiculturalism (often maintaining a dominant center while "including" others) and interculturalism (seeking mutual transformation and shared power). In a community or organization you know well, which approach seems more prevalent? What concrete steps would be required to move toward a more genuinely intercultural way of being? What are the potential risks, and the profound rewards, of such a shift?

6. Reflect on a time when you felt a deep, authentic sense of belonging within a community, a time when you felt truly seen, valued, and connected. What specific elements contributed to that profound experience of belonging? Was it shared values, mutual vulnerability, a sense of collective purpose, or something else? How might these insights inform how you endeavor to create or nurture such life-giving spaces of belonging for others in your various spheres of influence?

PART III

ABUNDANCE

Like a landscape in full bloom—unpredictable, varied, and deeply alive—these final chapters explore how vocational expression takes root and bears fruit in ways that nourish the world around us as well as ourselves. Here, we turn toward practices like accompaniment, storytelling, and ministry, not as final stages in a linear journey, but as expressions of a life continually attuning to call.

Too often, abundance is mistaken for harvest alone—the final product, the measurable yield. But abundance is also found in the overgrowth, the sharing, the cycles of giving and regrowth that defy easy accounting. It spills over borders. The vocational life, likewise, rarely proceeds in tidy sequence. These chapters honor the messier truth: the fruit of our lives appears at different times, in different forms, and often in collaboration with others.

Genuine abundance doesn't just fill our own baskets—it seeds future seasons, regenerates ecosystems, and sustains the flourishing of communities. In that spirit, what follows is not a conclusion, but a deeper unfolding of how our callings are lived out in relationship and shared life. True abundance is not the end of a process, but a part of a cycle of tending and caring and keeping seeds for the next growing season.

What the Farmers Knew

Outside of the headquarters of the Southern Poverty Law Center in Montgomery, Alabama, there is a monument dedicated to the memory of Dr. Martin Luther King Jr. It features a carved inscription of a quote from King's "I Have a Dream" speech, which paraphrases Amos 5:24: "Until justice rolls down like waters and righteousness like a mighty stream." The whole piece is a polished black granite fountain in the form of an inverted stone cone. A thin film of water flows over the base, which contains the names of forty-one martyrs of the civil rights movement. It is calm and reflective. Maya Lin, the sculpture's designer, is on record saying that the experience is rooted in the soothing and healing effects of water.

In the spring of my fourth-grade year, my family was living with my aunt. She lived in a condo that was large enough for our whole family to stay without being too much in the way as we got things figured out. Behind the edge of the back row of buildings, there was a patch of woods that had a creek in it that some of the kids in the area played around. I remember I was wearing overalls the day I fell in. I was never much of an athlete, so it shouldn't have surprised me that I didn't make the jump across. But others were there; I still hadn't gotten rid of all of my accent yet; and I'm sure the young me just wanted to fit in. So I jumped, and I missed. It was probably March or April, sometime before the full green of May took hold. And it was far smaller than a river, but shocked by the cold water, I gasped. I remember feeling how wrong it felt when I wanted air but instead breathed in spring stream. I don't remember the faces of any of the kids who made fun of me for falling, just the horrible sensation of water when there should have been air, and coughing and running to get away from that place and the kinds of people who would laugh when water had taken my breath away.

In the biblical narrative, the place where Amos spoke truth was initially called *Luz* but was renamed by Jacob after he had a dream of a ladder reaching to heaven. Today, it is the Palestinian village of Beitin, located in the West Bank, but for Amos, it would have been *Bethel*, the *Beth* of *El*, the house of God. And I don't blame Lin for wanting to make something that soothes the world. And Lord knows that the crimes of racism need every bit of healing that can be found. But when the prophet Amos gave his voice to God and offered that justice should roll down like water, something more than a quiet fountain was being called to.

Those who had lived through the *yoreh* and *malkosh*, the early and latter rains, would have known better. In the limestone hills there, dried riverbed *wadis* cut deep scars through the land, lined with sediment—sand, gravel, loose rocks—all pieces previous floods had carved and carried down. Each flood reshapes the channel, widening here, deepening there. Rich soil brought to unexpected places. These dry riverbeds could wake in a single storm. The farmers waited for it with hope and fear—too little meant hunger, too much meant destruction. Their calendar marked time by its rhythms: plant with the autumn rains, harvest before the spring floods. Amos knew these waters intimately, had probably seen flash floods tear through the hillsides of Tekoa, watched them carry away anything that was in their path.

So I wonder what those who first heard Amos felt. Did they remember the times they'd seen water tear through wadis, reshaping the land? Or did they think of standing in the temple, watching the careful streams of purification water flow through channels cut by generations of priests? Did they think of the stories their grandparents told of the great Flood, when water became God's judgment? I think Amos's words were meant to call up all of these, the wild and the tamed, the cleansing and the destroyed. What comes next will not be contained. Water keeps its own counsel.

We moved again later that spring. I never went back to that creek. I don't even know if I could find it today. But sometimes, when I swim, I can still feel that moment—the wrong rush of water instead of air, the burning in my lungs from a single half-breath of spring stream. Not the faces that laughed, not even the running away, but that primal knowing: Water doesn't care what we want from it. The farmers of God's House knew this.

And yes, water is life, but abundance isn't always about fullness. Sometimes it is, and I'm glad for those moments of reprieve and contentedness, especially for those who rarely get to rest. Other times, it is about standing at the edge of something wild and necessary, knowing it brings both gift and fear, leaving behind fertile soil and stripped bare rock.

He asked for justice to roll down. Not trickle, not seep, but roll. The question isn't whether the waters will come but whether we'll be ready when they do. And what we'll do with those who will not make the jump and are not prepared for what comes next. None of us crosses the water alone.

7

Accompaniment

To "listen" another's soul into a condition of disclosure and discovery may be almost the greatest service that any human being ever performs for another.

—Douglas Steere

There comes a time when silence is betrayal.

—Martin Luther King Jr.

The power of prayerful listening does not erase the numbing silence of inaction. There is indeed a profound transformation that can occur when we truly hear another,[1] but there will also be times when it is unfaithful to remain quiet in the face of injustice.[2] Between these two poles lies the rich, complex terrain of human connection and responsibility. Last chapter, I made the claim that our sense of self is inherently relational and communal. This understanding is part of the reason I think systems-thinking is so important. If we are, in our very sense of self, connected to others, to creation, and to God, then we have to think at the systems level if we want to understand ourselves.

Building on this foundation, I now turn my attention to some of the material consequences of this relational identity through the practice of accompaniment. As I see it,

---

1 Douglas V. Steere, *Gleanings: A Random Harvest* (Nashville: Upper Room, 1986), 3. See epigraph.
2 Martin Luther King Jr., "Beyond Vietnam: A Time to Break Silence," Speech, April 4, 1967, at Riverside Church in New York City. See epigraph.

this practice is more than a skill to be honed. Accompaniment is an embodied expression of our commitment to our interconnected nature. My goal is to affirm accompaniment as a dynamic, transformative process that goes beyond listening, silent contemplation, and passive reception. In doing so, I draw connections to my earlier discussions on spiritual formation and the interplay of joy and lament in our vocational journeys.

Deep listening creates space for both joyful revelations and painful lamentations to be expressed and held within community. This "holding" is part of the work of accompaniment and involves walking alongside others through seasons of celebration and struggle, echoing the rhythms of joy and lament we discussed earlier. These practices are integral to spiritual formation, helping us attune to God's presence and guidance in our lives and in others. They remind us that vocational discernment and spiritual growth occur not just in moments of quiet clarity, but also in times of doubt, difficulty, and resistance. By engaging in these practices, we create opportunities for mutual transformation, allowing both joy and sorrow to shape our understanding of vocation.

I am often reminded of the poet Rilke's line, where he has God speak to the reader: "You, sent out beyond your recall / go to the limits of your longing. / Embody me. // Flare up like flame / and make big shadows I can move in."[3] This powerful image from Rilke resonates with what I aim to explore in this chapter. Accompaniment, when done well, will push us beyond our comfort zones, inviting us to "go to the limits of our longing," creating space for us to experience the divine moving within our interactions and relationships. We can walk with each other into greater service, challenge, and joy.

Listening into Action

At its core, accompaniment is the art of journeying alongside others on their spiritual journey as they discern and live out their calling. As we move alongside them, we are called at times to offer support, guidance, accountability, and sometimes challenge. This practice is deeply rooted in Christian tradition, yet it continues to adapt and respond to the complexities of our modern world.

Accompaniment is not merely about offering advice or direction. Rather, it is a relational process that involves deep listening, mutual vulnerability, and a shared openness to the movements of the Spirit. It recognizes that vocational discernment is not a solitary endeavor but one that flourishes within community and through intentional relationships.

---

3 Rainer Maria Rilke, "Go to the Limits of Your Longing," in *Rilke's Book of Hours: Love Poems to God*, trans. Joanna Macy and Anita Barrows (New York: Riverhead Books, 1996), 85.

Accompaniment

In this section, we will explore the nature of accompaniment, drawing on rich theological traditions and contemporary insights. We'll examine how accompaniment can be both a nurturing and challenging practice, one that requires discernment, patience, and sometimes even disruption. By understanding the various dimensions of accompaniment, we can better equip ourselves to support others (and be supported) in the ongoing journey of vocational discernment. To do that, I'll begin with insights drawn from Pope Francis and the liberation theology tradition.

Theological Perspectives

The theological landscape of accompaniment is diverse, with numerous traditions offering valuable insights. However, for the purposes of our exploration, we will focus on two particularly complementary approaches: the teachings of Pope Francis and the insights of liberation theology.

I've come to use this pairing of theological perspectives because they provide a useful tension with each other. Just as a skilled gardener knows when to tenderly care for delicate shoots and when to prune for new growth, those engaged in accompaniment must discern what is needed in each unique moment of the vocational journey. In the cultivation of vocation, different seasons call for different approaches. From Francis, we find an emphasis on patient, compassionate accompaniment; from the liberation tradition, a call for prophetic disruption and solidarity. By examining these two perspectives, we can develop a nuanced understanding of accompaniment that is both pastorally sensitive and prophetically engaged.

At the heart of Francis's understanding is the concept that accompaniment is an "art." This practice involves walking alongside others with patience, compassion, and deep respect for each individual's unique process of growth. Francis emphasizes that accompaniment requires a profound openness to listen, not simply to correct or judge, but to foster a genuine encounter with God. He writes, "We need to practice the art of listening, which is more than simply hearing. Listening, in communication, is an openness of heart which makes possible that closeness without which genuine spiritual encounter cannot occur."[4] This perspective calls us to see accompaniment not as a passive act, but as an intentional and sacred process of mutual transformation rooted in relational depth and divine encounter.

Francis stresses that accompaniment should lead people toward deeper freedom in Christ, avoiding self-absorption and nurturing a pilgrimage toward God. He

---

[4] Francis, *Evangelii Gaudium: Apostolic Exhortation on the Proclamation of the Gospel in Today's World* (Vatican City, November 24, 2013), 171.

cautions against reducing accompaniment to mere therapeutic support, insisting that it should always orient individuals outward, toward God and the mission of the Church. As he puts it, "Far from setting us on a path of self-absorption, this enables us to discover more fully the God who seeks us out and challenges us to take a step beyond our own comfort."[5] This challenge is important. Without it, "accompaniment" can become just support. There's nothing wrong with support, but it alone is not accompaniment. A safe harbor is a good place for ships to weather a storm, but ships were meant for sailing.

As a harbor provides necessary shelter and safety for ships, accompaniment offers a supportive environment for individuals to find respite, healing, and reflection. However, the ultimate purpose of a ship is not to remain in harbor, but to venture out into open waters, exploring new horizons and fulfilling its intended purpose. Similarly, while accompaniment provides a safe space for personal growth and discernment, its goal is to empower individuals to move beyond their comfort zones, to "set sail" toward their calling. This involves taking risks, facing challenges, and actively engaging with the world.

The accompanier, like a skilled harbor master, must discern when to offer protection and when to encourage setting forth, mindful that the journey of vocation unfolds differently for each individual. For some, the harbor is a vital refuge, providing much-needed safety and stability amid ongoing challenges. For others, it serves as a launch point into the vast, complex waters of lived experience and service. Yet even for those who need to linger in the harbor, the ultimate purpose of accompaniment is to nurture readiness for eventual growth and exploration. The process of launching, though daunting, is an essential part of discerning and living out one's calling, as it allows individuals to engage with the fullness of their gifts and the needs of the world.

This holistic approach recognizes that vocational discernment is not just about making career choices but about integrating all aspects of one's life (spiritual, emotional, physical, and social) into a cohesive sense of calling. Francis calls for a "steady and reassuring" pace in accompaniment, reflecting closeness and a "compassionate gaze" that "heals, liberates and encourages growth in the Christian life."[6] Importantly, Francis emphasizes that accompaniment is not a hierarchical process where one simply imparts wisdom to another. Instead, it is a shared journey of discovery that reflects the incarnational nature of God's love. This mutual walking together embodies the Church's parental nature, nurturing and accompanying its

---

5 Ibid., 169.
6 Ibid.

members with tender care. Francis encourages pastoral workers to "take on the 'smell of the sheep,'" immersing themselves in the messy realities of people's lives.[7]

Francis highlights the importance of recognizing and embracing our own fragility in the process of accompaniment. This fragility is a deeply human quality. He suggests that our vulnerabilities, far from being weaknesses to be hidden, are "our true richness" that can make us more empathetic and understanding accompaniers.[8] This perspective encourages a model of accompaniment where both parties are open to growth and transformation, reflecting the mutual nature of the journey toward deeper faith and service. Francis also emphasizes the communal aspect of accompaniment, reminding us that "we are not alone, we belong to a people, a nation, a city that is on the move, a Church, a parish, this group ... a community on the move."[9] This communal dimension underscores that vocational discernment, while deeply personal, often unfolds within and contributes to the broader networks of community and belonging. At the same time, not everyone has access to supportive or dynamic communities; for some, the journey may involve seeking, creating, or imagining these spaces of belonging for themselves or others.

Within these networks of belonging, examples of individual accompaniment are vital to sustaining vocational discernment. Francis often turns to Mary as a model for discernment and accompaniment, offering a concrete example of the listening heart that is central to this practice.[10] In his teachings, the Pope highlights three key attitudes of Mary: she speaks little, listens a lot, and cherishes insights in her heart. This Marian approach provides a template for the kind of attentive, reflective presence that characterizes effective accompaniment. Francis points to Mary's rare but powerful words in scripture, such as her instruction at the wedding in Cana to "do whatever he tells you" (John 2:5). In Francis's reading, Mary's example highlights how accompaniment, while often characterized by patient listening, also involves knowing when and how to offer gentle guidance that directs individuals toward God's voice in their lives. By embodying these Marian qualities, accompaniers can foster an environment where vocational discernment can unfold naturally and meaningfully.

Mary's example encourages accompaniers to cultivate a posture of receptive listening, creating space for others to express themselves fully without rushing to offer solutions or judgments. Her practice of "cherishing in her heart" suggests a

---

7 Ibid., 24.

8 Francis, "Catechesis on Discernment. 14. Spiritual Accompaniment," Vatican.va (January 4, 2023). https://www.vatican.va/content/francesco/en/audiences/2023/documents/20230104-udienza-generale.html.

9 Ibid.

10 Ibid.

contemplative dimension to accompaniment, where insights and experiences are held with care, allowed to deepen and mature over time. This reflective stance can help both the accompanier and the accompanied to discern the subtle movements of the Spirit in their lives.

Although Francis's emphasis on Mary's listening heart and reflective stance offers valuable insights for the practice of accompaniment, it's important to acknowledge that this perspective might raise concerns for some readers. The focus on Mary's quiet, receptive nature could be interpreted as endorsing a passive or submissive role, particularly for women, in spiritual and vocational contexts. This interpretation might seem to reinforce traditional gender roles or a complementarian theology that assigns distinct and potentially limiting roles to men and women in the church and society.

However, it's useful to understand Francis's Marian model within the broader context of his teachings on accompaniment, which emphasize active engagement and the empowerment of all believers. The Pope's vision of accompaniment is not one of docile passivity, but of deep, active listening that leads to transformative action. Mary's "yes" to God's call was a profound act of courage and agency, not mere acquiescence. Similarly, effective accompaniment requires not just quiet reflection, but also the strength to speak truth, offer challenge, and encourage bold steps of faith when needed. As we consider Francis's Marian model, we must hold it in creative tension with the call for all believers (regardless of gender) to fully engage their gifts in service to God and others, recognizing that discernment and accompaniment involve both receptivity and active response to the divine call. This active response is present in Francis's vision, but it is not as emphasized, which is why I find that pairing it with perspectives from the liberation theology tradition can be beneficial.

Central to liberation theology's approach to accompaniment is its emphasis on critical awareness, deep solidarity with the marginalized, and the courage to confront systemic injustices. This framework challenges us to rethink normative assumptions and recognize the intersectionality of oppression. Paulo Freire, Gustavo Gutiérrez, James Cone, and Emilie Townes are the voices you'll hear from shortly. And although they do not directly offer perspectives on accompaniment, their work offers invaluable insights that can deepen our understanding of it.

Freire's critical pedagogy underscores the importance of developing consciousness that empowers individuals and communities to name and challenge their realities. Gutiérrez situates the struggle for justice within a broader theological vision that calls for active engagement with systemic inequities. Cone's work on racial justice reveals how accompaniment must center on God's alignment with the oppressed. Townes emphasizes the inclusion of often-overlooked voices, particularly those of women and communities of color. Examining accompaniment through their perspectives invites us to reimagine it as a collaborative and justice-oriented journey toward collective transformation.

Freire, while not a theologian per se, heavily influenced liberation theology through his work in critical pedagogy, which both Gutiérrez and Rubem Alves refer to in the first published works of liberation theology. Central to Freire's approach is the concept of conscientization (*conscientização*), which involves developing a critical consciousness that allows individuals and communities to name, analyze, and act upon the oppressive realities they face.[11] In the context of accompaniment, Freire's ideas challenge us to create spaces where both the accompanier and the accompanied can engage in dialogue that leads to greater awareness of social, political, and economic structures that affect their lives.

Richard Shaull, a long-time friend and supporter of Freire, has perhaps the most famous summary of Freire's work:

> There is no such thing as a neutral education process. Education either functions as an instrument which is used to facilitate the integration of generations into the logic of the present system and bring about conformity to it, or it becomes the "practice of freedom," the means by which men and women deal critically with reality and discover how to participate in the transformation of their world.[12]

This perspective invites us to see accompaniment as a mutual educational process, where both parties learn from each other and critically examine their realities.

For our purposes, I see Freire as challenging accompaniers to be aware of their own biases and assumptions, and to create spaces where those they accompany can develop their own critical understanding of their situations and possibilities for action.

> Through dialogue, the teacher-of-the-students and the students-of-the-teacher cease to exist and a new term emerges: teacher-student with students-teachers. The teacher is no longer merely the-one-who-teaches, but one who is himself taught in dialogue with the students, who in turn, while being taught, also teach. They become jointly responsible for a process in which all grow.[13]

---

11 Freire first details this in *Pedagogy of the Oppressed,* but for a more concise explanation of it, I recommend Regina Cortina and Marcella Winter, "Paulo Freire's Pedagogy of Liberation," *Current Issues in Comparative Education* 23, no. 2 (2021): 8–19.

12 Richard Shaull, foreword to *Pedagogy of the Oppressed,* by Paulo Freire, trans. Myra Bergman Ramos (New York: Continuum, 1970), 34.

13 Ibid.

Considering this perspective in regard to accompaniment means we have to recognize that accompanying someone is not about imparting wisdom from on high but about co-creating knowledge and understanding that can lead to mutually transformative action.

This dynamic of mutual teaching and learning reframes the roles of accompanier and accompanied as co-creators in a process of liberation. The accompanier is not a passive observer or detached guide but an active participant who engages their own experiences, biases, and assumptions alongside those they accompany. Similarly, the accompanied are not merely recipients of guidance but active agents in their own liberation, contributing essential insights and perspectives to the shared journey. This relational approach underscores that both parties have much to learn from each other, as their engagement with critical consciousness enables them to name the realities of injustice and imagine possibilities for transformation together. In this co-creative process, accompaniment becomes not only an act of solidarity but also a lived expression of shared growth, where learning and liberation are inseparable.

Building on Freire's foundational work in critical pedagogy, Gustavo Gutiérrez, often considered the father of liberation theology, translates these educational principles into a radical theological framework. Freire's concept of conscientization finds its theological counterpart in Gutiérrez's understanding of how faith communities come to recognize their role in social transformation. Where Freire saw education as a means of awakening critical consciousness, Gutiérrez envisions theology as a tool for awakening the church to its prophetic mission in the world.

Gutiérrez explicitly references Freire's work in *A Theology of Liberation*, drawing parallels between Freire's pedagogical approach and the process of theological reflection.[14] Just as Freire advocated for a dialogical method of education that empowers students to become subjects of their own learning, Gutiérrez proposes a theology that emerges from the lived experiences and struggles of the poor. He adopts Freire's concept of "generative themes" as a starting point for theological reflection. These themes are how Freire would teach his classes of adults who were learning to read: not starting with meaningless workbooks, instead gathering information about the key issues and struggles in people's lives, using that material to fuel a desire to read and engage.

This methodology shifts the locus of theology from academic institutions to the grassroots communities of the faithful, mirroring Freire's relocation of educational authority from teachers and the dispensing of expertise to learners and the space for questioning. Furthermore, Gutiérrez's insistence on praxis as the first act of theology,

---

14 Gustavo Gutiérrez, *A Theology of Liberation: History, Politics, and Salvation* (Maryknoll, NY: Orbis Books, 1973), 233–37.

followed by critical reflection, mirrors Freire's action-reflection cycle. This deep integration of Freirean thought leads Gutiérrez to a theology that is inherently tied to social transformation, expressed most powerfully in his concept of solidarity with the poor.

> The poor person does not exist as an inescapable fact of destiny. His or her existence is not politically neutral, and it is not ethically innocent. The poor are a by-product of the system in which we live and for which we are responsible. They are marginalized by our social and cultural world. They are the oppressed, exploited proletariat, robbed of the fruit of their labor and despoiled of their humanity. Hence the poverty of the poor is not a call to generous relief action, but a demand that we go and build a different social order.[15]

This perspective radically reshapes our understanding of accompaniment. It suggests that meaningful accompaniment cannot be divorced from the work of social transformation.

For Gutiérrez, to walk alongside someone necessarily involves engaging with the systemic injustices that shape their material reality. This approach to accompaniment challenges us to move beyond individualistic notions of calling and to consider how our vocations might contribute to building a more just social order. It demands that accompaniers not only listen to personal struggles but also help individuals contextualize their experiences within broader socioeconomic structures. This shift from a purely personal to a sociopolitical understanding of vocation has profound implications for how we practice accompaniment.

This sociopolitical understanding of vocation reshapes the practice of accompaniment in several key ways. First, it requires accompaniers to adopt a critical awareness of the systems and structures that perpetuate inequality, ensuring that their support does not unintentionally reinforce these dynamics. Second, it demands a commitment to advocacy and systemic change alongside personal care, recognizing that addressing immediate needs must be paired with efforts to transform the root causes of suffering. Finally, this approach broadens the scope of vocation itself, inviting individuals and communities to see their work not merely as personal fulfillment but as active participation in God's ongoing project of liberation and justice. In doing so, accompaniment becomes a shared journey of transformation, where both the accompanier and the accompanied are challenged to grow in their understanding of and engagement with the world's inequities.

---

15 Gustavo Gutiérrez, *The Power of the Poor in History: Selected Writings* (Maryknoll, NY: Orbis Books, 1983), 44.

Although Gutiérrez's work emerged from and spoke to the Latin American context, these ideas quickly found resonance in other parts of the world grappling with similar issues of systemic injustice. In North America, one of the early adopters of liberation theology's ethos was James Cone. While not in the direct lineage of Gutiérrez, Cone's work lifted up similar insights of liberation theology in the context of the African American struggle against racism, further expanding our understanding of what it means to accompany those on the margins of society.

Cone, a pioneer of Black liberation theology, brings a racial dimension to the practice of accompaniment. Cone argues that God is on the side of the oppressed, particularly Black people in the context of American racism. He states that "the task of theology is to criticize and show the inadequacies of old symbols and myths and to create new ones so that the people of God can fight for freedom."[16] In terms of accompaniment, Cone's work challenges us to critically examine the racial and cultural assumptions embedded in our understanding of vocation and calling. Cone further elaborates in his book *God of the Oppressed*:

> The black theologian must reject any conception of God which stifles black self-determination by picturing God as a God of all peoples. Either God is identified with the oppressed to the point that their experience becomes God's experience, or God is a God of racism.... The blackness of God means that God has made the oppressed condition God's own condition.[17]

This statement is not merely rhetorical; it represents a fundamental shift in theological thinking. Cone argues that a truly liberating theology must understand God as unequivocally on the side of the oppressed. This perspective has profound implications for accompaniment.

It suggests that accompaniment, particularly of marginalized individuals and communities, requires more than empathy or general goodwill. It demands a deep identification with the struggles of the oppressed and a commitment to their liberation. For Cone, this identification is not optional but essential to a true understanding of God's nature and work in the world. The God of liberation is not a passive observer but an active participant in the pain and resistance of the marginalized. For those who experience oppression firsthand, this theology resonates as an affirmation of their dignity, a validation of their struggles, and a source of divine solidarity in

---

16 James H. Cone, *A Black Theology of Liberation* (Maryknoll, NY: Orbis Books, 1970), 12.
17 Ibid., 63.

the face of systemic injustice. It transforms accompaniment into a sacred act of mutual empowerment, where the marginalized see their pain reflected in God's own experience and their liberation as central to God's mission.

For those with power and privilege, however, Cone's theology demands a more confrontational reckoning. It challenges them to relinquish their comfort and complicity in systems of oppression, to see accompaniment as a call to accountability and transformation, not as an act of benevolence. For the powerful, identifying with the oppressed means not only walking alongside them but also interrogating and dismantling the systems that perpetuate inequity: systems from which they often benefit. Without this deep commitment, accompaniment risks becoming performative, paternalistic, or complicit in maintaining the status quo. To genuinely engage in accompaniment, those with power must cultivate humility, listen deeply to the voices of the marginalized, and recognize that their own liberation is tied to the dismantling of unjust structures.

Building on Cone's insights into race and liberation, we must recognize that, even within liberation movements, there can be overlooked perspectives and marginalized voices. This limitation is central to the emergence of Womanist theology, which addresses the unique experiences and struggles of Black women in the fight for justice and liberation. Emilie Townes, an influential Womanist ethicist, enriches our understanding of accompaniment in the context of social justice. Townes's work on the cultural production of evil and the everyday nature of ethical action provides valuable insights into how we might conceptualize and practice accompaniment in ways that are truly transformative and liberating.

Townes emphasizes the importance of "everydayness" in ethical action and solidarity. She writes, "Solidarity comes from hard work, listening, hearing, analyzing, questioning, rethinking, accepting, rejecting. It comes from a place of respecting and being respected."[18] This perspective aligns closely with our understanding of accompaniment as a continuous, engaged presence that requires active listening and mutual transformation. In the context of accompaniment, Townes's words remind us that solidarity is not a passive state but an ongoing process of engagement, reflection, and action.

Townes underscores the collective nature of the struggle against systemic injustice. She argues that "tackling structural evil takes a whole bunch of folks with varieties of skills and insights because structures of domination rarely come in such pristine

---

18 Emilie M. Townes, *Womanist Ethics and the Cultural Production of Evil* (New York: Palgrave Macmillan, 2006), 155.

forms.... To speak of solidarity ... is to tempt the agony of the absurd, but frankly, I simply don't know what else to do and remain faithful."[19] This insight resonates deeply with our understanding of accompaniment as a communal practice that goes beyond individual relationships to engage with broader systemic issues.

Townes's emphasis on the everyday nature of ethical action reminds us that accompaniment is not limited to grand gestures or formal roles. Instead, it manifests in our daily interactions, choices, and commitments. This perspective encourages us to see accompaniment as a way of being in the world, a constant orientation toward justice and solidarity that infuses all aspects of our lives. Her insistence on the importance of particularity in addressing structural evil aligns with our understanding of accompaniment as a practice that honors the unique experiences and contexts of individuals and communities. It reminds us that effective accompaniment must be attentive to the specific ways in which systemic injustices manifest in people's lives, rather than relying on one-size-fits-all approaches.

In light of Townes's work, we can see accompaniment not just as walking alongside individuals in their personal journeys, but as a collective effort to dismantle structures of oppression, even when those structures appear within liberation movements. This approach challenges us to consider how our practices of accompaniment can contribute to broader movements for social justice. It invites us to see accompaniment as a form of solidarity that involves empathetic listening and support as well as active participation in the work of social transformation.

As we conclude this exploration of liberation theology perspectives on accompaniment, from Freire's critical pedagogy to Gutiérrez's solidarity with the poor, Cone's Black liberation theology, and Townes's Womanist ethics, we see an evolution of insight that pushes us to understand accompaniment as a deeply transformative and socially engaged practice. These thinkers challenge us to move beyond individualistic notions of vocation and accompaniment, urging us to consider the systemic and collective dimensions of our journeys.

As we move forward, the challenge before us is to hold these diverse perspectives in creative tension. The gentle, patient accompaniment emphasized by Pope Francis and the prophetic, justice-oriented approach of liberation theologians need not be mutually exclusive. Instead, they can inform a richer, more holistic practice of accompaniment. In the next section, I explore how these insights can be integrated into a three-dimensional model of accompaniment that honors both the personal and systemic dimensions of vocational discernment, always grounded in everyday ethical action.

---

19 Ibid., 156.

Toward a Three-Dimensional Model of Accompaniment

Drawing from the rich insights of Pope Francis's nurturing approach and liberation theology's prophetic stance, I frame accompaniment as having three dimensions: Companioning, Disruption, and Witness. These embody the yoked connection between reflection and formation discussed in the third chapter: Companioning often involves creating safe space for formation and vulnerable sharing; Disruption frequently prompts critical reflection and reorientation; and Witness integrates both, naming the sacred movements (reflection) that shape a person's ongoing journey (formation).

Effective accompaniment incorporates all three of these dimensions, each playing a role in providing a holistic and transformative experience. The art of accompaniment lies in discerning when to tend gently and when to prune boldly. Some seasons call for patient nurturing, creating a safe space for vulnerable exploration. Other times require prophetic challenge, spurring growth through disruption. Often, we need both simultaneously, compassionately holding space for someone's struggle while also gently challenging them to see beyond their current limitations.

Companioning embodies patient, compassionate presence and solidarity, creating the foundational trust and safety necessary for exploration and growth. It involves deep listening, empathetic understanding, and journeying alongside another in their vocational discernment. This dimension creates a space for vulnerability and self-expression, allowing journeys to unfold at their own pace while offering compassionate support through joys and struggles. In the Ignatian tradition, this is rooted in the concept of *cura personalis* (care for the whole person), recognizing that vocational discernment integrates all aspects of one's life.

Disruption acknowledges that growth often requires challenging comfortable assumptions and confronting both personal limitations and unjust systems. It incorporates loving correction and prophetic action, whether through gently pushing someone to consider new possibilities, asking probing questions that surface hidden assumptions embedded in their patterns of belief and behavior, or addressing oppressive structures. This dimension prevents accompaniment from becoming merely supportive or complicit in perpetuating harmful patterns. The accompanier must discern when to pose challenging questions, when to encourage broader thinking, and when to engage in loving confrontation. This could mean asking someone to reflect more deeply on their motives, consider perspectives they've overlooked, or examine how their choices affect others.

Through critical reflection on both personal and societal norms, this dimension challenges individuals to step out of their comfort zones and consider systemic injustices affecting vocational journeys. It reflects both Francis's recognition that growth sometimes requires loving correction and liberation theology's insistence on prophetic action. Thinking back to the fourth chapter's discussion of systems thinking, we could say that this dimension is often connected to the intentional disruption of an unhealthy but familiar equilibrium.

Witness connects individual journeys to larger spiritual and social realities, helping others notice and name God's movement in their lives while bearing witness to injustice and the transformative power of God's love. As discussed in the third chapter, theological reflection and spiritual formation require the ability to recognize and articulate God's presence in our daily experiences. Through careful attention and discerning conversation, we can help those we accompany develop their capacity to notice these sacred movements in their own lives. Sometimes, this means simply reflecting back what we observe ("It seems like there's a pattern of joy when you ..." or "I notice how your energy shifts when you talk about ..."), helping them recognize and name God's activity that they might otherwise miss.

> ### A Practice to Consider:
> # Witness and Walk
>
> *Recognizing and affirming the movement of God in another's life creates opportunities for shared growth and deepened callings. When we name the sacred in each other, we walk together toward greater purpose.*
>
> The next time you are in a conversation with someone and feel like you had the experience that they said something that felt prophetic or aligned with how that person might be called by God into service, let them know. You don't need to be certain: you can both wonder together if you are right.
>
> If you are, what might that mean? If naming this for the person you are with seems like it produces a significant reaction, be sure to stay in touch with them. Don't just say this and then walk away. A comment like that warrants ongoing connection.

Other times, witness grounds accompaniment in a larger context, linking individual experiences to broader narratives of faith and social change. By witnessing to what we see God doing in their lives, we help individuals develop their own theological reflection skills and recognize the holy in their everyday experiences. This witness nurtures their vocational integrity by deepening their awareness of God's presence, which in turn enriches their ongoing spiritual formation.

This integrated approach recognizes that vocational cultivation requires dynamic movement between all three dimensions. Like a skilled gardener who must discern when to nurture, when to prune, and when to simply witness growth, those engaged in accompaniment must develop sensitivity to which dimension is most needed in any given moment. Sometimes, this means dwelling primarily in one dimension, perhaps focusing on Companioning during times of crisis or loss. Other times, it requires fluid movement between dimensions within a single conversation, offering compassionate presence while also gently surfacing challenging questions, all while helping name where God seems to be moving.

Understanding these dimensions is valuable for those who may be called to accompany others and for anyone engaged in vocational discernment themselves. When we understand that effective accompaniment involves Companioning, Disruption, and Witness, we become better equipped to recognize and articulate what kind of support we need in different seasons of our journey. Perhaps we're in a period where we primarily need someone to walk with us through a difficult transition. Or maybe we sense we're stuck in patterns that aren't life-giving and need someone who can offer loving Disruption. Or we might be experiencing subtle movements of the Spirit that we need help naming and recognizing through attentive Witness.

Not all communities or potential accompaniers are equally skilled in all three dimensions. Some excel at compassionate presence but struggle to offer challenge. Others may be quick to push for change but are less adept at patient listening. Understanding these dimensions gives us agency in seeking out the kind of accompaniment we need. We can actively look for individuals or communities that can provide the specific type of support our current season requires. We might even seek out different sources of accompaniment for different dimensions: perhaps a spiritual director for Witness, a justice-oriented mentor for Disruption, and a trusted friend for Companioning.

This three-dimensional model offers distinct advantages over approaches that emphasize fewer aspects of accompaniment. First, it provides a flexible yet consistent framework that can adapt to diverse contexts and needs while maintaining clear guideposts for practice. Second, it promotes holistic growth by simultaneously attending to relational, challenging, and spiritual aspects of vocational discernment. Third, it maintains awareness of how personal vocations intersect with broader social realities, preventing an overly individualistic approach to discernment. Finally, it creates space for mutual transformation, recognizing that both the accompanied and accompanier are shaped through the process.

Perhaps most importantly, this model helps us navigate one of the core tensions in accompaniment: the balance between gentle support and prophetic challenge. By holding Companioning, Disruption, and Witness as equal dimensions rather than opposing forces, we can move beyond false dichotomies between "pastoral" and "prophetic" approaches. Instead, we recognize that truly effective accompaniment requires both deep compassion and loving challenge, both individual care and systemic awareness, both sacred witnessing and social transformation.

This integration equips us to both provide and seek out accompaniment that nurtures vocations that are simultaneously deeply rooted and boldly responsive to the needs of our time. It helps us create and identify spaces where individuals can explore their callings with both safety and courage, supported by communities that know how to tend, prune, and witness with wisdom and love. As we move forward to explore practical applications of this model, we'll see how these dimensions manifest in specific practices and approaches to accompaniment.

Practical Guidance for Accompaniment

As we move from theoretical understanding to practical application, it's helpful to consider how the principles of accompaniment manifest in real-world interactions. The art of companioning others in their vocational journeys is both profound and challenging, requiring sensitivity, discernment, and adaptability. In this section, we'll explore concrete strategies for both those providing accompaniment and those receiving it. The practices I'll discuss are grounded in the theological perspectives and three-dimensional model of accompaniment I suggested above. They aim to bridge the gap between our ideals of compassionate presence and prophetic disruption and the often messy, complex realities of human relationships and personal growth.

For Those Providing Accompaniment

When offering accompaniment, begin by taking time to understand the full context of the person you're walking alongside. What shapes their understanding of calling? How do their family and community view purpose and service? What traditions and practices have formed their spiritual journey? Rather than making assumptions, ask open-ended questions that invite them to share their story and perspective.

In the Companioning dimension, deep listening creates the conditions where trust can naturally develop and growth becomes possible. Pay attention to the language people use to describe their experiences and aspirations. Notice what matters to them, what energizes them, and what concerns them. When someone's background differs from your own, ask with genuine curiosity about their experiences and wisdom. Cultivating patience and humility is essential, as it allows space for the other person's voice to emerge fully without the need to rush to conclusions or offer solutions. Additionally, practice attentiveness to both verbal and nonverbal cues, as these can reveal unspoken truths or struggles that might otherwise remain hidden.

For the Disruption dimension, reflect carefully on the challenges and questions you pose. Consider whether your suggestions arise from understanding their specific situation or from projecting your own path onto theirs. Effective disruption requires a balance of courage and compassion, ensuring that your challenges are not dismissive or overly directive, but rather invitational and constructive. Sometimes, the nudge involves encouraging people to embrace disruption themselves, helping them to recognize when they need to challenge an unhealthy equilibrium in their lives, relationships, or environments. This might mean prompting them to reconsider a pattern that no longer serves them or supporting them in taking bold steps toward justice or growth. Ask open-ended questions that encourage self-reflection, helping them to explore areas they may not have considered while still honoring their autonomy. Be mindful of timing, as disruption offered too soon or too harshly can close someone off instead of fostering growth. Disruption is not about imposing your perspective but about lovingly inviting them to examine assumptions or habits that might be limiting their discernment or well-being. Recognize that this process requires trust, built through prior engagement in the Companioning dimension, and be prepared to sit with discomfort as they wrestle with the insights and challenges you offer.

In the Witness dimension, attune yourself to how the person experiences and names God's presence in their life. Different journeys lead to different ways of recognizing and articulating sacred movements, so learning to speak their spiritual language fosters deeper connections without imposing familiar patterns. Witnessing also means being present in moments of doubt or struggle, reflecting back signs of God's work that they may not yet see and gently helping them discern connections they might have missed. At times, this dimension extends beyond the individual to the broader community, requiring you to name and lift up someone's contributions and gifts that have been overlooked or taken for granted. Sometimes, the overlooking has occurred because the person you are accompanying has been hiding their light under a bushel, afraid to speak plainly about their labors for fear of being too egotistical. By witnessing to their value, both to them and to the community, you can help them see their worth in a new light, offering encouragement to embrace their gifts fully as a reflection of God's work in and through them.

Flexibility and openness enrich all aspects of accompaniment. Regularly ask if what you're offering serves their journey, and be ready to adjust your approach. This might mean changing how often or where you meet, exploring different spiritual practices together, or reconsidering what you're working toward. Be willing to step outside your usual methods if another approach would better serve their growth. At the heart of all three dimensions is the commitment to hold their unique story at the center, rather than imposing your own expectations. Each dimension also requires humility, as true accompaniment involves acknowledging what you don't know and remaining attentive to how God is at work in their life in ways you may not yet understand.

Embrace accompaniment as mutual learning. While you may have more experience in certain areas, the person you walk alongside brings their own wisdom and insight. Create relationships where you support and facilitate rather than direct. Be transparent about your limitations, and be willing to say, "I don't know." The practical theologian Annie Lockhart-Gilroy talks about "bi-directional mentoring," and I think this concept applies to accompaniment as well.[20] Accompaniment flourishes when both parties recognize they can learn from each other. This collaboration reflects the interconnected nature of spiritual journeys and deepens both participants' understanding of vocation.

Remember that individual journeys connect to the broader community and tradition. Help others see how their path interweaves with larger narratives of faith and service. This might mean introducing stories of others who have walked similar paths, facilitating mentor connections, or exploring how their gifts might serve community needs. Their unique calling exists within a web of relationships and possibilities that can enrich both their discernment and their eventual service.

Regular self-reflection strengthens your capacity to accompany others. Notice your reactions, assumptions, and emotional responses. Know your boundaries and move between the three dimensions as needed. While creating safe space for exploration (Companioning) forms the foundation, recognize when loving challenge (Disruption) might spark growth, always remaining attentive to how God moves in the process (Witness). This need to be aware of what the best form of accompaniment might be requires its own discernment. Even then, accompaniment is not always done well. Certain challenges commonly arise.

For those who accompany others on their spiritual journeys, whether as formal educators, mentors, or experienced lay ministers, the structured nature of institutional life can distance us from the daily realities of ministry, service, and student life. In a way, this tension can be a function of a power difference between professionals within an institution who have some level of security and students who may not be sure what the future has in store for them. Those in positions of institutional authority often have access to resources, networks, stability, and funding that students or mentees may

---

20 Annie Lockhart-Gilroy, *Nurturing the Sanctified Imagination of Urban Youth* (Skyforest, CA: Urban Loft Publishers, 2020), 79–80.

lack, creating an inherent imbalance. This dynamic can unintentionally lead to a lack of empathy or an overemphasis on institutional goals, which risks overshadowing the unique and vulnerable process of discernment unfolding for the individual.

I've heard of many times when assumptions from someone in an academic position can inadvertently narrow the paths students feel free to explore. For example, I can think of a student who hesitated to share his calling to arts ministry because it didn't fit what he thought a "serious" seminary professor would value and he knew he wanted to consider academic work. Instead of asking how it is that the arts might inform academic scholarship, he was considering pushing aside that part of himself to better fit what he had seen modeled for him. That experience, and others like it, have taught me to explicitly encourage exploration of unexpected paths and to share stories of diverse callings.

In Isaiah, I read that, even when God is doing a new thing, it is sometimes hard to notice at first (Isaiah 43:19). Reflecting on this, I've come to realize that what comes next often begins to take shape before we fully notice it, inviting us into a deeper awareness of the movements of the Spirit. What "comes next" has often already begun. I've also learned the hard way that trying to be everything to everyone who needs accompaniment can easily lead to burnout. Setting clear boundaries and tending to my own spiritual health actually makes me a better accompanier. I think this is true for most of us, not just professors.

In congregational settings, I've heard many stories about the challenge of viewing others' callings through the lens of one's own church experience. Other people aren't us in different bodies. Experience in ministry, while valuable, doesn't make anyone an expert about another's vocational journey. Each person's path with God unfolds uniquely. Faithful accompaniment means expanding our vision of how God calls people, recognizing that, while our own story may be useful at times, we shouldn't presume it to be normative for those we serve and walk with. Pastors and priests, in particular, have to be on guard to resist the temptation to shape someone's discernment around their congregation's immediate needs or denominational patterns. This temptation often arises from the pressures of institutional survival or a desire for predictability, which can inadvertently prioritize organizational goals over an individual's emerging call.

Regular self-reflection helps us notice when we're projecting our own paths onto others. Many accompaniers I know keep journals of their experiences, noting patterns in their responses and assumptions. This practice reveals common tendencies, like rushing to problem-solve when someone really needs space to explore, or avoiding challenging questions when tension makes us uncomfortable. Each dimension of accompaniment becomes more grounded when we're honest about our own limitations and growth edges.

For Those Receiving Accompaniment

Understanding the dimensions of accompaniment can help you actively shape your journey of vocational discernment. While others offer valuable guidance, you are ultimately the expert on your own experiences and calling. This understanding empowers you to seek out the kind of accompaniment you need in different seasons. Begin by reflecting on what kind of accompaniment would best serve your current situation. Not all potential accompaniers are equally skilled in all three dimensions. Some excel at compassionate presence but struggle to offer challenge. Others may be quick to push for change but are less adept at patient listening.

Do you need someone to primarily walk with you through a difficult transition? Are you feeling stuck in patterns that aren't life-giving and need someone who can offer loving Disruption? Or do you sense subtle movements of the Spirit that you need help naming through attentive Witness? When considering potential accompaniers, have initial conversations about their approach and experience. Ask about their understanding of vocational discernment, how they view their role, and what kind of support they're equipped to offer. Pay attention to the chemistry in these conversations. While accompaniment isn't friendship, there should be a basic comfort and trust in the connection.

Consider building a network of support rather than relying on just one person. You might seek different sources of accompaniment for different dimensions. Peer accompaniment can be particularly valuable alongside more formal relationships, offering perspective from others in similar life stages or transitions. As you engage in accompaniment, several common challenges can hinder genuine discernment and growth. I know of at least five ways that I see often. Understanding these helps you navigate more intentionally.

First, becoming overly dependent on guidance rather than doing your own discernment is a significant pitfall. While accompaniers offer valuable perspective, the work of discernment belongs to you, in relation to your community and God. You are the main part of the equation. Cultivate your own practice of noticing and naming alongside the accompaniment process. Keep a journal of your thoughts, questions, and insights. Pay attention to patterns in your experiences: What brings you joy? Where do you find challenge? When do you feel most alive? Reflecting on your answers to these questions can provide meaningful content for conversation with those accompanying you.

Second, practice active listening with your accompaniers, but don't shy away from respectfully challenging guidance that doesn't resonate with your experience or sense of calling. When receiving feedback or challenge, take time to discern what resonates with your journey. Sometimes initial resistance points to areas that need attention;

other times, it signals a mismatch between the guidance and your path. When you receive conflicting guidance from different accompaniers, use this as an opportunity for deeper discernment rather than seeing it as a problem to solve. What might these different perspectives reveal about your journey? How do they connect to your own inner knowing?

Third, the tendency to present only your "best self" in accompaniment can also be a limit to growth. While it's natural to want to make a good impression, sometimes it is the case that powerful growth can come from the honest sharing of struggles, doubts, and questions. This is where vulnerability becomes a key practice in being accompanied. Simply put, if you cannot be open, it is very hard to be accompanied in a meaningful way. The ability to trust someone enough to not only share your successes but to actively invite their concerns is a powerful catalyst for growth. Imagine finding someone you can honestly ask, "What about me and my current journey worries you?" and knowing that you both desire and can trust their response. That kind of exchange, where you are seeking loving critique rather than simple affirmation, can be profoundly liberating. It moves the relationship beyond performance and into a space of authentic mutual care where real discernment can happen.

Embrace vulnerability while knowing your boundaries. Share your challenges and uncertainties, but also recognize when you need privacy or when certain topics feel too raw to discuss. Recognize that spiritual accompaniment is not the same thing as getting professional mental healthcare. Both can be a part of your plan for accompaniment. And a plan *is* needed.

Fourth, it is important to remember that discernment doesn't happen in isolation. Stay connected to the broader community and tradition in which your discernment takes place. Participate in communal practices of worship, service, and reflection. Use these spaces to test and validate insights from your accompaniment relationships. Pay attention when individual discernment seems to conflict with community expectations: These tensions often hold important information about both personal calling and community needs. That being said, power dynamics can significantly affect accompaniment relationships, especially when your accompanier holds authority in your community or institution. Don't let their status prevent honest expression of your thoughts or disagreements. If you consistently feel intimidated or unable to speak freely, consider what that means for you and your journey.

Fifth, and finally, as your discernment unfolds, you may find your needs for accompaniment shifting. What served you well in one season might not fit in another. Sometimes you'll discover you've outgrown a particular relationship or need different support for a new phase of discernment. Learning to recognize these shifts and navigate them gracefully is itself part of the discernment process. Ending or changing an accompaniment relationship isn't a failure. It often signals growth and deeper understanding of your path.

The vocational journey rarely moves in a straight line. Periods of clarity alternate with times of confusion, and insights often emerge from wrestling with uncertainty rather than rushing toward answers. Make time for rest and practices that nourish your soul along the way. By engaging thoughtfully with accompaniment in all its dimensions, you create space for your calling to emerge and evolve, supported by wisdom that is both deeply personal and richly communal.

The Interplay of Giving and Receiving Accompaniment

As we navigate our vocational journeys, it's helpful to recognize that we often find ourselves simultaneously giving and receiving accompaniment. This dual role reflects the interconnected nature of our identities and the complex web of relationships in which we are embedded, as explored in the preceding chapter.

Our lives are not neatly compartmentalized into discrete roles of "accompanier" and "accompanied." Instead, we exist within a dynamic system of relationships where we may be offering guidance in one context while seeking it in another. A seminary professor, for instance, might be accompanying students in their vocational discernment while also receiving accompaniment from a spiritual director or mentor in their own ongoing journey of faith and service.

Understanding accompaniment through the lens of Companioning, Disruption, and Witness helps illuminate this dynamic interplay. When primarily offering accompaniment, we might feel confident Companioning someone through grief while simultaneously needing Disruption in our own stuck patterns. We might skillfully help others notice God's presence in their lives while yearning for someone to Witness sacred movements in our own journey. This recognition that we need different dimensions of accompaniment in different seasons can make us more attuned accompaniers, helping us notice what others might need.

The systems thinking approach we discussed earlier helps us understand these shifting roles. We are not isolated individuals but part of larger networks where our actions and experiences ripple outward. When I receive challenging feedback from my own accompanier, it might transform how I offer challenge to others. When someone I accompany shares a profound insight, it often shapes my own vocational understanding. Accompaniment becomes a form of mutual transformation, where every encounter has the potential to shape both parties. Recognizing this dual nature of accompaniment can enrich our practice in several ways.

First, it fosters humility. When we acknowledge that we are always both learners and teachers, we approach our role as accompaniers with greater openness and less presumption of expertise. This humility can create more mutually beneficial relationships. Even in moments when we feel confident in our ability to offer guidance, remembering our own need for accompaniment helps us stay grounded. We recognize that our insights and experiences, while valuable, are always partial and contextual. God's ways are always higher than our ways (Isaiah 55:8–9), so it is worth being attentive to the provisional nature of our understanding. This humility creates space for genuine dialogue where we can be surprised by wisdom that emerges from unexpected sources.

Second, the dual nature of accompaniment enhances our empathy. When we're actively engaged in both giving and receiving accompaniment, we're more attuned to the vulnerabilities and challenges on both sides of the relationship. We know firsthand how it feels to share difficult truths, to receive challenging feedback, and to wrestle with uncertainty. This lived experience of vulnerability can help us create safer spaces for others to explore how God might be calling them. I think often of Paul's reminder to the Thessalonians to "encourage one another and build each other up" (1 Thess. 5:11). When we are yoked to one other, we better understand the courage it takes to share doubts, the fear that can arise when facing disruption, and the deep need for witness to sacred movements in our lives. This dual perspective makes us more sensitive and responsive accompaniers, better able to notice and honor others' experiences.

Third, it promotes a more holistic view of vocational discernment. Rather than seeing it as a linear process with clear "experts" and "novices," we can appreciate it as a communal journey where insights and growth can come from unexpected sources. This view recognizes that God's calling often emerges through the interplay of relationships, where roles of giving and receiving shift fluidly. A student's genuine question might crack open new insight for a professor. A mentee's struggle might help a mentor recognize patterns in their own life. This more dynamic understanding helps us stay open to how the Spirit moves in all directions, often working through our relationships in surprising ways to shape both individual and communal vocational understanding.

For example, in my own Quaker tradition, we say that doing communal discernment doesn't always yield the answer we were looking for. Sometimes it doesn't yield any answer at all. But it always has the potential to deepen our capacity for discernment itself. The same is true in accompaniment. Every engagement in giving or receiving guidance strengthens our ability to notice and respond to God's movement, both in our own lives and in our communities. This mutual strengthening of discernment muscles helps us move beyond simplistic notions of expertise toward a more nuanced understanding of how vocational clarity emerges through relationship.

These enriching aspects of dual accompaniment don't emerge automatically. The humility, empathy, and holistic understanding it fosters all require intentional cultivation and careful attention to the complexities inherent in such relationships. These patterns mirror the systemic dynamics we explored in the fourth chapter, where we saw how changes in one part of a system ripple outward to affect the whole. Just as the reintroduction of wolves transformed Yellowstone's ecosystem, one person learning to give and receive accompaniment well can catalyze transformation throughout a community. This is the fractal nature of change: How we are in the small is how we are in the large. However, this dual role also presents unique challenges. It requires a high degree of self-awareness to navigate the shifting dynamics of when to speak and when to listen, when to offer guidance and when to seek it. It also demands flexibility, as we may need to quickly switch between these modes in different contexts or even within the same relationship.

The boundaries between giving and receiving accompaniment can sometimes blur, particularly in peer relationships or mentoring situations where the power dynamic is not clearly defined. This ambiguity can be both enriching and challenging, requiring careful discernment to ensure that both parties' needs are being met and boundaries are respected. For those in formal accompaniment roles, such as spiritual directors or mentors, it's important to create intentional spaces for receiving your own accompaniment. This might involve regular meetings with a supervisor, engaging in peer support groups, or maintaining your own spiritual direction relationship. I've heard more than one story from students in "supervised ministry" where they felt like their ministry mentor was using them to process stuff they probably ought to have been working through elsewhere.

This underscores the importance of having our own spaces for processing and growth separate from those we accompany. Just as we wouldn't expect a therapist to work through their personal issues during a client's session, we need to be mindful of maintaining appropriate boundaries in accompaniment relationships. This doesn't mean we can't learn from those we accompany. Indeed, as we've seen, mutual transformation is often part of the journey. But maintaining appropriate boundaries does mean being intentional about where and how we process our own vocational questions and challenges.

As we conclude this exploration of practical guidance for accompaniment, we return to the heart of what makes this practice transformative: its deeply relational nature and our experience of God in the midst of us. Whether giving or receiving, leading or following, teaching or learning, we remain connected to one another in ways that shape our understanding of calling and vocation. The three dimensions of accompaniment—Companioning, Disruption, and Witness—weave through all these relationships, sometimes flowing from us, sometimes toward us, always guided by the Spirit's movement in our midst. By remaining attentive to these dynamics and cultivating practices that support both giving and receiving well, we create spaces where vocational discernment can flourish, nurturing growth not just in individuals but in our communities as a whole.

A Possible Practice

As we consider how to move beyond silence into active engagement with our vocations, I'd like to share a practical approach I've developed and used in workshops over the years. This workshop, called "Stewarding Leadings and Gifts," provides a structured yet flexible framework for individuals and communities to discern, nurture, and act upon their callings. It embodies the transition from quiet contemplation to dynamic, communal engagement with vocation.[21]

The workshop is designed as a community practice to foster vocational discernment and nurture ministry. Ideally conducted in settings like church groups, professional cohorts, or ministry teams, this workshop creates a supportive environment where participants engage with the material both individually and collectively. The communal context is key, as it allows for continued exploration and application of the practices long after the workshop concludes. There are provided questions to consider and topics that are connected to those questions, but the heart of the workshop lies in the conversations, deep listening, and connections that participants forge or deepen with one another.

This workshop can be particularly powerful in lay ministry contexts. For example, a community Bible study group might use these practices to help members discover and nurture their gifts for service. A neighborhood ministry team might employ these tools to support each other's callings and strengthen their collective impact. The workshop's flexibility allows it to be adapted for any setting where people are seeking to better understand and live out their call to serve.

The flow of the workshop is that small groups of people jointly consider a paired set of ideas and then ask themselves and each other a set of questions about the ideas. This repeats three times; there's a break; and then it repeats two more times. Then, at the end, time is made for planning concrete next steps that the community can do to support one or more of the things they discussed. Functionally, this is a community practice that, when boiled down, is really just a facilitated conversation about a series of practices that can help provide the

---

21 I first co-led an early version of this workshop with my wife Kristina Keefe-Perry and Elaine Emily, who was providing accompaniment for us all as we served in the ministry among Quakers in Intermountain Yearly Meeting.

cultural container in which vocational discernment and the nurture of ministry are supported. There are four sets of questions that are asked five different times, each about a different topic.

The first pair of ideas is "Noticing and Naming." Below is the text I provide. Note that it provides some substantive food for thought without being overly long.

> Noticing is the practice of paying attention to the gifts, talents, and potential that may be emerging in an individual. Although it can involve spiritual sensitivity, at its core, it's about being intentional and caring in our observations of others. It's not about having special powers or insights, but rather about taking the time to really see people and what they might be capable of. This could be as simple as recognizing when someone consistently shows up to help, noticing the way a person lights up when talking about a particular topic, or observing how others naturally turn to someone for advice or support. Noticing doesn't require expertise or special training: it's something we can all do by being present and attentive in our interactions. It might involve seeing beyond someone's current role or status to recognize untapped potential. Although it can be strengthened with practice, noticing is fundamentally about being genuinely interested in others and their growth. It's a way of showing care through our attention, even before we put any observations into words.
>
> Naming goes beyond just recognizing. It is the act of articulating the gifts or callings you have noticed. This could be done formally, such as through a nomination for a specific role or responsibility, or informally, by expressing a simple observation over a conversation. Naming provides validation and acknowledgment to the individual, helping them recognize their own gifts or potential. However, not all responses to being named will be the same. Some people will feel joyful, while others may feel uncomfortable. Yet it's important to remember that the act of naming comes with responsibility. Follow-up is necessary to nurture what has been named. Finally, the ability to both notice and name emerging gifts in others is itself a unique gift.

There's much more that could be said about either of these topics, but, to help people dig into the material, it is often useful to pare down as much as possible. Each group reads the pairing aloud and has some time for the individuals to reflect on what they've read. I then ask the group to go through these questions:

1. Has anyone ever had an experience of [Noticing or Naming]? If so, what was it like?
2. Beyond any experiences shared, what other ways could this practice look like? That is, imagine how else it could be done. If a video camera were on while [Noticing or Naming] was happening, what would it record? Where? Who?
3. What life-giving things might emerge if more [Noticing or Naming] of this was done? How might it change the community? The individuals involved?
4. What obstacles might there be that prevent more [Noticing or Naming] from happening?

I emphasize that there's no need to rush through these questions. If the conversation becomes particularly engaging on one point, I encourage the group to stay with it. However, I also remind them to be mindful of group dynamics, suggesting that they try to avoid having the same person speak first each time. I stress that everyone brings wisdom to the conversation and diverse perspectives enrich the discussion.

In addition to noticing and naming, I include four other pairs of practices:

- Engagement and Encouragement: Both the individual and their community share responsibility in nurturing spiritual gifts, with the individual exploring their calling and the community offering support, resources, and opportunities for growth through active engagement.
- Prioritizing and Pruning: This practice requires mutual responsibility, as the individual clarifies priorities and sets boundaries, while the community supports these choices through understanding, dialogue, and respect for their redefined commitments.
- Exercise and Experiment: Both the individual and the community work together to move beyond theory, with the individual taking risks and trying new things, while the community encourages and provides space for these experiments in service of their calling.
- Rest and Reassessment: Reflection and growth are a shared responsibility, where the individual engages in practices of rest and discernment, and the community provides a space to celebrate growth, reassess direction, and offer support during the process.

It's important to note that, for each of these five pairs of practices, there is a shared responsibility between the individual stewarding their spiritual gifts and the community supporting them. This mutual engagement reflects the interconnected nature of vocational discernment we've discussed throughout this book.

For Noticing and Naming, while individuals must be open to recognizing their own gifts, the community plays a crucial role in affirming and articulating these gifts. In Engaging and Encouraging, both parties actively participate in nurturing the identified gifts. Prioritizing and Pruning requires the individual to set boundaries and make choices, while the community respects and supports (or challenges) these decisions. Exercising and Experimenting involves risk-taking by the individual, supported by a community that provides safe spaces for exploration. Finally, Resting and Reassessing is a shared process of reflection, where the individual takes time for discernment, and the community offers space for this reflection and helps celebrate growth. This collaborative approach underscores that vocational discernment is not a solitary journey but a communal process of mutual support and growth.

In the workshop, we explore the first three practice pairs, then take a break to allow participants to move, reflect, and recharge. Upon reconvening, we move into the final two pairs, followed by a collective share-out where groups have the opportunity to discuss their insights and experiences. The workshop then culminates in an action-planning phase. Here, participants collaborate to identify concrete, achievable steps they can take to foster a culture that supports ministry within their midst. Identifying what obstacles there might be to that support is useful to consider as well.

This process is particularly powerful when the entire group is already part of an established community, as it allows for immediate application and follow-through. However, even when participants come from diverse communities, this exercise remains valuable. It equips individuals with practical ideas and strategies they can adapt and implement in their home contexts, spreading the impact of the workshop far beyond the immediate group. This final stage transforms the theoretical discussions into tangible action plans, ensuring that the insights gained during the workshop have the potential to create lasting change in how communities support and nurture vocational callings.

In the workshop, participants often share powerful stories that illustrate both the presence and absence of support in their vocational journeys. They might describe the transformative impact of having a gift named by someone else, the growth that came from being encouraged to take on a new role, or the clarity that emerged from intentional periods of rest and reassessment. Equally important, and often more poignant, are the stories of times when individuals felt unseen, unsupported, or actively discouraged in their callings.

As a facilitator, I strive to create an environment where these sometimes-difficult stories can be shared and heard without defensiveness. I encourage participants to practice deep listening, embodying Douglas Steere's idea of "listening people into disclosure" that opened this chapter. This can be challenging, especially when I'm not intimately familiar with the communities represented in the workshop. This is one reason why I believe it's ideal for communities to run this workshop themselves. However, I approach the process with a presumption of best intentions and work to cultivate a space where discovery and vulnerability are not just possible but welcomed.

These reflections on both supportive and unsupportive experiences often spark the most profound discussions about the importance of community in vocational discernment. They highlight the real-world impact of the practices we're discussing and underscore the need for intentional, supportive communities. Stories of struggle can inspire participants to commit more deeply to creating environments where gifts are noticed, nurtured, and given space to flourish.

By creating space for both positive and negative experiences, the workshop acknowledges the complex reality of vocational journeys. It reminds us that the path of discernment is often marked by both joyful affirmations and painful setbacks. This honest approach allows participants to engage more meaningfully with the material, recognizing that the practices we're discussing aren't just theoretical ideals, but vital supports that can make a real difference in people's lives.

Through this process, the workshop becomes a microcosm of the supportive community we're aiming to create. It allows participants to experience firsthand the power of being truly heard and the transformative potential of a community committed to nurturing each other's gifts and callings. This approach often leads to more nuanced and compassionate discussions about how to create supportive environments for vocational discernment, moving us beyond silence into active, communal engagement with our callings. By culminating in concrete action planning, the workshop embodies the call to move beyond passive contemplation into active engagement with our callings. This aligns with our exploration of the limits of silence and the necessity of prophetic action in the face of injustice or unfulfilled potential.

I don't think this workshop is *the* answer to anything, but I do believe that it is a way to move toward a practical manifestation of the ideas we've explored throughout this chapter. By engaging in this process, participants move beyond theoretical understanding to active, communal engagement with vocation. They practice deep listening, share vulnerability, and collaboratively plan concrete actions to foster a culture of vocational support. This emphasis on shared responsibility echoes our discussion of the systemic nature of vocation, reinforcing the idea that vocational discernment is not a solitary pursuit but a communal process deeply embedded in our relationships and social contexts. This practical application helps bridge the gap between our ideals of accompaniment and the often messy realities of lived experience. However, the journey of vocational discernment doesn't end with a workshop or retreat; it's an ongoing process that requires continued commitment, reflection, and action. Like the quilted fragments of belonging we explored in the sixth chapter, ministry, too, is a pieced-together offering: imperfect, textured, and faithful in its incompleteness.

The Power and Limits of Silence

As I conclude our exploration of accompaniment, I want to return to Martin Luther King Jr.'s words that opened the chapter: "There comes a time when silence is betrayal." This statement encapsulates a central tension in the practice of accompaniment: knowing when to listen deeply and when to speak boldly. While contemplative traditions like my own Quakerism emphasize the transformative power of deep listening, King reminds us that listening alone is insufficient. Faithful accompaniment requires discernment about when to remain silent and when to break that silence.

The patient, attentive listening we discussed creates space for meaningful vocational exploration. It allows stories to unfold, doubts to be voiced, and sacred movements to be noticed. This kind of silence builds trust and nurtures growth. However, when we encounter injustice, oppression, or the suppression of genuine callings, remaining silent becomes complicity. Or, perhaps more pointedly, when those we *accompany* encounter injustice, we must be prepared to respond. The limits of silence become particularly apparent when accompanying those whose vocations challenge existing power structures or cultural norms.

When a woman experiences resistance to her calling to ministry in a patriarchal context, or when a person of color faces systemic barriers in pursuing their vocation, sympathetic listening without active advocacy can perpetuate harm. This highlights the need for accompaniment to integrate the kind of systems awareness discussed in the fourth chapter, recognizing that individual struggles are often intertwined with broader institutional patterns and power dynamics. Likewise, quietly supporting individuals without addressing institutional practices or cultural assumptions that stifle the flourishing of their callings fails to fully embody meaningful accompaniment.

We see these limits clearly in our discussion of liberation theology's perspectives. Freire, Gutiérrez, Cone, and Townes all emphasize that transformation requires more than contemplative witness. System-level change demands prophetic speech and action. Their insights remind us that vocational discernment happens within social contexts marked by power dynamics and systemic inequities. Effective accompaniment must engage with these realities, not just individual spiritual journeys. In this way, accompaniment becomes eschatological. Not because we await a future realm, but because we trust that the Divine is already among us, laboring toward wholeness. To accompany others in their suffering is to step into the ways in which the Reign of God is unfolding now.

The three dimensions of accompaniment help us navigate this balance. Companioning often requires the silence of deep listening. Disruption calls us to break silence when needed, challenging harmful patterns or systemic barriers. Witness demands we speak truth about both the sacred movements we observe and the injustices that impede them.

As we engage in accompaniment, may we cultivate the courage to listen deeply when silence serves growth and to speak boldly when silence would betray our calling to nurture vocation in ourselves and others. The art of accompaniment lies not in perfecting either silence or speech, but in learning to move faithfully between them in service of God's transforming work in our lives and communities.

Questions for Reflection

1. The chapter explores Pope Francis's emphasis on patient, compassionate accompaniment. Think of a time when someone companioned you with this kind of presence. What made their accompaniment meaningful? What did you learn from this experience?

2. Liberation theology perspectives, as explored in this chapter, urge us to connect individual accompaniment with the work of systemic change and solidarity with the marginalized. In your own context or areas of service, how do you see the relationship between supporting individual vocational journeys and the need to address broader social justice issues? Where do you feel the tension or synergy between pastoral care and prophetic action?

3. This chapter proposes a three-dimensional model of accompaniment: Companioning (patient presence), Disruption (loving challenge and prophetic action), and Witness (naming God's movement and bearing witness to injustice). How does this framework resonate with your understanding or experience of supporting others? Which of these dimensions feels most natural or intuitive for you to practice? Which one presents the greatest challenge or growth edge, and why might that be?

4. The idea of "bi-directional mentoring" or mutual learning suggests that in any accompaniment relationship, both parties can teach and learn from each other. Can you recall a time when someone you were intending to support or guide ended up teaching you something significant

about faith, vocation, or justice? Conversely, have you sensed moments where your presence or questions helped someone else see their own path more clearly?

5. Accompaniment relationships are rarely free of power dynamics, whether overt or subtle. Have you experienced challenges related to power differentials, either when you were accompanying someone or when someone was accompanying you? If so, how did you navigate those dynamics, or how might you strive to create more equitable and empowering accompaniment relationships in the future?

6. Toward the end of the chapter I discuss a workshop model that emphasizes both noticing and naming gifts in community. Can you imagine something like this being fruitful in any of your contexts? What would be the barriers? What are the opportunities?

8

Storytelling

Stories are the creative conversion of life itself into a more powerful, clearer, more meaningful experience.
—Robert McKee

The artist cannot and must not take anything for granted, but must drive to the heart of every answer and expose the question the answer hides.
—James Baldwin

In Matt Haig's novel *The Midnight Library* the boundaries between the present and the possible blur in a captivating exploration of life's pivotal moments.[1] The story introduces us to Nora Seed, a woman crushed by the weight of her regrets and unfulfilled potential. On the brink of taking her own life, Nora instead finds herself transported to a vast library where each book holds a different version of her life. Accompanied by Mrs. Elm, her childhood librarian turned metaphysical guide, Nora embarks on a journey through these alternate lives, each one a road not taken, each offering a glimpse of what might have been. Each book in the library represents a different life, a different version of Nora, based on the choices she might have made. Throughout the course of the book Nora explores lives where she is a rock star, a glaciologist, a successful Olympic swimmer, and a mother, among other possibilities. In each life, she experiences different levels of happiness, fulfillment, and disappointment.

---

1 Matt Haig, *The Midnight Library* (New York: Viking, 2020).

Like Nora exploring different versions of her life, we, too, engage in a journey of storytelling and exploration as we seek to understand and live out our calling. The shelves of our own "midnight libraries" are filled with narratives of who we are, who we might become, and what we're meant to do in this world. As I've said throughout this book, vocational discernment isn't about discovering a single, preordained path. In this chapter we'll look at how it can be seen as an ongoing process of narration and re-narration. Just as Nora's journey through the library leads her to confront her regrets, desires, and sense of purpose, our own process of vocational discernment invites us to examine the stories we tell about ourselves and to consider how these narratives might evolve.

Nora eventually realizes it is important to listen to Thoreau: "It's not what you look at that matters; it's what you see."[2] To that, I'd add that it also matters what you say about what you've seen. That being said, for many folk, systemic or social barriers restrict the ability to speak freely without a sense of potential repercussion. I take this as a reminder of the importance of finding (or creating) spaces where all voices can be heard and valued. Haig's metaphor underscores that our lives are composed of countless narrative possibilities, with each choice we make contributing to the evolving story of our vocation. Nora's journey through her alternate lives initially seems to offer answers to her most haunting questions: What if she had chosen differently? Who might she have become? Each life she explores offers a unique sense of clarity, turning abstract regrets into concrete experiences. She sees her "what ifs" materialize, each new possibility bringing a certain closure, a resolution to one of life's many unclosed doors. This process mirrors Robert McKee's view of storytelling as a way to transform experience into coherence, making life's ambiguities feel settled and more meaningful.[3]

But clarity alone, satisfying as it may be, doesn't bring Nora lasting fulfillment. As she dives deeper into the library of her possible lives, clarity transforms into something more ambiguous. Here, James Baldwin's charge for the artist to drive "to the heart of every answer" and expose the questions beneath it comes to life.[4] Nora's answers don't simply resolve her questions; they provoke new ones. Her experience reveals how story can illuminate but also disturb, drawing us into the hidden depths that clarity alone cannot reach. We begin to see that some stories, rather than providing a fixed

---

2 Ibid., 219.

3 Robert McKee, *Story: Substance, Structure, Style and the Principles of Screenwriting* (New York: ReganBooks, 1997). Also see epigraph.

4 James Baldwin, "The Creative Process," in *Creative America*, ed. John F. Kennedy, Dwight D. Eisenhower, Harry S. Truman, et al. (New York: Ridge Press, 1962). Also see epigraph.

meaning, unsettle our need for neat conclusions, pressing us to dwell in complexity and resist an easy satisfaction.

This is the duality in storytelling, providing clarity yet also unraveling it. From one view, narrative offers the comfort of form and coherence, of knowing and naming. Stories usually have a clear beginning, middle, and end. From another, meaningful storytelling can dislodge us from our assumptions, leading us into deeper ambiguities. As we engage in this process of vocational storytelling, we are invited to recognize the value in both: the moments of illumination that bring direction and the murkier revelations that require us to sit in the discomfort of unknowing.

There was a season when I stopped saying "I teach theology" and started saying, "I help people name what they care about most, and why." It changed more than just how others saw me. It changed how I saw myself. That small shift in story unsettled years of assumptions about what counted as legitimate work, about what kind of authority I thought I needed to have. It also surfaced deeper questions I hadn't yet asked: What do I really believe teaching is for? Whose questions am I helping people name? And who gets to call that holy work? The story gave shape, yes, but it also cracked something open.

Like Nora, I found myself not at the end of a discernment process, but at its beginning again, newly awake to the complex layers of meaning I hadn't yet understood. In the end, our journey becomes less about choosing between clarity and ambiguity, and more about allowing both to shape our understanding, challenging us to see our lives not just as tidy arcs but as layered, dynamic explorations.

In this spirit, the following pages will guide us through both aspects of storytelling: how it clarifies, comforts, and gives shape to our lives, and how it also disrupts, urging us to ask deeper questions that defy simple answers. Through this approach, we'll find that vocational storytelling requires us to both make sense of our past and remain open to the mysteries within it, a process that, much like Nora's midnight library, grows with us, always inviting us to look further and think deeper.

In the pages that follow, we'll examine how the practice of re-narration allows us to transform regret into wisdom, hesitation into action, and uncertainty into a deeper understanding of our calling. We'll consider how, like Nora, we have the power to reshape our stories in light of new experiences, insights, and reflections. Even more importantly, we'll wrestle with a truth that Nora discovers in her journey: that fulfillment isn't found in any one particular life path, but in how we choose to perceive and engage with the life we have.

Theological Perspectives on Storytelling

When I speak of storytelling in the context of vocational discernment, I'm not primarily referring to professional storytellers performing at libraries or festivals, though their work can certainly inspire us. Instead, I'm talking about the stories we tell about ourselves, our communities, and our faith. These are the stories that shape our understanding of who we are and what we're called to do in the world. These stories are told and retold in various settings: in places of worship, in small group discussions, in personal reflections, and in the day-to-day conversations we have with friends, family, and colleagues. The power of narrative to shape our understanding connects directly to our discussion of discernment in the second chapter.

Just as discernment involves sifting through various influences and promptings, storytelling helps us sort through different possible interpretations of our experiences and calling. Yet not all stories hold equal power or influence. The stories we tell (and those we have been taught to tell) are shaped by cultural, historical, and systemic forces that determine whose voices are amplified and whose are silenced. Patrick Reyes offers a profound critique of this dynamic.

> I, along with anyone educated in the United States, am uniquely qualified and proficient in the diversities of white storytelling. In fact, I have an elementary, high school, bachelor's, master's, and doctoral education in what amounts to white storytelling and meaning-making. I know these histories and their diversities. If Malcolm Gladwell is right about people becoming experts after dedicating ten thousand hours to a particular thing, then I am beyond an expert in white narratives.[5]

Reyes's reflection challenges me to interrogate the dominant narratives shaping how I understand vocation and purpose, particularly the ways well-meaning attempts at solidarity can miss the mark.

As Reyes observes, white liberals often respond to discussions of systemic injustice by narrating their own marginalization.[6] Stories of immigrant ancestors or personal struggles, while deeply meaningful, are frequently shared as a way for white folk to align with marginalized voices. Yet, as Reyes reminds us, this insistence on narrating solidarity often functions as a way to re-center whiteness, reinforcing rather than dismantling the systems that silence other voices. This dynamic reveals an important tension in vocational storytelling: Whose stories are being centered, and whose are being overshadowed?

---

5 Patrick Reyes, *The Purpose Gap* (Tantor Media, 2021), 37.
6 Ibid.

When dominant narratives dominate even spaces meant to amplify the marginalized, the result is not inclusion but a reassertion of privilege. As Reyes notes,

> To say that everyone in the room must share their stories equally is not inclusion. To require those from marginalized, colonized, and disenfranchised communities to share the narrative platform with every white, colonial story someone wants to spin is to dishonor the purpose of a preferential option for those voices that have been silenced or forgotten.[7]

This imbalance calls everyone to a collective reimagining of whose stories are centered, inviting both those benefiting from dominant narratives and those marginalized by them to create spaces where silenced voices are prioritized and allowed to inform a richer, more expansive understanding of vocation and purpose.

This critique calls for a broader, more reflective approach to storytelling in vocational discernment, one rooted in humility and a shared commitment to listening deeply. For those whose voices have historically been silenced or marginalized, the act of centering one's own story can be a radical and necessary assertion of agency and worth. At the same time, those whose voices have been privileged within dominant frameworks are called to de-center themselves, making space for others to share their narratives and ensuring these stories are heard and honored on their own terms. This approach invites each of us to ask: What stories have shaped my understanding of the world? How do these stories intersect with those of others? How can I contribute to a storytelling practice that fosters both truth-telling and justice? What systems and equilibriums are supported by a story? What is challenged? What would be most resonant with what we imagine God would want?

Like Paulo Freire's understanding of education, Reyes's work reminds us that storytelling is never neutral. The narratives we amplify reflect and reinforce the values and power dynamics within our communities. If storytelling is to align with God's mission in the world, it must resist the dominance of individualistic redemptive arcs, opening instead to a more communal, justice-oriented vision of purpose. Narrative theological reflection offers a transformative path, weaving together diverse stories (biblical, personal, and communal) to create space for richer, more inclusive understandings of vocation and God's work.

For those engaging this work as Christians, this involves honoring the stories of those who have been marginalized. That means not just holding them up not as side characters in a grander narrative but seeing them as central figures whose experiences reveal vital dimensions of God's liberation and redemption. Similarly, vocational

---

7 Ibid.

storytelling must move beyond centering the individual (especially those already privileged) to embrace the communal and relational nature of calling. This reframing invites us to see vocation not as a solitary pursuit but as a shared act of solidarity and justice. It reminds us that storytelling is not merely about self-expression or connection but about participating in God's work of renewal. To engage faithfully in this practice, we are called to amplify stories that challenge and expand our understanding of purpose, ensuring that our shared narratives reflect the diversity and complexity of God's mission in the world.

This understanding of storytelling as a communal and justice-oriented practice invites us to consider its deeper theological dimensions. Beyond shaping our vocational discernment and social engagement, storytelling holds the potential to connect us with the sacred, to reveal how God is at work in and through the narratives we share. This connection is not new; in many faith traditions, storytelling has long been recognized as a sacred act, one that transmits wisdom, values, and identity from one generation to the next.

I think about the Hebrew word for "word," דָּבָר (*dabar*), a lot. It holds so much more in it than just "a collection of sounds with meaning." Biblically, it is the word of God that comes to Abram in Genesis and tells him not to be afraid (Gen. 15:1). In Isaiah, the word is an active force, able to help God's children achieve what God wishes (Isaiah 55:11). This is the same force that comes through Ezekiel when he prophesied to the dry bones and the Spirit came into them and they lived (Ez. 37:4). We see also that the Gospel of John says. "The Word was with God, and the Word was God" (John 1:1), and the mystic Hildegard of Bingen says that "the Word is living, being, spirit, all verdant greening, all creativity. This Word manifests itself in every creature."[8] I think all of this points to the power that words and language can have to bring new life into being. This is even more true when those words are inspired by God and intended for service.

In the third chapter, I talked about how formation and reflection work together to deepen our understanding of vocation. Formation shapes us as we integrate our experiences, while reflection helps us draw meaning from them, aligning our sense of calling with God's ongoing work in our lives. Storytelling builds on these practices by inviting us to re-narrate our lives, actively revisiting and reshaping our personal stories. Through this process, we can see more clearly how the Spirit has been at work throughout our journey, prompting growth, transformation, and new insights into our purpose. By weaving our experiences into a cohesive narrative, storytelling

---

[8] Hildegard of Bingen, quoted in Matthew Fox, *Original Blessing: A Primer in Creation Spirituality Presented in Four Paths, Twenty-Six Themes, and Two Questions* (New York: Jeremy P. Tarcher/Putnam, 2000), 35.

enriches our self-awareness while strengthening our connection to the divine work of renewal within us, keeping us attuned to God's call. Yet in driving to the heart of these narratives, we expose the questions that our answers obscure, pushing us to stay open to deeper, often unsettling truths about our journey.

As we engage in the act of storytelling, particularly in the context of vocational discernment, we're called to navigate a delicate dance between patience and urgency. This equilibrium reflects an "already but not yet" tension. "Already but not yet" has been traditionally used to describe the idea that God's Reign is already present in our midst, yet not fully realized in its completeness. In the "already" aspect, we recognize that the Reign of God was inaugurated through Jesus's ministry, death, and resurrection. Christians who work in this frame see spiritual blessings like forgiveness, adoption, and the indwelling of the Holy Spirit as moments of the inbreaking Reign of God. Small moments or sensations of what God wants for us. We are considered citizens of God's kingdom and are called to live out kingdom values.

In terms of our vocations, this means that our callings are not merely future aspirations, but present realities that we're already living out, however imperfectly. On the other hand, the "not yet" aspect reminds us that the full manifestation of God's Reign is still future, awaiting the fullness of God's promise. The world continues to experience sin, suffering, and death. In our vocational stories, this "not yet" aspect acknowledges that our understanding and embodiment of our callings is incomplete and evolving.

Freire consistently wrote about how the primary vocation of all people is to become more deeply human.[9] This is a hard thought to think. By this, Freire *didn't* mean to suggest we are somehow lacking in our current level of humanity and need an upgrade. Rather, it is a call for us to see our humanity as a sacred, evolving process. To become more deeply human is not to correct a flaw but to grow into the fullness of who we are created to be, honoring the image of God within us that points to such a wellspring of Grace that it can't help but be an endless process. It is a call to live with greater courage and compassion, engaging with the world in ways that foster justice and healing.

Freire's vision invites us to embrace the tension between accepting ourselves as we are and recognizing the transformative possibilities of who we might become. This is not a rejection of the present but an affirmation that our growth is part of an unfolding story of redemption and renewal. In this sense, becoming more

---

9 There's much to recommend on this point, but I think a good starting point for folks interested in Freire and spirituality is Débora Junker's "The Poetic-Prophetic Dimension of Freirean Pedagogy to Imagine Another World Possible," *Quaestio: Revista de Estudos em Educação* 20, no. 2 (2018): 327–39, https://doi.org/10.22483/2177-5796.2018v20n2p327-339.

human aligns with the Christian call to live in the "already but not yet," embodying God's Reign while remaining open to the mysteries and challenges of its incomplete realization.

Living in this tension creates a dynamic existence for Christians that is reflected in how we approach our vocational storytelling. We're called to tell stories that honor both the "already" and the "not yet" of our callings, stories that celebrate the clarity and joy of moments when God's purpose is evident, while also holding space for the ambiguity and uncertainty that often accompanies discernment. There is a kind of oscillating awareness, a rhythm between clarity inbreaking and mystery persisting, that keeps us grounded in humility, reminding us that our understanding of our vocation is always partial and provisional. Yet this tension is not something to resolve or escape but to embrace as a vital part of the journey. By acknowledging both what we know and what remains unknown, we create space for God's ongoing work in our lives. Our vocational stories become acts of faith, proclaiming not only who we are now but also who we are becoming, as God leads us toward a future that is already being shaped in the present.

Just as the Reign of God grows like a mustard seed (Mark 4:30–32), our understanding of our calling often starts small and grows gradually, sometimes in ways we can't initially perceive. This patience requires a profound trust in God's guidance and a willingness to embrace the journey of discernment, even when the path ahead isn't clear. It involves sitting with uncertainty, being open to unexpected turns, and recognizing that our vocation may evolve over time. This patience isn't passive waiting, but an active engagement with the present moment, attentive to the subtle ways God might be speaking and leading. It requires us to resist societal pressure for immediate results or clear-cut answers. Instead, we're invited to find meaning and purpose in the process of discernment itself, recognizing that our understanding of our vocation deepens as we live it out day by day.

However, we're also called to a sense of urgency in responding to the pressing needs of our world. The stories we tell about our vocations aren't just for our own benefit or personal fulfillment. They're meant to inspire action and contribute to the transformation of our communities. This urgency echoes Jesus's words about the Reign of God being "at hand," calling us to active participation in God's work here and now (Mark 1:15). It challenges us to see our vocations not as distant ideals, but as immediate invitations to engage with the world around us. This sense of urgency doesn't mean hasty or ill-considered action, but rather a readiness to respond to the needs we see, using the gifts and understanding we currently have. It's about recognizing that, while our vocational journey is ongoing, we're called to act and serve in the present moment, even as our understanding continues to grow.

The tension between patience and urgency in our vocational storytelling mirrors the broader tension in Christian life between contemplation and action, between being and doing. It reminds us that our vocations are not static destinations but dynamic journeys of growth and service. This ongoing practice deeply resonates with the formation and reflection dynamic explored in the third chapter, where we saw how personal growth and theological understanding mutually reinforce each other. Just as reflection provides the substance for formation, our stories provide the raw material for understanding our calling. For those who have struggled to find voices or experiences like theirs in what they had been reading or seeing, finding and telling one's story can be both a radical act of reclaiming agency and purpose as well as a balm and gift to those who are coming up.

We're called to be patient with the process of discernment and growth, yet urgent in our response to the world's needs, to trust in God's timing, yet be ready to act when opportunities arise. This "already but not yet" framework provides hope amid present struggles, knowing that current hardships are temporary but ought not to be ignored. It calls believers to embody transformation and participate in God's mission in the present world, while also looking forward to a more just future. One way that this manifests in our lives practically is by sharing stories that testify to the transformative power of God's reign now, while also pointing toward the greater possibilities yet to come. The power of this everyday act of storytelling has long been recognized by theologians.

Taiwanese theologian C. S. Song, known for his trailblazing work on story theology and its significance in Asian cultural contexts, argues that stories carry a deep theological power.[10] They are not merely narratives; they are vessels through which divine purposes are revealed and enacted in the world. Song emphasizes that the power inherent in stories is polarized. It can build or destroy, heal or harm, empower or oppress. This polarization is not neutral but deeply connected to God's purpose for the world, challenging us to consider how our stories align with this divine mission. Unlike abstract theological propositions, stories enable us to see deeply into the human heart, connecting us to the experiences of others across cultural, temporal, and even religious boundaries. This power of empathy is crucial in the practice of ministry, as it allows us to connect our personal narratives with the broader community, fostering a sense of shared purpose and collective calling.

For example, in the practice of spiritual direction or in small group Bible studies, individuals share their life stories and spiritual experiences, revealing patterns and

---

10 C. S. Song, *In the Beginning Were Stories, Not Texts: Story Theology* (Eugene, OR: Cascade Press, 2011).

themes that might point toward their vocational call. This process of narrating and reflecting on one's journey can be transformative, as it opens up new possibilities for understanding yourself and how you are being called into service. Song argues that this transcendence inherent in storytelling bridges the gap between time and eternity, past and future, life and death. Stories help us connect with a broader, more eternal sense of purpose, making them powerful tools for navigating the complexities of vocation.

Song also warns that stories with theological seeds can be dangerous, especially to those in power. Such stories have the potential to subvert the status quo, challenge authority, and inspire change. This subversive potential aligns with the prophetic dimension of vocational discernment, where discerning one's calling often involves confronting and transforming societal norms and expectations. Vocational stories, therefore, are not just personal reflections; they can be radical acts of resistance and transformation, carrying within them the power to reshape our understanding of call in profound ways.

By recognizing the theological significance of these everyday acts of storytelling, we can approach our own narratives (and those of our communities) with greater intentionality and reverence. The stories we tell and retell, whether in formal religious settings or informal conversations, are a potent part of what shapes our understandings of self and call. This awareness invites us to engage more deeply in the storytelling processes that are already happening in our faith communities, creating new opportunities for meaningful storytelling. In doing so, we have the chances to align our narratives more closely with our hopes for the future and with the ongoing story of God's work in the world. It is my sense that this story arises in community and, when lived into, more closely binds us to community as well.

Storytelling isn't just about preserving tradition or entertaining an audience. It's a dynamic, interactive process where individuals and communities engage with their histories, their sacred texts, and their lived experiences to make meaning. In liberation theology, the practice of "base communities" (small groups of people from marginalized communities who gather to read the Bible and reflect on their lives) is a prime example of storytelling as theological reflection. In these gatherings, which might happen in someone's home or a community center, people share their daily struggles and joys, and together explore how their experiences connect with biblical stories. This process of sharing and reflecting often leads to new insights about individual and communal vocations. Whether it's a story shared during a Sunday sermon, a personal testimony offered in a small group, or a traditional tale told around a summer campfire, these acts of storytelling shape how people understand their place in the world and their unique vocations within it.

Context Collapse and Re-Narration

In our rapidly changing world, the ability to re-narrate our stories becomes an indispensable tool for navigating social transformations, cultural shifts, and personal transitions. Each of these is an opportunity to revisit and reshape the narratives that give our lives meaning. In the face of this constant change, understanding vocation as a dynamic, evolving process encourages ongoing reflection and adaptation. A useful concept for understanding how all this change enters our lives is the concept of "context collapse," an idea that comes to us from communications theory and media studies.

In the sixth chapter, we explored the relationship between identity and belonging, particularly how they influence and shape our sense of vocation. However, the fragmentation of identity and the complexities of belonging often make this process challenging, as we navigate various cultural, social, and personal influences that may conflict or compete with one another. Building on this, the concept of "context collapse" offers a powerful lens through which we can further understand the effects of this fragmentation. Context collapse emerged as a term in the early 2000s with the rise of social media platforms.[11] It refers to the merging of diverse social contexts and audiences into a single space, particularly in online environments.

For example, imagine posting a message on social media that is visible to your family, friends, colleagues, and acquaintances all at once. In the offline world, you might communicate differently with each of these groups, tailoring your language, tone, and content to fit the specific context. However, in the online world, these distinct contexts collapse into one, forcing you to navigate the challenge of addressing a wide and varied audience simultaneously. This can lead to difficulties in self-presentation, as it becomes harder to manage the expectations and perceptions of each group, potentially causing misunderstandings or conflicts.

Over time, many people have become so accustomed to this "collapse" that it extends beyond the online space. Even when we are not posting online, our sense of self is stretched and can fracture, as we carry the awareness of these multiple, overlapping audiences into our everyday lives. Even if we decide that we don't want to participate in the online spaces of social media, the fact is that many people are, and this is shaping how people interact, including how they interact with *you*, even if you've never opened Instagram or TikTok. This ongoing state of context collapse influences how we perceive and express our identities, making the task of articulating our sense of purpose and vocation even more complex. The lines between our private

---

[11] Alice E. Marwick and danah boyd, "I Tweet Honestly, I Tweet Passionately: Twitter Users, Context Collapse, and the Imagined Audience," *New Media & Society* 13, no. 1 (February 2011): 114–33.

and public selves blur, requiring constant adaptation as we navigate a world where the boundaries between different aspects of our lives are increasingly porous.

In this way, context collapse is not just a challenge of the digital age but a broader reflection of the fragmentation we explored earlier. Just as our fragmented identities demand creative assembly in our vocational journeys, the phenomenon of context collapse requires us to constantly renegotiate how we present ourselves and understand our calling in a world where the distinctions between different facets of our lives are increasingly fluid. It deepens the complexity of navigating identity and belonging, pushing us to develop new strategies for maintaining coherence and integrity across the various spheres in which we live and work. The benefit of developing these new strategies is why I think considering this idea can be so fruitful.

The concept of context collapse has its roots in the work of sociologist Erving Goffman, who argued that individuals engage in "audience segregation," carefully managing their self-presentation to suit different social contexts.[12] Social media platforms have made this careful management increasingly difficult. Context collapse can be categorized into two main types: context collusions and context collisions.[13] Context collusions are intentional mergers of different social contexts, such as when a user deliberately crafts a social media post to engage multiple social groups simultaneously. Context collisions, on the other hand, are unintentional and often unexpected mergers of distinct social contexts, such as when a post intended for a specific audience reaches a much broader, unintended audience due to sharing or algorithmic amplification.

Mary E. Hess, in her exploration of digital media and religious education, offers a useful reflection on how context collapse shapes our ability to narrate our stories, particularly within the realm of vocational discernment. She argues that the digital age, characterized by the pervasive influence of context collapse, has fundamentally altered the way we engage with and interpret our identities. She suggests that this phenomenon is not just about the loss of distinct social contexts but also about how we come to understand and present our narratives in a world where boundaries are increasingly blurred. As Hess puts it, "Context is an essential element of meaning-making, yet in many of the places we inhabit today, context is collapsing."[14] This collapse challenges

---

12 Erving Goffman, *The Presentation of Self in Everyday Life* (New York: Penguin Books, 1959).

13 Jenny L. Davis and Nathan Jurgenson, "Context Collapse: Theorizing Context Collusions and Collisions," *Information, Communication & Society* 17, no. 4 (2014): 476–85. https://doi.org/10.1080/1369118X.2014.888458.

14 Mary E. Hess, "Finding Learning amidst the Maelstrom: Storytelling, Trauma, and Hope," *Teaching Theology & Religion* 23, no. 4 (December 2020): 237–40, https://doi.org/10.1111/teth.12567.

our ability to anchor our stories in stable, shared understandings, requiring us to find new ways to create meaning amid the fragmentation.

I've felt this collapse firsthand.

In the first chapter, I described a season when the roles I had long inhabited began to shift. My energy changed. My attention narrowed, and my capacity to multitask faded. I stepped back from boards, said "no" to new projects, and gradually let go of the pace and posture that had once defined how I moved through the world. Practically, my life was contracting in deliberate ways. But online, it remained expansive. My digital presence still signaled availability. I was still tagged, still mentioned, still invited: perceived through the lens of who I had been, not who I was becoming.

And it started to feel suffocating. Every time I opened an app, I felt a spike of anxiety. Not because anyone was unkind, but because I was constantly being reminded of a self I could no longer sustain. In the language we developed for the Moral Orienting System in the first chapter, my internal coherence between values, relationships, and behaviors felt increasingly fragmented. Posts and messages pulled me back into rhythms I had consciously chosen to leave. I'd see conversations I once would've joined and feel a pang. Partly because of a fear of missing out, but also because I felt I was supposed to attend to things I no longer had the bandwidth to hold. It became harder and harder to tell where my attention ended and others' expectations began.

The dissonance wasn't dramatic, but it was persistent. What showed up in the feed didn't match what was happening in my body, my mind, or my spirit. And I didn't have the capacity to narrate the shift in real time. Platforms don't offer many graceful ways to grow quieter. I wasn't interested in performing transparency or curating a new identity. But the longer I stayed connected, the more fragmented I felt. So I stopped. No digital farewell. No big announcement. Just a quiet decision to log off.

What followed wasn't reinvention. It was right-sizing. I gave my attention to what was still mine to tend: my family, local relationships, students, writing, a smaller circle of work and witness. And in doing so, I began the slow work of re-narrating my call. Not with certainty, but with care. I scribbled notes in margins. I decided to practice writing differently. Talked with friends who could hold silence without rushing to fix. I traced the arc of what had been and slowly began to glimpse what might still be.

The story that began to emerge wasn't one of abandonment, but of evolution. I hadn't lost my calling, but I had been asked to carry it differently. And the act of telling that story, even just to myself, helped restore a sense of coherence. That's what storytelling does in the wake of disorientation. It helps us live forward by giving shape to what's behind us. Not to make everything tidy, but to make it possible to continue.

Bonnie Miller-McLemore writes powerfully about exactly the kinds of changes that I have experienced. She notes that, in later adulthood, it is common for individuals to face the challenge of relinquishing long-held callings, writing, "Relinquishing callings requires review and retelling of our lives, a going backward over life to go forward, a reversal and renewal of calling in a different form and direction."[15] This process often involves grief and lament but can also lead to new forms of service and a deeper understanding of one's life journey. By recognizing the value in both holding on to and letting go of callings, we can develop a more mature and flexible approach to vocation that adapts to the changing seasons of life.

When the stories we tell no longer fit our lived experience, we are not just narratively disrupted, we are spiritually disoriented. When our story falls apart, our sense of self can, too. As we explored through Willie James Jennings's work on fragments in the sixth chapter, this sense of rupture is often a core reality that we must navigate. The matrix of values, beliefs, behaviors, and relationships that once held us steady begins to slip, and re-narration becomes a form of moral reorientation. Storytelling allows us to reclaim a sense of agency, helping us make sense of our experiences and find clarity amid complexity.

For me, reflecting on my journey enabled me to reconnect with my purpose and discover new ways to live out my calling. This process of revisiting and reinterpreting our narratives often requires the kind of relinquishment and renewal that Miller-McLemore describes, where we reframe past callings to make room for new ones. Often, discernment begins not with a question, but with a story that no longer fits. We tell the truth slant, test out new versions, and listen for where coherence reemerges, not always in clarity, but in the felt sense that something has been re-stitched.

In this way, storytelling is not just how we remember, it's how we reorient. Yet this act of storytelling and discernment is about more than personal growth. It also draws us into the larger narrative of God's work in the world. Just as we explored through the lens of systems thinking and adrienne maree brown's writing on fractals in the fourth chapter, the stories we tell and the lives we lead are patterns that echo across scales. Our counternarratives are not just critiques: <u>They're</u> small-scale enactments of the world we long for.

Our Work in God's Work

If you're reading this and thinking it doesn't apply to you because you already know your calling and feel confident in your vocational path, let me suggest two things. First, I believe that attention to story offers a way to continually affirm and deepen

---

15 Bonnie J. Miller-McLemore, *Follow Your Bliss and Other Lies about Calling* (New York: Oxford University Press, 2024), 145.

your understanding of that calling, allowing you to articulate it with greater clarity and conviction. Whether through societal changes, personal growth, or new challenges, as contexts shift, revisiting and re-narrating your story can help you stay aligned with your core values and purpose.

Second, storytelling is not just for personal clarity; it's a powerful tool for communicating your journey to others, inspiring and guiding those who may be navigating their own uncertainties. For Christians, this practice takes on an even deeper significance because it is not solely about individual growth or understanding. Storytelling becomes a way to participate in the broader narrative of God's work in the world, what is known as the *missio Dei*, or the mission of God. By sharing your story, you are not just reflecting on your own life. You are contributing to the unfolding story of God's mission through the Church.

Your service and ministry are part of this larger divine narrative, and storytelling helps to situate your personal calling within the communal and global context of the *missio Dei*. It allows others to see how God is working through you, how your life intersects with the lives of others, and how together, we are all part of a greater purpose. Through storytelling, you can inspire others to see their own roles within this mission, encouraging them to discern how their gifts and callings contribute to the work of God in the world. In this way, storytelling is not just an act of self-reflection but a form of ministry, a way of bearing witness to the ongoing work of God and inviting others to join in that mission.

This emphasis on storytelling as a participation in the *missio Dei* naturally connects to Hess's use of the concept of *martyria*, or witness. She underscores that storytelling in the Christian context is not merely an act of personal reflection or self-expression but a profound engagement with the divine mission. Through storytelling, we bear witness to God's ongoing work in the world, aligning our individual narratives with the larger story of God's redemptive activity. Hess suggests that during context collapse and the fragmentation it causes, a "curriculum of *martyria*" is essential.[16]

This curriculum emphasizes the importance of testimony as a way of making sense of our experiences in light of God's mission. She writes that "we need to inhabit this kind of curriculum more than ever in the fraught places we find ourselves."[17] By sharing our stories as acts of witness, we participate in the *missio Dei* not just by recounting personal experiences but by testifying to the ways in which God is active in our lives and in the world. This kind of testimony invites others to see how their own stories might also be part of God's broader narrative, thereby fostering a communal understanding of vocation that transcends individualism and connects us to the divine purpose.

---

16 Hess, "Finding Learning amidst the Maelstrom," 223.
17 Ibid., 222.

In this light, storytelling as *martyria* is more than a personal exercise; it is a communal act that affirms and extends the reach of God's mission. It invites us to see our lives as interconnected with others, and with God's work in the world, encouraging a deeper engagement with our calling as participants in the *missio Dei*. Through this witness, our stories become a means of building up the Body of Christ, supporting one another in our vocational journeys, and contributing to the unfolding of God's Reign. In this sense, re-narration is not just about adapting to change but about actively shaping it. It's a practice of resilience and creativity that allows us to navigate life's uncertainties with a sense of purpose and direction. By re-narrating our vocational stories, we can respond to the challenges of our time in a way that remains faithful to our core values while also being open to new possibilities.

As I noted in the introduction of the book, *testimonio,* rooted in Latin American and Chicana feminist traditions, is not merely personal narrative or oral history. It is a political and conscientized account, offered in solidarity with others. Educational spaces shaped by a liberatory understanding of *testimonio* invite not just storytelling, but the deliberate naming of injustice and the voicing of agency. In this framing, the educator's task is not simply to deliver content, but to cultivate spaces where students can articulate their lived experiences as knowledge. These classrooms become sites of conscientization, where reflection and narration open paths toward healing and liberation. In vocational discernment, *testimonio* becomes a way of re-narrating one's life in light of communal struggle and hope, a space where the personal becomes political, and the telling itself becomes a form of action.

In an era of increasing awareness about systemic injustices and global challenges, how do we narrate our vocations in ways that respond to these realities? This might involve re-framing our understanding of success, reconsidering the relationship between work and personal life, or finding new ways to articulate the connection between our individual callings and the common good. Building on this, narrative theological reflection offers a way to deepen this alignment by weaving together the threads of our personal stories with the broader biblical narrative and the stories of our communities. This approach serves as a complement to the six-step theological reflection process outlined in the third chapter.

Although the structured model I shared provides a clear and methodical framework for discernment, it is not the only way to engage in meaningful reflection. Narrative theological reflection invites us into a more organic, story-driven process that emphasizes imagination, relationality, and context. Sun Hee Chang's concept of "weaving stories" provides a helpful lens for understanding this alternative method.[18]

---

18 Sun Hee Chang, "Exploring Weaving Stories: A Narrative Way of Theological Reflection in

Instead of following a fixed progression of steps, narrative theological reflection emerges through the interplay of divine and human narratives. By contrast to the six-step model, which asks us to analyze and discern specific actions or principles, narrative theological reflection focuses on integration and imagination. It encourages us to explore questions like: How does my story illuminate this scripture? How does this scripture challenge or affirm my story? What new possibilities emerge when these stories are woven together? Through this practice, we discover how our lives participate in God's unfolding work, both within us and through us.

This method also aligns with Hess's emphasis on storytelling as *martyria*. As Hess notes, storytelling is not just an act of personal expression but a communal act of witness that situates our lives within the broader context of the *missio Dei*. Through narrative reflection, we are invited to see our individual callings as interwoven with the collective work of God's people and the ongoing redemption of the world. This perspective reminds us that theological reflection, whether structured or narrative, is always about discerning our place in God's mission and responding faithfully to that call.

Ultimately, storytelling as narrative theological reflection is not just about re-narrating our lives; it is about imagining new possibilities for how we live out our faith. It invites us to listen deeply to the stories of others, recognize God's work in the world, and weave our lives into the fabric of God's ongoing mission. In doing so, we participate in a collaborative, hope-filled act of shaping the future, faithful to the past and yet open to the new. This weaving of stories becomes a means of resilience, creativity, and witness.

For Christians like myself, I'm inclined to talk about this as building up the Body of Christ and participating in what we call God's Reign on Earth, a vision of justice and healing that, I hope, might resonate with others across traditions and commitments. What's at stake is not merely individual fulfillment or private meaning-making, but the kind of collective transformation that becomes possible when people attend to the sacred within and around them, however they name it. Our stories, shared honestly and interpreted with care, can disrupt injustice, nurture solidarity, and point toward more generous ways of being in the world.

Exploring the Future

I've suggested that storytelling and re-narration are powerful tools for making sense of our past and present. However, vocational discernment isn't just about understanding where we've been or where we are now. It's also about imagining where we might go.

Field Education," *Reflective Practice* 44, no. 44 (2024), https://journals.sfu.ca/rpfs/index.php/rpfs/article/view/1809.

The practice of exploring possible futures is a vital component of discernment, allowing us to envision new possibilities for our calling and our world. This forward-looking aspect of vocational discernment invites us to engage our imagination in profound ways. It challenges us to look beyond the constraints of our current circumstances and consider what might be possible. It can help us pierce through the comfortable assumptions we hold about the present, compelling us to consider the questions that lie beneath our visions. This process of imagining future possibilities isn't mere daydreaming or wishful thinking. Rather, it's a purposeful and hope-filled practice that can shape our actions in the present and guide us toward more intentional and meaningful paths of service.

> **A Practice to Consider:**
> # Re-Frame and Re-Tell
>
> *The stories we tell shape the way we see ourselves and our purpose. By reframing these narratives, we open new pathways for growth, healing, and deeper alignment with our calling.*
>
> 1. Choose a part of your story you tell often, especially one that feels unresolved or needs fresh perspective. Find a way to tell that story a different way, reframing it so that it might mean something new to you. For example, a perceived failure, like not getting a job you wanted, could become the moment you discovered a new passion or path that better suited your gifts. Or a difficult relationship might be retold as the experience that taught you how to set boundaries or care for yourself.
> 2. Share this reframed story with someone you trust, and pay attention to their response, whether they see something you missed or challenge you to consider another angle. Let this process help you see your story in a new light and identify what it might be teaching you.

Paulo Freire has been one of the most helpful people for helping me think about the connection between possible futures and stories in the present. Freire was clear that social transformation requires a set of double imaginative actions. Change comes about due to the "dialectical relationship between denouncing the present and announcing the future. To anticipate tomorrow by dreaming today."[19] This is a little jargony, but I think that the point is very important. Any complaining (denouncing) without

---

19 Paulo Freire and Ira Shor, *A Pedagogy for Liberation: Dialogues on Transforming Education* (South Hadley, MA: Bergin & Garvey Publishers, 1987), 187.

speaking of a vision for what else might be possible (announcing) is insufficient. Likewise, it is hollow to voice hope without plans for removing the obstacles to get there. For Freire, dreaming is necessary, as it is how the present mingles with the possible, seeding in the dreamer a desire that demands tilling by material response.

For Freire (and me), the "material response" is profoundly important. He calls talk without action "verbalism." On the other hand, when people are just interested in "mere activism," without reflection and reconsideration, the situation isn't much better. He uses the term *praxis* to stand in for the cyclical interaction of observation that leads to reflection and discussion that leads to action that leads to observation.[20] In the context of Christian ministerial formation, this is often framed as the "pastoral cycle," the roots of which are the "see-judge-act method," formalized by the Belgian Cardinal Joseph Cardijn in the early twentieth century.[21]

Just as Freire emphasizes the importance of dialogue in education, vocational discernment becomes a kind of ongoing dialogue between our ideals, our experiences, and the needs of the world around us. During this dialogue, Freire thinks it is important to support dreaming and imagining ways things could be different. However, dreaming for justice must have its roots in the stuff of this world.

> I do not understand human existence, and the struggle needed to improve it, apart from hope and dream. Hope is an ontological need.... I do not mean that, because I am hopeful, I attribute to this hope of mine the power to transform reality all by itself, so that I set out for the fray without taking account of concrete, material data, declaring, "My hope is enough!" No, my hope is necessary, but it is not enough. Alone, it does not win. But without it, my struggle will be weak and wobbly. We need critical hope the way a fish needs unpolluted water.[22]

Importantly, this imaginative work isn't about fantasy or escapism. Rather, it's a serious engagement with possibility, grounded in our values, gifts, and sense of calling. It's about asking ourselves: "What if?" What if I pursued this path? What if I developed this gift? What if I really spent the time to learn about the hurt of the world and responded?

This kind of imagination invites us into an honest assessment of our capacities and a courageous exploration of our calling. It's a practice of opening ourselves to the risks

---

20 Freire's early writing on this topic is in *Pedagogy of the Oppressed*.

21 Justin Sands, "Introducing Cardinal Cardijn's See–Judge–Act as an Interdisciplinary Method to Move Theory into Practice," *Religions* 9, no. 4 (2018): 129, https://doi.org/10.3390/rel9040129[3].

22 Paulo Freire, *Pedagogy of Hope: Reliving Pedagogy of the Oppressed*, trans. Robert R. Barr (London: Bloomsbury Academic, 2014), 8.

and responsibilities that come with living into our gifts, especially when those gifts call us into spaces of discomfort or challenge. Such reflection pushes us beyond simply seeking personal fulfillment and into a deeper commitment to the needs around us. Imagination, in this sense, becomes a tool for liberation, inviting us to envision ways our unique strengths can contribute to justice, healing, and reconciliation. By framing our vocational questions in the language of "What if?" we create space for action, fueled by a genuine desire to make a difference, one aligned with who we are and who we may become.

This work of exploring possible futures is deeply tied to the stories we tell ourselves and others. Stories are how we make sense of the world, and they often shape the boundaries of what we believe is possible. Seen this way, imagination becomes an act of moral repair: a way to integrate what has been fractured and to envision a coherent future, even amid uncertainty. This is not escapism or fantasy. It's a necessary part of reorienting ourselves when our old frameworks no longer hold. When we reframe our narratives with an eye toward justice and hope, we are engaging in more than just creative re-imagining: we are participating in an act of resistance. When we live as though the world is already being made new, we participate in its becoming. Rather than waiting passively for change, we act in trust that God's reign is already near, already stirring in our relationships, our traditions, and our commitments. This is the eschatology of the everyday. By choosing to tell stories that center on transformation, resilience, and the ways God is at work in the world, we challenge the status quo and open new pathways for action. These stories remind us that hope is not passive; it is active and transformative, demanding courage and commitment.

Hope as Resistance

Hope and dreaming the way Freire thinks about it are not merely optimism about the future, but transformative forces that change how we live in the present. It is a *critical* hope, yes, grounded in the promise of God's future, but calling us to active participation in the present. In this light, re-narration becomes a powerful tool of hope and resistance. When we re-narrate our stories, we're not just changing our personal narratives. We can challenge dominant narratives of cynicism, individualism, and despair. We're declaring that a different world is possible and that we have a role to play in bringing it about. That being said, I am aware that sometimes people can be critical of "too much hope."

For example, the ethicist Miguel De La Torre says that "hope, as a statement of unfounded belief, serves an important middle-class purpose. All too often, hope becomes an excuse not to deal with the reality of injustice."[23] De La Torre's critique of hope stems from his observation that it can sometimes serve as a barrier to addressing present injustices, particularly for those in positions of privilege. He argues that hope can become a form of complacency, allowing people to believe that things will improve without requiring immediate action or confrontation with systemic injustices. This perspective is rooted in his understanding of the lived experiences of marginalized communities, who often face persistent, generational struggles that don't align with optimistic narratives of progress. I understand the argument, but I find I can't get on board with it. Not quite. But I do understand his worry.

Hope makes me nervous. Not because I think it should be banned or condemned, but because I am afraid that sometimes hope becomes an idol at which we worship, looking to the future, when our God of transformation, renewal, and resurrection stands nearby and invites us to change now. The thing is, people who talk about hopelessness make me even more nervous. I understand the theoretical logics by which minimizing hope ought to force people into a more serious engagement with the material present. But I think hope is always *already* bound up in the present. So then what?

It is sloppy and inelegant, but when I have come to talk about hope I usually couch it in a clause: I want a *material* hope, a hope that begins with the physical stuff of life and unfolds into what might be. I want a *critical* hope, a hope that resists any insistence that what already is is all there will ever be. I want a hope that is an experience of what the theologian Grace Jantzen called the "sensible-transcendent," a hope that grounds us more deeply into where we are and simultaneously flings us out beyond our recall, out to the limits of our longing. This critical perspective on hope aligns with the reflections on joy and lament in the fifth chapter, reminding us that real hope calls us to respond actively to present injustices rather than merely holding out for future change. The concept of "prefigurative politics" from social movement theory offers an interesting parallel here.

Prefigurative politics is a concept within social movements that emphasizes embodying and enacting the social and political practices that activists wish to see in the broader society. This approach to activism involves creating and practicing alternative social structures and relationships in the present, which reflect the desired future society. It is characterized by principles such as participatory democracy, horizontality, inclusiveness, and direct action.[24] The term

---

23 Miguel A. De La Torre, "Toward a Theology of Hopelessness," http://drmigueldelatorre.com/2015/toward-a-theology-of-hopelessness/.

24 Guilherme Fians, "Prefigurative Politics," in *The Open Encyclopedia of Anthropology*, ed. Felix Stein. facsimile of the first edition in *The Cambridge Encyclopedia of Anthropology*, 2022.

"prefiguration" itself has historical roots that extend back to Christian theological concepts of salvation.

The commitment to embodying the future now finds deep resonance within the Christian tradition itself. The Apostle Paul's understanding of God's call (*klēsis*), for instance, was not merely an individual summons but a force that created a fundamentally new community identity, one intended to transcend the deeply ingrained social categories of his time; that is, "neither Jew nor Greek … slave nor free … male and female" (Gal. 3:28). This early Christian vision can be seen as a form of theological prefiguration: living now as members of an alternative community grounded in Christ rather than empire or existing social hierarchies. As I see it, a theology of vocation committed to justice ought to take this Pauline social transformation seriously, applying its potential critically to the contemporary divisions of race, class, gender, and other dimensions of oppression that continue to fracture the "one body."

This concept was adapted by political activists to signify a different kind of transformation, one that seeks to build the desired future society through present actions. Over time, the concept has been associated with a wide range of social movements, including those opposing neoliberal globalization and advocating for new forms of democracy.

For instance, if we envision a more just and equitable society, prefigurative politics would encourage us to embody those values in our current work and relationships. This might involve creating collaborative decision-making processes in our organizations, prioritizing diversity and inclusion in our teams, or developing more sustainable practices in our daily operations. By doing so, we're not just working toward a distant goal for society writ large, but actively creating pockets of that desired future within our present reality. Prefigurative politics suggests we shouldn't just complain (verbalism) or resist without a plan for transformation (mere activism). We should try to live into the vision of a future, more just society today, knowing that we'll never get there in its fullness but that every step along the way is right to take. Telling the stories of our experiments and exploration of these "pockets" is sometimes called a "counternarrative," a powerful tool for challenging dominant societal narratives and imagining new possibilities.[25]

These counternarratives serve multiple purposes: They document our efforts, inspire others, and contribute to a collective reimagining of social structures. By sharing our experiences of prefigurative politics in action, we not only reinforce our

---

[25] Daniel G. Solorzano and Tara J. Yosso, "Critical Race and LatCrit Theory and Method: Counter-Storytelling," *International Journal of Qualitative Studies in Education* 14, no. 4 (2001): 471–95.

own commitment to these alternative ways of being but also invite others to join in the process of creating change. This storytelling becomes a form of resistance in itself, highlighting the viability of alternative models and expanding our collective vision of what's possible. Counternarratives also create spaces where truth and challenge coexist, where storytelling illuminates while courageously confronting the places where vision grows too complacent and complicit.

In this way, these stories echo the original use of gospel (*euangelion*), a term first used to announce Roman military victories and the reign of Caesar, but taken up and radically subverted by Jesus in the opening of Mark's Gospel to proclaim a different kind of reign entirely: one rooted in justice, healing, and the nearness of God's liberating presence.[26] His proclamation was not just spiritual, but social, a public declaration that another world was possible and already breaking in. When we tell stories that name alternative ways of living and organizing our lives, we participate in that same tradition of subversive proclamation.

In the context of vocational discernment, these counternarratives can help us reframe our understanding of what it means to live out our calling, encouraging us to see our work not just in terms of personal fulfillment or career advancement, but as part of a larger movement toward social transformation. Through this lens, our vocations become sites of experimentation and embodied hope, contributing to a growing tapestry of stories that challenge the status quo and point toward more just and equitable futures. This approach aligns closely with the systems thinking perspective discussed in the fourth chapter.

As we explored there, systems thinking encourages us to see the interconnectedness of various elements and to recognize how small changes can ripple out to affect the entire system. The concept of fractals, as articulated by adrienne maree brown, is particularly relevant here. Remember that brown argues that "how we are at the small scale is how we are at the large scale."[27] The practices we cultivate in our immediate spheres can have profound impacts on larger scales. Prefigurative politics, then, can be seen as a practical application of this fractal principle.

By embodying our values and desired social structures in our immediate contexts, we're creating microcosms of the larger changes we hope to see. Our workplaces, communities, and relationships become sites of change that seed hopes for larger transformation as well. This connects back to brown's emphasis on "small is good, small is all," which encourages us to value and cultivate small, everyday actions that

---

26 Rowland Onyenali, "The Markan Proskuneo (Mark 5:6; 15:19) as Anti-Roman Motif in Mark's Gospel," *Biblical Theology Bulletin* 52, no. 2 (2022): 77–87, https://doi.org/10.1177/01461079211027703.

27 adrienne maree brown, *Emergent Strategy: Shaping Change, Changing Worlds* (Chico, CA: AK Press, 2017), 51.

align with our sense of calling. By focusing on these small-scale practices, we can engage in deliberate and hopeful work that feels manageable while planting the seeds for larger social and global transformations. These small acts of resistance and creativity take root in the immediate and ripple outward, shaping both our lives and the communities we inhabit.

In the sixth chapter, I explored the connected relationship between identity and belonging, the ways in which we both make and are made by community. Building on this, the choices that each of us makes to embody creative expressions of resistance and hope in our everyday lives have a ripple effect, influencing the shared practices and stories of our communities as well as our own individual lives. By living out our values and desired futures in the present, we're not just telling stories about what could be, we're actively writing new narratives through our actions. These lived stories become powerful tools for inspiring others, challenging dominant narratives, and expanding our collective imagination of what's possible.

By cultivating our capacity for imagination, we open ourselves to new possibilities for our vocation. We become more adaptable, more resilient, and more attuned to the ways God might be calling us to serve in a changing world. We're co-creating our vocational story with God, living into new ways of being, always aware that God's ways are higher than our ways and there is ever a new thing being done, a new way in the wilderness and new stream in the wasteland (Isaiah 43:18–19).

More Than a Wish

I know that storytellers and "story time" are often associated with young children. The truth is, though, that storytelling isn't just about entertainment or understanding our past. Stories, particularly the ones we tell about ourselves, take root in our imagination and gradually shape the landscape of what we believe is possible. This forward-looking aspect of storytelling invites us to look beyond the constraints of our current circumstances and consider what more is yet to come. Particularly in the context of vocation, this process of imagining future possibilities isn't mere daydreaming or wishful thinking. Rather, it's a purposeful and critically hope-filled practice that can shape our actions in the present and guide us toward more intentional and meaningful paths of service.

This is particularly powerful in "everyday" contexts, where stories often arise from the intersection of faith and daily life. The account of how a casual conversation led to a prayer group, how a workplace crisis became an opportunity for spiritual care, or how a neighborhood need sparked a new ministry: These stories help us recognize God's work in unexpected places. Lay ministers often excel at seeing and naming these sacred moments precisely because they're so embedded in the ordinary rhythms of life. When we engage in vocational storytelling with this kind of hope, we're declaring that we believe that positive change is possible, that our efforts matter, and that God is working in all things.

Next time that you find yourself telling a story from your own life that you've told before, see if you can end it a different way. Instead of concluding with the usual ending, reflect on how that experience might connect to God's work in your life or the lives of others. Consider what new insights you can draw out of the story: Was there an unexpected blessing? A lesson learned? A way in which you were shaped or called? Sharing this fresh perspective with your listeners might not only deepen their understanding but also help you recognize new dimensions of God's presence in your journey. Over time, this practice can transform familiar narratives into dynamic reflections of hope, growth, and divine creativity.

In many ways, this imaginative work in vocational storytelling mirrors the Christian understanding of hope. Biblical hope is not just optimistic wishing, but a confident expectation grounded in faith. It's a hope that acknowledges the brokenness of our present reality while also asserting that this is not the end of the story. Part of the challenge to those of us who are people of faith is that there are so many other stories we swim in that press us into the status quo. It takes work to begin to see ourselves as part of a plot that involves change. Imagination is where the present and the possible meet, and storytelling is one way to change what we can imagine as possible.

I recently came across an interview with the musician Nick Cave that really drove this home for me. In it, he read aloud a letter from a fan and his response to it:

> Following the last few years I'm feeling empty and more cynical than ever. I'm losing faith in other people, and I'm scared to pass these feelings to my little son. Do you still believe in Us (human beings)?[28]

I won't quote the whole thing here, but I'd recommend that you check it out if you get a chance. He speaks powerfully in a way that is very resonant with our purposes here. I think he is spot on.

> You are right to be worried about your growing feelings of cynicism and you need to take action to protect yourself and those around you, especially your child. Cynicism is not a neutral position—and although it asks almost

---

[28] Nick Cave, "Issue #190 / April 2022," *The Red Hand Files*, April 2022, https://www.theredhandfiles.com/do-you-still-believe-in-us/. Accessed November 21, 2024.

nothing of us, it is highly infectious and unbelievably destructive. In my view, it is the most common and easy of evils.... Unlike cynicism, hopefulness is hard-earned, makes demands upon us, and can often feel like the most indefensible and lonely place on Earth. Hopefulness is not a neutral position either. It is adversarial. It is the warrior emotion that can lay waste to cynicism. Each redemptive or loving act, as small as you like ... such as reading to your little boy, or showing him a thing you love, or singing him a song, or putting on his shoes, keeps the devil down in the hole. It says the world and its inhabitants have value and are worth defending. It says the world is worth believing in. In time, we come to find that it is so.[29]

In a world often characterized by cynicism and despair, the act of hoping, of imagining, and working toward a better future can be a profound form of resistance.

This is particularly the case in the context of vocation, where hope allows us to envision and strive for meaningful ways of serving God and our communities, even in the face of challenges and setbacks. Cave's words resonate deeply with my sense of the practice of vocational discernment. To discern and pursue our calling in a world often marked by injustice, suffering, and seeming meaninglessness is an act of hope. It is, as we saw in the fifth chapter, a pursuit of joy as an act of resistance. It's a statement that our lives and our actions matter, that we can make a difference, and that God is still at work in the world. By exploring our call in story, we're not only shaping our own paths but also contributing to a larger narrative of possibility, inspiring others to see places of change and renewal in their own lives and communities.

As we cultivate this practice of storytelling and exploration in our vocational discernment, we're invited to hold the tension between the "already" and the "not yet" of God's Reign. We tell stories that acknowledge the reality of our present circumstances while also pointing toward the possibility of transformation and renewal. In doing so, we participate in entering more fully into God's Reign in our own lives and in the world around us. As I see it, the practice of vocational storytelling is an invitation to live more fully into our identity as co-creators with God. It challenges us to see our lives and our work as part of a larger narrative of God's work in the world. As we continue to explore, to imagine, and to tell our stories, may we do so with courage, creativity, and a critical, material hope that all things can be made new.

---

29 Ibid.

Questions for Reflection

1. The chapter discusses ways in which storytelling can be a tool for vocational discernment. Think about a significant moment in your vocational journey. How might you narrate this experience differently now compared to when it first occurred? Does this "re-narration" offer any insights?

2. Think of someone whose vocational journey you admire. If possible, have a conversation with them about how they've experienced and navigated their sense of calling. What aspects of their story resonate most with you? What challenges you?

3. The chapter presents the idea of vocational discernment as an ongoing process of re-narration rather than a one-time discovery. What parts of your vocational story might need re-examination or re-telling in this season of your life?

4. The concept of "context collapse" is discussed as a challenge in modern storytelling and identity formation. How, if at all, has this phenomenon affected your ability to articulate your sense of calling across different areas of your life? How might you address these challenges?

5. The chapter introduces the concept of prefigurative politics, the idea of embodying the future we hope to see in our present actions. Can you identify ways you're already "prefiguring" aspects of your calling, or areas where you could start to do so? What are some ways you are trying to live into the vision of the life and service you feel called toward?

6. The chapter discusses Freire's concept of "critical hope" as something that isn't naïve or "wishful thinking." How do you understand this idea of hope that is both grounded in reality and oriented toward change? Can you recall a time when you practiced this kind of hope in your own vocational journey? How might cultivating critical hope shape your approach to ministry or service?

9

Ministry

The function of freedom is to free someone else.
—Toni Morrison

The moments, hours, and days of self-giving must be balanced by moments, hours, and days of withdrawal into, and enrichment of, her individual selfhood if she is to remain a whole person.
—Valerie Saiving

This book began with a chapter on vocation. Now, we conclude with an exploration of ministry as the manifestation of that call, a topic that is both challenging to contemplate and rich with potential for profound joy and meaning. In opening with Toni Morrison's insight about freedom's function,[1] we return to themes that opened our journey: the delicate interplay between individual calling and communal flourishing, between "freedom from" and "freedom for."

These dynamics, first explored through Ignatian spirituality and deepened with emphasis on communal liberation, now find their practical expression in how we understand and embody ministry.

Now that we've journeyed through almost the whole of the book, we arrive at a familiar but complex word: ministry. And honestly? It's one of the hardest to pin down because it's so tangled up in theology, history, and all the baggage we carry

---

[1] Toni Morrison, "Cinderella's Stepsisters," Commencement address presented at Barnard College, New York, NY, May 28, 1979.

about what "serving" really means. Though this is a liberation theology of *vocation*, I see vocation as the seedbed of ministry, which means reimagining extends there as well. When we free vocation from individualism, credentialism, and abstraction, we also reconfigure ministry, not as a role reserved for the few, but as a shared, Spirit-led practice of collective discernment and liberative presence. Ministry becomes less about fitting into institutional positions of authority and more about participating in the world's repair.

Viewed this way, Valerie Saiving's observation about the necessity of balancing self-giving with self-enrichment takes on particular significance.[2] Her insight, emerging from reflection on women's experiences, reminds us that calls to service and self-giving are never gender-neutral. They land differently on different bodies, shaped by social location and systemic power. Many Christians wrestle with how to interpret Jesus's ultimate example of faithfulness in light of their everyday responsibilities and relationships. What does it mean to revere his willingness to face death on the cross?

If being Christlike means being "faithful unto death," how do we navigate this call while honoring our commitments to families, jobs, and communities? This tension becomes particularly acute when we consider those whose caregiving responsibilities or economic circumstances don't easily allow for dramatic gestures of self-sacrifice. A parent providing for children, a worker supporting elderly relatives, or someone managing chronic illness must weigh their desire to serve against their obligations to themselves and others. Rather than seeing this as a failure of discipleship, we might understand it as an invitation to discover how faithfulness manifests differently across various life circumstances. Perhaps being Christlike involves not just grand sacrifices, but also the patient, steady work of showing up day after day for those who depend on us.

This tension between service and self-realization, between giving and being, mirrors our opening discussions about vocation. Just as we began by examining how personal calling interweaves with community needs, we now explore how ministry manifests this dynamic relationship. Today's world is marked by power imbalances, diverse experiences, an unfolding climate crisis, and evolving spiritual landscapes. All of these invite new ways of reimagining the meaning of service. As a Christian called to support people in discerning call, my task is to understand ministry in ways that honor both the call to serve and the need for all people, especially those historically marginalized, to fully develop their gifts and presence in the world.

This is the case because, as a Christian, I follow a God who consistently shows preferential concern for the marginalized and oppressed throughout scripture. From

---

2 Valerie Saiving, "The Human Situation: A Feminine View," *Journal of Religion* 40, no. 2 (April 1960): 108.

the liberation of the Israelites in Exodus to the prophetic calls for justice in the Hebrew Bible, and ultimately to Jesus's ministry, which prioritized the poor, the outcast, and the overlooked, the biblical narrative demonstrates God's commitment to those on the margins. For Christians, Jesus's life and teachings emphasize that the Reign of God is one where the last are first, where every person is valued, and where systems of exclusion are dismantled. Thus, I believe that those of us who claim to follow Christ are called to reflect this divine concern in our own lives and ministries, aligning our work with God's redemptive mission to restore dignity, equity, and flourishing for all, particularly those historically excluded or devalued. This focus is not optional; it is intrinsic to embodying the Gospel and participating in God's work in the world.

These insights about power, gender, and the varied demands of daily life matter for everyone engaging in ministry, not just those who identify as marginalized. For those in positions of relative privilege, understanding these dynamics is vital for effective and ethical service. Without recognizing how calls to sacrifice and service land differently on different bodies, well-intentioned ministry efforts can unintentionally perpetuate harm. Additionally, those with social privilege often face their own forms of constraint. There are perhaps subtle but real pressures to maintain appearances, meet others' expectations, or uphold institutional traditions that may no longer serve. Regardless of social location, understanding the complex interplay between power, responsibility, and service helps all of us to minister more wisely and compassionately. It enables us to create spaces where everyone's gifts can flourish and where service becomes truly life-giving rather than depleting for both those who give and those who receive.

The circle closes, but not as a simple return to beginning. Rather, we spiral upward, carrying forward the insights about systems thinking, accompaniment, identity, and belonging that we've gathered along the way. These perspectives now inform our understanding of ministry as both a manifestation of personal calling and a catalyst for communal transformation. In this final chapter, we examine how ministry can embody the paradoxical truth that meaningful service both requires and creates freedom: freedom from oppressive constraints and freedom for life-giving engagement with God, creation, and community.

Servitude, Power, and the Call to Serve

The challenge of ministry lies partly in the biblical language that associates service, faithfulness, and ministry with concepts of servitude and slavery. Scriptures like Mark 10:43–45, which states, "Whoever wants to become great among you must be your servant, and whoever wants to be first must be slave of all," present us with a paradox. These texts, while emphasizing humility and selflessness, can be problematic when applied uncritically, especially in contexts of oppression or marginalization. How do we interpret these calls to servitude in a way that empowers rather than diminishes? How can we honor the spirit of these teachings while being mindful of the potential for misuse?

While pride and ego can certainly obstruct effective ministry, my experience with students and in congregations is that a far more prevalent struggle is the tendency for people to "hide their light under a bushel" (Mt. 5:14–16). This reluctance to fully embrace one's gifts and calling is particularly pronounced among those from marginalized groups, reflecting deeper systemic issues of power, representation, and internalized oppression within religious structures. This isn't to say that there aren't some ministers with big ego problems. There are. But when all the attention is paid there, larger issues can be missed. The trailblazing white feminist theologian Valerie Saiving shed light on this issue in her groundbreaking essay, "The Human Situation: A Feminine View," which is quoted in the epigraph.

Saiving challenged the notion that sin is universally rooted in pride and self-assertiveness, arguing that, for many women, the greater spiritual danger lies in self-negation and the underdevelopment of self. As we saw in the opening to this chapter, she wrote, "The moments, hours, and days of self-giving must be balanced by moments, hours, and days of withdrawal into, and enrichment of, her individual selfhood if she is to remain a whole person."[3] To say that women need to be more self-negating, decrease further, and be less self-assertive could result in the "underdevelopment or negation of the self."[4] In a society where male dominance has been a social norm and presumed truism, a male view saying that pride was the issue is sensible ... for men. For women, though, the problem of sin is far more likely to be a lack of self-realization: hiding light under the bushel basket.

> Today, when at last women might seem to be in a position to begin to be both feminine and fully developed, creative human beings; today ... theology, to the extent that it has defined the human condition on the basis of masculine experience, continues to speak of such desires as sin or temptation to sin. If such a woman believes the theologians, she will try to strangle those impulses in herself.[5]

In addition to our understandings of sin and virtue, this insight invites us to reconsider how we conceptualize and practice ministry. By imagining that the experience of men was the experience of humanity writ large, theology was making a biased mistake. The

---

3 Saiving, "The Human Situation," 108.
4 Ibid., 109.
5 Ibid., 110.

problem here is failing to take context into consideration. Though we are all made in God's image, we are not all the same and do not occupy the same social location and the privileges they afford.

Building on Saiving's groundbreaking work, subsequent generations of feminist and womanist theologians have further expanded our understanding of how social location and identity shape experiences of faith, sin, and ministry. These scholars have emphasized the importance of intersectionality, recognizing that individuals often embody multiple, overlapping identities that influence their spiritual journeys and ministerial callings. This intersectional approach reveals that the dynamics Saiving identified are often compounded for women of color, who face interconnected systems of oppression based not only on gender but also on race, class, and other factors.

One particularly influential voice in this ongoing conversation is the womanist theologian Delores Williams. Williams's work not only reinforces Saiving's critique of male-centric theological frameworks but also pushes us to reconsider fundamental Christian concepts like redemption and ministry through the lens of Black women's experiences. Her insights offer a powerful challenge to traditional understandings of service and sacrifice, especially for those who have historically been marginalized and unable to easily access social centering, power, and the benefits that comes from such access.

Williams's assertion that "Jesus came to show humans life—to show redemption through a perfect ministerial vision"—represents a profound shift in understanding Jesus's mission and the nature of redemption.[6] Traditional Christian theology often emphasizes Jesus's death as the primary means of redemption, focusing on concepts like substitutionary atonement. However, Williams challenges this view, arguing that it can perpetuate harmful ideas about the redemptive nature of suffering, especially for those who have historically been expected to suffer while their exploited labor helped others to thrive.

Instead, Williams posits that Jesus's redemptive work was primarily enacted through his life and ministry, not his death. By saying Jesus came "to show humans life,"[7] she suggests that Jesus's purpose was to demonstrate a way of living that brings wholeness, justice, and abundant life. This "perfect ministerial vision" that Williams describes is not about suffering or self-negation, but about actively working to right relationships and restore balance in all aspects of human existence.

Williams argues that the synoptic gospels "provide resources for constructing a Christian understanding of redemption that speaks meaningfully to Black women,

---

6 Delores S. Williams, *Sisters in the Wilderness: The Challenge of Womanist God-Talk* (Maryknoll, NY: Orbis Books, 1993), 164.

7 Ibid.

given their historic experience." This ministerial vision, according to Williams, involves "righting relations between body (individual and community), mind (of humans and of tradition) and spirit." It's a vision that includes "raising the dead (those separated from life and community), casting out demons (for example, ridding the mind of destructive forces prohibiting the flourishing of positive, peaceful life) and proclaiming the word of life that demanded the transformation of tradition so that life could be lived more abundantly."[8] This is a vision of ministry as repair: a practical, relational, and world-mending vocation.

Williams reinterprets the cross not as a symbol of redemptive suffering, but as "an image of defilement, a gross manifestation of collective human sin."[9] She argues that Jesus conquered sin in life, not in death, "by resisting the temptation to value the material over the spiritual," and by refusing "to allow evil forces to defile the balanced relation between the material and the spiritual, between life and death, between power and the exertion of it."[10] This perspective challenges us to rethink ministry not as self-sacrifice or suffering, but as life-affirming action that rights relations and promotes flourishing.

Engaging with such reinterpretations isn't about abandoning core Christian beliefs, but about seeing them with new eyes, allowing the wisdom and experiences of those historically on the margins to illuminate overlooked dimensions of God's love and liberation. It's an invitation to a fuller, more inclusive understanding of the Gospel. It invites us to consider how our understanding of ministry might need to shift to "respond meaningfully to Black women's historic experience."[11] This kind of responsive and inclusive reevaluation doesn't just reshape our theology; it necessarily calls us to a more nuanced understanding of how we embody our faith in diverse human contexts.

Given Saiving's work and the insights from Williams, I think we are invited to consider how different individuals, based on their social location and intersecting identities, might need to hear and apply biblical teachings on service and humility differently. For those in positions of power and privilege, the call to "decrease" so that Christ might increase may indeed be appropriate and necessary (John 3:30). Other traditions might frame this as yielding to love, community, or a deeper truth. The impulse to step back so something larger can emerge can be powerfully corrective. However, for those who have been historically marginalized, the message may need to be one of empowerment, self-realization, and the courageous use of their God-given gifts.

---

8 Ibid., 130.
9 Ibid., 166.
10 Ibid.
11 Ibid., 165.

To complicate matters further, many individuals embody multiple, intersecting identities, each carrying unique dynamics and demands. Some aspects of a person's identity may call for humility and "decreasing," while others require empowerment and "increasing." This interplay underscores the need for a nuanced, contextual approach to ministry that moves beyond one-size-fits-all prescriptions and instead honors the complexities of human experience. As we navigate these intricate realities, it is vital to remember that obedience and submission in Christianity are not ends in themselves but are intended to contribute to the liberation and empowerment of all people.

The challenge lies in interpreting and applying teachings on ministry in ways that foster justice, flourishing, and the full realization of human potential, rather than perpetuating cycles of oppression or self-negation. This requires a communal approach to discernment, one that engages honestly with scripture, tradition, and our lived experiences, while remaining attuned to God's guiding presence. By holding these tensions together, we may uncover new ways of living out our ministries that affirm the dignity of all and lead to profound joy and meaning in our shared spiritual journeys.

Scriptural Foundations of Christian Ministry

The concept of ministry in Christianity is deeply rooted in biblical teachings, with both the Hebrew Bible and Christian scriptures providing rich insights into what it means to serve God and community. From the prophetic calls to justice in the Hebrew Bible to the teachings of Jesus on love, humility, and service, ministry is framed as a dynamic and relational commitment. It involves not only the act of serving others but also a continuous alignment with divine purpose, seeking to embody compassion and integrity in all aspects of life. In the New Testament, this call to ministry expands, inviting Christians to understand themselves as "co-workers with Christ," participating in a mission of reconciliation and healing.[12] That sense of being summoned toward repair and care, of being accountable to something larger than ourselves, is not unique to Christianity. Ministry, therefore, is not merely a role or position within a church; it is a lived expression of existential commitment encompassing any profound responsibility to work toward the flourishing of individuals and communities.

Indeed, some of the most powerful ministry happens through leaders who, without formal theological degrees, bring deep wisdom, practical experience, and meaningful connection to their service. These ministers often have an intimate understanding of their communities' needs and can bridge gaps between formal church structures

---

12 See 2 Corinthians 5:18–20; 1 Corinthians 3:9; Romans 12:4–8 for examples of the New Testament call to ministry as participation in Christ's work of reconciliation and healing.

and daily life. Their calling is no less profound for being lived out in ways that don't require academic or ordination credentials. Understanding ministry through this broader lens challenges us to consider how our unique gifts and callings can contribute to a vision of justice, mercy, and love.

In the Hebrew scriptures, we see various forms of ministry embodied in the roles of prophets, priests, and kings. These biblical models also remind us of the systems-thinking approach that we discussed in the fourth chapter, encouraging us to see ministry not as isolated acts but as interconnected responsibilities within a larger spiritual ecosystem. The prophets, such as Isaiah, Jeremiah, and Amos, served as God's messengers, calling people to faithfulness and justice. Their ministry often involved challenging societal norms and speaking truth to power.[13] The priesthood, established in the line of Aaron, focused on mediating between God and the people through ritual and sacrifice.[14] Kings, at their best, were called to lead with justice and compassion, serving as shepherds to God's people.[15] Throughout these scriptures, the Hebrew word עָבַד (abad) is often translated as "serve" or "work." It appears frequently, conveying the idea of service to God and others. This concept lays the groundwork for understanding ministry as fundamentally about service.

In the Christian scriptures, several Greek words are used to convey the concept of ministry, each adding nuance to our understanding. The most prominent is διακονία (diakonia), which fundamentally means "service." This term emphasizes that, at its core, biblical ministry is about serving others. We see this word used in key passages such as 1 Corinthians 12:5 and Ephesians 4:12, where it describes the diverse ways believers serve within the body of Christ.

Jesus himself embodies the ultimate model of ministry, describing his mission as one of service: "For even the Son of Man did not come to be served, but to serve, and to give his life as a ransom for many" (Mark 10:45). Jesus's ministry encompassed teaching, healing, and compassion, often directed toward the marginalized in society. His washing of the disciples' feet (John 13:1–17) provides a powerful image of humble service that has shaped Christian understanding of ministry for centuries. While these passages don't use *diakonia* specifically, they use verbs like βόσκω (bosko, "to feed") and ποιμαίνω (poimaino, "to shepherd"), which describe ministerial actions.

---

13 See Isaiah 1:17; 58:6–7; Jeremiah 22:3; 7:5–7; Amos 5:24; 2:6–7 for examples of prophetic ministry challenging societal norms, denouncing oppression, and calling people to justice and faithfulness.

14 See Exodus 28:1; Leviticus 9:7; Numbers 18:1–7 for examples of the priesthood's role in mediation, ritual, and sacrifice.

15 See 2 Samuel 23:3–4; Psalm 78:70–72; Ezekiel 34:2–4 for examples of the ideal vision of kingship, emphasizing justice, compassion, and shepherding leadership.

Another significant term is δοῦλος (doulos), meaning "slave" or "servant." This word is used by Paul, James, Peter, and Jude to describe themselves in relation to Christ (Romans 1:1; Phil. 1:1; James 1:1; 2 Peter 1:1; Jude 1:1). The use of *doulos* emphasizes the complete devotion and submission of the apostles and leaders to Christ, portraying ministry as a form of radical servanthood, where one's entire identity is shaped by their relationship to Christ as master. However, this term carries a historical and cultural weight that must be approached with care, especially given its associations with the atrocities of slavery and oppression. When taken out of its first-century context, the term can be misunderstood or even weaponized, obscuring the transformative theological message it was intended to convey: a redefinition of servitude as an act of love and liberation in Christ. When considered in context, however, the apostles' use of the term was a profound act of theological subversion, a deliberate rejection of worldly status to claim allegiance to a crucified Lord over and against the claims of Caesar.

The early church, as depicted in Acts and the Epistles, saw ministry as a diverse and Spirit-empowered activity. Paul's letters, in particular, offer rich insights into the nature of Christian ministry. In 1 Corinthians 12, Paul describes the church as a body with many parts, each with its own function but all working together for the common good. This metaphor underscores the diverse and complementary nature of ministry within the Christian community. By emphasizing that an eye cannot do the work of a hand, nor a foot the work of an ear, the image insists that true unity is found not in uniformity, but in the healthy interdependence of different, essential functions. Paul also uses familial metaphors to describe his own ministry, portraying himself as a nursing mother and a father (1 Thess. 2:7; 1 Cor. 4:15). These images highlight the nurturing and parental aspects of ministry.

In Ephesians 4:11–16, Paul outlines various ministerial roles (apostles, prophets, evangelists, pastors, teachers) whose primary function is to equip other believers for ministry. Helping ministry come to life in others *is* ministry. The ultimate goal is the edification and maturity of the entire body of Christ, indicating that ministry is not an end in itself but a means to build up the community of faith. Beyond these core concepts, biblical ministry encompasses several other important aspects. Preaching and teaching are emphasized in passages like 2 Timothy 4:2 and Romans 10:14–15, using Greek terms such as κηρύσσω (*kerusso*, "to preach") and διδάσκω (*didasko*, "to teach"), highlighting the importance of communicating and explaining God's word. Stewardship and accountability are addressed in 1 Corinthians 4:1, which uses the term ὑπηρέτης (*hyperetes*, "servant" or "minister"), and in James 3:1, which warns of stricter judgment for teachers, underscoring the responsibility that comes with ministry roles. Humble leadership is another aspect, as highlighted in 1 Peter 5:1–4, where elders are exhorted to shepherd God's flock willingly and eagerly, not for personal gain or domination, but as examples to others. Proclamation, responsible stewardship, and servant leadership are additional dimensions of ministry that each complement and enrich the broader biblical understanding of ministry as service to God and community.

It's important to note that, while the Christian scriptures do describe some specific ministerial roles, they don't present a rigid structure for ministry. Instead, they emphasize the diverse gifts given by the Spirit for the building up of the church, suggesting a more fluid and inclusive understanding of ministry. This biblical portrayal of ministry as service encompassing pastoral care, teaching, leadership, and the use of diverse gifts for the benefit of the community, provides a rich foundation for understanding Christian ministry today.

Interpretive Strategies

This is not a book about biblical interpretation, but when approaching scriptural passages on ministry with an eye toward issues of justice, power, and marginalization, it's useful to employ a nuanced and contextually aware interpretive strategy. This approach involves several key elements that help us understand these texts in ways that promote liberation and empowerment rather than reinforce unjust structures.

First and foremost, we must consider the historical and social context in which these texts were written. Many of the Christian scripture passages addressing ministry and service were directed to early Christian communities that were often marginalized within the broader Roman society. Recognizing this context can significantly shift our understanding of what terms like "servanthood" or "slavery" might have meant to the original audience. For instance, the radical call to servanthood in Mark 10:43–45 takes on new meaning when we consider that it was addressed to a community already experiencing societal powerlessness. In this light, Jesus's words can be seen as a critique of existing power structures rather than an endorsement of subservience.

Closely related to this is the need to carefully consider the use of metaphorical language in these texts. The imagery of "slave" and "servant" is often employed metaphorically to convey deep spiritual truths about one's relationship with God and others. We should resist the temptation to interpret these metaphors as literal endorsements of unjust power structures. Instead, we must ask what these metaphors were intended to convey about devotion, humility, and the nature of spiritual leadership. This approach allows us to honor the text while also critically examining how such language has been misused historically to justify oppression.

The concept of intersectionality, modeled by theologians such as Delores Williams, is life-giving in our interpretive strategy. One's social location significantly affects how these texts are experienced and should be interpreted. Social location includes factors like race, gender, class, ability, and cultural background. For those in positions of power and privilege, these texts may indeed call for humility and the use of their privilege for the benefit of others. However, for those who are already marginalized, these same texts may need to be read as affirming their inherent worth and the value of their gifts. This intersectional approach reminds us that there is no single, universal interpretation of these texts, but rather a range of valid readings shaped by diverse life experiences.

In light of this, we should always ask how these passages can be understood in ways that liberate and empower, rather than oppress. The call to serve in Mark 10:43–45, for example, can be seen as a radical inversion of power structures, challenging those with authority to use it for the benefit of others rather than for self-aggrandizement. This reading aligns with Jesus's own ministry, which consistently elevated the marginalized and challenged oppressive systems. He and his story ought to be a major part of the basis upon which interpretation is done. That is, I think it is useful to read these passages holistically, situating them within the broader biblical narrative. The Bible contains overarching themes of justice, liberation, and the inherent dignity of all people created in God's image. How do specific texts about ministry align with or challenge these broader themes? This holistic reading increases the likelihood that our interpretation of ministry is consistent with the Bible's overall message of love, justice, and human flourishing.

We must be willing to wrestle honestly with the ways these passages have been used historically to justify oppression and marginalization. This doesn't mean dismissing or discarding difficult texts, but rather engaging with them openly, acknowledging their potential for both liberative and oppressive interpretations. This critical engagement requires us to center the voices of those who have been harmed or silenced by these texts. For those of us who have benefited from dominant cultural norms, this means listening with humility, allowing our own perspectives to be corrected and expanded. For those whose communities have been on the receiving end of oppressive interpretations, this work is a vital act of survival, reclamation, and theological truth-telling. By centering these perspectives, we move toward a more faithful and honest reading of scripture, one that is accountable to the full body of Christ and better equipped to challenge long-held assumptions about meaning and application.

Finally, we must consider the practical implications of our interpretations. How might different understandings of these texts affect real-world power dynamics and the treatment of marginalized groups? What are the concrete consequences of how we apply these passages in our communities and ministries? This practical focus ensures that our interpretive work isn't merely academic but has real-world relevance for how we understand and practice ministry in diverse contexts.

By employing these interpretive strategies, we can approach biblical texts on ministry in ways that honor their spiritual depth while also addressing critical issues of justice, power, and marginalization. This approach allows us to develop a more nuanced, contextually aware, and ultimately more faithful understanding of Christian ministry for our contemporary world. Of course, we also need to realize that the meaning of things doesn't get frozen in time based on what is in the Bible. The meaning of "ministry" and what was meant by it developed over time like most meanings. Looking at that development helps us get a sense of the history of the terms and reminds us (for better or worse) that the present state of things is not how it always was or always will be.

The Historical Evolution of Ministry

The way we understand and practice ministry has been continuously shaped and reshaped across the centuries by cultural, social, and theological currents, both within the Christian tradition and in response to the world around it. As a result, it's worth reflecting on where we've been to get a better sense of where we are. From its beginnings in the life of Jesus and the early church, through the rise of complex institutions, and into our own era of global and digital realities, ministry has always been a living, evolving thing. Trying to map this evolution across two millennia is, to put it mildly, a humbling task. Therefore, what follows is my attempt to offer a bird's-eye view of these vast changes, knowing full well that any such an overview can only scratch the surface. My hope is that this glimpse into ministry's dynamic past will provide a helpful backdrop for understanding where we find ourselves now.[16]

The Apostolic Age (30–99) saw ministry deeply rooted in Jesus's approach in first-century Palestine. His ministry encompassed teaching, preaching, healing, exorcism, discipleship, and compassionate service, often focusing on marginalized groups within Jewish society. Jesus's emphasis on service over domination set a foundational principle for Christian ministry that influenced subsequent generations and regions (Mark 10:42–45).

As local congregations began to form throughout the Mediterranean world, leadership roles started to diversify. The Didache, an early Christian text likely originating in Syria, mentions apostles, prophets, and teachers as key figures. House

---

16 This whole section draws heavily upon Justo L. González, *The History of Theological Education* (Nashville, TN: Abingdon Press, 2015), as well as H. Richard Niebuhr and Daniel D. Williams, eds., *The Ministry in Historical Perspectives* (New York: Harper & Brothers, 1956).

churches, often led by both men and women, like Priscilla, Aquila, and Lydia, became central to Christian community life from Rome to Ephesus. Women such as Phoebe (described as a deacon) and Junia (referred to as an apostle) held notable positions, reflecting a level of gender inclusivity that varied over time.[17] This period was marked by a fluid understanding of ministry, deeply rooted in the Jewish synagogue tradition yet increasingly distinct as the young faith spread beyond its Jewish origins.[18]

The Ante-Nicene Period (100–312) witnessed the development of a more structured church hierarchy as Christianity spread throughout and beyond the Roman Empire. This early period saw Christianity expanding beyond the Greco-Roman world, reaching regions like Persia, India, and Ethiopia. Each of these regions developed unique expressions of Christian ministry, influenced by local cultures and traditions.[19] For instance, the Church of the East, centered in Persia, developed a strong emphasis on monastic and scholarly traditions that would later influence Christian thought in China and Central Asia. The early church was known for its emphasis on spiritual gifts, social care for widows, orphans, and the poor, and a strong focus on evangelism.[20] During times of persecution, martyrdom became a powerful form of witness and ministry, particularly notable in the North African church, which produced figures like Perpetua and Felicity.[21]

The Age of Christian Empire (312–590) brought profound changes to the practice of ministry as Christianity transitioned from a persecuted faith to the state religion of the Roman Empire. The church hierarchy became more elaborate, mirroring imperial structures. Bishops took on civic responsibilities, including judicial roles, blurring the lines between religious and secular authority.[22] This period also saw the rise of desert monasticism and the development of liturgical practices that would shape Christian

---

17 Bernadette J. Brooten, "Women and the Early Churches: The Challenge of Early Christian History," in *Women and the Early Churches: The Challenge of Early Christian Women* (Minneapolis: Fortress Press, 1996), 1–23.

18 Judith M. Lieu, "The Synagogue and the Separation of the Christians," in *The Ancient Synagogue from Its Origins until 200 CE*, ed. Birger Olsson and Magnus Zetterholm (Stockholm, Sweden: Almqvist & Wiksell, 2003), 189–207.

19 George H. Williams, "Ministry in the Later Patristic Period," in *The Ministry in Historical Perspectives*, ed. H. Richard Niebuhr and Daniel D. Williams (New York: Harper and Brothers, 1956), 33–80.

20 Vincent E. Faherty, "Social Welfare before the Elizabethan Poor Laws: The Early Christian Tradition, AD 33 to 313," *Journal of Sociology & Social Welfare* 33, no. 2 (June 2006): 107–22.

21 Jan N. Bremmer, "Felicitas: The Martyrdom of a Young African Woman," in *Perpetua's Passions: Multidisciplinary Approaches to the Passio Perpetuae et Felicitatis*, ed. Jan N. Bremmer and Marco Formisano (Oxford: Oxford University Press, 2012), 35–53.

22 Williams, "Ministry in the Later Patristic Period," 81–110.

worship for centuries. As Christianity spread along trade routes and beyond imperial borders, we have some evidence suggesting that early contact was made with India and China.[23]

The Early Middle Ages (600–1000) saw the practice of ministry profoundly shaped by the spread of Christianity across Europe and the establishment of monasticism. Under the influence of figures like Benedict of Nursia in the West and Basil of Caesarea in the East, monasteries became centers of spirituality, learning, and social service.[24] Missionary work flourished during this period, with figures like St. Patrick in Ireland, St. Augustine of Canterbury in England, and St. Boniface in Germany establishing churches, baptizing converts, and setting up ecclesiastical structures. These missions often involved a complex interplay of evangelization, cultural exchange, and sometimes suppression of local practices, foreshadowing later colonial dynamics.[25]

The High Middle Ages (1000–1300) witnessed significant developments in church structure and the formalization of ministry roles. The East-West Schism of 1054 led to divergent approaches to ministry and ecclesiology. In the West, the role of priests in administering sacraments became central to church life, while the East maintained a more mystical approach to sacramental theology. Scholasticism, exemplified by theologians such as Thomas Aquinas, developed complex theological systems that influenced ministerial education and practice in Western Europe. Meanwhile, the Eastern church, particularly in Byzantium, maintained a more contemplative approach to theology.

This period also saw the emergence of new forms of religious life, such as the mendicant orders (e.g., Franciscans and Dominicans), which emphasized preaching and service to the poor.[26] The Crusades represented a controversial form of "ministry," blending religious fervor with political and military objectives, and had far-reaching consequences for Christian-Muslim relations and the future of Christianity in the Middle East.

Navigating these centuries, we see the tension between ministry as pastoral care and spiritual development, and ministry entangled with institutional power and geopolitical ambition, a tension that, in many ways, continues to shape religious

---

23 Barbara Watson Andaya, "Christianity in Asia," *Oxford Research Encyclopedia of Asian History* online (June 25, 2018).

24 Roland H. Bainton, "The Ministry in the Middle Ages," in *The Ministry in Historical Perspectives*, ed. H. Richard Niebuhr and Daniel D. Williams (New York: Harper and Brothers, 1956), 111–45.

25 See, for example, Peter Brown, *The Rise of Western Christendom: Triumph and Diversity*, AD 200–1000, 10th anniversary revised ed. (Chichester, West Sussex: John Wiley & Sons, 2013), 321–54.

26 Caroline Bruzelius, "The Architecture of the Mendicant Orders in the Middle Ages: An Overview of Recent Literature," *Perspective*, no. 2 (2012): 365–86.

life today. This ongoing tension takes on new textures as we enter the Late Middle Ages (1300–1512). This era, far from resolving earlier complexities, presented its own distinct set of significant challenges and profound changes to the practice and understanding of ministry. It was a period where societal shifts, institutional strains, and even devastating events like plague and schism created fertile ground for both spiritual searching and the retrenchment of established power, leading to diverse and sometimes contradictory expressions of religious life and service.

The development of mysticism, represented by figures such as Hildegard of Bingen and Julian of Norwich in the West, and Symeon the New Theologian in the East, offered alternative models of spiritual leadership. However, formal ministerial roles for women became increasingly restricted in both East and West, though some found expression through mysticism and monastic leadership.[27] Meanwhile, the Coptic Church in Egypt and the Ethiopian Orthodox Church continued to develop their own distinct traditions of ministry, largely isolated from European conflicts.

The Age of Reformation (1517–1648) dramatically reshaped the understanding and practice of Christian ministry. Martin Luther's emphasis on the priesthood of all believers challenged the hierarchical structure of the Catholic Church and redefined the role of clergy. Various Protestant movements emerged, each developing distinct approaches to ministry and church leadership, while Catholic reforms, including the Counter-Reformation, brought significant changes to Catholic ministerial practices worldwide.[28] This era also saw the emergence of radical reformation groups like the Anabaptists and the Peace Churches, who challenged both Catholic and mainstream Protestant understandings of ministry and church-state relations.[29]

The Post-Reformation Era (1603–1773) witnessed the consolidation of Protestant denominations and the Catholic Counter-Reformation. This period saw Christianity's global spread accelerate alongside colonial expansion, particularly in the Americas, Africa, and Asia. Missionaries played a deeply complex and often contradictory role in this expansion. Although some individuals advocated for Indigenous rights or demonstrated genuine care, the broader missionary enterprise was frequently entangled with colonial power, leading to the suppression of Indigenous cultures, spiritualities, and sovereignty.[30] The establishment of seminaries and mission training schools reshaped ministerial formation, integrating academic study with practical

---

27 Barbara Newman, "Annihilation and Authorship: Three Women Mystics of the 1290s," *Speculum* 91, no. 3 (2016): 591–630.

28 Kevin Burrell, "How the West Was Won: Christian Expansion Before and After the Protestant Reformation," *Andrews University Seminary Studies* 56, no. 1 (2018): 115–40.

29 Alister E. McGrath, *Christianity's Dangerous Idea: The Protestant Revolution—A History from the Sixteenth Century to the Twenty-First* (San Francisco: HarperOne, 2007), 77–82.

30 Burrell, "How the West Was Won."

ministry experience in an apprenticeship model.[31] Influenced by Pietism and other renewal movements, some Protestant training programs began to emphasize personal spiritual formation alongside intellectual development. This holistic approach sought to nurture both the mind and heart of future ministers, recognizing that effective pastoral leadership required more than just theological knowledge.

The Early Modern Era (1783–1865) brought significant challenges and changes to Christian ministry. In the United States, the Second Great Awakening led to new forms of evangelism and social reform efforts. This period saw the birth of many missionary societies, driving a new wave of global evangelization often closely tied to colonial expansion.[32] The industrial revolution brought massive social changes, challenging ministers to address new forms of poverty and labor exploitation. The establishment of the University of Berlin in 1810 marked a pivotal moment in the evolution of theological education. This institution revolutionized the approach to theological studies, inspired by Friedrich Schleiermacher's vision of theology within the university setting as a rigorous field of academic inquiry.

This "Berlin Model" introduced the influential fourfold curriculum, identifying the areas in which a minister was supposed to have mastery: biblical studies and languages, systematic theology, church history, and practical theology.[33] This structure would come to dominate graduate theological education globally and persists to this day. You might even recognize echoes of this fourfold pattern in how theological topics are often presented or discussed in your own communities or studies, so pervasive has its influence been.

The Late Modern Era (1870–1945) was characterized by significant social and political changes that profoundly affected the practice and understanding of Christian ministry. The rise of the Social Gospel movement in Protestantism and the development of Catholic Social Teaching emphasized the church's role in addressing societal issues, expanding the concept of ministry beyond individual spiritual care to include social reform and justice.[34] Figures such as Pope Leo XIII and Walter Rauschenbusch articulated theologies that integrated social engagement into the Christian mission.[35]

---

31 González, *The History of Theological Education*, 95–105.

32 Hadley Kruczek-Aaron, "The Second Great Awakening and the Remaking of Everyday Life," in *Everyday Religion: An Archaeology of Protestant Belief and Practice in the Nineteenth Century* (Gainesville: University Press of Florida, 2015).

33 González, *The History of Theological Education*, 105–17.

34 Ibid.

35 See, for example, Pope Leo XIII, *Encyclical Rerum Novarum* ("Rights and Duties of Capital and Labor") (May 15, 1891); Walter Rauschenbusch, *A Theology for the Social Gospel* (New York: Macmillan, 1917).

This period also saw the growth of ecumenical movements, fostering cooperation across denominational lines in ministry efforts. In colonized regions, Indigenous Christian leaders increasingly challenged the paternalism of Western missionaries, asserting their right to contextual expressions of faith and laying the groundwork for independent national churches. This shift toward indigenization would have far-reaching effects on global Christianity in the following decades. Additionally, the traumatic experiences of two World Wars and the Holocaust forced many ministers to grapple with questions of suffering, evil, and the role of faith in times of crisis, further shaping ministerial approaches and theologies.

The post–World War II Era (1946–1989) saw transformative shifts in Christian ministry, profoundly influenced by the threat of nuclear annihilation. This existential crisis reshaped theological reflection and ministerial practice globally. Christianity's rapid growth in the Global South spurred contextual theologies such as Latin American liberation theology, which criticized the ways in which unchecked capitalism damaged communities. In the United States, the Civil Rights Movement and Black Theology reframed ministry through racial justice, and student movements pushed for social engagement. Pentecostal and Charismatic movements expanded globally, emphasizing spiritual gifts and greater lay involvement. Decolonization fostered Indigenous church leadership, and many traditions began ordaining women. The Cold War context, defined by nuclear deterrence, shaped ministry differently across regions. Ecumenical efforts encouraged cooperation, often united by concerns over nuclear proliferation. By 1989, these diverse influences had dramatically altered the landscape of Christian ministry, setting the stage for the post–Cold War era's challenges and opportunities.

The Global-Digital Era (1989–present) has witnessed dramatic shifts in Christian ministry, increasingly influenced by growing awareness of globalization, technological advancements, and human-caused climate change. On the whole, Christianity has declined in the West, with a parallel rise in "nones" and the "spiritual but not religious," especially in the United States. Simultaneously, though, Christianity has experienced explosive growth in the Global South, particularly sub-Saharan Africa, regions often most vulnerable to climate change impacts. This has led to new forms of contextual theology and ministry practices, including eco-theologies and creation care ministries. The era has been marked by a divergence in approaches: some embracing a pluralistic, culturally sensitive ministry integrating spiritual care with social and environmental justice, while others have aligned with religious nationalism and are often skeptical of climate science.

Megachurches and Pentecostal movements have gained prominence, further diversifying the ecclesiastical landscape. The COVID-19 pandemic accelerated many of these trends, necessitating rapid adaptation to digital platforms and a reassessment of the church's role in supporting crisis-stricken communities. These developments reflect broader societal changes, challenging churches to navigate complex cultural, political, and environmental terrains while maintaining their spiritual mission. The existential threat posed by climate change has become a central concern for many ministries, influencing everything from theological education to practical outreach efforts, and pushing churches to consider their role in advocating for and implementing sustainable practices. It's a dizzying array of shifts to witness, let alone navigate faithfully, in just a few decades.

Throughout this historical development, we can trace both continuity and change. While the forms and understandings of ministry have evolved dramatically across diverse cultural contexts, the core concept of ministry as service to God and community has remained constant. From the early church's focus on communal care to the modern era's engagement with global and digital realities, ministry has consistently sought to meet the spiritual and practical needs of people in their specific contexts. The historical journey of Christian ministry reflects an ongoing dialogue between tradition and innovation, as each era has grappled with the challenge of embodying timeless truths in ever-changing circumstances. And that, I believe, is a dance we're still learning today.

And so this rapid journey across centuries and continents comes to a pause. If attempting to map this evolution felt humbling at the outset, summarizing its many turns in these few pages feels doubly so. Each era, each movement, and every shift in understanding "ministry" carries with it countless stories, struggles, and sparks of divine insight that a brief overview like this can only acknowledge. My hope, reader, is that this quick survey serves not as an exhaustive catalog, but as a clear reminder: The ways we understand and embody service are not fixed. They continue to develop and change. As we turn now to how ministry is understood in our contemporary landscape, perhaps we can carry this sense of a dynamic, evolving inheritance with us. The call remains, but how we hear it, and how we respond, continues to be shaped by the realities of our time.

As we turn our attention to contemporary understandings of ministry, we must recognize that we stand on the shoulders of this rich and complex history. From traditional pastoral roles to innovative forms of digital outreach, the diversity of approaches we see today are all part of this continuing story. In the following section, I explore how current practitioners and theologians are defining and reimagining ministry for the twenty-first century, building on the lessons of the past while responding to the unique challenges and opportunities of our time. This exploration will help us consider how we might faithfully and creatively engage in ministry in our own contexts, honoring our inherited wisdom while remaining open to the Spirit's ongoing work of renewal and transformation.

Contemporary Understandings of Ministry

Though I think it is useful to know some of the historical and biblical underpinnings of the meaning of ministry, I recognize that people's current experience of things rarely resembles scenes from Corinth in the year 50 CE or Cold War Era Europe. That is, how communities have come to understand ministry is often quite diverse, even if they haven't explicitly redefined it. There are numerous overlapping ways in which ministry is understood and practiced today. The following "understandings" of ministry are not formal definitions in the strict sense, nor are they all mutually exclusive categories. Rather, they represent functional definitions: ways of thinking about ministry that I have observed in both scholarly literature and practical service contexts. Over the years, as I've heard people talk about how they feel called, I've added to the list if I felt like I was hearing something new.

These understandings often coexist within individuals and communities, sometimes complementing each other, other times creating tension. Within a given community, it is likely that, if everyone was polled, there would be several understandings of ministry present. I don't mean to suggest that the right way to do things is to try to get everyone to focus on a single perspective. Rather, I'd encourage you to treat the list below as a field guide of sorts, helping you identify and reflect on the various assumptions about ministry that shape your understanding and practice as well as those of your communities.

For better or worse, all the lenses I offer here are drawn from Christian perspectives and experiences. Other faith traditions and secular contexts will undoubtedly have their own rich ways of categorizing and understanding what it means to serve the good. What follows reflects the landscape I know best. Some may resonate strongly with your experience, while others might challenge your preconceptions or open new avenues for considering what ministry entails. This evolving view of ministry reflects the continuous journey of discernment we discussed in the second chapter, where each generation interprets and lives out its calling in response to changing contexts.

For the sake of organization, I've organized it from perspectives that are individual and internally focused to those that are more collective and external. I've also noted when particular spiritual gifts seem especially connected to that emphasis on ministry. Finally, in each, I've included a brief comment about the possible opportunities and challenges present. My point here is not that there is one "best" view on ministry, but that they each contribute different things and we ought to consider the consequences of excluding some or intensely emphasizing only a few. In some ways, this is a paired understanding to the spiritual "sliders" from the third chapter.

There I used the metaphor of a musician's mixing board to describe spiritual sliders, a dynamic framework for understanding spiritual formation. Each slider represented a dimension of spiritual growth, such as intellectual engagement, community connection, or the exercise of spiritual gifts. These sliders highlighted how spiritual formation involves both sources (practices and experiences that shape us) and evidence (observable signs of that growth). The metaphor also underscored the cyclical and evolving nature of formation, where growth in one dimension often leads to engagement in another.

The understandings of ministry presented here serve as a paired framework, extending this dynamic, "mixing board" model to practice. Just as the spiritual sliders help us assess and visualize the interior consequences of spiritual formation, these perspectives on ministry provide a practical way to reflect on the diverse ways ministry is understood, practiced, and made manifest in the world.

Both frameworks recognize that growth and discernment are not static. Just as our spiritual sliders shift in prominence based on our context and needs, so, too, do our perspectives on ministry. We may emphasize different understandings of ministry at different times, depending on the gifts we're stewarding, the needs of our communities, and the Spirit's movement in our lives. It is also the case that you can experience God calling you into multiple types of service simultaneously.

As you read through these understandings, I encourage you to reflect on which ones align more with your own experiences and call. Consider how they might shape your practice or the practices of your faith community. Be open to perspectives that might initially seem foreign or challenging: They may offer valuable insights for expanding or deepening your conception of ministry in our complex, rapidly changing world.

1. *Living Relationship with God*

This view, rooted in personal spirituality, posits that ministry is fundamentally about cultivating and expressing an intimate relationship with God. It's particularly emphasized in Charismatic and Pentecostal traditions and draws from Jesus's teaching in John 15:4–5 about abiding in Him. This approach aligns with the spiritual gift of faith (1 Corinthians 12:9), which enables believers to trust God deeply and inspire others to do the same. Contemporary examples include ministries like Bethel Church or IHOP (International House of Prayer). Adherents often focus on personal spiritual growth and intimacy with God as the foundation for all ministry. They might particularly value practices like personal devotions and small group gatherings, encouraging a vibrant, experiential faith. While this approach cultivates a culture of personal spirituality, it might sometimes struggle to balance inward spiritual growth with outward expressions of faith and service.

2. *Word Ministry*

Building on personal spiritual growth, this interpretation frames ministry primarily in terms of the proclamation and teaching of God's Word. It's common across various Protestant denominations and is rooted in 2 Timothy 4:2, which instructs us to "preach the word." This conception aligns with the spiritual gifts of teaching, wisdom, and knowledge (Romans 12:7, 1 Corinthians 12:8). It's particularly emphasized in Reformed traditions and can be seen in ministries like John MacArthur's Grace to You or R. C. Sproul's Ligonier Ministries. Proponents often emphasize biblical instruction, manifesting in sermons and Bible studies. It can include versions of digital ministry as well, where technology is used to proclaim the Word of God. They might particularly value biblical literacy and the authority of Scripture in the life of the church. While this focus on the Word is important, those who hold this view may sometimes struggle to integrate solid biblical teaching with other aspects of ministry and practical application of faith in daily life.

3. *Mentoring and Accompaniment Ministry*

This model emphasizes the importance of one-on-one or small group mentorship and accompaniment in ministry. It draws biblical support from relationships like Paul and Timothy (2 Timothy 2:2) and aligns with the spiritual gifts of exhortation and discernment (Romans 12:8, 1 Corinthians 12:10). It involves guiding and nurturing individuals in their faith journey, providing support, and fostering deep spiritual growth and accountability. Contemporary examples include mentorship programs for new believers, leadership training groups, and spiritual direction sessions. This approach recognizes the power of interpersonal relationships in fostering spiritual growth and leadership development. While it can lead to deep, transformative experiences, it may face challenges in scaling to larger communities and ensuring healthy boundaries in mentoring relationships.

4. *Service and Sacrifice*

Moving from internal growth to outward action, this paradigm emphasizes that ministry is primarily about offering oneself in sacrificial service to God and others. It's deeply rooted in the Protestant Reformation's emphasis on the priesthood of all believers and finds its biblical basis in passages like 1 Peter 2:5, which calls believers to "offer spiritual sacrifices acceptable to God through Jesus Christ." This approach aligns with the spiritual gift of service (Romans 12:7). Many evangelical and mainline Protestant denominations embrace this view, as do service-oriented organizations such as World Vision or Samaritan's Purse. Adherents often see ministry as an act of devotion that elevates service to a divine level. They might be particularly drawn to volunteering and charity work, viewing these activities as ways to emulate Christ's sacrificial example in daily life. This perspective challenges believers to consider how they can serve sacrificially while maintaining their own spiritual, emotional, and physical health.

5. *Universal Service*

Expanding the concept of service to encompass all aspects of life, this notion frames ministry as humble service to others, reflecting Christ's example. It's particularly prevalent in Evangelical and Baptist traditions and is based on Jesus's words in Matthew 20:28 and Mark 10:45, where He states that He came "not to be served, but to serve." This understanding aligns with the spiritual gifts of service and helps (Romans 12:7, 1 Corinthians 12:28). Contemporary expressions of this idea can be seen in organizations such as Habitat for Humanity or local church outreach programs. Those who embrace this understanding often see ministry as an inclusive and accessible practice, allowing all believers to participate through various forms of service. They might be particularly involved in community outreach and help ministries, viewing everyday acts of kindness as expressions of ministry. The concepts of Work-as-Calling, which views one's profession as a mission field, also fits within this category, emphasizing service through daily work even if conventionally seen as "secular." This approach encourages a culture of humility and service but may struggle to balance this general call with the recognition of specific gifts and callings.

6. *Pastoral Care*

Focusing more explicitly on care for others, this conceptualization views ministry as providing emotional and spiritual support to individuals and communities. It's common across most Christian denominations and finds biblical support in passages such as James 5:14–15, which speaks of caring for the sick. This approach aligns with the spiritual gifts of mercy and pastoring (Romans 12:8, Ephesians 4:11). Contemporary expressions include chaplaincy service and counseling programs such as Stephen Ministries. This perspective views ministry as fostering physical, emotional, and spiritual healing and wholeness. It encompasses such practices as healing prayer, pastoral counseling, wellness programs, and holistic health initiatives. This approach recognizes the interconnectedness of body, mind, and spirit and aims to promote overall well-being. It might include support groups, retreats focused on mental health, and integrating alternative healing practices with spiritual care. While this ministry is vital for building strong, supportive faith communities, those who practice it may struggle to maintain healthy boundaries while offering genuine, empathetic support.

7. *Reconciliation and Conflict Mediation*

This approach views ministry as facilitating reconciliation and mediating conflicts within the church and broader community. It's rooted in Jesus's teaching on peacemaking (Matthew 5:9) and Paul's description of the "ministry of reconciliation" (2 Corinthians 5:18–19). This understanding aligns with the spiritual gifts of wisdom, discernment, and exhortation (1 Corinthians 12:8, Romans 12:8). It's prevalent across various Christian traditions, particularly emphasized in peace churches such as the Mennonites and Quakers. Contemporary expressions include conflict resolution programs in churches, community mediation centers with faith-based roots, and such organizations as Christian Peacemaker Teams or the Center for Justice and Peacebuilding at Eastern Mennonite University. Adherents often see ministry as creating spaces for dialogue, healing, and restoration of relationships. They might be particularly involved in interpersonal conflict resolution, restorative justice initiatives, or even international peace-building efforts. This approach encourages a culture of peace and reconciliation within the church and beyond, viewing conflict as an opportunity for growth and transformation. While this ministry is needed for fostering healing and unity, it may sometimes struggle with balancing the pursuit of peace with the need for justice and accountability, potentially leading to situations where deeper systemic issues or power imbalances are not adequately addressed.

8. *Hospitality Ministry*

This approach emphasizes creating welcoming, inclusive environments as a form of ministry. It aligns with the spiritual gift of hospitality (1 Peter 4:9–10) and focuses on making people feel at home in the church or ministry setting, addressing both physical and social needs. This perspective recognizes the importance of creating spaces where people can experience God's love and acceptance tangibly. It extends beyond mere friendliness to encompass a holistic approach to welcoming and including others in the life of the community. It can also encompass the creation of liturgical spaces that invite participation and foster a sense of belonging and sacredness within the community. While Hospitality Ministry can greatly enhance community building and outreach, it faces several challenges, including balancing openness with the need for structure and boundaries, avoiding surface-level friendliness without deeper relational engagement, navigating cultural differences in understanding and expressing hospitality, maintaining consistency across different church contexts and interactions, and addressing potential burnout among those heavily involved in hospitality roles.

9. *Priestly Service*

Bridging individual service and communal roles, this interpretation emphasizes ministry as a priestly role of offering spiritual sacrifices and mediating between God and people. While most formally expressed in Catholic and Orthodox traditions, the function of priestly service appears in many contexts. Even in Protestant traditions that strongly emphasize the "priesthood of all believers" (a concept rooted in passages like 1 Peter 2:9, which describes the faithful as a "royal priesthood"), the pastor is often set apart to perform uniquely priestly duties. These can include consecrating communion elements, pronouncing blessings, leading the congregation in confession, and serving as a spiritual guide who helps connect the community with the sacred. Adherents often focus on the sacred duty of ordained ministry, manifesting in these liturgical and sacramental rites. They might particularly value the continuity of this function from the biblical witness, underscoring the importance of ordained ministry. A central challenge in this approach is balancing the sacred responsibility of this role with the call to empower all believers in their own ministry.

10. *Lay Ministry*

This model expands the very definition of who a minister is, emphasizing the vital role of non-ordained individuals in the church's mission. "Lay ministry" itself is not a single type of service; rather, it is the recognition that ministry is the shared responsibility of the entire community. Grounded in the concept of the "priesthood of all believers" mentioned above, and revitalized in Catholic life after the Second Vatican Council, this approach sees ministry as the exercising of the diverse spiritual gifts mentioned in 1 Corinthians 12 and Romans 12. Contemporary expressions include the rise of lay ecclesial ministers, catechists, and pastoral care providers in the Catholic Church and the emphasis on every-member ministry in many Protestant traditions. This perspective challenges the church to recognize and empower the gifts of all members, though it may sometimes struggle with questions of authority and the specific role of ordained ministry.

11. *Governance and Operations*

Moving toward more organized, communal expressions, this framework views ministry primarily in terms of structured organization and implementation of church activities to meet community needs. It's common in Mainline Protestant churches and finds biblical precedent in passages like Acts 6:1–7, which describes the early church organizing to meet community needs. This approach aligns with the spiritual gifts of leadership and administration (Romans 12:8, 1 Corinthians 12:28). Many established denominational structures, such as the United Methodist Church or the Presbyterian Church (USA), reflect this understanding. Adherents often value clear structure and organization, manifesting in formal church service and work on congregational committees. They might see ministry as supporting communal worship and education, reflecting a culture of organized religion. While this approach can provide clarity and efficiency, it may sometimes struggle to remain flexible and responsive to individual needs and the Holy Spirit's leading.

12. *Administrative Ministry*

This perspective views ministry as effectively managing and coordinating church or ministry operations. It aligns closely with the spiritual gifts of administration and helps (1 Corinthians 12:28). This approach focuses on the behind-the-scenes work that enables other ministries to function smoothly, including tasks like organizing events, managing resources, and coordinating volunteers. It can include versions of digital ministry as well, where technology is used as part of the underlying support needed for other ministries to function effectively. While vital for effective ministry operations, this approach may sometimes struggle with maintaining a spiritual focus amid practical demands.

13. *Resource Mobilization Ministry*

Supporting communal efforts, this approach frames ministry in terms of mobilizing resources to support various church activities and outreach efforts. It finds biblical precedent in passages like 2 Corinthians 8–9, where Paul encourages generous giving to support other believers. This approach aligns with the spiritual gift of giving (Romans 12:8). Many churches and faith-based nonprofits, such as World Vision or Compassion International, embody this understanding in their approach to ministry. Those who embrace this view often see fundraising and resource mobilization as spiritual acts that enable the church to fulfill its mission. They might be particularly involved in stewardship campaigns, charity events, or grant-writing. This approach encourages a culture of generosity and good stewardship but may sometimes struggle with the tension between faith and financial pragmatism.

14. *Great Commandment and Commission*

Expanding to a broader communal mission, this conception views ministry as the fulfillment of the dual mandates to love God and neighbor (the Great Commandment, Matthew 22:36–40) and to make disciples (the Great Commission, Matthew 28:18–20). It aligns with the spiritual gifts of evangelism and apostleship (Ephesians 4:11). It's common in Evangelical and Missionary circles, with organizations such as Campus Crusade for Christ (Cru) or the International Mission Board embodying this approach. Adherents often see clear, actionable goals for ministry in evangelism and discipleship programs. They might emphasize love and evangelism as central tenets of the Christian faith, fostering a mission-oriented culture within the church. While this approach provides clear direction, it can sometimes become overly task-oriented, potentially overlooking other aspects of Christian life and ministry.

15. *Charismatic Ministry*

Emphasizing empowered communal witness, this paradigm views ministry as a divinely empowered mission to be witnesses for Christ. It's prevalent in Pentecostal and Charismatic traditions and draws its biblical basis from Acts 1:8, where Jesus promises power to His witnesses. This approach aligns with spiritual gifts like prophecy, miracles, healing, and speaking in tongues (1 Corinthians 12:8–10). Contemporary expressions include ministries like Reinhard Bonnke's Christ for All Nations or Heidi Baker's Iris Global. Proponents often emphasize divine empowerment for service, manifesting in evangelistic campaigns and pastoral care. They might particularly value the supernatural aspects of ministry, including spiritual gifts and divine guidance. While this approach can be deeply motivating, it may sometimes be perceived as overly mystical or abstract, struggling to balance divine empowerment with practical, grounded ministry approaches.

16. *Works of Mercy*

Focusing on communal action for those in need, this interpretation emphasizes that ministry is fundamentally about performing acts of compassion and kindness, particularly for those in need. It's rooted in the biblical tradition of the corporal works of mercy, which find their basis in Matthew 25:35–36, where Jesus identifies himself with the hungry, thirsty, naked, sick, and imprisoned. This approach aligns with the spiritual gifts of mercy and service (Romans 12:7–8). This view is particularly prominent in Catholic social teaching, but it's also embraced by many Protestant denominations and ecumenical organizations. Groups such as the Society of St. Vincent de Paul or the Salvation Army exemplify this approach. Adherents often see ministry as a practical expression of faith through direct service to others. This also includes crisis and disaster response ministry or programs where folks are committed to feeding the hungry, sheltering the homeless, or visiting the sick and imprisoned. This perspective challenges believers to see Christ in every person they serve, emphasizing the inherent dignity of all people.

17. *Educational Ministry*

This perspective views ministry as encompassing educational efforts within the church and community. It aligns closely with the spiritual gifts of teaching and knowledge (Romans 12:7, 1 Corinthians 12:8). It finds biblical basis in passages like

Deuteronomy 6:6–7 and Matthew 28:19–20. Contemporary expressions include Sunday school programs, theological education, and church-run literacy or vocational training programs. Adherents highlight the importance of knowledge and learning in spiritual formation and community development. This approach recognizes the transformative power of education in both individual spiritual growth and broader community empowerment. However, it may sometimes struggle with balancing academic rigor and practical application of faith.

18. *Arts and Creative Ministry*

This category focuses on the use of various art forms as a means of ministry and worship. Although not tied to a specific spiritual gift in biblical lists, it can be seen as an expression of diverse gifts used creatively. It draws biblical support from passages such as Exodus 35:30–35 and Psalm 150. Contemporary examples include church music ministries, liturgical dance teams, and visual art installations in worship spaces. Proponents emphasize the role of creativity in expressing faith and engaging the broader community. It also can be understood to exist outside of the congregation in which the creative practice itself is understood as ministry. This approach recognizes the power of art to communicate spiritual truths and evoke emotional and spiritual responses. While it can be a powerful means of engagement and expression, it may sometimes face challenges in balancing artistic expression with traditional forms of worship and ministry.

19. *Interfaith and Ecumenical Ministry*

This approach emphasizes building bridges between different faith traditions or Christian denominations, promoting understanding, and finding common ground for collaboration. Although not directly tied to a specific spiritual gift, it draws on gifts like wisdom, knowledge, and discernment. It finds biblical support in passages like John 17:21 and 1 Corinthians 12:12–27. It often involves interfaith dialogue initiatives, collaborative community service projects, and ecumenical worship services. Organizations such as the World Council of Churches and local interfaith councils exemplify this approach. This view fosters a culture of unity and cooperation, highlighting the shared values and goals among diverse religious communities. While this approach can lead to powerful partnerships and broaden perspectives, it may sometimes struggle with balancing openness to other traditions with maintaining distinct faith identities.

20. *Social Justice and Outreach*

Representing the broadest societal engagement, this model emphasizes that ministry is about advocating for and serving the marginalized in society. It's often emphasized in progressive Christian groups and draws biblical support from passages like Isaiah 1:17 and Matthew 25:35–40, which call for justice and care for the vulnerable. Although not tied to a specific spiritual gift, it draws on such gifts as mercy, service, and prophecy (in terms of speaking truth to power). Contemporary examples include organizations such as Sojourners and Bread for the World. Proponents often focus on community service and advocacy, manifesting in social programs and activism, including environmental stewardship. They might particularly value the integration of faith with social action, seeing social engagement as a meaningful expression of Christian faith. While this approach powerfully demonstrates faith in action, those who embrace it may sometimes struggle to balance social engagement with other aspects of spiritual life and ministry.

A Practice to Consider:
Your Ministry Recipe

Ministry, like a recipe, requires intentionality in choosing and blending its ingredients. Reflecting on your unique combination helps to align your gifts with the diverse needs of the world.

1. Consider the "Contemporary Understandings of Ministry" from this chapter as ingredients for your unique approach to ministry. What proportions feel right for you?
2. Choose Your Ingredients: From the list of 20 manifestations of ministry, pick the ones that resonate most with your own sense of calling.
3. Decide on Proportions: Assign an amount to each ingredient. For example, two parts social justice, one part pastoral care, a dash of teaching. What mix feels closest to your sense of call? Remember that what you're good at and what you are called to are not always the same thing.
4. Reflect on the Blend: In a journal entry or conversation with a peer, explore why you chose each ingredient and its amount. How do these elements complement each other to shape your approach to ministry?

Ministry in a Changing Spiritual Landscape

As we consider the perspectives above, I think it is worth acknowledging the shifting spiritual landscape in which those understandings exist, particularly in the United States. Recent decades have seen a significant increase in the number of people identifying as "spiritual but not religious" (SBNR) or as religious "nones," those unaffiliated with any organized religion. This trend presents both challenges and opportunities for Christian ministry, calling us to reimagine how we understand and practice ministry in this evolving context.

This changing landscape particularly highlights the growing importance of lay ministry. As traditional church attendance patterns shift and communities seek spiritual nurture in diverse ways, lay ministers often serve as crucial bridges, bringing spiritual care and leadership to spaces formal religious structures might not reach. Increasingly, I see people called to chaplaincy in this way, but it is certainly not limited to that. Community organizers, policy advocates, and "social bankers" of all sorts can join with the work of God.[36] Their intimate knowledge of their communities, combined with their meaningful calling to serve, allows them to minister effectively in workplaces, neighborhoods, and informal gatherings where traditional ministry might not penetrate.

The concept of ministry has found resonance far beyond traditional Christian contexts, expanding into realms that might surprise or even unsettle some traditional practitioners. Life coaches, mentors, and counselors often describe their work as ministry, focusing on personal growth and holistic well-being. Environmental stewardship, community service, and various healing practices are increasingly viewed as forms of ministry by those who consider themselves spiritual but not religious. In secular contexts, the term "ministry" is sometimes adopted to describe community service and humanitarian efforts. These activities, although not explicitly religious, often align with the original Christian concept of serving others, reflecting a broader understanding of ministry as service to humanity and the planet.

Organizations such as Volunteers of America, for instance, focus on service without necessarily emphasizing a particular religious framework. Similarly, many environmental activists consider their work a form of ministry, committed to the stewardship and conservation of our planet. This perspective aligns with our understanding of ministry as any faith-inspired action intended to serve as a catalyst

---

36 I'm grateful to my colleague De'Amon Harges for introducing me to the idea of "social banking." As he sees it, this role entails "bringing neighbors and institutions together to discover the power of being a good neighbor," building "on the strengths that are already present in the neighborhood," and using those assets "to empower and connect rather than working from the community's needs and deficits." More information can be found here: https://www.investedfaith.org/deamon-harges.

for growth, healing, or positive change. It challenges us to expand our notion of what constitutes "faith-inspired" action and to recognize the diverse ways in which people are responding to what they perceive as sacred callings.

Interestingly, we've also seen the emergence of secular communities that mirror certain aspects of religious gatherings. The Sunday Assembly, often referred to as the "Atheist Church," and the Oasis Network are prime examples of this phenomenon.[37] These organizations provide community, inspiration, and opportunities for personal growth and service, all without a theological framework. They offer a space for those who seek the social and emotional benefits traditionally associated with religious communities, but without presuming a certain religious belief system. The existence and growth of such groups underscore the persistent human need for community and meaning-making, even as traditional religious affiliations decline. This trend invites us to reflect deeply on what vital human needs our ministries are meeting (or failing to meet).

The rise of SBNR and "nones" reflects a complex set of factors, including growing disillusionment with traditional religious institutions and practices.[38] Many individuals, especially younger generations, are seeking spiritual fulfillment outside the confines of organized religion. This is part of a much broader societal trend, as public confidence in nearly every major institution has been in steady decline for decades, with faltering trust everywhere from the government and the press to the medical establishment and large corporations.[39] People may be skeptical of religious authority, wary of perceived hypocrisy, or simply find traditional religious expressions irrelevant to their lives. However, this shift also indicates a persistent spiritual hunger, suggesting that, while many are turning away from organized religion, they are not necessarily abandoning spiritual pursuits altogether. This presents both a challenge and an opportunity for Christian ministry.

In light of these realities, I think there is good reason to consider how, if at all, ministry can be reimagined in ways that can speak more meaningfully to this changing context while remaining attentive to the tradition. Ministry in this landscape must prioritize helping people make meaning they find useful and demonstrate its relevance to everyday life. This means moving beyond formulaic answers and being willing to

---

[37] You can learn more about these groups at https://www.sundayassembly.org/ and https://www.oasisnetwork.com/.

[38] Pew Research Center. "Religious 'Nones' in America: Who They Are and What They Believe," Pew Research Center, January 24, 2024, https://www.pewresearch.org/religion/2024/01/24/religious-nones-in-america-who-they-are-and-what-they-believe/.

[39] Pew Research Center, "Americans' Deepening Mistrust of Institutions," Pew Research Center, Fall 2024, https://www.pew.org/en/trend/archive/fall-2024/americans-deepening-mistrust-of-institutions.

engage honestly with doubt, questioning, and the complex realities of modern life. Rather than adopting a defensive posture, Christian ministry can seek opportunities for dialogue and collaboration with those outside traditional religious structures, recognizing that we might have much to learn from their perspectives and experiences.

As we move forward, it's important to remember that the rise of the SBNR and "nones" doesn't signal the end of Christian ministry, but rather calls for its transformation. The core of Christian ministry remains as relevant as ever: love for God and neighbor, pursuit of justice, cultivation of spiritual depth, and creation of meaningful community. The challenge and opportunity before us is to embody these timeless values in ways that speak to the unique spiritual longings of our time. Sometimes, this embodiment will happen within familiar congregational contexts. Other times, our most faithful ministry will take place far beyond the church walls, offering spiritual nourishment to those who may never seek institutional belonging. To serve the world as it is—and not only as we wish it were—is itself a profound act of faithfulness to the church's deepest calling.

In this evolving landscape, Christian ministry has the potential to offer something profoundly valuable: a holistic spirituality that integrates personal experience with communal support, ethical living with spiritual depth, and ancient wisdom with contemporary relevance. By embracing this potential, we can continue to fulfill our calling to be salt and light in the world, offering hope, meaning, and transformation in an age of spiritual seeking and religious disaffiliation.

Moreover, these shifts in the spiritual landscape don't just affect institutions and communities. They reshape individual ministers and their callings as well. A changing system inevitably leads to changes in those who serve within it. What began as a call to congregational leadership might evolve into a ministry of community organizing. Someone who starts in youth ministry might find themselves drawn to spiritual direction or chaplaincy. A worship leader might discover their gifts are particularly suited to digital ministry or creative arts. These evolutions in personal calling aren't failures or detours from an original path, but natural responses to an ever-changing context. Just as the broader religious landscape adapts to new realities, individual ministers must remain open to how their particular expressions of service might need to shift and grow. This dynamic interplay between systemic change and personal adaptation is part of what keeps ministry vital and responsive to the Spirit's ongoing work in the world.

For those engaged in theological education and ministerial formation, these shifts present both challenges and opportunities. How do we prepare ministers to serve effectively in contexts where traditional religious language and structures may be met with skepticism or indifference? How do we cultivate a spirit of innovation and adaptability while remaining rooted in the rich soil of Christian tradition? These questions invite us to reimagine not just the content of our ministerial training, but its very form and structure.

Implications of Emphasis

As we conclude our exploration of ministry, it's important to reflect on why we've taken this journey through biblical foundations, historical developments, and contemporary understandings. My aim hasn't been merely academic; rather, my hope is that this comprehensive view equips you to engage more thoughtfully and effectively with the challenges and opportunities that lie ahead. By understanding the contours of ministry's past and present, we're better prepared to navigate its future with wisdom and intentionality. Throughout this book, we've examined various aspects of vocational discernment and ministerial formation. Now, as we consider the implications of our evolving understanding of ministry, we see how our conception of ministry shapes both our theology and our practical approaches to serving God and neighbor.

These reflections barely scratch the surface of where we might look, so consider this exploration as an introduction rather than an exhaustive study. The issues we've examined reveal just how deeply ministry intersects with both our theological convictions and our practical approaches to living out our call. As we move forward, we are invited to consider how these insights reshape not only our beliefs but also the concrete ways we engage in service. This journey has laid the groundwork for a richer understanding of ministry, one that both challenges and deepens our theological frameworks and inspires more thoughtful, intentional approaches to practice. By reflecting on the intersections of theology and ministry, we prepare ourselves to engage with real-world needs, making our faith an active, lived reality.

Impacts on Theology

As we reconsider what ministry means and how it's expressed, we're invited to revisit core doctrinal areas, seeing them through new lenses. This theological reflection isn't an abstract exercise. It's a vital process that grounds our ministry in deep, life-giving truths while allowing those truths to speak afresh to our changing context. The interplay between our theology, our understanding of ministry, and our sense of calling is dynamic and reciprocal: As our concept of ministry expands, it challenges us to broaden and deepen our theology and reimagine how we discern and live out our vocations. Conversely, as our theology develops and our vocational understanding matures, it informs and shapes our approach to ministry. Let's examine how our evolving view of ministry intersects with, and may influence, key areas of Christian doctrine, inviting us into a richer, more nuanced theological framework for ministry and vocational discernment in the twenty-first century.

For example, the doctrine of Scripture may need reassessment in light of our changing views on ministry. Grappling with different approaches to interpretation could reshape our understanding of ministry roles and practices. This might involve revisiting passages traditionally used to define ministry, considering them in light of contemporary contexts and diverse cultural perspectives. The tension between historical interpretation and contemporary application presents both challenges and opportunities for ministerial formation. How do we balance biblical authority with the need for contextual interpretation in our approach to ministry?

Shifting perspectives on ministry may challenge us to reconsider our theology proper, our understanding of God's nature and attributes. As we encounter diverse forms of ministry, we might find ourselves reflecting on how our concept of God shapes our approach to service. For instance, our understanding of divine love could inform how we approach pastoral care and counseling. Yet we must also wrestle with how other divine attributes, such as justice and holiness, inform our ministry practices. How might our doctrine of God challenge or reshape our current models of ministry?

Christology takes on new significance as we reimagine ministry. We might be challenged to consider how we can embody Christ's presence in our various ministry contexts and vocational roles, and how we could practice a self-giving love that reflects Christ's own kenosis (self-emptying). This invites us to reflect on the interplay between Christ's divinity and humanity in our own ministries, balancing authority with humility. This reflection on Christology encourages us to explore how embodying the incarnation can inspire ministries that are simultaneously grounded in divine purpose and attuned to human vulnerability. What happens if we take Delores Williams seriously and consider the possibility that Christ's ministry was less about self-sacrificial death and more about the liberative power of life-affirming survival and relational solidarity? How might a renewed understanding of the incarnation reshape our own approach to service and presence in the world?

Rethinking pneumatology becomes ever more important as our view of ministry evolves. A robust doctrine of the Holy Spirit could remind us that ministry is not merely a human endeavor, but possibly a participation in the ongoing work of the Spirit in the present. This perspective may challenge us to cultivate practices of discernment in our vocational journeys. At the same time, we must consider how to distinguish between the Spirit's leading and our own desires or cultural influences. How do we discern and respond to the Spirit's leading in our ministries while maintaining accountability and order within our faith communities?

Theological anthropology, or the study of humanity in the context of God, can take on new dimensions when we adopt an inclusive understanding of ministry. This perspective may challenge us to see community members not just as recipients of ministry, but as possible ministers, perhaps called and gifted by God for service. However, this view also raises questions about the nature of spiritual authority and the role of specialized training in ministry. This dual perspective on humanity challenges us to navigate the tension between celebrating divine potential and confronting the complexities of our shared human condition. How do we balance the affirmation of the *imago Dei* with the reality of human fallenness in our ministry practices?

Hamartiology and soteriology, our sense of sin and salvation, may need reexamination as our understanding of ministry shifts. We might be challenged to consider how our doctrine of sin shapes our approach to pastoral care, counseling, and social engagement and vice versa. This invites us to reflect on the relationship between personal transformation and social justice in our understanding of salvation. This interaction between personal and communal aspects of salvation encourages us to evaluate how theological frameworks inform, and are informed *by*, our lived experiences of brokenness and restoration. How do our understandings of sin and salvation shape our approach to holistic ministry that addresses both spiritual and social needs?

Ecclesiology, the study of the church, comes into question as we reimagine ministry. A more inclusive view might push against traditional hierarchical models, potentially emphasizing the priesthood of all believers and the diverse gifts distributed throughout the body of Christ. This shift could lead to a reevaluation of the role of ordained clergy and the nature of spiritual authority within the church community. This reimagining of ecclesial structures compels us to explore how authority and leadership can reflect both the diversity and unity of the faith community, fostering collaboration without sacrificing coherence. How do we balance the need for ecclesiastical order with a more distributed and inclusive model of ministry?

Finally, eschatology, or the study of ultimate Christian hope, may need reconsideration as our perspective on ministry changes. We may need to reflect on how our doctrine of last things shapes our present ministry practices. This invites us to consider how our understanding of the Reign of God influences our approach to social engagement and cultural transformation. This reflection challenges us to hold in tension the already and the not-yet, inspiring ministry that is both deeply rooted in the present and profoundly oriented toward the future fulfillment of God's promises. How do we maintain a sense of ultimate hope and urgency in our ministries while also engaging in long-term, sustainable efforts for change and transformation in the world?

These theological reflections underscore that our understanding of ministry is not just a practical matter, but potentially a deeply doctrinal one that touches on every aspect of systematic theology. As we navigate the changing landscape of ministry in the twenty-first century, we may need to remain grounded in thoughtful theological reflection, possibly allowing our practice to inform our theology and our theology to shape our practice. This ongoing dialogue between doctrine and praxis might be vital as we seek to discern and live out our vocations in ways that are both faithful to our traditions and responsive to the needs of our world. However, these theological considerations don't exist in a vacuum. They have profound implications for how we actually do ministry on the ground.

Impacts on Practice

Our understanding of ministry profoundly shapes our practices, with far-reaching implications across various aspects of church life and service. These practical implications are deeply intertwined with the theological reflections we explored earlier. Just as our doctrine of Scripture, theology proper, Christology, and other theological areas are influenced by our understanding of ministry, so, too, are our day-to-day practices and structures. This interconnection between theology and practice underscores the importance of thoughtful, critical engagement with both our commitments and our attempts to embody them in practice. As we consider the practical implications of our ministry perspectives, we must remain mindful of how they reflect and reinforce our theological commitments, and vice versa. This dynamic interplay between belief and action invites us into a continual process of reflection, adaptation, and renewal in our approach to ministry.

When I speak of "practice," I mean more than just repeated actions or routines. For me, a practice is a dynamic pattern of behavior deeply rooted in context, intention, and meaning. It encompasses the interplay between what we do and why we do it, embedding shared imaginations about what is possible within the actions themselves.[40] Practices are not static; they are shaped by historical and cultural conditions and are capable of shaping those conditions in turn. They serve as sites of both continuity and transformation, embodying the potential to maintain, disrupt, or create new imagined visions of the world and God's work in it. In this sense, a practice is not merely about what is done but also about the possibilities it opens for reflection, resistance, and renewal. By attending to practices as living, contextual expressions of belief and community, we engage with them not just as acts to be performed but as spaces for discernment and transformation.

---

40 L. Callid Keefe-Perry, "Schooling the Imagination: A Practical Theology of Public Education," PhD diss., Boston University, 2020.

In the realm of leadership development, the way we conceptualize ministry significantly influences our approach to preparing individuals for service. If ministry is primarily seen as the work of ordained clergy, leadership development might focus intensively on seminary education and formal ordination processes, potentially limiting opportunities for those without access to such resources. However, if ministry is viewed as the calling of all believers, leadership development might shift toward more inclusive, accessible training programs that equip lay members for various forms of service and leadership within and beyond the church walls.

This broader view could lead to more diverse leadership but might also raise questions about maintaining theological depth and pastoral competence. How can we balance the need for specialized training with the desire to empower all believers for ministry? The approach we take to leadership development not only shapes who leads in our churches but also influences how ministry is understood and practiced throughout the congregation. It also influences what we think it is important to learn when you're training in ministry, either in school or in a church program.

Church structures, too, are deeply affected by our understanding of ministry. A hierarchical view might lead to more centralized decision-making processes and clearly defined roles within the church structure, potentially offering clarity and efficiency but at the risk of stifling innovation and individual initiative. Conversely, if ministry is seen as a collaborative effort among all members, church structures might evolve toward flatter hierarchies, team-based leadership, and more participatory governance models. Much like the role of accompaniment we discussed in the seventh chapter, collaborative ministry recognizes that each person's gifts contribute uniquely to the community's spiritual health, fostering a culture of mutual support and shared leadership.

While this approach could foster greater engagement and ownership among members, it might also present challenges in terms of coordination and accountability. What organizational structures might best reflect our theological understanding of ministry while also meeting practical needs for effectiveness and accountability? The structures we choose not only shape how decisions are made but also communicate our values about the nature of ministry and the role of each member of our community. They can either reinforce or challenge traditional power dynamics within the church, potentially opening up new avenues for diverse voices and gifts to be expressed.

Our approach to discipleship and spiritual formation is similarly shaped by our ministry perspective. If ministry is primarily understood as teaching and preaching, discipleship programs might emphasize biblical and theological knowledge acquisition, potentially creating a well-informed congregation but possibly neglecting practical application. However, if ministry is viewed more holistically as living out one's faith in all aspects of life, spiritual formation approaches might focus more on practical application, experiential learning, and integrating faith into daily decision-making. This approach could lead to more well-rounded disciples but might risk undervaluing the importance of solid theological grounding. How can we develop discipleship approaches that effectively balance theological depth with practical life application? The way we approach discipleship not only shapes individual believers but also influences the overall spiritual health and maturity of the church community. It can determine whether faith remains an intellectual exercise or becomes a transformative force in people's lives and in society.

Community engagement strategies are also influenced by how we understand ministry. A perspective that sees ministry as primarily focused on spiritual matters might lead churches to prioritize evangelism and Bible study in their community outreach, potentially having a strong spiritual impact but possibly overlooking pressing social needs. On the flip side, a view of ministry that emphasizes social justice and holistic care might result in churches developing more comprehensive community programs addressing physical, social, and economic needs alongside spiritual concerns. Although this approach could have a broader impact, it might also risk diluting the church's distinctively spiritual mission. How can churches engage their communities in ways that honor both spiritual and community care dimensions of ministry without compromising either? The approach we take to community engagement not only affects our impact on society but also shapes our witness as the church. It can either reinforce or challenge perceptions about the relevance and role of faith in addressing real-world issues.

Last, our approach to pastoral care is deeply affected by our ministry perspective. If ministry is viewed through a professional lens, pastoral care might be seen primarily as the responsibility of trained clergy, emphasizing formal counseling sessions and crisis intervention. This approach ensures a high level of professional care but might overlook the potential for mutual care within the congregation. Alternatively, if ministry is understood as mutual care within the body of Christ, pastoral care approaches might involve training lay members in basic caregiving skills, developing support groups, and fostering a culture of everyday compassion and support among church members.

Although this approach could create a more caring community, it might also raise concerns about maintaining appropriate boundaries and ensuring adequate care in complex situations. How can we develop pastoral care models that leverage the strengths of both professional expertise and community-based support? The pastoral care approach we adopt not only affects how individuals are supported in times of need but also shapes the overall culture of care within the church. It can influence how members view their responsibilities toward one another and how the church is perceived as a place of healing and support in the broader community.

These varying implications illustrate the profound impact our understanding of ministry has on our practices. As we navigate the changing landscape of ministry in the twenty-first century, it's vital to reflect on how our theological perspectives inform our practical approaches. This reflection invites us to continually reassess and potentially reimagine our methods of leadership development, church organization, discipleship, community engagement, and pastoral care. By thoughtfully examining these implications, we can develop more intentional, theologically grounded, and contextually relevant approaches to ministry. This process of reflection and adaptation is vital as we seek to faithfully live out our callings and effectively serve our communities in an ever-changing world. As we conclude, what steps can we take to ensure that our ministry practices remain both theologically sound and contextually relevant in our rapidly changing world?

Ministry as Manifestation of Call

If you look back over the perspectives on ministry throughout this chapter, you'll note that I frame ministry both by what it is (its essence) and by what it does (its effect). This oscillating understanding of the term is how *I* define ministry. In essence, I talk about ministry as "the practice of intentionally stewarding spiritual gifts and responding to divine leadings for the benefit of others." This practice involves deep listening, discernment, and a commitment to nurturing one's spiritual life in service of a greater good. It's about cultivating a posture of openness to the sacred and allowing that connection to guide our actions in the world. In effect, I talk about ministry as "any faith-inspired action that serves as a catalyst for growth, healing, or positive change." It can comfort the afflicted and afflict the comfortable. It may inspire individuals to deepen their spiritual lives, empower communities to work for justice, or challenge societal structures that perpetuate harm. The effects of ministry can be seen in renewed hope, strengthened relationships, increased compassion, and concrete actions that make the world a little more just and loving.

I like holding the essence and effect of ministry in tension because it provides a fuller understanding of this complex and vital aspect of spiritual life. Focusing solely on the essence of ministry can sometimes lead to an overly introspective or abstract approach that might lose sight of its real-world impact. However, on the other side of the coin, we must also be cautious about equating the "success" of ministry solely with its visible outcomes. It's about the integrity of our response to the divine call, not the measurable results of that response. The parable of the sower reminds us that the seeds of ministry may fall on various types of soil, and the fruit of our efforts is not always immediately apparent or measurable (Mt. 13:1–23, Mark 4:1–20, Luke 8:4–15). Some ministries may seem to bear abundant fruit quickly, while others may take years or even generations to show their full impact. Some may appear to fail entirely, yet still plant seeds of transformation that will sprout in unexpected ways and times. That our work is to sow seeds faithfully, trusting God with the harvest, whatever it may be, is so central to my understanding of ministry that the image on the cover of this book is a linocut I made inspired by this very parable.

This view reminds us that ministry flows from a place of deep spiritual grounding and intentionality, while also challenging us to manifest that inner work in ways that affect material conditions, benefit others, spiritually deepen the church, and contribute to positive change in the world. As we move into discussing ministry in our changing spiritual landscape, this dual perspective of essence and effect will help us navigate the complexities and challenges ahead. It provides a framework for understanding how traditional forms of ministry can adapt to new contexts and how emerging forms of ministry relate to our spiritual heritage. In the face of shifting religious affiliations and evolving spiritual needs, remembering both the essence and effect of ministry can help us stay grounded in our calling while remaining responsive to the world around us. As I see it, the ability to remain grounded and responsive is a foundational dynamic of both ministry and the callings that lead one into that service.

Throughout this book, I've framed vocation as a dynamic, evolving process rather than a fixed destination. It's a continuous process of growth, adaptation, and discovery, deeply embedded in our personal experiences and communal contexts. Vocation encompasses discovering and nurturing our unique gifts and passions, which are then used in service to the common good and its broader spiritual ecosystem. In this light, ministry can be seen as the manifestation of vocational call. It's the intentional stewarding of our spiritual gifts, nurtured through spiritual formation, and the active response to divine leadings, discerned through theological reflection, the very same practices central to the framework developed in the third chapter. Essentially, ministry bridges our inner spiritual lives with our outward engagement in the world. That is, ministry takes various forms, but, at its core, it's about translating our sense of calling into tangible service to God, community, and creation.

When we serve as ministers, we are not simply enacting a job description, we are stewarding a way of being in the world that reflects our deepest convictions about what is meaningful, sacred, just, and life-giving. That reflection is always in process. The structures that orient our inward lives into action must be tended over time. The values, relationships, beliefs, and practices that orient us require maintenance at times. Ministry is one way that tending happens.

The relationship between vocation and ministry is deeply interconnected. Your vocational journey will require different types of attention in different seasons. Some periods call for active planting and pruning, others for patient waiting and watching.

Trust the organic unfolding of your calling. Vocation provides the foundational sense of calling and purpose, while ministry is the active expression of that calling in material, service-oriented actions. Both require ongoing discernment, reflection, and engagement with our communities. They involve a delicate balance between individual introspection and communal affirmation.

Our sense of vocation is shaped by personal reflection and community feedback, while effective ministry requires both personal spiritual grounding and communal support. Importantly, both vocation and ministry emphasize adaptability and responsiveness to changing contexts. Just as our understanding of vocation evolves with new insights and life stages, our approach to ministry must adapt to meet the spiritual and practical needs of people in diverse and evolving contexts. This adaptability is a boon in our rapidly changing world, where the nature of community, the expression of faith, and the needs of society are constantly shifting. The way our inner stirrings develop outward expression is part of the interplay between vocation and ministry. This is not a distant idea for me. It's the core of my life's journey. And it has required profound reorientation.

As I write this in the spring of 2025, it has been twenty years since two Quaker ministers spoke words to me that I hadn't yet learned to speak for myself: "You are carrying gifts of vocal ministry." I was in my early twenties, grieving a breakup, floundering in dangerous depression, and only beginning to explore faith and spiritual community. I didn't grow up with religious language. I didn't have a theology of call. But their naming, that clear, grounded recognition, gave shape to something I had only vaguely intuited. It gave me direction.

That initial call moved outward, fast and bright. I felt summoned to public ministry: to teach, to preach, to speak truthfully and creatively about God, justice, and the human condition. I gathered people, created workshops, told stories that carried theological weight. I found joy in bridging intellect and spirit, in turning dense ideas into shared experiences of meaning. It was a season of momentum and imagination.

And I was built for it. Or, I at least believed I was. I made connections quickly, recalled texts easily, improvised in the moment. I didn't need many notes. I could walk into a room with a half-formed idea and trust that something would emerge. That kind of mental sharpness became central to how I saw myself as a minister. It was not just a tool. It felt like the vehicle of the call.

And then, quietly, it unraveled.

Not because the work stopped being meaningful, but because I couldn't keep up. I missed details. Forgot deadlines. Began falling behind. It wasn't because I didn't care, but because something in me had changed. My cognitive ease wasn't there. My social energy waned. And I didn't know how to say any of that out loud. Not yet. I hadn't accepted the truth of what was happening inside me. And I definitely didn't want to admit it publicly.

It was personal. It shook the frame I had built around my sense of call. I had understood ministry to mean visibility, eloquence, responsiveness. When those tools stopped working, I wasn't sure who I was anymore.

But vocation doesn't disappear when the outward form of ministry changes. Over time, slowly, through grief and reorientation, I began to understand that the call had not ended. It had changed. It had moved from the front of the room to the side of the circle. From performance to presence. From creating the spark to helping others tend their flame.

Now, I serve as a theological educator. One of the great joys of my life is working with students. Companioning people who are asking brave questions, imagining just and faithful futures, and stepping into ministries of their own. My work now shows up in companioning students as they wrestle with vocation and context, building programs and theological frameworks that support their growth. I help shape learning environments that prioritize reflection and clarity. At my best, I hold space rather than fill it. Space where others feel seen, supported, and called forward.

The heart of the call has remained constant: to help people live lives shaped by imagination, discernment, and justice. To make the life of the Spirit tangible, livable, and accountable in the world as it is.

Twenty years ago, I was called to be a public minister in the form of a preacher, performer, and convener. Someone who lit sparks through presence and improvisation. Today, I am called to be a mentor, builder, and accompanier, someone who tends the scaffolding that helps others find their fire and stay faithful to tending it.

The work is slower now. More deliberate. I can't do nearly as much as I used to, and what I do isn't always done as well as it would have been done before. Sometimes, it looks like staying put. Listening closely. Asking careful questions. Holding others gently as they find their own way.

The call remains. And so do I.

But, if there's anything this journey has taught me, it's that remaining is not the same as staying still. Ministry, like vocation itself, must be tended as living terrain. The form of our faithfulness changes, sometimes gradually, sometimes all at once. When the conditions around us shift, when our capacities rise and fall, or when the world breaks open in some new way, we may find ourselves disoriented. But disorientation is not failure. It is often a sign that our inner guide is doing its work, refusing to settle for incoherence or drift. In those moments, the call doesn't disappear. It emerges through new questions.

And so, we return to where we began: with vocation as a response to what is sacred, just, and necessary. With a reclaimed sense of grounding. Rooted in what we love, who we travel with, and what we know to be true, we can begin again to ask where we are, who we're alongside, and what faithfulness looks like now. The story I've just told is not simply about changes in my role or identity; it's about reorienting to a call that remains, even when my capacities and context were changing. It's about tending coherence in a shifting landscape.

As we've explored the various theological and practical implications of our understanding of ministry, we've seen how deeply it affects every aspect of church life, from leadership development to pastoral care. Each of these areas is, functionally, a manifestation of how we understand our collective and individual callings. The way we structure our churches, approach discipleship, engage with our communities, and care for one another all stem from and contribute to our sense of vocation. In this light, ministry becomes not just a set of tasks or roles, but a holistic expression of our response to God's call. It's about creating spaces and structures that allow all believers to discern and live out their vocations. It's about fostering communities where diverse gifts are recognized, nurtured, and employed for the common good. It's about engaging with the world in ways that bring hope, healing, and transformation.

As we move forward in our vocational journeys and our ministries, we're invited into a continuous process of reflection and adaptation. Individually and collectively, we're called to remain open to new understandings of how we might experience God calling us to serve in our changing world. We're challenged to create ministry structures and practices that are both theologically grounded and contextually relevant. This journey requires a delicate equilibrium that honors our traditions and embraces innovation, between nurturing our personal spiritual lives and engaging with the broader community. It calls us to recognize the value of being both contemplative and active, rooted in our faith while reaching out to a world in need. We know we can't do it all ourselves, but we also know that we're not alone.

As we navigate this path, we must be willing to grapple with difficult questions, confront our biases, and sometimes step out of our comfort zones. We're invited to see ministry not as a fixed set of practices, but as a dynamic, evolving expression of God's love in the world. This perspective challenges us to continually reassess our understanding of ministry, to be open to new forms of service, and to remain attentive to the diverse ways in which God's call manifests in our lives and in the lives of others. It reminds us that ministry is about participating in God's ongoing work of redemption and renewal in the world, a work that often unfolds in surprising and unexpected ways.

How might we cultivate a deeper awareness of the connection between our sense of vocation and our practice of ministry? What would it look like to approach ministry not as a fixed set of tasks, but as a dynamic expression of our evolving sense of call?

How can we create spiritual communities that nurture vocational discernment and empower all to engage in ministry?

These questions invite us into ongoing dialogue and discernment. They challenge us to remain attentive to the movement of the Spirit in our lives and communities. As we conclude, may we approach ministry with a renewed sense of its connection to our deepest callings. May we remain open to the ways God might be inviting us to manifest our vocations in service to the church and the world. May our ministries become ever more meaningful expressions of God's love and grace in our diverse and changing contexts. And you—reader, minister, seeker, friend—may you carry forward this sacred work, not alone, but alongside others who are listening too. Stay close to the ache and the joy. Your call is unfolding even now.

Questions for Reflection

1. The opening of this chapter grapples with the biblical language of ministry as "servitude," alongside Valerie Saiving's insight that for some, particularly women or marginalized individuals, the spiritual danger might be self-negation rather than pride. How do you personally navigate the call to humble service with the need to affirm your own gifts and well-being? Where have you seen this tension play out in your own life or in the ministries you've witnessed?

2. This chapter traces the historical evolution of ministry and presents a wide array of contemporary understandings, from "Word Ministry" to "Social Justice and Outreach." As you reflect on this diversity, which of these expressions of ministry most resonate with your own sense of what it means to serve? Were there any historical shifts or contemporary forms that surprised you or challenged your previous assumptions about what counts as ministry?

3. The chapter defines ministry by both its "essence" (intentionally stewarding spiritual gifts in response to divine leading) and its "effect" (being a catalyst for growth, healing, or positive change). In your own experience of ministry, or in what you hope to offer, which of these aspects do you find yourself emphasizing more, the inner intention or the outer impact? How do you hold these two in a healthy tension?

4. The idea that ministry is a "manifestation of call" suggests a deep link between our inner vocational journey and our outward service. Can you trace how your own evolving sense of vocation has shaped, or is currently shaping, the form and focus of your ministry or service in the world?

5. Considering the rise of people who identify as "spiritual but not religious," and the need for ministry to be relevant in diverse, sometimes secularized contexts, how might your primary faith tradition or community need to adapt its understanding or practice of ministry to effectively meet the spiritual hungers of today? What innovative or "intercultural" approaches might be needed?

6. The chapter concludes by affirming that ministry, like vocation, is a dynamic and evolving journey, one that requires us to balance honoring tradition with embracing innovation, and personal spiritual life with communal engagement. As you look toward your own future in service, what is one way you hope to intentionally tend to your ministry as living terrain, remaining rooted in your core calling while staying responsive to the shifting capacities within you and the changing needs of the world around you?

In Closing

Throughout this book, I've used the metaphors of seeds, growth, and abundance to structure our exploration of vocation and ministry. The reality is that our vocational journeys rarely follow such a neat, linear progression. At any given moment, we might find ourselves simultaneously planting new seeds of possibility in one area of our lives while experiencing profound growth in another and sharing abundantly from yet another. Some gardens in our lives may lie fallow while others flourish; some plantings may require pruning while others need nurturing. As you continue your own journey, may you find comfort in knowing that this mixture of experiences is not a sign of confusion or failure. If you are currently experiencing moments of careful seeding, challenging growth, or joyful abundance (or all three at once!), remember that you are part of a larger story of divine love unfolding in the world, called to serve in ways that bring life to yourself and others. May you continue to cultivate your calling with patience, courage, and hope, knowing that each season brings its own gifts and challenges to your ongoing journey of faithful service.

How to Listen for What Comes Next

1.

You will hear it on the seventh day of waking to a dream where everything was right; it was clear what your next step was; and you knew just what to do with that long weekend you still have open. You know, the space you want to use for something, but you've been pulling back from it since you couldn't think of anything just right to do with the time you have. And you want a perfect fit. Yes, the hackneyed hand in glove, and your favorite jacket, but also the first hug and conversation with your dear friend, long-missed and still loved, the joy of becoming a parent, or grandparent, or auntie, the smell of cocoa when you are ten and snow has called you all day. The smell of July and nothing but basketball until Monday. Greens and warm bread. Being seen as you are. Attention given to small joys.

2.

When the memory of that fit lingers, call it back to you daily. Ask it what it needs. What would it like? Are there any special purple socks it prefers? A particular bakery that is *the* spot? Make that memory a friend. The dream wants you as a conspirator and confidant. The dream wants to share with you the shapes of what can be, contours of priority and passion that lead out to a place where things are the way they should be. Even before your friendship is cemented, tell others about this new relationship. How there's a certain something that captivates you even though you can't put your finger on it. Talk about what it is like to learn about what you've always wanted and rarely known. Always known and rarely felt. Listen to others and what they say to you when you tell them how good the news is. Ask if they've been hearing it too. They'll have stories of their own.

3.

Eat food that nourishes your body and spirit. Eat it with those you love. Raise your voices in laughter, love, frustration, and—as needed—rage. If you cannot get to any of the tables that make you feel whole and home, or you need to turn away and walk toward new ideas of holiness and hearth, do whatever you need to find a place where you feel like you are becoming more of what you are supposed to be. Learn what the space feels like inside. Move your body as needed, in dance, in love, out into the street, into hills where tall trees call you down into the earth. The details are less important than the reminder that your flesh and bone is worthy of love and attention. Scream and cry or stand silently. Spin clockwise under the stars; lose yourself in a crowd; make something small; or bury yourself in soil until you touch the roots. Remember that you can be part of what will come next.

4.

There will be moments when you will want a life you do not have. Days that call not for ease or lushness but ask you to do the hard thing. You will wonder if someone like you should be living like that. On the edge of change. Rough. Sometimes, that is the life you will need to be building. Stone on stone, walls rising slowly and made to last. Good work. Calluses on your spirit. Heft. Other days, you will not want rest because you know how much is left to be done. You will remember the faces that have been lost and rage at those who seed loss. And on some of those days, you will need to sleep. To watch your favorite film again, mouthing the lines along with each actor just to feel like you know where you are. And I don't know when those days will come. Or what other walks you will take. Or stumbles. So, listen. Remember the things that call you and stay calling. Know that you can be called, then called away, and then back. That your respite is sometimes shorter than you would have liked. Longer. Far longer. Too short.

5.

...and work together.
Resist together.
Rest together.
Dream.
Build.
Listen.
Grow.

Appendix

This appendix offers a collection of additional materials designed to support your continued exploration of vocational discernment. These practical exercises and frameworks for deeper reflection are intended to be useful as you engage with the ideas presented in this book and apply them to your own life and work.

The tools and practices included here are offered to assist you, particularly during moments when you seek greater clarity, need new ways to approach a challenge, or wish to deepen your understanding. Many of these materials have been developed and refined through years of teaching and communal discernment. They are not presented as definitive solutions, but as invitations to further your own process of listening, thinking critically, and responding faithfully to your sense of call.

You are encouraged to use these resources in ways that best suit your individual needs and learning style. Adapt them, discuss them with others, and revisit them as your journey unfolds. Please feel free to use them with your community—however it is that you define that. Just let them know where you got the tool or exercise, and you're welcome to use any of these.

Theological Reflection in Practice

A Step-by-Step Guide

This section offers a structured, step-by-step process for theological reflection, expanding on the practice introduced in chapter 3. It is designed to guide you in analyzing significant experiences by connecting them to scripture, tradition, or other theological sources. Use this framework to make intentional meaning from life events, discern God's movement, and bring clarity to your vocational path. This guide is well suited for individual reflection, academic assignments, and ministry development, and can also serve as a practical resource for facilitating theological reflection in adult faith formation groups or classroom settings.

Theological reflection is more than an academic requirement: it is a discipline that deepens spiritual awareness, strengthens ministerial practice, and fosters the integration of faith and life. As you begin this work, your first step will be engaging with chapter 3, "Formation and Reflection," which introduces the why behind theological reflection: its role in spiritual formation, its capacity to bring theological and experiential knowledge into dialogue, and its potential to shape one's sense of vocation.

This guide takes the next step, offering a structured yet flexible process for engaging theological reflection with depth and intentionality. Moving beyond abstract concepts, it provides a clear, step-by-step approach, equipping you with the tools to critically examine experience, engage theological insights, and consider how reflection shapes practice. With detailed explanations, guiding questions, and sample reflections, this guide is designed to help you not only write strong reflections but also cultivate a habit of attentiveness that becomes part of your daily life.

Theological reflection is not a one-time exercise but an ongoing practice. A way of seeing, thinking, and responding that shapes how you engage the world. This guide will support you in developing that practice, ensuring that your reflections are both rigorous and meaningful, deeply personal yet theologically rich.

Step 1: Experience

The "Experience" section of your theological reflection paper asks you to narrate a specific encounter, event, or moment that has stayed with you. This experience serves as the foundation for your reflection, providing a concrete moment from which to engage deeper theological inquiry. It does not need to be dramatic or extraordinary; sometimes, the most meaningful theological reflection arises from ordinary moments.

Your experience can take different forms. It might be a single event that stood out to you, or it may be a pattern of events that you've observed over time. It can be something that happened directly to you or something you encountered (a news story, a public event, or a situation that you've found yourself thinking about repeatedly). What matters is that it lingers with you in some way, prompting questions, emotions, or curiosity.

Why It Matters

Theological reflection is not merely an intellectual exercise; it is yoked to spiritual formation. Naming and reflecting on an experience is part of the larger work of developing attentiveness to the movement of God in our lives and the world. Jesus often drew theological insights from everyday encounters: observing farmers sowing seeds, watching guests choose seats at a banquet, or noticing the faith of a stranger. These moments were not incidental; they revealed deep truths about God's kingdom, human nature, and discipleship. In the same way, theological reflection invites us to slow down and pay attention, recognizing that divine wisdom is often embedded in the ordinary.

Christian theology does not emerge solely from abstract reasoning or doctrinal study but is shaped by lived experience. Our encounters with joy, suffering, justice, and struggle are not just personal moments; they are theological texts in their own right. When we take time to reflect theologically, we are engaging in a process that integrates what we have read, studied, and believed with what we have seen, felt, and lived. This practice helps us bridge the gap between what we profess in faith and how we embody that faith in the world.

Taking time to describe an experience in detail fosters self-awareness, helping us recognize the assumptions, emotions, and reactions we bring to ministry and to life. Our habits of perception (what we notice, what we ignore, how we interpret events) are shaped by our upbringing, theological traditions, and social location. Without reflection, these patterns remain unexamined, potentially limiting our ability to see where God is at work. By naming and reflecting on our experiences, we begin to uncover not only our biases but also the deeper truths that shape our calling and response to God.

Theological Reflection in Practice

This kind of reflection is an essential practice for growth, deepening both personal formation and the capacity to minister with wisdom and attentiveness. In ministry, theological reflection helps us move beyond instinctive or surface-level responses, allowing us to engage with others with greater depth, humility, and insight. It cultivates the ability to listen well, discern wisely, and act with theological integrity. Over time, those who practice theological reflection regularly develop a richer, more nuanced sense of vocation, one that is not merely about what they do but about who they are becoming in relationship with God and the world.

Guidelines for Selecting an Experience

For students in a course that remains in the classroom, something like *Theological Reflection for Ministry*, the experience you choose can come from any area of your life, your studies, work, relationships, or something from public life that has captured your attention.

For students in a contextual education placement course, something like *Internship Reflection Group*, your experience should come from your internship site. Think about a moment or pattern of interactions that stood out to you. Perhaps a challenge in leadership, an unexpected insight, or a situation that has made you reflect more deeply on ministry.

Questions to Guide Your Reflection

To describe your experience with depth and clarity, consider these questions:

- What happened? Be specific in describing the setting, people involved, and sequence of events.
- What did you see, hear, and feel in that moment?
- What was your initial reaction? How did others respond?
- What about this experience made it stand out to you?
- What questions did it raise for you?

At this stage, the goal is to describe the event as clearly as possible. Later sections of your reflection will invite you to analyze, interpret, and make theological connections.

Theological Implications

The experience itself is just the beginning of theological reflection. While later sections will invite you to connect this moment to scripture, tradition, and theological themes, it is essential to first dwell on the details of the experience itself. Too often, we rush to interpretation, seeking to categorize, explain, or justify what happened, without fully sitting with the experience. By pausing to describe what actually took place, we cultivate the kind of attentiveness that forms the foundation of spiritual wisdom. In doing so, we resist the urge to impose meaning prematurely and instead allow the experience to speak for itself before placing it within a broader theological framework.

This practice of dwelling on experience mirrors the way scripture often unfolds theological insight. The Bible is full of stories in which meaning is revealed gradually, rather than being imposed immediately. Think of Moses at the burning bush, Mary pondering the angel's words in her heart, or the disciples on the road to Emmaus, who only later recognized Jesus in their midst. In each of these moments, God was present before the people involved understood what was happening. Similarly, by taking time to describe and reflect on our experiences without rushing to conclusions, we open ourselves to discovering God's presence in ways we might not have noticed otherwise.

By engaging with this section with care and honesty, we also develop the habit of seeing God at work in everyday life. Theological reflection is not just an academic exercise; it is a way of training our perception to notice the sacred in the ordinary. This attentiveness is not just for moments of crisis or profound revelation but for the seemingly mundane and routine encounters of daily life. When we practice naming our experiences with depth and clarity, we create space for God's activity to become more visible, shaping how we understand our calling and vocation.

Taking this step seriously lays a strong foundation for deeper theological insight. When we eventually move to connecting our experiences with scripture, tradition, and theological themes, we do so with a fuller sense of the reality we are reflecting on. Rather than making superficial or forced connections, our theological engagement will be more grounded, personal, and meaningful. The discipline of dwelling in experience allows us to bring our full selves, our emotions, uncertainties, and questions, into the process of discernment, making our reflections not just intellectually rich but spiritually transformative.

Sample

I was at the grocery store, waiting in line at the checkout. The line was moving slowly, and the cashier looked tense, their hands shaking slightly as they punched in numbers on the register. A small error popped up on the screen, and they hesitated, biting their lip before trying again. The customer ahead of me let out a loud sigh and shifted their weight impatiently, tapping their fingers against the counter. Someone behind me muttered, "Come on ... learn your job," just loud enough for others to hear.

The cashier apologized, their voice barely above a whisper. The bagger next to them glanced over, waiting, but didn't say anything. The delay stretched on ... five seconds, ten ... and the customer ahead of me finally shook their head, grabbing their bags a little too quickly when the transaction finally went through.

When I stepped forward, the cashier barely met my eyes. "Sorry for the wait," they said again, voice tight. I nodded as they started scanning my items, their movements quick but stiff, like they were bracing for another mistake. The tension in the line was still there, lingering even as the next customer shifted forward behind me.

After paying, I took my bags and made my way toward the exit. The automatic doors slid open, and I stepped outside. I walked to my car and as I reached for my keys, I realized my shoulders were still tense. I loaded my bags into the trunk, shut it, and stood there for a second, staring at the ground before finally getting into the driver's seat.

Step 2: Contextualize

The "Contextualize" section of your theological reflection paper invites you to explore why a particular experience stood out to you. This section helps you recognize how your background, past experiences, personal values, and emotional responses shape the way you perceive and interpret events. By examining what made this moment significant for you, you gain insight into how your own story intersects with the experience and why it continues to resonate.

Why It Matters

We do not experience events in isolation. Our reactions, thoughts, and emotions are shaped by our upbringing, cultural background, prior experiences, and theological assumptions. The process of contextualizing an experience allows us to slow down and ask, *Why did this moment affect me? Why am I still thinking about it?*

Theological reflection is not just about analyzing external events. It is also about understanding ourselves in relation to them. In doing this work, we recognize that spiritual formation is ongoing and that the lens through which we view the world is always being shaped by our experiences. This awareness is crucial for developing the self-reflective habits necessary for ministry, leadership, and discipleship.

Additionally, it is important to recognize that we do not always see events objectively. Two key psychological concepts (countertransference and projection) can shape how we interpret situations. Projection occurs when we attribute our own emotions, experiences, or struggles to someone else, assuming they must feel as we do. Countertransference is when an event, person, or interaction stirs something unresolved in us, often based on past experiences, and we react not just to what is happening but to what it reminds us of.

For example, if I once struggled in a job where I felt constantly scrutinized, I might see a struggling cashier and immediately feel a strong sense of injustice or anger toward the impatient customers. But am I reacting to what actually happened, or to my own past feelings of insecurity? If I grew up in a household where mistakes were met with criticism, I might assume the cashier felt deep shame, when in reality, they may simply have been having an off day and moved on quickly. Recognizing how our own experiences shape our reactions is an essential step in reflection, allowing us to engage more deeply and honestly with the event.

Questions to Guide Your Reflection

To help you think more deeply about why an experience stood out to you, consider the following:

- Have you encountered similar situations before? If so, how did this compare?
- Did this moment challenge or affirm something you already believed?
- Was there something about your personal history, upbringing, or past experiences that made this moment especially striking?
- Did the experience evoke a strong emotional response? If so, why might that be?
- Could projection be influencing your reaction? Are you assuming something about another person based on your own emotions or experiences?
- Could countertransference be occurring? Does this moment remind you of something from your past that may be influencing how you see the situation?
- What assumptions (about people, work, power, fairness, kindness, or responsibility) were revealed in your reaction?
- Have you ever been in a similar role or position as someone in the situation? Did that influence how you saw things?

This section is not about drawing theological conclusions yet: that comes later. Instead, it is about identifying what was already present in you that shaped your experience of the moment.

Example of Why This Matters

Imagine two people witness the same event: a young intern in a church staff meeting hesitates when asked a question, stumbles over their words, and then grows quiet for the rest of the discussion. One observer feels deeply uncomfortable, sensing that the intern must be feeling ashamed and unsupported. Another barely notices the moment at all. What's the difference? The first person might have had experiences of feeling dismissed in meetings and unconsciously projected that history onto the intern. The second person, never having felt silenced in a professional setting, sees nothing remarkable.

If we don't take the time to ask why an experience stands out to us, we risk misunderstanding what really happened. We might center our own emotions rather than the reality of the situation, or we might assume we fully understand someone else's experience when in fact we are filtering it through our own. By slowing down and reflecting on why something resonated, we become more aware of our own biases, assumptions, and emotional triggers, allowing us to engage more honestly and deeply with the event.

Theological Implications

Contextualizing an experience is a crucial part of developing the capacity for discernment. Every event we reflect upon is filtered through our own lens: our story, biases, and expectations inevitably shape how we interpret what happens around us. Theological reflection invites us to recognize this reality rather than ignore it. When we become aware of the assumptions we bring to an experience, we create space for deeper understanding and more faithful engagement with God's movement in our lives. Without this awareness, we risk seeing only what we expect to see, rather than being open to what God may actually be revealing.

This process of self-examination is not about self-doubt or overanalyzing every experience, but rather about cultivating a posture of humility and openness. Scripture shows us that even the most faithful individuals sometimes misinterpret their circumstances. Elijah expected God to be revealed in the wind, earthquake, and fire but instead encountered God in a still, small voice. The disciples struggled to understand Jesus's teachings because they were shaped by expectations of a different kind of Messiah. By reflecting on our own contexts, we follow in the biblical tradition of learning to listen more carefully: to others, to scripture, and most importantly, to the Spirit at work within and around us.

Developing this awareness also strengthens our ability to listen well in ministry and community. If we can acknowledge how our perspectives shape what we see, we are better able to hear the experiences of others with clarity and compassion. This is especially important in ministry, where the ability to step outside our assumptions and truly witness the struggles, joys, and insights of those we serve is essential. The more we engage in this practice, the more we cultivate the patience and humility necessary for meaningful pastoral care, justice work, and faithful leadership.

By engaging this section with honesty, you are strengthening the spiritual practice of attentiveness, a key element of theological reflection and ministerial formation. Attentiveness is more than passive observation; it is an active, intentional practice of noticing, of asking not just "What happened?" but also "What might I have missed?" and "What is God revealing here?" Over time, this kind of theological reflection becomes not just an academic discipline but a way of living—one that keeps us continually open to God's presence and guidance in our lives and ministries.

Sample

I've worked in customer service before, and I remember how it felt to be in that cashier's position: nervous, trying to keep up, aware that every second of delay was frustrating the people around me. I know what it's like to be on the receiving end of impatient sighs, to feel my own hands tremble as I rushed to avoid making another mistake. Seeing it happen to someone else, from the other side of the counter, stirred something familiar and uncomfortable in me.

Or maybe it was because I've always been sensitive to moments where people seem powerless or vulnerable. I grew up watching my parents work in jobs where they had to navigate customers' moods and expectations, and I know how easy it is for frustration to turn into dismissiveness, for someone's dignity to be chipped away by a single offhand comment. The way the cashier braced for criticism, how they wouldn't even meet my eyes, made it clear this wasn't the first time they'd been treated this way.

It could also be that I have always struggled with my own discomfort in tense situations. I don't like conflict, and I tend to freeze when I witness it, unsure whether to step in or just keep my head down. This moment may have stuck with me because I left the store feeling like I had been a passive observer to someone else's discomfort, as if I had let something play out without knowing what to do about it.

Or perhaps it wasn't just about the cashier at all. Lately, I've been noticing how often small, everyday moments feel charged with something bigger: how quickly impatience and frustration flare up in public spaces, how disconnected people seem, how easily we turn irritation into cruelty. Maybe this moment stood out because it felt like one more example of how transactional and impersonal the world can be. I'm not sure, I guess.

Step 3: Social Dynamics

The Social Dynamics section of your theological reflection paper asks you to examine how broader social systems shape the experiences you are reflecting on. This section helps us move beyond individual perspectives to see how power, privilege, and systemic structures influence situations, interactions, and even our own theological interpretations.

Why It Matters

Many people engaging in theological reflection for the first time may not immediately see social analysis as essential to the process. At first glance, identifying who is on the margins and why may seem like an aside, an ethical consideration added onto theological reflection rather than something inherent in it. But in reality, learning to recognize social dynamics is not an optional component of faithful reflection; it is fundamental to understanding how God is at work in the world and how we are called to respond.

Jesus's ministry was deeply concerned with those on the margins of society, the poor, the oppressed, and those excluded by dominant systems. His parables, healings, and interactions were not only about individual spiritual transformation but also about revealing and challenging the social and religious structures that kept people marginalized. Theological reflection that ignores these dynamics risks missing an essential part of the gospel message. When Jesus says, "Whatever you did for one of the least of these ... you did for me" (Matthew 25:40), he is making care for the marginalized central to discipleship. Recognizing and reflecting on social location, privilege, and exclusion is not a distraction from theology. It *is* theology.

For many, theological reflection begins with personal experience, asking, "Where is God in this moment?" However, the ability to discern God's movement requires us to consider not just our own position but also the positions of those whose voices are often unheard. If we only reflect on our own experiences without considering how power, privilege, and marginalization shape those experiences, our reflections may reinforce blind spots rather than illuminate deeper truths. Learning to see "the least of these" means learning to notice patterns of inclusion and exclusion, to ask who is present and who is missing, and to recognize how systems shape people's access to resources, opportunities, and dignity.

In many ways, identifying who is on the margins and why is a spiritual discipline in itself, shaping our ability to minister with justice, compassion, and integrity. Just as prayer and scripture study train us in attentiveness to God's voice, training ourselves to see social dynamics sharpens our ability to witness truthfully and respond faithfully. It is not enough to seek God in isolated moments; we must also seek God in the systems that govern our lives and in the lives of those who experience oppression most acutely. Theological reflection that includes social awareness is not only more faithful but also more transformative, calling us beyond passive contemplation into meaningful action.

What Are Social Factors?

Social factors are the elements of society that shape human interactions, power structures, and access to resources. These can be explicit (clear and visible) or implicit (subtle but influential). Here are some key social factors to consider:

- *Race/Ethnicity:* How does racial or ethnic identity impact people's experiences in this situation?
- *Gender:* Are men and women (or nonbinary individuals) treated differently in this setting? Who is expected to speak, lead, or remain silent?
- *Economic Status (Class):* How does wealth or poverty shape who has access to resources, opportunities, or leadership?

- *Education Level:* Does the level of education influence whose voices are heard and respected?
- *Nationality/Immigration Status:* How does being an immigrant, refugee, or citizen affect how people are included or excluded?
- *Language:* Who speaks the dominant language fluently, and who does not? How does language create barriers or access?
- *Disability (Physical/Mental Health):* Are spaces and conversations accessible to those with disabilities? Are mental health concerns acknowledged or stigmatized?
- *Age:* How do different age groups experience this situation? Are elders listened to? Are young people dismissed?
- *Religious Identity:* How does faith tradition influence participation, leadership, or marginalization?
- *Sexual Orientation:* Are LGBTQ+ individuals included, affirmed, or excluded in this setting?
- *Family Structure:* Are certain types of families (married with children, single parents, chosen families) privileged over others?
- *Cultural Norms and Expectations:* What behaviors are considered "normal" or "acceptable," and who defines them?

Questions to Guide Your Reflection

When writing this section, consider the following questions:

- Who is included and who is excluded in this situation?
- What social factors (e.g., economic status, ethnicity, language, gender) shape this experience?
- How do power and privilege operate in this encounter? Who has authority, and who does not?
- How might my own identity (cultural, social, theological) shape how I interpret this situation?
- What implicit or explicit biases might be at play?
- What does this situation reveal about the structures that shape human interactions?
- Where do I see a need for justice, healing, or transformation?

Theological Implications

Jesus consistently challenged systems that devalued people based on their social position. Whether overturning tables in the temple, healing those deemed "unclean," or dining with outcasts, his ministry disrupted social norms that reinforced oppression. His actions were not merely acts of personal kindness; they were profound theological

Theological Reflection in Practice

statements about the nature of God's reign, a way of being where the last are first, where the powerful are brought low, and where the marginalized are honored. If theological reflection is to be truly Christ-centered, it must follow this example, moving beyond individual spiritual insight to examine the ways social structures shape human dignity and flourishing.

Seeing social dynamics through a theological lens invites us into the work of justice and reconciliation, but it is important to remember that analyzing these dynamics does not mean we have fully "figured out" what caused a particular experience. Social factors might be deeply relevant, but they also might not be the primary forces at play. Even when we cannot determine with certainty how social positioning influenced a given situation, the practice of wondering about it remains valuable. By consistently asking questions about power, marginalization, and belonging, we cultivate a habit of attentiveness that trains us to see the world more like Christ does. This discipline shapes our instincts, helping us remain open to the presence of social injustice while avoiding assumptions that oversimplify complex realities.

Engaging in this kind of reflection ensures that our theological insights are not just personal or abstract but transformative. It allows us to align our ministry with Christ's mission, ensuring that our responses to the world's brokenness are not just well-intended but deeply informed. Over time, this practice fosters both humility and clarity. Humility in recognizing that we may not always fully understand what is happening beneath the surface of a given moment. Clarity in seeing patterns of inclusion and exclusion more readily. This habit of reflection helps us become people who are not only aware of injustice when it is obvious but are also attuned to the quieter, subtler ways it operates in daily life.

By engaging this section with depth and honesty, you are not simply applying a social framework to an experience: you are forming yourself to see more like Christ. Jesus did not merely react to social conditions when they were explicitly named; he moved through the world with an awareness of who was being centered and who was being overlooked. Cultivating this awareness in ourselves takes time, but by making space for these reflections, we train our hearts and minds toward the kind of vision that allows us to respond to the world with both compassion and wisdom. Theological reflection does not require us to reach definitive conclusions about every experience, but it does invite us to keep looking, keep questioning, and keep growing in our ability to see and serve as Christ does.

Sample

One clear dynamic was economic class and labor expectations. The cashier was in a service role, responsible for keeping the line moving, while the customers (including me) were in the role of consumers, expecting efficiency. Low-wage workers, especially in customer service, are often expected to absorb frustration without complaint, apologizing even when the problem isn't their fault. The tension in the line (customers sighing, muttering) suggests that this unspoken expectation was in play.

Race, age, and power imbalances may have also contributed. The cashier was young, likely in her late teens or early twenties, and appeared to be Latina. Most of the customers in line were white. The impatience of the customers and the cashier's quiet, almost shrinking response made me wonder if racial or age-based biases were shaping the moment. Would an older, white cashier have been met with the same level of irritation? Or would the same customers have been more understanding? Research shows that service workers of color, especially young women, often face more scrutiny and harsher reactions from customers, even when performing at the same level as their peers.

Another possible factor was language and perceived competence. While the cashier spoke fluent English, I noticed a slight accent. It made me wonder whether some of the frustration in the line was amplified by unconscious bias. Studies suggest that customers can be quicker to express impatience with workers who have accents, associating hesitation or mistakes with incompetence rather than inexperience or stress.

Finally, public stress and emotional regulation may have played a role. People in public spaces carry private frustrations, and small inconveniences (like a slow checkout) can become lightning rods for bigger anxieties. The customers ahead of me might have been rushing home, dealing with personal stress, or simply reacting to the overall pace of life. It's possible the cashier had been managing this kind of impatience all day.

Step 4: Connection

The "Connection" section of your theological reflection paper invites you to bring your experience into conversation with scripture, tradition, theology, and other sources of insight. This is not just about finding a relevant Bible verse or theological concept to attach to your experience. It is about discovering which connection serves as the clearest lens through which you can understand what is most significant about the experience.

Why It Matters

Christian theology is not developed in isolation; it emerges from the interplay between lived experience and theological reflection. When Jesus taught, he drew from the Hebrew scriptures, reshaping familiar stories and laws to uncover deeper truths. In a similar way, theological reflection invites you to consider multiple possible connections (each offering a different way of seeing) before settling on the one that most clearly reveals what you need to see about your experience.

By making connections in this way, you allow your experience to be shaped and informed by faith traditions, while also recognizing that your lived reality brings new insight into those traditions. Some connections may affirm what you already know to be true, while others may challenge or even unsettle your assumptions. The goal is not just to apply theology to experience but to use theology as a lens to sharpen your understanding of what this experience is revealing.

Theological Implications

The process of selecting a connection is part of the work of discernment. Some connections may seem obvious at first but fail to fully illuminate what is at stake in your experience. Others may be surprising, initially seeming unrelated until they unlock something deeper. The practice of weighing different possibilities before selecting the most revealing connection strengthens your ability to engage in theological inquiry with depth and attentiveness.

How to Choose Your Theological Lens

Selecting a theological lens for reflection is a crucial step in moving from personal experience to deeper insight. The right lens will help you see new meaning in your experience, revealing connections that may not have been obvious initially. Below are four approaches to help guide your selection.

Scriptural Parallel—Where Does This Story Show Up in the Bible?

Ask:

- Does this experience remind me of a specific story, teaching, or parable from scripture?
- Is there a biblical figure who might relate to this experience?
- How does this moment reflect broader scriptural themes of justice, mercy, suffering, redemption, or transformation?

Example: If your reflection involves witnessing an act of kindness toward a stranger, you might choose The Parable of the Good Samaritan (Luke 10:25–37) as your lens.

Theological Themes—What Doctrine or Concept Sheds Light on This?

Ask:

- What Christian beliefs are at play in this experience? (e.g., grace, vocation, suffering, resurrection, sin, hospitality)

- Does this moment challenge or affirm my understanding of God, humanity, or the church?
- Are there theological tensions here where my experience feels at odds with what I have been taught?

Example: If you are reflecting on exhaustion in ministry, you might choose Sabbath and Rest as your lens, drawing from scriptural teachings on God's rhythm of work and rest (Genesis 2:2–3, Exodus 20:8–11) and theological discussions on self-care in ministry.

Church Tradition & Historical Witness—Who Else Has Wrestled with This?

Ask:

- Have theologians, saints, mystics, or reformers written about similar experiences?
- Does church history offer wisdom or warnings related to this reflection?
- Are there prayers, liturgies, or practices in my tradition that speak to this moment?

Example: If your reflection involves struggling with uncertainty in discernment, you might use Ignatian Discernment (from St. Ignatius of Loyola's Spiritual Exercises) as a theological lens.

Contemporary Voices & Contextual Theology—What Speaks to Today?

Ask:

- Are there theologians or faith leaders from diverse perspectives who provide insight into this experience?
- How does this moment connect to issues of race, gender, class, ability, or other social dynamics?
- Are there songs, poems, films, or art that reflect the theological significance of this experience?

Example: If your reflection is on systemic injustice, you might use Liberation Theology as your lens, drawing from voices like Gustavo Gutiérrez, James Cone, Delores Williams, or Patrick Reyes (*The Purpose Gap*).

Putting It into Practice

Once you have a few possible lenses in mind, ask:

- Which lens clarifies something I hadn't noticed before?
- Which lens helps me see where God is at work in this experience?

- Which lens moves me toward deeper reflection, not just confirmation of what I already believe?

By choosing a lens with intention, you allow your reflection to move beyond personal interpretation into a meaningful theological dialogue, one that is both faithful to tradition and responsive to the realities of your life.

Example

For my experience, I was at the grocery store, watching as an overworked cashier struggled to keep up while impatient customers sighed and muttered under their breath. The tension in the line made me uncomfortable, and I left the store feeling burdened by the quiet disregard I had witnessed.

Exploring Possible Connections

1. The Parable of the Rich Man and Lazarus (Luke 16:19–31)
   → This story explores the consequences of ignoring suffering and failing to recognize the humanity of those in difficult positions. The impatient customers and my own passive observation could be read in light of the rich man's failure to see Lazarus.
2. Catholic Social Teaching: The Dignity of Work and the Rights of Workers
   → This connection places the experience in a broader societal context, considering how service workers are often undervalued and mistreated. It might lead to reflection on structural injustices rather than individual actions alone.
3. Jesus Washing the Disciples' Feet (John 13:12–17)
   → This passage speaks to the dignity of service and how Jesus models honoring those in roles often overlooked. It might highlight the failure of the customers (and myself) to embody that ethic in a moment of tension.
4. Dorothy Day and the Catholic Worker Movement
   → Dorothy Day emphasized the dignity of workers and the sacredness of everyday encounters, urging solidarity with those in service roles. Her perspective challenges the tendency to treat labor as transactional rather than relational. Through her lens, this grocery store moment reveals a missed opportunity to affirm dignity and practice justice in daily interactions.

Selecting the Lens

While each of these connections could be fruitful, the one that feels most *revealing* is Jesus washing the disciples' feet. The contrast between Jesus's act of honoring service and the disregard shown toward the cashier sheds light on a deeper truth: dignity is something that can be recognized or ignored in small, everyday moments. This connection doesn't just analyze what happened—it reveals what I *need to see* about it.

Expanding the Theological Lens

Although many people primarily engage in theological reflection through scripture and doctrine, over time, many find it freeing to realize that God's wisdom is not confined to these traditional sources. Theological insight can emerge from music, art, oral traditions, lived experience, and the wisdom of diverse communities. Recognizing these as valid sources of reflection does not diminish the centrality of scripture or doctrine but rather deepens and expands our awareness of how God speaks in the world.

For example, the spirituals sung by enslaved Africans in the United States carried profound theological reflections on liberation and suffering, just as Indigenous storytelling traditions express deep wisdom about creation and communal identity. Contemporary music, poetry, and visual art can also function as theological texts, offering insights into justice, longing, and divine presence.

Lived experience, especially as shaped by race, gender, class, and ability, can also serve as a theological lens. Liberation theologians emphasize that theology is not only something we read but something we live, shaped by our encounters with struggle, joy, and community.

When reflecting theologically, consider:

- Does a story, song, or image help express what I am experiencing?
- Have I seen this theme or question arise in a place I didn't expect?
- What insights emerge when I pay attention to how God speaks through everyday life?

Engaging these non-traditional sources does not replace scripture or doctrine but enhances reflection by recognizing that God is present in more places than we sometimes assume.

Sample

As I reflect on this moment, I am reminded of the story of Jesus washing his disciples' feet (John 13:12–17). In that passage, Jesus takes the role of a servant, embodying humility and care for others. The contrast between Jesus's actions and the impatience I observed at the checkout line is striking. If Christian discipleship calls us to imitate Christ in acts of love and service, how often do we fail to see the dignity of those who serve us?

Jesus's washing of the disciples' feet was not merely an act of kindness; it was a radical reordering of social expectations. In his time, foot-washing was a task reserved for the lowest-ranking servants. Yet Jesus, teacher and Lord, took on that role willingly, showing that true leadership and love are found in service, not status. The patience and tenderness with which he approached the task stand in stark contrast to the scene I witnessed in the grocery store, where the social order remained unchallenged, and frustration dictated behavior.

This connection helps me see that my discomfort in the grocery store was not just about witnessing a tense interaction but about recognizing a failure of attention, the failure to see the cashier's dignity. While Jesus deliberately took notice of those in service and elevated them, I remained passive, watching but not intervening, present but not engaged. The discomfort I felt walking away was not simply empathy for the cashier's struggle but the realization that I had an opportunity to respond differently and failed to take it.

But Jesus did not stand by when others were in a position of service; he honored them. He acknowledged their work not as something to be ignored or endured but as something worthy of reverence. What might it mean for me to follow that example? In a world that often treats service work as invisible or unimportant, embodying the ethic of Christ means not just being polite but intentionally recognizing the dignity of those who labor, whether through small acts of kindness, advocacy for just working conditions, or simply slowing down enough to acknowledge their humanity.

This reflection challenges me to reconsider my habits of attention and response. How often do I allow myself to be a bystander, assuming my presence is neutral when in fact, my silence upholds the status quo? Jesus's example reminds me that discipleship is active. It requires seeing, responding, and honoring others in ways that disrupt patterns of indifference. This experience leaves me with a renewed commitment to practicing that attentiveness in my daily life, learning to recognize dignity where it is too often overlooked.

Step 5: Reconsideration

The *Reconsideration* section of your theological reflection paper invites you to take a second look at your experience, not with fresh eyes, but with a fresh lens. Now that you have placed your experience in conversation with scripture, tradition, theology, or history, how does that connection sharpen or shift your understanding? If making the connection was like putting on a new pair of glasses, *Reconsideration* is about noticing what becomes clearer and what still remains fuzzy.

Without a lens, an experience may seem scattered, ordinary, or even confusing. But once we apply a theological or historical connection, the contours of meaning come into focus. This is the moment where theological reflection moves beyond simply *naming* a connection and begins to reveal something new about the experience itself.

Why It Matters

Before you put on glasses, the world isn't *empty*—you can still see something—but details remain unclear. Similarly, before theological reflection, an experience may seem like *just* a frustrating grocery store interaction, *just* a difficult conversation, *just* a moment of discomfort. But once a connection is in place, what seemed insignificant may now appear deeply meaningful.

For example:

- Without the connection lens: This moment was just a frustrating example of how impatient people can be. The cashier had a tough day, and that's unfortunate, but it happens.
- With the connection lens (Jesus washing the disciples' feet): This moment is not just about impatience; it reveals how easily we fail to recognize dignity in service. Jesus took on the role of a servant and honored those in service, while here, a worker's struggle was met with frustration and disregard. My discomfort wasn't just about witnessing an awkward moment: it was about failing to *see* the sacredness of service.

This step helps us realize that theological reflection is not about attaching a passage or doctrine to an event to make it "fit." Instead, it is about learning to see what is at play in an experience and how God may be speaking through it.

Questions to Guide Your Reflection

To engage deeply in this process, ask yourself:

- Without the lens of my theological connection, how did I originally interpret this experience? What seemed most important?
- Now that I have applied this lens, what has come into focus? What seems newly significant?
- What details, emotions, or dynamics were blurry before that now seem clearer?
- Has this reconsideration challenged or expanded any of my prior assumptions?
- Are there any aspects of the experience that remain unclear or unresolved? What tensions still exist?
- How does this new perspective shape my understanding of God, ministry, or discipleship?

Theological Implications

Reconsideration is where theological reflection moves beyond observation to transformation. It is not merely an intellectual exercise of reviewing an experience but an intentional practice of discerning its deeper significance. This step challenges us to go beyond recalling what happened and begin asking: What does this mean? How is God present here? What is being revealed that I had not seen before? Some connections that emerge in this process may offer clarity, sharpening our understanding of an experience and helping us draw out new meaning. Others may introduce complexities, raising tensions that we had not previously noticed: disrupting assumptions, surfacing contradictions, or revealing gaps in our understanding. Both outcomes are valuable.

Transformation occurs not because we resolve every tension or arrive at a neatly packaged insight, but because we allow ourselves to remain engaged in the questions. Theological reflection does not seek to force quick conclusions; rather, it invites us to sit with ambiguity, to hold together moments of insight and uncertainty, and to trust that even unresolved tensions can be meaningful. This kind of reconsideration cultivates a theological lens through which we learn to perceive God's movement in the world, not just in dramatic revelations but in the quiet, ordinary moments of life that, upon reflection, contain far more than we first realized.

This process also challenges us to expand our ways of seeing. Sometimes, we think we understand an experience fully, only to discover that new perspectives or theological insights shift our interpretation. Scripture itself models this kind of unfolding revelation: Jesus's own disciples frequently had to reinterpret what they thought they understood, gradually realizing the deeper meaning behind his words and actions. Likewise, we must be willing to let go of initial impressions when reflection reveals something more complex or profound than we first assumed.

By engaging this section with curiosity and openness, you are not simply interpreting an experience: you are allowing yourself to be changed by it. True theological reflection shapes the way we move through the world, forming us into people who are more attuned to God's presence, more aware of the layers of meaning in our daily lives, and more willing to embrace transformation. Over time, this practice becomes more than a method; it becomes a way of being. One that deepens our faith, sharpens our discernment, and equips us to engage life's moments, both ordinary and extraordinary, with greater depth, wisdom, and openness to God's ongoing work.

Sample

Placing this experience in conversation with Jesus washing the disciples' feet (John 13:12–17) has made something clear that was fuzzy before: this was not just about impatience; it was about the dignity of those who serve and how easily we overlook it. Jesus did not simply acknowledge service; he elevated it, making it central to discipleship. With that lens in place, I now see the moment differently: the tension in the checkout line was not just about slow service; it was about the way we treat those whose labor makes our daily lives easier.

Now, instead of viewing myself as a passive bystander to an awkward situation, I recognize my complicity in a larger pattern, one in which service workers are often expected to absorb frustration, perform flawlessly, and remain invisible unless they make a mistake. My discomfort walking away was not just secondhand awkwardness; it was the realization that I had an opportunity to affirm dignity and remained silent. I didn't sigh or mutter like the others, but I also didn't offer a kind word, a smile, or even eye contact that might have signaled to the cashier: *I see you.*

I think this is the first time I realized the real point of theological reflection. It is to help me see that there are lessons God is offering to teach me all the time, lessons I guess I'm always missing. Now that I think of it, it's so obvious that this grocery store moment could help me become more deeply committed to dignity for workers. But if I hadn't done this reflection, I probably would have just forgotten about it. How many other moments have passed me by that could have shaped me if I had paid attention?

This reconsideration challenges me to think differently about what discipleship looks like in everyday life. It's easy to admire Jesus washing the disciples' feet in a theological sense, but am I willing to actually embody that ethic? What would it mean to enter spaces like the grocery store with the same attentiveness Jesus had toward those in service? How might I practice seeing dignity where I might otherwise be distracted or impatient?

Step 6: Integration into Action

The *Integration into Action* section is where theological reflection moves beyond insight into lived practice. It asks: *Now that I see this moment more clearly, what will I do differently?* This is not about having the "right answer" to an experience but about developing the habit of responding to what we see, allowing our theological reflection to shape our choices, relationships, and ways of being in the world.

Theology is not meant to remain theoretical. It is not an abstract exercise removed from daily life but a way of knowing that is formed and refined in practice. Across Christian traditions, wisdom and spiritual formation are understood as being shaped in action, not just in thought. Just as faith without works is dead (James 2:26), theological insight without engagement risks becoming stagnant, detached from the lived realities it is meant to illuminate. Theological reflection is valuable precisely because it is not confined to contemplation, it is a process that should lead to response.

Different Christian traditions express this integration of reflection and action in distinct ways. Jesuits speak of "Reflection-in-Action," recognizing that we do not first learn in theory and only later apply what we have learned. Instead, understanding develops as we engage in practice, testing our insights in the lived realities of ministry, service, and community. Similarly, the See-Judge-Act method, developed by Joseph Cardijn and widely used in the pastoral cycle, offers a structured approach to this interplay. It begins with seeing a situation clearly, then judging it in light of faith and ethics, and finally acting in response. This method acknowledges that theological discernment is incomplete if it does not move us toward faithful engagement with the world.

Likewise, the Quaker tradition emphasizes acting in "Gospel Order" (a commitment to discern and act in alignment with divine leading), even when the full path is not yet clear. Rather than waiting for perfect understanding before taking action, this approach trusts that ongoing faithfulness will reveal the next step as long as the person taking action remains radically open to the prompting of the Holy Spirit. This resonates with the way Jesus called his disciples to follow him, not giving them a detailed roadmap but instead inviting them to walk in faith, learning as they went. In each of these traditions, there is a shared understanding that theological reflection is not simply about gaining new insights but about being shaped by them in ways that transform how we live and serve.

Each of these approaches affirms that understanding and action must remain in constant dialogue, a dynamic process of reflection, response, and re-evaluation. Theological reflection should never be an end in itself; its purpose is to refine our perception so that we can move through the world with greater wisdom and faithfulness. Even small changes (shifting our posture toward someone in need, speaking up where we once remained silent, adjusting the way we engage in ministry) can be meaningful responses to what we discern. The point of theological reflection is not just to understand a moment differently, but to let it shape our actions, however small, so that we are continually formed into people who more fully embody the love and justice of God.

Questions to Guide Your Reflection

What is one concrete thing I can do differently because of this reflection?

- How might this insight change the way I approach everyday situations?
- Is there a habit of attention or a small practice I can commit to?
- Does this reflection invite me to take a larger action, advocating for justice, shifting a behavior, or having a conversation I've been avoiding?
- How can I make sure I don't just move on and forget this insight?

Theological Implications

Theology, at its heart, is not just about understanding the world but about transforming it: beginning with ourselves. Throughout scripture and Christian tradition, faith is never presented as a passive belief system; it is a way of life. Jesus did not just tell his disciples to honor service; he demonstrated it by washing their feet (John 13:12–17).

He didn't simply teach about love, he embodied it in action, healing the sick, feeding the hungry, and welcoming the outcast.

Paul similarly insists that faith is not an abstract ideal but something made visible through our lives: *"Be doers of the word, and not merely hearers who deceive themselves"* (James 1:22). Faith without action, without tangible expression in how we treat others, is incomplete. Theological reflection is not meant to end at insight—it must propel us into lived faithfulness.

At the same time, Christian tradition reminds us that small, consistent actions matter. Not every moment calls for grand gestures, but every moment invites faithfulness. The Benedictine principle of *ora et labora* (prayer and work) suggests that everyday life, whether in study, service, or simple attentiveness, can become an act of prayer when done with intention. Dorothy Day's Catholic Worker Movement embraced this, emphasizing that justice and holiness are practiced in small, daily ways, such as recognizing the dignity of workers, sharing a meal, or standing in solidarity with the poor.

This section asks you to commit to one tangible step forward. Maybe it's simply remembering to look a service worker in the eye and recognize their dignity. Maybe it's practicing patience in moments where frustration would be easier. Maybe it's advocating for fair labor practices or finding ways to support those who serve in unseen ways.

The point is not that every reflection must lead to massive transformation overnight. Rather, it cultivates the habit of responsiveness, training you to not only see the world through a theological lens but to act accordingly, one small decision at a time. Over time, these small choices shape who we are, forming us into people who are more attuned to God's presence and more faithful in our discipleship. Theological reflection is not just about deepening understanding; it is about deepening commitment. Seeing differently is the first step. Learning to respond differently is what makes that vision manifest.

Sample

The lens of *Jesus washing the disciples' feet* has sharpened my understanding of why this moment stuck with me: it revealed how unnoticed labor is a spiritual issue, not just a social one. My call as a disciple is not just to avoid impatience, but to actively practice recognition—to develop the habit of seeing and honoring the dignity of others, especially in places where it is often ignored.

That said, I know myself, and I know that if I set some big, abstract goal—like "always standing up for worker justice" or "never missing an opportunity to recognize dignity"—I'll probably get overwhelmed and end up doing nothing. So instead, I'm going to start small. The next time I'm at the grocery store, I'll make sure to actually *see* the cashier. I'll look them in the eye, say hello, and try (just for a moment) to see them as God sees them: as a beloved child, not just someone scanning my food. It's not a grand act of justice, but it feels like something I can actually do. And maybe if I get in the habit of noticing, of paying attention, it will help me be ready for the bigger things when they come.

I don't expect this one reflection to transform me overnight, but I do think it's nudging me in the right direction. If Jesus calls us to honor those who serve, then I want to practice doing that in the small, ordinary places first—because that's probably where I'll spend most of my life anyway.

Guidelines for Writing Theological Reflection Papers

As I hope I've shown above, theological reflection is more than a personal or academic exercise. It is a way of engaging with experience, faith, and community to discern meaning and direction. The previous sections have explored how theological reflection deepens spiritual formation, fosters attentiveness to God's movement, and integrates faith with lived experience. Now, this section provides specific guidelines for translating that reflective process into a structured written assignment.

Writing a theological reflection paper requires more than simply recounting an experience or offering personal insights. It invites you to engage in a disciplined process of analysis, interpretation, and response, using theological themes, scripture, and tradition to illuminate your experience in new ways. The goal is not just to describe what happened, but to explore its significance in light of faith, ministry, and ethical engagement.

The guidelines that follow outline key expectations for structuring your reflection paper. They are designed to help you move beyond surface-level observations and into deeper engagement with the theological dimensions of your experience. Whether you are reflecting on a ministry encounter, a social issue, or a personal moment of insight, these guidelines will help you articulate your learning and connect it meaningfully to the broader work of theological reflection.

An Exercise in Awareness

Intentional reflection on one's experience from the perspective of one's theology or values is one of the key skills students can cultivate more deeply in contextual education. In *How to Think Theologically*, Howard Stone and James Duke describe the differences between embedded theology and deliberative theology. Theological reflection facilitates dialogue between the two.[1]

---

[1] Howard W. Stone and James O. Duke, *How to Think Theologically*, 4th ed. (Minneapolis: Fortress, 2023).

Embedded theology or embedded values are those that, for many of us, are relatively unconscious or seem "normal." Embedded theology is often a result of early formation in a faith tradition or other set of values and provides the foundation for patterns of behavior and attitudes that shape an individual or community. They form the paradigm, or to use Stone and Duke's word, the "template" from which our opinions and behaviors arise, the "lens through which [a person] look[s] at the world."[2]

Deliberative theology seeks to bring embedded theology into awareness. Deliberative theology or practice asks questions that can evaluate the consistency between one's stated beliefs or values and one's practice. It can allow new information to inform and even call into question embedded beliefs or values that an individual or community hold. Deliberative theology can aid the student in discerning how to integrate new information into their theological or value-based framework.

Theological reflection in this manner does not require a particular doctrinal basis or membership in a specific religion. At its core, theological reflection asks the question, "What part(s) of how I understand and make meaning of the world come from my religious or spiritual commitments?" If you imagine that religious, spiritual, and/or philosophical convictions function as a lens that frames how you see/interpret experiences, then the role of theological reflection is to (1) help clarify what lenses you tend to use, (2) identify how they shape your interpretations of experience, and (3) "polish" and refine them so that they serve you with greater nuance and depth.

For example, consider someone who was a Christian and wanted to reflect theologically on a conversation they recently had with a stranger at the library. The key question of theological reflection for that person would be, "What parts of Christianity (including scripture, theology, history, and/or my experience as a Christian) frame or tint how I think or feel about that conversation?" What theological reflection does is help to surface some of the ways in which our spiritual convictions form how we think and act in the world.

Format

Theological Reflection papers will be written with six separate sections each with a heading corresponding to the topics below. The length of each paper should come in between 1,000 and 1,200 words total (4–5 pages double-spaced) and each section should have roughly the same amount of content (approximately 175–225 words), though sections 4–6 may often be longer than sections 1–3.

1. *Experience*: Describe a personal encounter or dynamic which you have experienced or noticed. What moment from your site or recent life experience stayed with you and/or gave you pause?

---

2 Ibid., 45.

2. *Contextualize*: Reflect on why this particular experience stood out to you as significant. What was it about your own background, personal history, or prior experiences that may have contributed to this event striking you as it did? Are there any bodily sensations that arise when focusing on the selected experience?
3. *Social Dynamics*: What aspects of the experience or dynamic described were influenced by the role of structural systems of power, privilege, and/or marginalization?
4. *Connection*: Relate the experience or dynamic to scripture or another sacred text, theology, tradition, religious history, personal experience from a faith community, and/or value system. What about the selected source connects to the experience or dynamics being reflected upon? What is the "lens" you are using to reflect on this experience or dynamic?
5. *Reconsideration*: Reflect on what insights the connecting pieces provide for understanding the experience in a new or changed way. Having brought your experience into conversation with something outside yourself, what new understandings or perspectives, if any, emerge? How does the "lens" you are using offer you new or more nuanced interpretations about how it is you understand divinity/God to be at work in the world?
6. *Integration into Practice*: Ask what this reconsideration suggests for changes in practice or perspective in the future. How might you do things differently? What different attitudes or understandings might you bring to a similar experience in the future?

When you think you're finished with a reflection, make sure you can easily and clearly fill in the blanks on these questions. A good reflection will have concise and specific answers.

1. *Experience*
   → The experience I'm reflecting on is _____.
2. *Contextualize*
   → This experience mattered to me because _____.
3. *Social Dynamics*
   → Social or systemic factors that may have influenced this experience were _____.
4. *Connection*
   → The single lens I am using to reflect on this experience is _____.
5. *Reconsideration*
   → When I look at this experience through my lens, what I see (that I wouldn't have without it) is_____.
6. *Integration into Practice*
   → One way this reflection may shape my actions in the future is _____.

Possible Questions to Aid in Your Reflection

Inspired by and adapted from *Shaping Spiritual Leaders* by Abigail Johnson.[3]

Experience

- What happened?
- Who was involved?
- What did you see, hear, and/or experience?
- How did you respond? How did others respond?
- What feelings were evoked by the event?
- What did you find challenging or stimulating?
- Why was it significant to you?

Contextualize

- Are there any bodily sensations that arise when focusing on the selected experience?
- What personal experiences or background influences made this event striking for you?
- Could your reaction be shaped by countertransference, that is, projecting past emotions onto the present?
- How might your unique perspective affect your interpretation of the event's significance?
- Are you responding more to the circumstances or to something it brings up internally?
- What deeper personal or spiritual issues might this experience be highlighting?

Social Dynamics

- What larger social or structural realities may have influenced the event or dynamic being reflected upon?
- What role(s) do gender identity, race, ethnicity, mental health, physical ability, nationality, sexual orientation, education, trauma history, and/or economic status play in the experience or dynamic being reflected upon?
- What unspoken norms might be part of the organizational culture of the institution(s) in which the experience or dynamic took place?

---

3 Abigail Johnson, *Shaping Spiritual Leaders* (Herndon, VA: Alban Institute, 2007).

Connection/Lens

- What stories, events, images, or insights from your faith tradition and heritage does the event bring to mind?
- Did you experience transcendence in the experience or dynamic? If so, where? How?
- What specific theological or value issues are raised as you reflect on this event or dynamic?
- What points of connection with your own previous experiences or the experience of your faith tradition and heritage do you see?

Reconsideration

- What implications does this situation have for your understanding of the nature of your faith? The human condition? Vocation?
- How was your faith or value system deepened or challenged as a result of this event?
- How might you interpret the experience or dynamic differently if you did not have the knowledge you referred to in the connection component?

Integration into Action

- How might you act or think differently in the future, given your reflections above?
- What have you learned about yourself? Others? What bearing does this have on your work, service, and/or sense of self and calling?
- What questions still linger that you want to engage with?

A (Non-Exhaustive) List of Theological Connection Points / Lenses

What kinds of things are viable to make connections to in theological reflection?

Doctrines

1. Theology Proper
2. Christology
3. Pneumatology
4. Anthropology
5. Soteriology
6. Ecclesiology
7. Revelation
8. Eschatology

Church History and Tradition

1. Lives of the Saints
2. Ecumenical Councils
3. Schisms and Heresies
4. Monastic Movements
5. Reformation and Counter-Reformation

Catholic Teachings and Traditions

1. Magisterium and Papal Authority
2. Marian Devotion and Apparitions
3. Saints and Intercession
4. Eucharistic Adoration
5. Catholic Social Teaching
6. Holy Days
7. Religious Orders and Consecrated Life

Protestant Teachings and Traditions

1. Sola Scriptura and Biblical Authority
2. Justification by Faith Alone
3. Priesthood of All Believers
4. Predestination and Election
5. Dispensationalism
6. Believer's Baptism

Sacraments and Rituals

1. Baptism
2. Eucharist/Communion
3. Confirmation
4. Marriage
5. Anointing of the Sick
6. Funerals and Memorial Services

Spiritual Practices

1. Prayer (Contemplative, Intercessory, Liturgical)
2. Fasting and Asceticism
3. Lectio Divina and Biblical Meditation
4. Ignatian Spirituality and the Examen
5. Pilgrimage and Retreat Experiences
6. Spiritual Direction and Mentorship
7. Centering Prayer and Mysticism

Meaningful Non-Scriptural Texts

1. Prayers
2. Liturgies
3. Films, stories, poems
4. Devotional readings

Personal Faith Experiences

1. Conversion or "Born Again" Moments
2. Experiences of Divine Presence or Guidance
3. Moments of Doubt or Spiritual Dryness
4. Experiences of Forgiveness and Reconciliation
5. Encounters with Religious Communities or Mentors

Interfaith Dialogue

1. Similarities and Differences with Other Faith Traditions
2. Experiences of Religious Pluralism
3. Interfaith Cooperation and Conflict
4. Theology of Religions
5. Missiology and Evangelization

Theological Themes

1. Theodicy
2. The "Omni-problem"
3. Vocation
4. Discernment
5. Authority
6. Social Justice and Ethics
7. Ecological Stewardship
8. Pastoral Care
9. Spiritual Formation
10. Religious Education

Scripture Passages

1. Any that work!

Tips for Excellence in Theological Reflection Papers

This guide provides specific tips and reminders for each section of your theological reflection paper to help you achieve excellence in your writing and reflection.

1. *Experience (The Foundation)*
    - Choose a moment that genuinely "grabbed" you emotionally, intellectually, or spiritually
    - Include rich sensory details. What did you see, hear, feel?
    - Describe both external events AND your internal response
    - Focus on a specific moment rather than a general period
    - Show why this experience lingered with you
    - *Remember:* You're not just reporting what happened, but conveying its impact

2. *Contextualize (The Personal Lens)*
    - Examine your bodily responses and emotional reactions closely
    - Connect to specific events from your past that might influence your interpretation
    - Consider your cultural background and how it shapes your perspective
    - Be honest about potential biases or assumptions
    - Look for patterns in how you tend to interpret similar experiences
    - *Remember:* This part should answer, "Why did THIS particular moment stay with me?"

3. *Social Dynamics (The Broader Picture)*
    - Look beyond individual actions to systemic factors: experience happens within larger social contexts
    - Consider multiple forms of privilege and marginalization
    - Race, gender, class, ability, sexuality, nationality, etc.
    - Examine institutional cultures and unspoken norms
    - Think about who holds power and who doesn't in the situation
    - Consider whose voices are centered and whose are peripheral
    - *Remember:* You don't need to "prove" that any of these dynamics impacted the situation; you're just wondering and reflecting on what *might* have had an impact.

Theological Reflection in Practice

4. ***Connection (The Theological Bridge)***
   - Choose a theological lens that genuinely illuminates the experience
   - Make explicit connections to a specific text or tradition
   - Consider multiple possible theological connection points to see what feels most right, but select one single lens through which to reflect. You ought to be able to fill in the blank: "The Theological Lens I am using for this reflection is _____."
   - Your lens can have multiple supporting elements from different sources, but should center on a single theological theme.
   - Explain why this particular theological lens is meaningful and is a good fit. Why does it feel right?
   - *Remember:* The goal is meaningful connection, not forced parallels

5. ***Reconsideration (The New Perspective)***
   - Show how the theological lens changes your understanding
   - Compare your initial reaction with your post-reflection insights
   - Consider what you might have missed in your first interpretation
   - Examine how your chosen theological lens reveals new meanings
   - Be open to surprising or challenging new perspectives
   - Ask: "How do I see this differently through this theological lens? If I didn't have the lens I selected, how would things look different?"
   - *Remember:* This section should demonstrate genuine transformation in understanding. It doesn't need to be epically revelatory. Small realizations and noticings are great, too!

6. ***Integration into Practice (The Way Forward)***
   - Be specific about concrete changes you'll make: the goal is transformed practice, not just new ideas.
   - Consider both immediate and long-term applications
   - Address both personal growth and professional development
   - Include both attitudinal changes and practical steps
   - Make commitments that are realistic and measurable
   - Connect your proposed changes to your theological insights
   - *Remember:* You don't need this to be huge. I'm not looking for every reflection to capture a moment of total transformation.

Set Your Sliders

A Tool for Assessing Spiritual Formation Dimensions

This tool employs the metaphor of a soundboard or mixing board, as introduced in chapter 3, "Formation and Reflection," to help you visualize and assess how different aspects of spiritual formation are emphasized in your life and community. By "adjusting sliders" for dimensions such as Intellectual Engagement, Community Connection, Mystical Experience, Spiritual Practices, and the Exercise of Spiritual Gifts, you can gain insight into your personal spiritual emphases and compare them with those of your faith community. This exercise can be used individually or in groups to foster awareness, spark discussion, and identify areas for intentional growth and adjustment in spiritual life and practice.

※

This exercise helps you visualize and assess how different aspects of spiritual formation are emphasized in your life and community. Like a sound engineer adjusting levels on a mixing board, you'll consider how various dimensions of spiritual formation are "turned up" or "down" in different contexts.

Part 1: Understanding the Dimensions

Intellectual Engagement encompasses the study, reflection, and exploration of theology, scripture, and faith traditions. This dimension involves actively seeking to understand the intellectual foundations of one's beliefs, which could include engaging with religious texts, theological works, and historical context. Intellectual engagement allows individuals to deepen their understanding of their faith, question and clarify their beliefs, and connect their spiritual life with broader knowledge frameworks. It nurtures critical thinking and self-reflection, encouraging practitioners to reconcile modern knowledge and scientific insights with spiritual beliefs. When the slider for Intellectual Engagement is "turned up," individuals may regularly study scripture, participate in theological discussions, or pursue academic study related to spirituality. However, if underemphasized, intellectual growth may be limited, and spiritual practices might lack depth or understanding. A balanced intellectual engagement enhances one's ability to articulate beliefs and understand the nuances of their faith tradition, enriching both personal and communal spiritual experiences.

Community Connection involves relationships, shared spiritual practices, and the collective life within a faith community. This dimension highlights the importance of belonging and engaging actively with others who share similar values and spiritual aspirations. Community Connection is built through shared rituals, worship services, communal prayers, social events, and support networks. A strong emphasis on this dimension encourages individuals to participate in group settings, where they can both give and receive encouragement, guidance, and accountability. When this slider is set high, individuals find strength in collective wisdom, forming bonds that help sustain their faith and provide a sense of accountability. Conversely, minimal community involvement can lead to isolation, making it difficult to sustain spiritual growth and motivation. Balancing this dimension involves not only finding community but also engaging meaningfully within it, fostering relationships that support individual and collective spiritual journeys.

Mystical and Personal Experience focuses on direct, personal encounters with the divine or transcendent, often experienced through contemplation, prayer, or meditation. This dimension encourages openness to the inner, mystical aspects of spirituality: moments of awe, personal revelations, or experiences of inner peace that transcend ordinary understanding. Such experiences can provide profound insight, grounding individuals in their spiritual beliefs in ways that feel deeply personal and often ineffable. When this slider is "turned up," individuals may regularly seek contemplative practices or engage in solitude to deepen their connection to the divine. A low emphasis on this dimension can lead to a more intellectual or ritualistic approach to faith, potentially missing out on the mystery and intimacy that mystical experiences offer. Those with high engagement in mystical experiences often find renewed inspiration and guidance, feeling a personal connection with the sacred that complements communal and intellectual practices.

Spiritual Practices include the regular habits and disciplines that nurture one's relationship with the divine, such as prayer, meditation, worship, fasting, and other rituals. This dimension is the foundation of a daily spiritual life, providing consistency and structure that allow individuals to deepen their faith over time. Engaging in spiritual practices on a regular basis supports alignment with one's values, encourages self-discipline, and fosters mindfulness. When this slider is high, individuals may find themselves deeply embedded in a rhythm of worship, prayer, and devotion, which can bring comfort and stability. A lower setting on this dimension might suggest a more sporadic or informal approach, potentially leading to a sense of disconnection from spiritual goals. An intentional focus on spiritual practices helps individuals maintain a centered, purposeful life that aligns with their faith commitments, even amid daily challenges.

Exercise of Spiritual Gifts refers to using one's unique talents and abilities in service to others and the community. This dimension emphasizes the practical outworking of faith through actions and contributions, be it through teaching, leadership, healing, hospitality, or other forms of service. Spiritual gifts are often seen as callings or talents bestowed by the divine for the purpose of uplifting others and advancing the common good. High engagement in this dimension involves regularly using these gifts in specific contexts, such as church, volunteer work, or personal relationships, fulfilling a sense of purpose through practical expressions of spirituality. When underemphasized, one might feel a lack of purpose or clarity in how to contribute meaningfully to the lives of others. Actively exercising spiritual gifts can create a sense of fulfillment and interconnection, fostering a vocation that aligns with one's talents, passions, and values.

Part 2: Setting Your Sliders

Your Community's Settings

- For each dimension, assign a number (1–10) reflecting your community's emphasis
- Note specific examples that justify your rating
- Consider: Are these levels consistent or do they fluctuate?

Remember: There are no "right" settings. The goal is awareness and intentionality in your spiritual formation journey. Use this tool to foster dialogue, guide decisions, and support your ongoing growth. For each dimension, consider what different levels might look like:

INTELLECTUAL ENGAGEMENT (Study, learning, theological reflection)
    1–3:   Minimal emphasis on study; rare engagement with theological texts
    4–7:   Regular biblical study; occasional deeper theological exploration
    8–10: Intensive study; regular theological discussion; academic pursuit

COMMUNITY CONNECTION (Relationships, shared practices, tradition)
    1–3:   Limited community involvement; mostly individual practice
    4–7:   Regular community participation; some shared spiritual practices
    8–10: Deep community integration; strong emphasis on collective wisdom

MYSTICAL AND PERSONAL EXPERIENCE (Direct spiritual experiences, contemplation)
- 1–3: Rare focus on mystical experiences; emphasis on rational understanding
- 4–7: Openness to mystical experiences; some contemplative practice
- 8–10: Regular mystical encounters; deep contemplative life

SPIRITUAL PRACTICES (Prayer, meditation, ritual, worship)
- 1–3: Occasional or informal spiritual practices
- 4–7: Regular engagement in traditional spiritual practices
- 8–10: Daily disciplined practice; multiple forms of spiritual exercise

EXERCISE OF SPIRITUAL GIFTS (Service, ministry, using talents for others)
- 1–3: Limited expression of gifts; unclear sense of how to serve
- 4–7: Regular use of gifts in specific contexts
- 8–10: Frequent and varied expression of gifts; continuous service

Your Personal Settings

- Now rate your own emphasis or desired emphasis for each dimension
- Be honest about where you actually are, not where you think you "should" be
- Consider: Do these levels reflect your current reality or aspirations?

For each dimension, consider what different levels might look like:

INTELLECTUAL ENGAGEMENT (Study, learning, theological reflection)
- 1–3: Minimal emphasis on study; rare engagement with theological texts
- 4–7: Regular biblical study; occasional deeper theological exploration
- 8–10: Intensive study; regular theological discussion; academic pursuit

COMMUNITY CONNECTION (Relationships, shared practices, tradition)
- 1–3: Limited community involvement; mostly individual practice
- 4–7: Regular community participation; some shared spiritual practices
- 8–10: Deep community integration; strong emphasis on collective wisdom

MYSTICAL AND PERSONAL EXPERIENCE (Direct spiritual experiences, contemplation)
- 1–3: Rare focus on mystical experiences; emphasis on rational understanding
- 4–7: Openness to mystical experiences; some contemplative practice
- 8–10: Regular mystical encounters; deep contemplative life

SPIRITUAL PRACTICES (Prayer, meditation, ritual, worship)
- 1–3: Occasional or informal spiritual practices
- 4–7: Regular engagement in traditional spiritual practices
- 8–10: Daily disciplined practice; multiple forms of spiritual exercise

EXERCISE OF SPIRITUAL GIFTS (Service, ministry, using talents for others)
- 1–3: Limited expression of gifts; unclear sense of how to serve
- 4–7: Regular use of gifts in specific contexts
- 8–10: Frequent and varied expression of gifts; continuous service

Part 3: Analysis and Reflection

Compare your community and personal settings:

ALIGNMENT QUESTIONS:
- Where do your settings most closely match your community's?
- What does this alignment tell you about your fit with this community?
- How does this alignment support your spiritual growth?

DIFFERENCE QUESTIONS:
- Where are the biggest gaps between your settings and your community's?
- How do these differences affect your spiritual life?
- Are these differences sources of growth or tension?

GROWTH QUESTIONS:
- Which dimensions would you like to adjust up or down?
- What resources or support would you need to make these adjustments?
- How might changes in one dimension affect the others?

Part 4: Action Steps

Based on your reflection:
1. Identify 1–2 dimensions where adjustment feels most important
2. List specific steps you could take to make these adjustments
3. Consider what support you might need from your community
4. Think about how these changes might affect other dimensions

EXAMPLE:

Sarah's Assessment:

Community Settings:
- Intellectual Engagement: 8
- Community Connection: 7
- Mystical Experience: 3
- Spiritual Practices: 6
- Exercise of Gifts: 5

Personal Settings:
- Intellectual Engagement: 6
- Community Connection: 8
- Mystical Experience: 7
- Spiritual Practices: 7
- Exercise of Gifts: 5

Sarah's Analysis: The biggest gap is in mystical experience, where she desires more than her community typically emphasizes. She might need to seek additional support outside her primary community for this dimension while maintaining the valuable intellectual and community aspects her tradition provides.

System Mapping Me

A Visualization of Vocational Influences

The "System Mapping Me" exercise guides you in creating a personal visual map to better understand the complex systems influencing your vocational journey, a theme explored in chapter 4, "Systems Thinking." By identifying key systems in your life, such as family, work, and community, and mapping their connections and influences (both supportive and challenging), this tool helps you gain clearer insight into how these networks shape your sense of calling and where you might focus your attention for growth and discernment.

This exercise allows you to create a personal map, helping you visualize the complex systems influencing your calling. By identifying and connecting the various factors and relationships in your life, you can gain insight into how different networks shape your sense of vocation.

Step-by-Step Guidelines
1. *Start with "Me" at the Center*
    - Draw a central circle and label it "Me." This circle represents you: your values, goals, and sense of calling. All other circles will connect to this center, highlighting their influence on you.
2. *Identify and Map Key Systems*
    - Around the central "Me" circle, add additional circles for key systems in your life. Examples include:
        - *Family*: Immediate and extended family members who influence your decisions, either through support or expectation.
        - *Work*: Colleagues, mentors, or organizational culture in your workplace.

- *Community*: Faith groups, local organizations, or friends who shape your spiritual and social life.
- *Finances:* Economic factors, financial obligations, or resources that influence your choices.
- *Education*: Schools, programs, or mentors influencing your intellectual growth and vocational direction.
→ You may add other systems that play significant roles in your life, such as health, social networks, or creative pursuits.

3. *Draw Connections*
   → Draw lines from each system circle to the central "Me" circle. This shows the connection and level of influence between each system and your sense of calling.
   → Use *solid lines* for strong, direct influences and *dotted lines* for weaker, indirect influences.
   → If certain systems influence each other, connect those circles as well. For instance, *family* and *finances* might be closely linked.

4. *List Key Influences within Each System*
   → Inside each system circle, list the specific people, organizations, or factors that influence you.
   → Examples:
     - *Family*: Parents, spouse, siblings, children, family expectations.
     - *Work*: Supervisors, work culture, career goals, team dynamics.
     - *Community*: Faith leaders, friends, volunteer groups, social norms.
   → Be specific. If certain individuals or factors play a prominent role, list them clearly for a more personalized map.

5. *Use Colors to Indicate Type of Influence*
   → Use colors within each circle to show different types of influence:
     - *Green* for supportive influences that positively affect your calling.
     - *Red* for challenges or obstacles that may complicate or hinder your vocation.
     - *Blue* for resources: people, assets, or programs that you can draw on to strengthen your vocational journey.

6. *Reflection Questions*
   → Once your map is complete, take some time to reflect on the following:
     - Where do you see the strongest connections, and what might this say about the current influences on your calling?
     - Are there systems or individuals exerting more pressure than others?

System Mapping Me

- ▸ Where are your primary sources of support, and how can you lean into them?
- ▸ Do certain areas feel under-resourced? Consider how you might find additional support or balance.
- → Reflecting on your "System Mapping Me" visualization can reveal patterns in your life that either support or challenge your calling. It might also highlight areas where you need more balance or connection.

This map is a dynamic tool that evolves alongside your personal and spiritual growth. Consider revisiting and adjusting it periodically, as your life circumstances, relationships, and vocational focus shift. Each time you return to the map, you have an opportunity to assess how different systems and influences have developed or changed, revealing new insights about your calling. Over time, this visual becomes both a diagnostic tool and a roadmap for growth. As a diagnostic, it allows you to identify supportive structures, challenges, and gaps in resources that may need attention. As a growth map, it helps you see how each system contributes to your spiritual journey and where you might lean in or pull back to foster a more balanced and purposeful vocational life.

Organizational Boundary Audit Worksheet

The "Organizational Boundary Audit Worksheet" offers a structured method for communities and organizations to assess the clarity and effectiveness of their operational and relational boundaries, a key aspect of healthy systems discussed in chapter 4. This tool guides your group in examining dimensions such as information flow, decision-making processes, internal and external relationships, and overall organizational culture. Use this worksheet to identify current boundary strengths, pinpoint areas for improvement, and collaboratively define actionable steps toward fostering clearer and more functional organizational dynamics.

Boundaries are vital for creating healthy, balanced organizations. They help clarify roles, define relationships, guide ethical behavior, and ensure clear channels for communication and decision-making. This audit is designed to help communities and organizations examine the boundaries across various dimensions, assess their effectiveness, and identify areas for improvement.

Conducting a boundary audit can reveal strengths in how the organization communicates, collaborates, and upholds values. It can also uncover areas where boundaries may need to be strengthened, clarified, or adapted to meet current needs. This worksheet encourages thoughtful reflection, highlights specific boundary areas for review, and supports concrete goal-setting for ongoing growth and clarity.

Instructions for Using the Worksheet

1. *Complete each section thoughtfully*: Each section includes prompts to evaluate boundaries in that area. If possible, gather feedback from different levels within the organization to gain a holistic view.
2. *Use rating scales*: For each boundary dimension, use the 1–10 scale to provide a snapshot of current conditions. This can help prioritize areas needing immediate focus.

3. *Discuss and Reflect on Findings*: After completing the audit, review the ratings and reflections as a group. Discuss how each boundary influences day-to-day interactions and organizational culture.
4. *Identify action steps*: In the final section, summarize boundary strengths, select areas for improvement, and define actionable steps. Setting a timeline and defining metrics for success can help track progress.
5. *Schedule regular audits*: Boundaries evolve as needs and dynamics shift within an organization. Plan regular audits (e.g., annually) to revisit these areas, assess progress, and make necessary adjustments.

Boundary Audit Worksheet

1. *Information Flow*
    - How does information typically flow within our organization?
    - Are there any bottlenecks or barriers to information sharing?
    - Do all members have equal access to necessary information?
    - Rate the transparency of information flow on a scale of 1–10: _____
2. *Decision-Making Processes*
    - Who is typically involved in major decisions?
    - How are decisions communicated to the wider organization?
    - Is there a clear process for challenging or appealing decisions?
    - Rate the inclusivity of decision-making on a scale of 1–10: _____
3. *Internal Relationships*
    - How do different departments or groups interact?
    - Are there any silos or divisions that hinder collaboration?
    - How are conflicts typically resolved?
    - Rate the health of internal relationships on a scale of 1–10: _____
4. *External Relationships*
    - How does our organization interact with external partners or stakeholders?
    - Are there clear guidelines for these interactions?
    - How responsive are we to external feedback or concerns?
    - Rate the effectiveness of external relationships on a scale of 1–10: _____
5. *Organizational Culture*
    - What unspoken rules or norms exist in our organization?
    - How do these norms influence inclusion and diversity?
    - Are there any cultural practices that might be exclusionary?
    - Rate the inclusivity of our organizational culture on a scale of 1–10: _____

6. *Structural Boundaries*
   - How clear are reporting structures and job responsibilities?
   - Are there areas where roles or responsibilities overlap or are ambiguous?
   - How flexible are these structures in responding to change?
   - Rate the clarity of structural boundaries on a scale of 1–10: _____
7. *Ethical Boundaries*
   - What ethical guidelines govern our organization's actions?
   - How are these communicated and enforced?
   - Are there mechanisms for reporting ethical concerns?
   - Rate the strength of ethical boundaries on a scale of 1–10: _____
8. *Technology and Data Boundaries*
   - How is data protected and shared within the organization?
   - Are there clear policies on technology use and data access?
   - How are privacy concerns addressed?
   - Rate the effectiveness of technology/data boundaries on a scale of 1–10: _____
9. *Denominational/Regional Influence (for religious organizations)*
   - How does our larger denominational or regional context influence our practices?
   - Are there any tensions between local needs and broader organizational expectations?
   - How do we maintain our unique identity within this larger context?
   - Rate the balance of local autonomy and denominational alignment on a scale of 1–10: _____
10. *Reflection and Action Steps*
    - Based on this audit, what are our organization's boundary strengths?
    - What are the primary areas needing improvement?
    - List three specific action steps to address boundary issues:
      1. _____.
      2. _____.
      3. _____.
    - How will we measure progress on these action steps?
    - When will we conduct our next boundary audit? Date: _____

Trauma-Informed Culture Self-Assessment Tool

"4 People Encounter 5 Values in 4 Places"

This is a worksheet designed to help your department, institution, or community evaluate its implementation of trauma-informed care principles, vital for fostering the supportive environments as discussed in chapter 5. Using a "4 People Encounter 5 Values in 4 Places" framework, which considers such values as safety, trustworthiness, choice, collaboration, and empowerment across various interactions and settings for all community members, this tool enables you to identify strengths and areas for improvement. Its purpose is to guide reflection and action toward building a more resilient, inclusive, and healing culture that tends to the fractures within your community for everyone involved. For more about the origins of this framework check out Maxine Harris and Roger D. Fallot, Using Trauma Theory to Design Service Systems (San Francisco: Jossey-Bass, 2001).

This self-assessment worksheet is designed to help you evaluate how well your department or context implements trauma-informed care principles, with a focus on relationship building and tending to the fractures within your community. By reflecting on five core values (safety, trustworthiness, choice, collaboration, and empowerment) across four key places (first contact, physical settings, relationships, and events) and considering the experiences of four kinds of people (students, faculty, staff, and administrators), you can identify strengths and areas for improvement. Implementing trauma-informed care is crucial in creating a supportive and inclusive environment that enhances the well-being and success of all individuals within your institution. This process can help foster a culture of safety, trust, and mutual respect, ultimately contributing to a more resilient and thriving campus community.

Note: If you're looking for an example as to what it might look like to make some changes that are actionable and actually feasible, there is a scenario to consider at the end of this document.

Instructions

Use this worksheet to evaluate how well your department or context implements trauma-informed care principles. Reflect on each of the five values and the four places, considering the experiences of the four kinds of people (students, faculty, staff, and administrators). Identify which values, places, and people are most relevant and important to your context, and consider what actions you can take and what support you need from the organization.

Values

Safety:
- Establish a learning and living environment that prioritizes acceptance, fosters a sense of security, and normalizes the process of learning from mistakes.
- Relationship Building: Create safe spaces for open communication and trust, where individuals feel heard and supported.

Trustworthiness:
- Communicate course and campus life expectations clearly, maintain consistency in application, respect appropriate boundaries, and strive to minimize student disappointment.
- Relationship Building: Build trust through transparency, reliability, and consistent follow-through on commitments.

Choice:
- Create opportunities for students to exercise agency, express their perspectives, cultivate skills, and build self-assurance and proficiency.
- Relationship Building: Encourage individuals to voice their opinions and participate in decision-making processes, respecting their choices and autonomy.

Collaboration:
- Foster a partnership-oriented approach with students, sharing power and encouraging collaborative decision-making processes.
- Relationship Building: Promote teamwork and mutual respect through group activities and shared goals, involving all stakeholders in collaborative efforts.

Empowerment:
- Facilitate student access to suitable peer and professional support systems that enhance their academic, personal, and professional development.
- Relationship Building: Empower individuals by recognizing their strengths, celebrating their achievements, and providing resources to help them succeed.

Places

First Contact:
- How are initial interactions with your department (e.g., orientation, admissions) handled?
- What steps are taken to make these first points of contact welcoming and supportive?
- Relationship Building: Ensure first contacts establish a foundation of trust and openness, setting a positive tone for ongoing interactions.

Physical Settings:
- How are the physical spaces (e.g., classrooms, offices, dormitories) designed to be safe and inclusive?
- What improvements could be made to enhance these environments?
- Relationship Building: Create physical environments that encourage positive interactions and community building.

Relationships:
- How are relationships between students, faculty, staff, and administrators nurtured and supported?
- What practices are in place to ensure positive and healthy interactions?
- Relationship Building: Prioritize relationship-building activities that strengthen community bonds and foster mutual respect.

Events:
- How are events (e.g., lectures, workshops, social activities) planned and executed with a trauma-informed approach?
- What steps are taken to ensure these events are inclusive and considerate of diverse needs?
- Relationship Building: Design events that promote inclusivity, engagement, and connection among all participants.

Self-Assessment

Step 1: Reflect on the 5 Values for Each of the 4 People

For each group of persons (students, faculty, staff, and administrators), consider the following questions:

Safety:
- How is safety ensured for this group?
- What actions can be taken to improve their sense of safety?

Trustworthiness:
- How is trust built and maintained for this group?
- What actions can be taken to enhance trustworthiness?

Choice:
- How is this group given choices and agency?
- What actions can be taken to provide more choice and autonomy?

Collaboration:
- How is collaboration fostered with this group?
- What actions can be taken to encourage more collaboration?

Empowerment:
- How is this group empowered?
- What actions can be taken to enhance their empowerment?

Step 2: Reflect on the 5 Values in Each of the 4 Places

For each type of place (first contact, physical setting, relationship, event), consider the following questions:

Safety:
- How is safety ensured in this place?
- What actions can be taken to improve safety?

Trustworthiness:
- How is trust built and maintained in this place?
- What actions can be taken to enhance trustworthiness?

Choice:
- How is choice and agency provided in this place?
- What actions can be taken to offer more choice and autonomy?

Collaboration:
- How is collaboration fostered in this place?
- What actions can be taken to encourage more collaboration?

Empowerment:
- How is empowerment facilitated in this place?
- What actions can be taken to enhance empowerment?

Reflection and Action Plan

Most Relevant and Important Areas

Identify which values, places, and people are most relevant and important to your context.

Personal Actions:
- What can you personally do to better address these areas?

Organizational Support:
- What do you need to ask for at the organizational level to support these efforts?

Action Steps:
- What is one specific action you want to take?
- What is one specific action you want to ask for from your organization/department?

Sample Scenario

Alex and a Trauma-Informed Admissions Process

Before

Alex had been working in student admissions for several years. He took pride in his work, ensuring that prospective students received all the necessary information about the university. His approach was thorough, but it primarily focused on efficiency and the logistical aspects of admissions. Alex scheduled campus tours, organized open houses, and provided detailed presentations about the university's programs. However, his focus was more on delivering information than on the emotional and psychological experiences of prospective students.

When prospective students and their families arrived for campus visits, Alex greeted them warmly but quickly moved into a structured itinerary. He ensured they met with faculty and current students, but these interactions were often rushed and formal. Alex did not consider how overwhelming or intimidating the admissions process could be for some students, especially those coming from backgrounds without parental experience with college.

Feedback from prospective students sometimes mentioned that the process felt impersonal. Some students expressed feeling anxious or lost during their visits, and a few even mentioned feeling unwelcome or misunderstood.

After

After participating in a workshop on trauma-informed care practices and learning about the 4-5-4 model, Alex realized the importance of creating a trauma-informed admissions process. He recognized that small changes could significantly impact prospective students' experiences.

Changes Alex Plans to Make

1. *Physical Settings:*
    - Before: The admissions office and event spaces were functional but somewhat impersonal.

- After: Alex arranges comfortable seating areas, ensures clear signage, and creates a more relaxed atmosphere. He adds elements like artwork from diverse cultures and calming colors to make the environment more inviting.
- Values: Safety, Empowerment

2. *Relationships:*
   - Before: Interactions with prospective students were formal and focused on delivering information.
   - After: Alex prioritizes building genuine connections. He encourages informal conversations and personal stories from current students and faculty. He trains his staff to be more empathetic and approachable, focusing on making every interaction meaningful and supportive.
   - Values: Trustworthiness and Transparency, Collaboration

3. *Events:*
   - Before: Admissions events had rigid schedules and a formal structure.
   - After: Alex rethinks the structure of events. He incorporates flexible activities that allow students to explore at their own pace. He includes interactive sessions where students can ask questions and share concerns in a safe environment. He also ensures that events are accessible to students with different needs, providing necessary accommodations.
   - Values: Choice, Safety

4. *First Contact:*
   - Before: Initial contact was informative but lacked warmth and personalization.
   - After: Alex improves the initial contact process by providing clear, concise information in a friendly and reassuring manner. He makes sure emails and phone calls are not just informative but also welcoming and supportive. Alex creates a FAQ section addressing common concerns and provides resources for additional support.
   - Values: Trustworthiness and Transparency, Empowerment

5. *Values Applied:*

Safety:
- Before: Safety was considered in a general sense, but not explicitly focused on emotional safety.
- After: Alex ensures the environment is safe for all students, providing clear guidelines and expectations, making students feel secure and respected.

Trustworthiness and Transparency:
- Before: Information was provided but sometimes lacked consistency.
- After: Alex maintains honesty and consistency in all communications, clearly explaining the admissions process and setting realistic expectations, building trust with prospective students and their families.

Sample Scenario

Choice:
- Before: Limited options for engaging with the admissions process.
- After: Alex offers multiple ways for students to engage, such as virtual tours, in-person visits, and one-on-one meetings, allowing students to choose what works best for them.

Collaboration:
- Before: Limited involvement of faculty and current students in the admissions process.
- After: Alex involves faculty, current students, and staff in the admissions process, encouraging a team approach and ensuring everyone works together to create a supportive environment.

Empowerment:
- Before: Prospective students were provided with information but not actively empowered.
- After: Alex empowers prospective students by providing them with the information and resources they need to make informed decisions. He encourages questions and expressions of concern, helping students feel confident and supported.

Outcome

With these changes, Alex notices a significant improvement in feedback from prospective students. They feel more welcomed, understood, and supported throughout the admissions process. The environment becomes more inclusive and less intimidating, leading to a more positive experience for everyone involved. Alex feels proud of the transformation and continues to look for ways to improve, fostering a trauma-informed culture in every aspect of his work.

Group Reflection on the NEPER Practices

This guide facilitates a "Group Reflection on the NEPER Practices" (Notice & Name, Engage & Encourage, Prioritize & Prune, Exercise & Experiment, and Rest & Reassess) which are five interrelated practices of accompaniment detailed in chapter 7. It offers a structured process with guiding questions for small groups to explore each practice through shared conversation and storytelling. Use this tool to deepen your community's understanding of these accompaniment practices, reflect on lived experiences with them, identify potential obstacles, and discern how to more intentionally foster these approaches to nurture spiritual growth and vocational clarity among members.

※

NEPER stands for five interrelated practices of accompaniment: Notice & Name, Engage & Encourage, Prioritize & Prune, Exercise & Experiment, and Rest & Reassess. These practices describe how we can journey alongside others in ways that nurture spiritual growth, clarity of call, and faithful living. Taken together, they offer a framework for intentional, communal discernment, helping individuals and communities alike to listen deeply for how the Spirit is moving, what gifts are emerging, and where God might be inviting transformation or care.

The reflection process below is designed to help small groups explore each practice more fully through shared conversation. It centers real experience (both past and imagined) and invites thoughtful curiosity, honest storytelling, and mutual listening. The guiding questions are meant to open space, not dictate outcomes. Whether you've engaged in these practices often or are encountering them for the first time, the goal is not mastery, but attentiveness to one another, to the practices themselves, and to the Spirit of accompaniment that weaves through them all. Hopefully, coming out of this activity, you'll have a clearer sense of how these practices already live among you and where there may be invitations to deepen them further.

A Process for Reflecting on the Practices

In small groups, read aloud the description of the practice being discussed. After reading, proceed to share reflections on the following four sets of questions, one at a time, allowing for sharing after each question:

1. Has anyone ever had an experience of this? If so, what was it like?
2. Beyond any shared experiences, what other ways *could* this practice look like even if you haven't experienced it yet? If a video camera recorded it, what would it capture?
3. What life-giving things might emerge if more of this were done? How might it change the community or individuals involved?
4. What obstacles might prevent more of this from happening?

Feel free to spend as much time on each question as feels right. If the conversation comes alive at any point, stay with it. Be mindful of the group and try not to have the same person speak first every time. Everyone brings wisdom! After each set of questions in small groups, there will be an opportunity for large group sharing about any particularly powerful or quickening conversation that emerged. After the large group sharing, people return to the same small groups for the next practice, going through the same questions again.

A Preparatory Note

Sometimes even when these practices are not done well, or not done at all, or, worse yet, done so poorly that they wound, gifts still emerge for use in service, and people still find callings in their lives. The following practices are not a foolproof recipe for ensuring vibrant and robust callings or ministries; rather, they are exercises that help us corporately deepen in faithfulness and service. These practices don't always occur in a particular order, nor do they always need to. They serve as a guide to becoming more intentional stewards of spiritual gifts.

Notice and Name

Noticing is the practice of paying careful attention to the gifts, talents, and spiritual callings that may be emerging in an individual. It is not passive observation; it requires discernment to recognize what is developing, sometimes quietly, in someone's life. The practice of noticing is akin to having spiritual sensitivity, being tuned in to what might be growing beneath the surface in others, and being open to what is emerging.

Naming goes beyond just recognizing. It is the act of articulating the gifts or callings you have noticed. This could be done formally, such as through a nomination for a specific role or responsibility, or informally, by expressing a simple observation over a conversation. Naming provides validation and acknowledgment to the individual, helping them recognize their own gifts or potential. However, not all responses to being named will be the same. Some people will feel joyful, while others may feel uncomfortable. Yet it's important to remember that the act of naming comes with responsibility: follow-up is necessary to nurture what has been named. Finally, the ability to both notice and name emerging gifts in others is itself a unique gift.

Engage and Encourage

Engaging with an individual stewarding a gift or calling requires consistent, active involvement. This means taking the time to connect with the person, not just on the surface, but in a way that fosters their development. Engagement is about asking questions, listening deeply, and maintaining a supportive relationship. It's not enough to notice someone's gift or calling; engagement means stepping into a space where you can walk alongside them as they explore their calling.

Encouraging complements engagement by offering the affirmation, support, and positive reinforcement needed to help individuals grow in their gifts and callings. Encouragement involves more than just words. It can include providing resources, suggesting new opportunities, or offering guidance for deeper growth. At times, encouraging someone may mean challenging them to step into new roles or take on new responsibilities. However, this must be done carefully, as personal growth may lead to shifts in relationships or community dynamics. Encouragement also helps individuals face the challenges that may arise as they begin to reorient their lives around their gifts or callings. Taken together, engagement and encouragement help individuals and communities grow in life and faithfulness.

Prioritize and Prune

Prioritizing goes hand-in-hand with pruning. Once unnecessary elements are removed, the individual must identify what is most essential and life-giving. This involves clarifying what needs to take precedence in their lives to fully live into their gifts and callings. Prioritizing requires careful discernment about where to invest time, energy, and resources. It can also involve asking for help in making decisions about which areas to focus on. Together, pruning and prioritizing help ensure that the individual is devoting their attention to what matters most, allowing their gifts to flourish in alignment with their spiritual calling.

Pruning is the process of removing anything that drains energy or attention from the gifts or callings someone is trying to steward. Just as plants sometimes need their leaves or branches trimmed to focus energy on new growth, individuals may need to identify and eliminate things in their lives that are distractions or obstacles to their service. Pruning may involve letting go of commitments, habits, or even relationships that no longer serve their deeper purpose. It can also mean stepping away from past roles or responsibilities that were once helpful but are now burdensome. Pruning isn't easy, but it helps an individual create space for more focused and fruitful growth.

Exercise and Experiment

Exercising one's gifts or callings means putting them into practice regularly. Just as physical exercise strengthens the body, exercising spiritual gifts and callings strengthens their capacity. This involves taking action and stepping into roles or situations where these gifts can be applied. Exercise often requires persistence and the willingness to repeat actions until one becomes more adept. Whether through service, leadership, or another type of engagement, exercising a gift is a way to develop confidence and skill.

Experimenting takes this a step further by inviting the individual to try new things, stretch beyond what they already know, and explore uncharted territory with their gifts or callings. Experimenting allows space for trial and error, where failure is not seen as a setback but as part of the learning process. It is through experimenting that individuals discover new possibilities for how their gifts can be used, sometimes uncovering abilities they didn't know they had. Experimentation can also involve stepping into roles they've never considered or testing a calling in a completely different context. Together, exercising and experimenting open up pathways for growth, insight, and creative exploration of one's gifts and callings.

Rest and Reassess

Resting is a necessary pause from active work, a time to step back and recover both physically and spiritually. Rest is more than a break. It is an intentional practice that allows for rejuvenation and connection with the deeper currents of life. In the spiritual context, rest can involve Sabbath time, silence, or retreat, where one reconnects with the Spirit and finds renewed energy. Resting also gives space for joy and laughter, particularly after periods of heavy work or challenging tasks. It is important to remind ourselves that rest is not indulgence but a vital part of maintaining balance in service.

Reassessing complements rest by providing an opportunity to reflect on the journey so far and discern the next steps. After a period of work, rest creates a space where individuals can look back on what they have done, evaluate its impact, and listen for guidance on how to move forward. Reassessing may involve asking: What has gone well? What needs adjustment? What changes are needed in the future? By integrating both rest and reassessment, individuals and communities can ensure that they remain aligned with their deeper callings and continue to serve faithfully while avoiding burnout.

In Closing

If time permits, after the last all group share-out, I strongly encourage individuals to take a few moments at the end of the conversation to consider what might come next. Listening well to one another is sacred work, but when possible, it's also valuable to ask: *What now?* Were there particular stories or ideas shared in your group that seem to invite concrete steps? Are there ways you or your community might act differently in light of what you've heard?

This could mean following up with someone you've noticed a gift in, suggesting a small experiment, offering support for someone feeling called to make a change, or even committing to rest or reassessment. These practices are not only for discussion: They are meant to shape how we live. So if something from this conversation stirred your imagination or gave you clarity, take it seriously. Even a small decision can be a powerful next act of accompaniment. If you feel like there is something from the activity you want to make sure to remember, write yourself a note and consider sharing your inclination with someone. You might not act on it right away, but sometimes, we all need reminders.

In Closing

Seeding Change with Story

This is a guide that outlines a practice for reclaiming narrative power by consciously listening to and rewriting the stories that shape your understanding of yourself and your calling, a theme central to chapter 8. Drawing on feminist and liberationist insights, this process helps you identify and resist limiting narratives, especially those imposed by dominant systems. Use these steps to reconstruct your personal and vocational stories in alignment with your deepest values and faith, fostering self-legislation, moral accountability, and the courage to live more authentically from your vocational voice.

Seeding Change with Story is a practice of reclaiming narrative power. It invites you to listen deeply to the stories that have shaped you, especially those imposed by systems of dominance, and to consciously rewrite them in alignment with your values, faith, and vocation. Drawing on feminist insights and liberationist frameworks, this practice understands storytelling not just as expression, but as resistance and renewal. It's a way to resist internalized limitations, honor your full humanity, and take seriously your evolving sense of call. Whether you're discerning next steps or simply seeking to live with more integrity, Seeding Change with Story offers tools to help you hear your own voice more clearly, and to live from it with courage.

Storytelling is a powerful way to explore who we are and what we're meant to do. It helps us shape our sense of purpose and take charge of our journey, particularly in a world that often tries to impose restrictive ideas about who we should be. This guide is deeply influenced by the work of Farah Godrej, whose research highlights how storytelling can be a tool for reclaiming identity and resisting dominant, often oppressive, narratives.

In her article, "Spaces for Counter-Narratives: The Phenomenology of Reclamation," Farah Godrej[1] explores how marginalized groups, particularly women and other

---

1 Farah Godrej, "Spaces for Counter-Narratives: The Phenomenology of Reclamation," *Frontiers: A Journal of Women Studies* 32, no. 3 (2011): 111–33.

historically oppressed communities, use storytelling as a form of resistance against the dominant cultural narratives that attempt to define and limit them. Her work is deeply rooted in feminist theory, emphasizing how patriarchal structures often shape the stories told about women, reducing their agency and reinforcing systems of power that keep them marginalized.

Godrej argues that storytelling is not merely a way of sharing personal experiences; it is an act of reclaiming power and autonomy. By crafting and asserting their own narratives, individuals and communities can challenge the status quo, resist the imposition of limiting identities, and create spaces where their evolving selves can be recognized and validated. This reclamation of narrative is vital in a world where dominant voices often seek to silence or distort the experiences of those who are marginalized.

The feminist nature of Godrej's work is particularly important because it highlights the intersection of storytelling with broader struggles for gender justice and equality. She demonstrates that by creating "counternarratives," women and other oppressed groups can actively resist the cultural scripts that have historically constrained them. These counternarratives do more than just provide alternative stories; they actively dismantle the structures that uphold inequality and create new possibilities for personal and collective liberation.

This guide is indebted to Godrej's insights because it draws on her understanding of storytelling as a transformative practice. Just as she describes the power of counternarratives to challenge and reshape societal norms, this guide encourages you to use storytelling as a way to initiate and sustain meaningful changes in your life. Whether you are navigating your sense of vocation or simply trying to understand your place in the world, the steps outlined here are rooted in the belief that storytelling is not just about self-expression: It is about reclaiming your power, redefining your identity, and contributing to a more just and equitable world.

For people of faith, this approach to storytelling is particularly relevant because it offers a way to stay grounded and attuned to your calling in a world that often moves too fast for deep reflection. In the midst of a culture that frequently values speed and superficiality over depth and discernment, storytelling can be a spiritual practice that allows you to pause, reflect, and listen for the voice of your calling. By reclaiming your story and aligning it with your faith, you can find clarity and direction, even in a noisy world that doesn't always make space for such important work.

While Godrej's work emphasizes feminist theory and the ways storytelling can resist patriarchal structures, storytelling as a tool for change is just as powerful in challenging all forms of social power that seek to limit or silence. Whether confronting class, racial, economic, or cultural dominance, storytelling offers a means of reclaiming identity and purpose, making space for those whose voices have been marginalized across various contexts. This guide is for anyone seeking to reshape their narrative in a way that reflects and honors their full humanity, standing as a response to any dominant forces that attempt to define or diminish them.

Step 1: Gatekeep the Narratives You Encounter

- *Description:* The first step in storytelling into change is the critical assessment of the narratives and messages that shape your self-conception and vocational understanding. In a world saturated with information and external expectations, it's easy to absorb stories that don't serve you. As a gatekeeper of your consciousness, you must discern which stories deserve space in your life and which should be set aside.
- *Action:* Begin by intentionally slowing down and creating moments of stillness in your daily life, whether through meditation, prayer, or quiet reflection. In these moments, take inventory of the dominant narratives that influence you, both those imposed by society and those you've internalized over time. Are these narratives rooted in your values, or do they reflect external pressures and expectations that distance you from your calling? Engage in practices like journaling to map out these influences. Ask yourself: Are these stories helping me listen to my inner voice, or are they drowning it out with noise? Cultivating awareness of these narratives allows you to consciously choose which stories to let in and which to reject.
- *Caution:* Be wary of narratives that, while seemingly comforting, may actually hinder your growth. For example, societal norms that prioritize stability over exploration might tempt you to settle for what is safe rather than pursuing your calling. Similarly, narratives from well-meaning friends or family might reflect their desires for you rather than your own. In a fast-paced world, these narratives can be hard to notice because they often operate in the background, subtly influencing your decisions. The challenge is to stay vigilant and ensure that the stories you allow into your life align with your deepest values and aspirations.

Step 2: Actively Reconstruct Your Narrative

- *Description:* Once you've identified and filtered out limiting narratives, the next step is to actively reconstruct your own story. This process involves not only crafting new narratives that reflect your strengths and aspirations but also embracing the fluidity and evolving nature of your vocational journey. Your narrative should be a dynamic, living document that grows and adapts as you do.

- *Action:* Begin the process of narrative reconstruction by setting aside time to reflect deeply on your past experiences, current challenges, and future hopes. Use creative practices like writing, art, or storytelling exercises to explore different versions of your future self. What paths might you take if certain constraints were lifted? How do these possibilities align with your sense of calling? Consider creating a "vocation journal" where you regularly record insights, reflections, and evolving stories about who you are and where you're headed. In this journal, articulate your core values and how they inform your narrative. As you reconstruct your story, regularly revisit and revise it, allowing it to evolve as you gain new insights and experiences. Ask yourself: How does this narrative help me stay grounded in my faith and to my calling, even in a world that pulls me in many directions?
- *Caution: Avoid the temptation to create a narrative that is too idealized or disconnected from reality. While it's important to dream and aspire, your narrative should also acknowledge the challenges and uncertainties that are part of any journey. An overly rigid or idealistic story can lead to frustration when life inevitably presents obstacles. Instead, embrace the ambiguity and complexity of your journey, allowing your narrative to remain flexible and responsive to change. This will help you stay grounded and adaptable, even as you strive to fulfill your calling.*

Step 3: Seek and Share with a Supportive Community

- *Description:* Storytelling is most powerful when it is shared and affirmed within a supportive community. This step involves finding or cultivating a community where your narrative can be heard, validated, and refined. The community's recognition and feedback are crucial for solidifying your vocational narrative and ensuring that it resonates with both your internal sense of calling and the broader social context.
- *Action:* Actively seek out or build a community that values deep reflection, honesty, and mutual support, whether it's within a faith community, a small group of trusted friends, or a circle of mentors. In this community, share your reconstructed narrative and invite feedback. Listen to the stories of others, recognizing how their experiences and insights might inform and enrich your own. This communal storytelling process not only helps refine your narrative but also grounds you in a sense of shared purpose and collective wisdom. Consider creating or joining a regular discussion group where members can share their evolving stories and support each other in their vocational

Seeding Change with Story

journeys. In these spaces, storytelling becomes a sacred practice, one that helps everyone involved stay connected to their deeper calling amid the distractions of everyday life.
- *Caution: Be mindful of communities that may unconsciously reinforce limiting beliefs or resist the changes you're making. Some groups may be invested in maintaining the status quo and could subtly discourage you from pursuing a more adventurous or unconventional path. Additionally, avoid becoming too reliant on external validation; while community feedback is valuable, your sense of vocation should ultimately be guided by your inner convictions and discernment. The goal is to find a balance where community support strengthens your narrative without overshadowing your own voice.*

Step 4: Practice Self-Legislation in Your Internal Dialogue
- *Description:* Sustaining the change initiated through storytelling requires disciplined internal dialogue. Self-legislation involves setting clear boundaries and guidelines for how you think about and engage with yourself. In a world full of distractions and external pressures, maintaining an empowering, compassionate internal narrative is vital for staying attentive to your calling.
- *Action:* Establish a regular practice of self-reflection to monitor your internal dialogue. Pay attention to patterns of negative self-talk, self-doubt, or criticism that may undermine your reconstructed narrative. When these thoughts arise, consciously challenge them and replace them with affirmations that reflect your potential and the story you've chosen to live by. Consider using tools such as meditation, prayer, or positive affirmations to cultivate a healthy and empowering internal conversation. These practices can help you stay grounded and focused on your calling, even when the world around you is chaotic. Additionally, engage in periodic "spiritual audits" where you assess whether your internal dialogue aligns with your faith and values. This ongoing self-regulation ensures that your inner narrative remains a source of strength and guidance.
- *Caution: Beware of the persistent nature of old habits and negative self-talk. These can resurface, particularly during times of stress or uncertainty, and may attempt to sabotage your efforts to sustain a new narrative. It's also important to avoid becoming overly rigid in your self-legislation; allow for flexibility and compassion, recognizing that growth often involves missteps and recalibration. Maintaining a balance between discipline and self-compassion is vital for nurturing your vocational journey and staying attentive to your calling.*

Step 5: Embrace Moral Accountability in Your Storytelling

- *Description:* Creating change through storytelling also requires a deep commitment to moral accountability. This means holding yourself responsible for the narratives you choose to accept, the stories you tell about yourself, and the actions you take based on these stories. In a world where it's easy to get swept up by trends or external pressures, moral accountability ensures that your storytelling remains grounded in your values and aligned with your calling.
- *Action:* Engage in regular moral reflection, considering how your narrative aligns with your core values, ethical principles, and the broader mission of your faith. Ask yourself: Does this story reflect the kind of person I strive to be? Does it honor the responsibilities I have to others and to my community? Does it contribute to the common good? When you identify discrepancies between your actions and your narrative, take steps to realign them. This might involve revising your narrative, making amends, or changing your behavior to better reflect your values. Consider engaging in practices such as spiritual direction, ethical reflection groups, or journaling to deepen your moral accountability. These practices help ensure that your storytelling is not only about personal growth but also about contributing positively to the world around you.
- *Caution: Avoid rationalizing or justifying actions that are inconsistent with your values or the narrative you wish to live by. This can create cognitive dissonance, weakening your sense of purpose and integrity. Also, be careful not to become too rigid or self-critical in your moral accountability; recognize that growth is a process, and allow room for grace and self-forgiveness when you fall short. The goal is to cultivate a narrative that is both aspirational and compassionate, guiding you toward greater alignment with your vocation and ethical commitments.*

Conclusion

Storytelling as a means of navigating vocational discernment isn't a quick fix or guaranteed solution. It's an ongoing practice that demands effort, reflection, and openness to growth. This approach isn't about crafting a perfect narrative that neatly wraps up your life. Rather, it's about engaging with your story as it unfolds, recognizing its dynamic nature and embracing the revisions that come with new experiences and insights.

This practice is more about staying attuned to your journey than reaching a final destination. It's about listening carefully to your sense of calling and making adjustments as needed. There will be times when your story feels uncertain, when old narratives resurface, or when external pressures challenge your new narrative. These moments aren't failures but opportunities to deepen your practice, inviting you to revisit the steps we've discussed with renewed commitment and patience.

Remember, this process is deeply relational. It's not just about the stories you tell yourself, but also those you share with others and the feedback you receive. Your narrative will be shaped by your interactions with your community, your engagement with the world, and your faith. By remaining open to this relational dynamic, you allow your story to be a living dialogue between your inner convictions and the outer world, enriching your understanding of who you are and where you're called to go.

In a world that often moves too quickly for deep reflection, storytelling offers a way to stay grounded, to listen for the quiet whisper of your calling, and to make choices aligned with your sense of self. It takes courage and faith to continually revisit and reshape your narrative, trusting that through this practice, you're not only navigating your own path but also contributing to a broader, more just and compassionate world.

As you move forward, remember that storytelling into change is a lifelong journey. It demands your attention, honesty, and willingness to grow. There will be no final draft of your story, but rather a series of iterations reflecting your ongoing process of becoming. Embrace this practice with patience, knowing that each time you return to your narrative with intention, you're participating in the work of crafting a life that is attentive to your calling and aligned with the values you hold dear.

Index

Abrams, David, 4
abundance, 207, 210, 316
accompaniment, 19, 22, 45, 71, 241, 292
    deep listening in, 214, 218, 225, 228, 242, 243
    disruption in, 225–28, 229, 230, 234, 236, 243
    Francis, nurturing approach to, 215–18, 224, 243
    giving and receiving, interplay of, 234–37
    interconnection, as commitment to, 213–14
    liberation theology perspective, 215, 218–24, 243
    NEPER accompaniment practices, 377–81
    power dynamics in accompaniment relationships, 244
    practical guidance for those providing, 228–31
    practical guidance for those receiving, 232–34
    three-dimensional model, 225–28, 236, 243
accountability, 19, 38, 181, 184, 354, 388
    in accompaniment approach, 214, 223
    gendered expectations for, 131
    in ministry context, 280, 292, 294, 304, 307
    in Quaker tradition, 66, 67, 71
Adler, Jonathan, 159
After Whiteness (Jennings), 185
Alves, Rubem, 165, 219
Amos, 209, 210, 211, 279
Anabaptists, 286
Ano, Gene, 158–59
Ante-Nicene Period, 284
Anthony, Susan B., 67
anxiety, 14, 49, 125, 332, 373
    COVID-19 pandemic, anxiety during, 37–38
    in the dizziness of freedom, 46
    organizations as managing, 120–22, 133, 134
    triangulation in attempts to lower anxiety, 130–31
Arendt, Hannah, xvii
Arrupe, Pedro, 65
Atheist Church (Sunday Assembly), 301
attentiveness, 35, 69, 182, 229, 337, 340
    in Benedictine thought, 342
    cultivating the habit of, 331
    equilibrium, as part of, 39
    to God's voice, 329
    in Ignatian spirituality, 57, 59
    in Quaker practice, 67
    in storytelling setting, 377
    in theological reflection, 321, 322, 323–24, 327, 333, 343
authority, 24, 127, 233, 247, 282, 284
    biblical authority, 292, 304, 348
    in Confucian framework, 128
    in congregational settings, 123
    educational authority, 220
    institutional authority, 230, 273
    in ministry, 295, 305
    in Quaker tradition, 66, 68
    skepticism of religious authority, 301
    storytelling, challenging authority in, 254
    theological reflection on, 330. 349
    in Ubuntu context, 139

Baker, Heidi, 297
Baldwin, James, 246
Baptist tradition, 293
Barrett, Lisa Feldman, 160
base communities, 254
Beall, Sandra K., 158
belonging, 69, 178, 198, 201, 217
    ancestral belonging, 184
    communal belonging, 36, 120, 173, 205, 206, 354
    creating spaces of, 197, 202
    fragmentation, impact on, 191–94, 194–95
    identity and belonging, 177, 179–82, 255, 256, 268
    institutional belonging, 302
    intersectional approach to, 200
    moral belonging, 20, 21
    sense of, 27, 95, 96, 114, 125, 154, 174, 185, 187, 190, 294
See also identity
Berlin Model, xxii–xxiii, 287
Bethel Church, 291

Beyond Majority Rule (Sheeran), 65
BIPOC leaders, 131
Blake, William, 3
Bonnke, Reinhard, 297
Book of Revelation, 142
Bowen, Murray, 118, 119
Bowen Family Systems Theory (BFST). *See under* systems thinking
Branigan, Christine, 157
Bread for the World, 299
broaden-and-build theory, 157
brown, adrienne maree, 116, 134, 258, 267
Brown, David, 96–97, 101
Brueggemann, Walter, 163–64, 167, 174
Buechner, Frederick, 7, 144
burnout, 21, 33–34, 172, 231, 294, 380

Cahalan, Kathleen, 39–40
Caldeira, Cleusa, 182, 183
Campus Crusade for Christ, 296
Cardijn, Joseph, 263, 340–41
Catholic Social Teaching, 287, 297, 335, 348
Catholic Worker Movement, 335, 342
Cave, Nick, 269–70
Center for Justice and Peacebuilding, 294
Chang, Sun Hee, 260
chaplaincy, 113, 293, 300, 302
Charismatic tradition, 50, 288, 291, 297
Christ for All Nations, 297
Christian Empire, 284–85
Christian Peacemaker Teams, 294
Christology, 304, 306, 347
colonialism, 206, 249, 285, 288
    colonial fragments, 185–88, 189–90, 193, 204
    Doctrine of Discovery as fueling, 178
    global evangelization tied with, 286–87
    land justice and colonization, 151–52
    leadership styles, decolonial critique of, 143–44
    resistance to colonial empire, 182–83
commodity fragmentation, 185, 188–89, 190, 193, 204
common good, 142, 260, 310, 388
    the church as working for, 280
    diverse gifts as employed for, 313, 388
    service to the common good, 43, 72
community connection, 88, 103, 291, 354, 355, 356, 357
Companioning, dimension of, 225–29, 230, 234, 236, 243
compassion, 19, 81, 140, 229, 251, 331
    in accompaniment context, 215, 216, 225, 227, 228, 232, 243
    in Bowen Family Systems Theory, 119
    community conflicts, navigating with, 197
    discernment, approaching with, 30, 43
    in a holding environment, 168
    in Jesus's ministry, 279, 283
    lament, grounding in compassion, 156, 164
    in ministry, 274, 278, 297, 308, 309, 327, 329
    in *mujerista* framework, 79
    self-compassion in the vocational journey, 387
    spiritual formation, role in, 76, 84, 95
    in storytelling framework, 387, 388, 389
    suffering as a catalyst for, 166
    in vocational discernment, 117, 241
Compassion International, 296
complementarian theology, 218
Cone, James, 218, 222–23, 224, 242, 334
conflict mediation, 294
Confucius, 128, 129
conscientization, 219, 220, 260
context collapse, 206, 255–57, 259, 271
contextual education, 323, 343
counternarratives, 43, 258, 266–67, 384
Counter-Reformation, 286, 348
countertransference, 325, 326, 346
COVID-19 pandemic, 37, 288–89
Crazy Quilts, 203, 204–5
Crenshaw, Kimberlé, 199–200, 201, 205
Crusades, 285
cultivation, 34, 57, 302
    in accompaniment practice, 235–36
    of collective joy, 152
    viveka as emphasizing, 54
    vocational cultivation, 35, 215, 227
cultural commute, 197–98

Dalit Christians, 55–56
Davidson, Richard, 157
Day, Dorothy, 335, 342
deep listening, 35, 184, 309
    in accompaniment framework, 214
    in Companioning practice, 225, 228, 243
    Quakerism as emphasizing, 242
    in Stewarding Leadings and Gifts workshop, 237, 240–41
deification. *See* theosis
De La Torre, Miguel, 264–65
deliberatio process, 64–65
deliberative theology, 343–44
diakonia (service), 279
Didache (Christian text), 283
discernment, 25, 72, 100, 102, 218
    accompaniment as a safe space for, 216
    as an adaptive, dynamic process, 36, 201
    ambiguity as accompanying, 192, 252

Index   393

communal discernment, 22, 64–71, 94–95, 96, 235, 278
compassion, approaching with, 30
connection selection as part of, 333
definitions and perspectives, 49–52
divine guidance and, 55, 66
as an embodied experience, 25
equilibrium in the process of, 44
etymology of discernment, 47
exile, discernment beginning in, 184
in Ignatian spirituality, 14, 57, 58–62, 334
individual discernment, 56–62, 63
joy and lament in discernment process, 150, 156
ministry, discernment in, 73, 273, 304
moral discernment, 20, 160
questions for reflection, 73–74
reorientation, as a process of, 112
systems perspective, cultivating, 113, 146, 147
through theological reflection, 329, 341
word study of discernment, 52–56
See also spiritual formation; vocational discernment
disordered attachments and affections, 14, 43, 59
disorientation, 19, 22, 114, 151, 194
in Brueggemann framework, 163, 174
failure, not a sign of, 18, 312
integrity in the face of, 76
as an invitation to reconsider, 101
moral disorientation, 20–21, 112
storytelling in the wake of, 257
systemic injustices, as a response to, 117
Disruption, dimension of, 225–28, 229, 230, 234, 236, 243
divine guidance, 49, 53, 62, 70, 92
in charismatic ministry, 297
discernment and, 55, 66
in Ignatian spirituality, 50
privilege as shaping understanding of, 69
in Quaker framework, 67, 68
divine presence, 9, 64, 71, 84, 95, 336, 349
dizziness of freedom, 46, 74
Doctrine of Discovery, 178–79
doubt, 94, 159, 229, 302, 349
in accompaniment approach, 233, 235, 242
self-doubt, 21, 24, 189, 327, 387
in vocational discernment, 163, 166, 168, 171, 214
doulos (radical servanthood), 280
Duke, James, 343–44

Early Modern Era, 287
ecclesiology, 10, 285, 305, 347
Elijah, 15, 16–17, 327

embedded theology, 54, 343–44
emergent strategy, 116–17, 134
emotional dialectics, 159
emotional granularity, 160, 161
emotional triangles, 130–35, 147
Engage and Encourage practice, 239, 240, 379
equilibrium, 13, 72, 127, 201, 313
already-but-not-yet tension, reflecting, 251
reaching an equilibrium, 36–44
between stability and adaptability, 95, 104
system equilibrium, 120–25, 132, 133, 134, 147, 195, 226
unhealthy equilibrium, 195, 226, 229
eschatology, 264, 305
Evangelical tradition, 292, 293, 296
evangelism, 287, 296–97, 308, 349
Exercise and Experiment practice, 239, 240, 380
exhaustion, 32, 33, 38, 39, 41, 46, 334
Exline, Julie, 158
external call, 26–28
Ezekiel, 250

Failure Fridays, 170, 171
faith, 12, 61, 98, 273, 291, 347
accompaniment and formation
faith in accompaniment framework, 217, 218, 226, 230, 234, 244
faith in the discernment process, 102
faith in the formation process, 88–90
spiritual practices deepening faith, 354, 384
actions and expression
actions in alignment with faith, 77
creativity in expressing faith, 298
faith in *lo cotidiano*, 78
love and evangelism as tenets of faith, 296
social action, integrating with faith, 299
community and practice
faith in ministry, 297, 300–301, 302, 303, 307–8, 309, 313, 339
Quaker tradition, ongoing faithfulness in, 341
tradition and faith, 96, 97–98, 99, 101, 104
experiences and challenges of faith
childhood faith, 192
colonial impacts on faith, 187–88
fragments of faith, 184, 185–86, 190, 206
lament, effect on faith, 155, 159, 163–64, 167, 174
prophet Elijah, faith of, 15, 16
Ricœur's vision of, 8, 9, 10
in theological reflection, 80, 81–84, 103, 321, 322, 342, 343
faith communities, 92, 103, 135, 220, 254
BFST, applying to, 111, 120, 125

faith communities *(continued)*
  communal discernment in, 69
  community connections and, 81, 88, 345, 354, 386
  in ministry context, 153, 291, 293, 304, 305
  quilting traditions and, 205
  in Set Your Sliders practice, 90
  synodal process as strengthening, 95
  theological reflection and, 93, 101
Fantastic Hegemonic Imagination, 42, 72
feedback, 26, 35, 61, 232, 389
  challenging feedback, 129, 234, 235
  community feedback, 311, 386, 387
  feedback loops, 89, 115, 130, 148
  inner voice, balancing with, 44
  organization engagement with, 129, 363, 364
  from prospective students, 373, 375
  situational affirmations as offering, 27
  willingness to accept, 123, 124
Feuerbach, Ludwig, 3
Foley, Edward, 78
formation. *See* spiritual formation
fractals, 134–35, 258, 267
fractured callings, 117
fragmentation, 179–91, 191–94
Francis, Pope, 94, 101
  on accompaniment, 215–18, 224, 243
  on growth requiring loving correction, 225–26
  on vocation, 11, 17
Fredrickson, Barbara, 157
Freire, Paulo, 115, 242, 249
  on becoming more deeply human, 12, 251
  conscientização, on the discomfort of, 181
  on critical hope, 263, 264, 271
  critical pedagogy of, 218–19, 224
  Gutiérrez, as integrating thought of, 220–21
  on *inedito viavel*, 164–65
  on possible futures, 262–63
  reading of the world, on true learning requiring, 76
Frijda, Nico, 159

Gee's Bend quilts, 203–4, 205
Gladwell, Malcolm, 248
Global-Digital Era, 288
God of the Oppressed (Cone), 222
Godrej, Farah, 383–84
God's will. *See* will of God
Goffman, Erving, 256
grace, 39, 251, 333
  cooperation with grace, 90
  in discernment, 10, 31, 51, 55, 56, 63
  in Ignatian spirituality, 14, 59, 60
  in the Reformed tradition, 50
  sanctification and, 87
  in the theosis process, 85, 86
Great Commandment and Commission, 296–97
guilt, 14, 19, 20–21, 160, 180, 181
Gutiérrez, Gustavo, 218–19, 220–21, 222, 224, 242, 334

Habitat for Humanity, 293
Haig, Matt, 245, 246
hamartiology, 305
Hershfield, Hal, 159
Hess, Mary E., 256, 259, 261
Hicks, Edward, 108
Hildegard of Bingen, Saint, 250, 286
Hinojosa, Carolina, 192
holding environment, 167–69, 174
holiness, universal call to, 6, 12
Homer, 99
hope, 123, 262, 269
  in already-but-not-yet framework, 253
  critical hope, 263, 264, 265, 271
  joy, lament and, 150, 156, 164, 165, 169, 170, 174, 265
  in *mujerista* theology, 78
  resistance, hope as a form of, 152, 264–68, 270
  theology of human hope, xxviii–xxix
  in vocational discernment, 43–44
hospitality, 294, 333, 355
house churches, 283–84
How to Think Theologically (Stone/Duke), 343–44
"The Human Situation" (Saiving), 275
Humboldt, Wilhelm von, xxii

identity
  context collapse, effect on, 256
  identity and belonging, 177, 179–82, 255, 256, 268
  identity-based challenges, 154
  identity formation, 191, 271
  intersections of identity, 199
  See also belonging
Ignatian spirituality, 50, 272, 348
  cura personalis concept, 225
  Ignatian discernment, 13, 57–59, 61, 334
  indifference, cultivating a state of, 14
  Spiritual Exercises, 58, 60, 63, 334
Ignatius of Loyola, Saint, 14, 58, 59, 61, 64
injustice, 8, 102, 213, 325, 335
  in accompaniment framework, 174, 220, 242

active response to, 241, 265
bearing witness to, 226, 243
economic injustice, 39
internalized systems of, 72
lament in reaction to, 150, 155, 164, 173
macro-level injustices, 118
resistance to, 42, 183
social injustice, 43, 331
in storytelling context, 261
suffering as used to justify injustice, 166
systemic structures as perpetuating, 115, 122
theological insights emerging from, 79
vocational discernment in a world marked by, 9, 270
See also social injustice; systemic injustice
inner voice, 24, 44, 176–77, 385
intellectual engagement
formation, as a dimension of, 88, 103, 291
positive feedback loop, creating, 89
in Set Your Sliders exercise, 353–54, 355, 356, 357
traditional academic models as prioritizing, 168
interconnectedness, 28, 94, 173
in emergent strategy, 134
in ministry framework, 293
in systems thinking, 112, 135, 148, 267
Tutu's emphasis on, 138, 139
Vine and the Branches, in metaphor of, 136
interculturalism, 196–97, 199, 201, 205, 206
interfaith dialogue, 298, 349
internal call, 23–26
International House of Prayer, 291
International Mission Board, 296
intersectionality, 69, 78, 118, 199–201, 205, 218, 276, 282
interstitium, 107
Iris Global, 297
Isaiah, 108, 231, 250, 279
Isasi-Díaz, Ada María, 7, 78–80

Jantzen, Grace, 99, 104, 265
Jennings, Willie James, 190, 204
fragments framework, 185–89, 190, 206, 258
on joy as an act of resistance, 149–50, 173, 175
on white self-sufficiency, 15–16, 184
Jeremiah, 164, 165, 279
Jesuit Guide to (Almost) Everything (Martin), 59
Jesuits, 58, 59, 64–65, 68, 340
Jesus Christ, 59, 98, 178, 292, 322
accompaniment and formation
Christ-likeness, continuous striving toward, 31
deeper freedom in Christ via accompaniment, 215
image of Christ in spiritual formation, 84–85, 86, 87
sense of purpose in following Christ, 151
biblical and historical context
in Christian prefiguration, 266
Jesus movement, earliest years of, 141
Jewishness of Jesus, 12
Quaker reenactment of Christ's entry into Jerusalem, 66
on the road to Emmaus, 324
disciples and followers
disciples as known for their love for one another, 11
doulos, disciples as, 280
honor for those who serve, Jesus calling for, 343
ongoing faithfulness encouraged in Christ followers, 341
struggle to understand the teachings of Jesus, 327
washing of disciples' feet, 279, 335, 336–37, 338, 339, 340, 341, 342
doctrine and theology
abiding in Jesus, 291
Christ in every person, 297
Church as the Body of Christ, 136–37, 138
deeper truths of Jesus, 332, 339
Jesus in fragments of faith, 185, 186
the kingdom of God, 136, 183, 252, 267
sin, Jesus conquering, 277
the values of Christ, 60–61
ministry and mission
existing power structures, critiquing, 281
faithfulness of Jesus, 273
the marginalized, paying particular attention to, 81
ministry of Jesus, 43, 136, 251, 276, 278, 279, 282, 283, 294, 304, 329, 330
service, Jesus's gift of, 293
social conditions, awareness of, 331
Johnson, Abigail, 346
joy, 24, 154, 161, 165
creating space for, 160, 162, 167–72, 173–74, 214
faith as fostered by embrace of joy, 164
as a fruit of the Spirit, 56
in *lo cotidiano*, 8, 79
in ministry, 177, 272, 278, 311

joy *(continued)*
    in Noticing and Naming practice, 238–39, 379
    resistant joy, 149–50, 152, 156, 173, 175, 183, 270
    in storytelling framework, 252, 254
    in vocational discernment, 149–50, 151, 153, 155, 157, 159, 162–63, 166, 169–72
    See also lament
justice, 144, 178, 211, 229, 251, 279
    accompaniment and communal frameworks
        in accompaniment context, 218–19, 221, 224
        collective struggle for, 55
        justice-oriented mentors, 227
    biblical and prophetic imagery
        Amos, imagery of justice in, 209, 210, 211
        Jesus as bringing justice, 276
        kings called to lead with, 279
        prophetic calls for justice, 274, 278
    commitment to justice, maintaining, 166, 181
    discernment and, 43, 56, 72
    disorientation beneath calls for justice, 194
    dreaming for justice, 263
    ecological justice, 139
    gospel, justice rooted in, 267
    inclusivity and, 156
    joy, lament and, 164
    ministry and practice
        in liberation theology framework, 10, 190
        in ministry framework, 281, 282, 283, 287–88, 294, 302, 304, 309, 311, 312, 327, 329
        in reframing of narratives, 264
        in storytelling framework, 249, 250, 384
        theological reflection on, 322, 330, 331, 333, 336, 341
    racial justice, 218, 288
    refusing to give up on, 165
    resistance and, 189
    in small, daily interactions, 79, 147, 335, 342–43
    vocation in working toward, 115, 266
    See also injustice; social injustice; systemic injustice

kenosis (self-emptying), 86, 304
Kierkegaard, Søren, 46
King, Martin Luther, Jr., 209, 242, 286
Kingdom of God. *See* Reign of God
klēsis (God's call), 266

lament, 160, 164, 174, 205, 265
    cathartic nature of, 158
    cultural contexts to expressing, 161
    Elijah's sense of lamentation, 17
    fostering space for lamentation, 167–72
    frustration and lamentation, 154, 165
    injustice, lament over, 151–52, 155–56, 173, 175
    new stories, lament when learning to tell, 41
    in relinquishing calling, 47, 258
    songs giving voice to lament, 96
    in vocational discernment, 149–51, 153, 157, 159, 162–63, 166
    in the vocational journey, 105, 169–72, 174, 214
    See also joy
Lamott, Anne, 47
Lange, Alex C., 199
Late Modern Era, 287
Lay, Benjamin, 67
Lee, Boyung, 196, 197, 199, 200, 201, 205, 206
LenkaBula, Puleng, 139–40
liberating interdependence concept, 200
liberation theology, 69, 193, 254, 288, 334, 336
    in accompaniment framework, 215, 218, 222, 224, 242, 243
    Freire as an influence on, 219, 220
    injustice, resisting, 115, 166
    prophetic stance, 225, 226
    of vocation, 10, 69, 190, 273
Ligonier Ministries, 292
Lin, Maya, 209, 210
Lizardy-Hajbi, Kristina, 143–44
Lockhart, Lakisha, 24–25, 189, 196
Lockhart-Gilroy, Annie, 230
lo cotidiano (everyday realities), 7, 9, 78–80
Lonsdale, David, 50–51
Lorde, Audre, 177, 179
Luther, Martin, 7

MacArthur, John, 292
Mainline Protestants, 292, 295
Make America Great Again movement, 113
the marginalized, 42, 281, 299, 350
    biblical messages for, 276–77, 282–83
    ministry of Jesus as directed toward, 279, 282, 283, 329, 331
    preferential option for the marginalized, 249, 273–74
    storytelling, marginalized groups using, 383–84
Marian model, 217–18
marriage, 70–71, 348
Martin, James, 59
martyria (witness), 259–60, 261
Mary, Blessed Virgin, 217–18, 324
May, Gerald, 90
McKee, Robert, 246
McLuhan, Marshall, 3

Mennonites, 294
mentors, 153, 171, 174, 235, 300
  in accompaniment framework, 227, 234, 236, 292
  bi-directional mentoring, 230, 243
  connections through, 348, 349
  mutual learning for mentors, 152
  resonating deeply with the work of, 26–27
  supportive community for mentors, 386
mercy, 42, 333
  Jesus's life as rooted in, 43
  in ministry context, 279, 297
  spiritual gift of, 293, 297, 299
Methodists, 57, 84–85, 97, 113, 295–96
Middle Ages, 285–86
The Midnight Library (Haig), 245
Miller-McLemore, Bonnie, 115, 117
  on the burdens of vocation, 165–66
  Follow Your Bliss and Other Lies about Calling, 41, 114
  on relinquishing a calling, 47, 257–58
ministry, 32, 308
  in accompaniment paradigm, 231, 236, 242
  call to ministry, 150, 309–14
  challenges and contexts of ministry
    in a changing spiritual landscape, 300–303
    contemporary understandings of, 290–99
    emotional costs of, 170, 172, 173
    new perspectives on, 30, 33, 83
    systemic injustices in ministry contexts, 159
  as dynamic and evolving, 74, 315
  faith community in ministry context, 153, 291, 293, 304, 305
  formation and training
    attentiveness in ministerial formation, 327
    deeper formation, call to, 190
    encouraging others to pursue ministry, 27, 29
    ministry training programs, 167, 168
    in Stewarding Leadings and Gifts workshop, 237, 238, 240
  forms and expressions of
    lay ministry, 150, 179–80, 202, 230, 237, 268–69, 295, 300
    marriage as a ministry, 70–71
    ordained ministry, 150, 288, 295, 307
    practice, ministry as shaping, 306–9
    public ministry, call to, 152
    servitude, power, and the call of service, 274–78
    storytelling as a form of, 259
    women in ministry, 101
  fragmented understanding and, 188, 193, 194
  historical evolution of ministry, 283–89, 314
  Jeremiah, prophetic ministry of, 164
  of Jesus, 43, 136, 251, 276, 278, 279, 282, 283, 294, 329, 330, 331
  pastoral care, 38, 172, 304, 308, 349
    Berlin Model for, xxii
    doctrine of sin in approach to, 305
    ministry as pastoral care, 281, 285, 293, 297, 299, 309
    patience and humility needed for, 327
    prophetic action, synergy with, 243
    in a Quaker setting, 71
    as a spiritual gift, 29, 295
  scriptural foundations of Christian Ministry, 278–83
  spiritual and emotional dimensions
    critical hope in approach to ministry, 271
    empathy as critical for ministry, 253
    exercising ministry as a spiritual gift, 356, 357
    joy and lament in ministry, 151, 155, 156, 157–58, 160–62, 168, 174
  in systems thinking, 111, 112–14
  theological reflection and, 322, 323, 325, 334, 338, 340, 341, 343
  theology, impacts on ministry, 303–6, 321
missio Dei (mission of God), 259–60, 261
missional spirituality, xxiii–xxiv
monastic tradition, 284–85, 286, 348
Moon, Zachary, 18, 21, 160
Moore, Mary Elizabeth, 97–98, 101
Moral Orienting System (MOS), 44, 93, 113, 160, 191, 257
  disorientation, accounting for, 20–22, 101, 114
  four vital aspects to, 18–20
  institutional betrayal as disrupting, 154
Morrison, Toni, 272
Mott, Lucretia, 67
mujerista theology, 78–79
Mulholland, M. Robert, 84–85
multiculturalism, 196, 197, 199, 201, 206
mycorrhizal networks, 107–8
mystical and personal experience, 88, 103, 354, 356, 357, 358
mysticism, 286, 348

Nayler, James, 66, 68
nepantla (in-betweenness), 192–93
NEPER practices guide, 377–81
Nirmal, Arvind P., 55
nones (religiously unaffiliated), 288, 300, 301, 302
Notice and Name practice, 238–39, 240, 378–89
novelty worship, 100
Oasis Network, 301

Organizational Boundary Audit Worksheet, 363–65
Orthodox traditions, 85, 286, 295

Palmer, Parker, 5, 6, 36–37
parables, 136, 309–10, 329, 333, 335
Pargament, Kenneth, 158
The Peaceable Kingdom (painting), 108
Peace Churches, 286
Penington, Isaac, 9
Penn, William, 108
Pennebaker, James W., 158
Pentecostalism, 89–90, 288, 291, 297
percy, rose j., 169
Phan, Peter, 100–101
plea-to-praise movement, 163
pneumatology, 304, 347
power dynamics, 98, 122, 147, 199, 242, 282
  in accompaniment relationships, 233, 244
  belonging and, 200–201
  the church, power dynamics within, 307
  decolonial critique of, 143
  discernment, interaction with, 24, 68–69, 72
  Jesuit tradition as a model for, 65
  storytelling as reflecting and reinforcing, 249
  in systems-aware approach, 145
The Powers, 140–44, 148, 190
practices to consider
  Condensed Examen, 60
  Double Journal, 162
  Failure Fridays, 170
  A Fragment Inventory, 191
  Leave the Cave, 16
  Life Review, 12
  Re-Frame and Re-Tell, 262
  Seeing Angels, 145
  Set Your Sliders, 90, 353–58
  Systems Mapping Me, 119, 359–61
  Tending the Web, 198
  Theological Reflection, 84, 321–51
  Tracing the Call, 28
  Witness and Walk, 226
  Your Ministry Recipe, 299
praxis, 10–11, 76, 220, 263, 306
prayer, 13, 87, 213, 329, 334
  communal prayer, 354
  dance as embodied prayer, 25
  in *deliberatio* context, 64
  in the discernment process, 51, 54, 68
  healing prayer as part of pastoral care, 293
  in Ignatian spirituality, 14, 50, 58, 59, 60
  lay ministers as conducting, 202
  in *ora et labora* principle, 342
  "Shema Yisrael" prayer, 12
  as a spiritual tool, 88, 96, 348, 349, 356, 387
  in the vocational path, 42–43
prefigurative politics, 265–67, 271
Presbyterian Church, 295
priesthood of all believers, 286, 292, 295, 305, 348
priestly service, 294–95
Prioritize and Prune practice, 239, 240, 379–80
projection, 325, 326
prophets and prophecy, 52, 67, 150, 250, 254
  in accompaniment framework, 215, 224, 225–28
  Amos, 209, 210, 279
  in the Didache, 283
  ecological awareness in prophetic writings, 135–36
  Elijah, 15, 16–17, 327
  fragments of faith in the words of prophets, 185–86
  future harmony, prophetic vision of, 108
  Jeremiah, 164, 165, 279
  justice, prophetic calls for, 156, 274, 278
  prophecy as a spiritual gift, 297, 299
  prophetic action, 225, 226, 241, 243
  prophetic mission of the church, 220
  system-level change and, 242
Protestant Reformation, 7, 286, 292, 348

Quakers. *See* Religious Society of Friends
quilombos communities, 182–84
quilts, 202–5
Qur'an, 54

Rah, Soong-Chan, 150, 175
reconciliation, 294, 394
rectification of names, 128–29, 133, 141
redemption, 249, 251, 261, 276–77, 313, 333
Reflection-in-Action, 340
Reformed tradition, 50, 292
Reign of God, 97, 243, 253, 260, 274, 305
  alignment with, 136
  as already-but-not-yet, 251
  as being "at hand," 252
  the marginalized as honored in, 331
  participation in, 261, 264, 270
  as a subversive notion, 43, 183, 267
  theological reflection on, 322
religious education, 97–98, 109, 256, 349
Religious Society of Friends (Quakers), 9, 13, 108, 153, 294
  clearness committee work, 70–71

communal discernment, approach to, 65–67, 68, 235
  deep listening, emphasizing, 242
  Doctrine of Discovery, addressing legacy of, 178–79
  Gospel Order, emphasis on acting in, 341
  vocal ministry, recognizing gift of, 311
reorientation, 17, 112, 204
  Disruption as prompting, 225
  in ministry setting, 311, 312
  in MOS framework, 18–20, 21–22
  re-narration as moral reorientation, 258
  spiritual reorientation through dance, 25
  in systems-informed approach, 113
  in Ubuntu context, 138
resistance, 4, 22, 36, 39, 42, 123, 306
  change, resistance to, 120, 122
  communal discernment as met with, 66
  feedback, resistance when receiving, 232
  hope as a form of, 152, 264–68, 270
  identity, resistance as shaping, 177
  Jennings on resistance, 184, 189
  joy as an act of, 149–50, 152, 156, 173, 175, 270
  lament due to meeting resistance, 155, 165
  in liberation theology, 10
  the marginalized and, 222, 242
  of *quilombos*, 182–83
  in rigid boundary systems, 126
  storytelling as a form of, 383, 384
  in system equilibrium framework, 146, 147
  vocational discernment during times of, 214
  vocational stories as acts of resistance, 254
Rest and Reassessment practice, 239, 240, 380
resurrection, 251, 265, 333
retreat, 29, 60, 172, 293, 348, 380
revelation, 28, 29, 42, 96–97, 339, 347
Reyes, Patrick, 13–15, 248–49, 334
Ricœur, Paul, 8, 9, 10
Rilke, Rainer Maria, 214

Saiving, Valerie, 214, 273, 275–76, 277
Salvation Army, 297
Samaritan's Purse, 292
sanctification, 86–88, 103
Sappho, 99
saudade (holy discontent), xviii, 165
schism, 285, 286, 384
Schleiermacher, Friedrich, xxii, 287
Scholasticism, 285
Second Great Awakening, 287
Second Vatican Council, 65, 68, 295
See-Judge-Act method, 263, 340–41

sensible-transcendent experience, 265
servant leadership, 143–44, 281
Shakur, Tupac, 3
Shaping Spiritual Leaders (Johnson), 346
Shaull, Richard, 219
Sheeran, Michael J., 65
signs of the times, 94
sin, 14, 60, 118, 275–76, 305, 333
"small is good, small is all" concept, 116, 148, 267–68
social factors, 329–30, 331
Social Gospel movement, 287
social justice, 24, 30, 128, 169, 243, 349
  in accompaniment context, 223, 224
  in discernment process, 73
  in ministry framework, 308, 314
  in *nepantla* dimension, 193
  personal transformation and, 305
  social justice advocates, 32
Society of St. Vincent de Paul, 297
Sojourners, 299
solidarity, 20, 56, 190, 225, 304
  in the Catholic Worker Movement, 335, 342
  in communal lament, 175
  leadership arising through, 197
  in liberation theology, 215, 218, 220, 221, 222–24, 243
  in *lo cotidiano*, 79
  in storytelling framework, 248, 250, 260, 261
Song, C. S., 253–54
soteriology, 10, 305, 347
"Spaces for Counter-Narratives" (Godrej), 383–84
spiritual but not religious (SBNR), 77, 81, 288, 300, 301, 302, 315
spiritual direction, 62, 133, 172, 302
  in accompaniment framework, 236, 292
  in Ignatian spirituality, 61
  as a spiritual practice, 348, 388
  vocational call and, 253–54
Spiritual Exercises of Ignatius Loyola, 58, 60, 63, 334
spiritual formation, 349
  discernment, role in, 51, 73, 99
  image of Christ in, 84–85, 86, 87
  in living ecosystem of tradition, 91–95
  ministerial formation, xxiii, xxxiii
  reflection, as intertwined with, 75–76, 91
  sliders tool, use in, 88–89, 90, 353–58
  spiritual practices and, 88, 103
  tradition, contending with, 95–103
  See also Moral Orienting System; theological reflection

spiritual gifts, 239, 284
  of administration, 295, 296
  of discernment and exhortation, 292, 294
  exercise of spiritual gifts, 88, 103, 291, 355, 356, 357, 380
  Holy Spirit, in traditions honoring, 50, 288
  ministry as the stewarding of spiritual gifts, 309, 310, 314
  of pastoral care, 29, 295
  of service, 292, 293, 297
  in vocation fulfillment, 126, 138
spiritual practices, 327, 348, 384
  accompaniment and, 229–30
  Indigenous spiritual practices, 188, 193
  spiritual formation, as a dimension of, 88, 103, 353, 354–55, 356, 357
  vocational discernment and, 144, 168
  See also practices to consider
Sproul, R. C., 292
Steere, Douglas, 240
Stephen Ministries, 293
Stewarding Leadings and Gifts workshop, 237–42
stewardship, 280–81, 296, 299, 300, 349
Stone, Howard, 343–44
storytelling, 267, 336, 389
  change, storytelling into, 385–88
  context collapse and re-narration, 246, 250, 255–61, 264, 271
  forward-looking aspect of, 123, 261–64, 268
  marginalized groups, use of, 383–84
  narrative reconstruction, 20, 386
  in NEPER practice, 377
  reframing narratives, 250, 258, 262, 264
  Seeding Change with Story guide, 383–89
  theological perspectives on, 248–54
  vocational storytelling, 171, 247, 248, 249–50, 253, 269, 270, 386–87
suffering, 8, 10, 243, 251, 276, 335
  hope in a world marked by, 270
  in Ignatian spirituality, 59
  joyful resistance and, 150
  lament and human suffering, 163
  misinterpreting suffering, 174
  naming and challenging the sources of, 165
  redemptive suffering of the cross, 277
  romanticizing suffering, refraining from, 166
  root causes, attempting to transform, 221
  sinful systems as creating, 118
  theological reflection on, 322, 333, 336
  traumatic experiences as linked with, 288
Sunday Assembly, 301
synodality, 94–95

systemic injustice, 20, 45, 152, 225, 260, 265
  accompaniment approach to, 221–24
  disorientation as a response to, 117
  lament over, 151, 156, 159, 175
  liberation theology as addressing, 218
  theological reflection on, 334
  white liberal response to, 248
systems thinking, 180, 213, 234
  Bowen Family Systems Theory, 111–12, 118, 119–20, 201
    system boundaries, 125–30, 133, 147
    system equilibrium, 120–25, 132, 133, 134, 147, 195, 226
    triangle formation, 120, 130–35
  fractal nature of systems, 134–35, 258, 267
  ministry, viewing through, 112–13, 279
  the power of systems, 114–18
  The Powers, systems-aware approach to, 140–44, 148, 190
  System Mapping Me tool, 119, 359–61
  Ubuntu theology and, 137–40, 200

teleios (maturity in character), 31
testimonio tradition, xxvii, 260
theological anthropology, 305, 347
theological education, 188, 193, 287, 289, 298, 302
  fragment framework, taking into account, 185, 186
  joy and lament in, 157, 160
  systemic racism in, 154
  theological reflection in, 83
  white self-sufficiency as part of, 15–16, 184
theological reflection, 101, 103, 220, 254, 310, 321
  connection as a lens for, 332–37, 345, 351
  contextualizing reflection, 325–28, 345, 350
  core doctrinal areas, revisiting, 303, 305–6
  educational and methodological guidance
    guidelines for writing theological reflection papers, 343–47
    practice of theological reflection, 77–84
    tips for excellence in theological reflection papers, 350–51
  experience, reflecting on, 322–25, 344, 345, 350
  formation and spirituality
    integration into practice, 340–43, 345, 351
    spiritual formation and, 75–76, 91, 204–5, 226
    as a spiritual tool, 96
  intellectual engagement and, 355, 356
  narrative theological reflection, 249, 260–61
  post-WWII era as reshaping, 288
  reconsideration with a fresh lens, 337–40, 345, 351

Index

social dynamics, analyzing, 53, 328–32, 345, 350
theological connection points, 347–49
A Theology of Liberation (Gutiérrez), 220
theoquilombism, 182–84
theosis, 85–86, 87–88, 103
Thurman, Howard, 179, 205
  on the Fantastic Hegemonic Imagination, 42, 72
  on the sound of the genuine, 34–35, 36, 41–42
  unknown and undiscovered siblings, on resistance to, 177
Townes, Emilie, 42, 72, 218, 223–24, 242
traditionalism, 97, 100
trauma, 20, 24, 62, 177, 288
  post-traumatic growth, 158–59
  trauma-informed admissions process, 373–75
  trauma-informed care, 367–71
  trauma-informed culture, 124, 168–69, 375
triangulation, 127, 130–35, 147
"true calling" concept, 30
Tutu, Desmond, 5, 37, 137, 138, 139–40

Ubuntu ("I am because we are"), 17, 137–40, 190, 200
United Methodist Church, 57, 113, 295
University of Berlin, xxii, 287

Vasconcelles, Erin, 158–59
Vatican II, 65, 68, 295
verbalism, 263, 266
Visio Divina Gallery practice, 63
vocation, 50, 115
  as co-created, 9, 42–43, 45, 72, 268
  consequences of call, 32–36
  divine vocation of The Powers, 142–43
  as a dynamic process, 5, 9, 11, 17, 20, 31, 39–40, 48, 72
  evolving nature of, 5, 11, 17, 41, 44, 147, 246, 252
  experiences of call, 22–32, 75
  high expectations, contending with, 152–53, 154–55
  listening in vocational exploration, 51, 242
  moral orientation and the shape of vocation, 17–22
  personal and communal purposes, as serving, 205
  perspectives and definitions, 6–17
  questions for reflection, 44–45
  reaching an equilibrium, 36–44
  reframing in the vocational journey, 48, 116–17, 267
  struggle, as entailing, 165–66
  systems-aware approach to, 112–14, 115–18, 145–47
  theological education and, xxii–xxvi
  trauma-sensitive approach to exploration of, 168–69
  Vocational Formation programs, 171
  vocational influences, visualizing, 359–61
  vocation journal, creating, 386
  whiteness as shaping dominant visions of, 184
  See also spiritual formation; theological reflection; vocational discernment
vocational discernment, 164, 263
  accompaniment and relational dimensions
    in accompaniment framework, 214–15, 217, 224, 232, 234
    as a communal process, 240–41
    Companioning in journeys of discernment, 225, 227
    in a holding environment, 167–69, 174
    the relational and communal self, approaching with, 138
  analytical and systemic perspectives
    context collapse within the realm of, 256
    core principles, applying to, 116–17
    systemic deformation, being alert to, 114
    systems thinking, applying to, 134, 137, 148
  colonial and decolonial contexts
    colonial fragments manifesting in context of, 187
    decolonial approach to, 193
    multiculturalism *vs.* interculturalism, understanding the dynamics of, 197
  formation and inner integration
    commodity fragments, resisting, 188–89
    deep formation, requiring, 156
    everyday realities, as rooted in, 7–8, 58, 80
    holistic approach to, 216
    interconnected approach to, 118, 239
    inward affirmation and being drawn outward, 26–28
    stillness and awareness practices, cultivating, 35
  learning and narrative frameworks
    quilt making as mirroring the journey of, 204
    Stewarding Leadings and Gifts workshop as fostering, 237–38
    in storytelling framework, 248–51, 254, 270, 271, 388
    testimonio tradition and, 260
  in ministry context, 303, 314
  moral and psychological dimensions
    in conditions of threat or exclusion, 22

vocational discernment *(continued)*
  consequences of taking vocational discernment seriously, 6
  in MOS framework, 19, 20
  rational and affective dimensions of, 23–26
  as an ongoing process, 10–13, 16–17, 28, 31, 246
  as personal and communal, 5, 28, 56, 118
  reflective and experiential aspects
    episodic nature of vocational experiences, 29, 30–31
    four connected questions on, 48
    hope and possibility, approaching with a sense of, 43–44
    identity and belonging as part of, 181
    illusion of completeness in, 185
    inclusive spaces, as envisioning, 198
    portfolio approach to calling, developing, 194
    power dynamics, navigating, 242
    release, as a process of, 46–47
  resistance, taking into account, 184, 214
  theoretical and reflective analyses
    broader implications of calling, understanding, 144
    counternarratives in, 267
    evolving nature of, 41
    fragmentation, contenting with, 186, 191
    no single, correct way for, 98
    possible futures, taking into account, 261–62
    "seeking fragments" in the context of, 99
    tradition, engagement with, 101, 103
  See also joy; lament
Volunteers for America, 300

Washington, Karen, 4
Westwood, Lynne, 109
Williams, Delores, 276–77, 282, 304, 334
will of God, 14, 166
  discerning God's will, 52–53, 64–65
  as dynamic and relational, 49, 74
  exercise of freedom and, 50–51
  Ignatian discernment of, 58–59, 61
  sanctification as conforming to, 86–87, 103
Wink, Walter, 140–44, 148, 190
Winnicott, D. W., 167
Witness, dimension of, 225–28, 229, 230, 234, 243
wolves, reintroduction of, 115, 236
Womanist scholarship, 189, 196, 223, 224, 276
Woodley, Randy, 151–52
word ministry, 292
Work-as-Calling concept, 293
World Council of Churches, 298
World Vision, 292, 296

Yang, Hwajin, 157
Yang, Sujin, 157
Yellowstone National Park, 115, 124–25, 236

"*Tending Call* reframes vocation as a liberatory practice, integrating spiritual formation with structural critique. It offers a guide that connects personal direction with collective transformation. . . . A vital resource for anyone who yearns to understand how their sense of identity and purpose intersects with God's liberating work in the world."

—**John Senior, Assistant Dean of Vocational Formation and Doctoral Education, Wake Forest University School of Divinity**

"At this moment of both danger and opportunity for theological education, Keefe-Perry shows us a way to engage vocation that tends lovingly to the rich and varied stories, contexts, and paths of those who embark on theological education today. . . . [and he] may just point us towards what might be emerging from the rubble."

—**Elizabeth W. Corrie, Professor, Candler School of Theology, Emory University**

"Brilliant yet accessible, this wonderful resource challenges traditional approaches to ministry while offering concrete tools for discernment that honor and center voices historically marginalized in and by theological education."

—**Colin Yuckman, Senior Director, Hybrid Programs, Duke Divinity School**

"Keefe-Perry weaves the personal and communal aspects of call, offering a beautiful, disquieting, and practical view of what it means to wrestle with questions of meaning and purpose in a broken world, and he provides us with practical tools for implementing these ideas in our own lives."

—**Christina Repoley, Vice President of Program, Forum for Theological Exploration, and Founder, Quaker Voluntary Service**

"An evocative and image-rich text that moves with ease and interpretation of Catholic and Protestant theological sources, psychology, ecology, and sacred text."

—**Kate Lassiter, Senior Director, Lifelong Learning, Meadville Lombard Theological School**

"*Tending Call* invites readers to imagine a hopeful future for faith—one that is attentive to God's call and is carried by faith communities who nourish vocation within their midst. . . . A guide to those discerning God's call and a companion to faith communities and educational institutions who nurture God's call through liberative practice."

—**Dustin D. Benac, Director and Co-founder, Program for the Future Church, Truett Theological Seminary at Baylor University**

"*Tending Call* serves as a compelling *testimonio* that affirms the process of discovering one's calling in community while simultaneously challenging readers to clarify the many sources of that calling. It is a must-read for ministers tending to the signs of the times today."

—**Luis Melgar, Director, Campus Ministry, Assumption University**

"Faithfully discerning vocational call is often disruptive, discomforting, and disorienting. This book is clear, concise, and compelling, meeting us in the murk where we grovel, second-guess, and grasp for courage, compassion, and creativity. Here is a gift for those of us weary and wandering souls."

—**Zachary Moon, Director, Chaplaincy Studies, Brite Divinity School**

"Keefe Perry's book came like an answer to a prayer when I was personally wrestling with the vocational question of 'what is my work to do in the world?' I felt profoundly challenged, both practically and theologically, to stretch my vocational responsibility and imagination to meet the urgent call for collective liberation."

—**Madeline Bugeau-Heartt, Program Associate, The BTS Center**

"Unlike traditional treatments of vocation, this book broadens our vision and reorients our hearts, inviting us to rediscover and reimagine the true meaning of our calling. *Tending Call* is not just a reflection—it's a revelation."

—**Sung Hee Chang, Associate Professor, Union Presbyterian Seminary**

Advance Praise for *Tending Call*

"For educators, clergy, and religious leaders, Keefe-Perry offers liberative practices and frameworks that empower individuals and communities to discern their vocation toward freedom. [He] . . . echoes the spiritual depth of Henri Nouwen [and] . . . evokes the prophetic insight of Walter Wink."

—**Patrick B. Reyes, author,** *Nobody Cries When We Die* **and** *The Purpose Gap*

"Drawing on years of mentoring students, creative scholar Callid Keefe-Perry provides an incredible range of practices and insights, broadening common conceptions of calling from the pursuit of self-fulfillment to a deeply moral and social endeavor. A fundamental guide for flourishing in our callings *and* resisting unjust systems."

—**Bonnie Miller-McLemore, author,** *Follow Your Bliss* **and** *Other Lies about Calling*

"With a pastoral sensitivity, Keefe-Perry honors the best aspects of multiple traditions, gently eschews a one-size-fits-all approach, and champions the liberating, mutual, dynamic, and ever-evolving work of vocational discernment. Complete with rich and thought-provoking exercises, this book . . . invites readers to celebrate discernment as a co-creative process with God, inexorably bound to the pursuit of human flourishing."

—**Stephen Cady, President, Brite Divinity School**

"*Tending Call* breathes life into how we engage identity, vocation, and the spiritual journey. More broadly, these pages invite liberative possibilities across the whole of theological education . . . to reclaim formation as a deeply embodied, community-rooted, and hope-filled endeavor."

—**Kristina Lizardy-Hajbi, Associate Professor, Iliff School of Theology**

"At last—a book that refuses to reduce vocation to career counseling or individual self-actualization! Callid doesn't shy away from hard truths: systems of power deform our calling, anger at injustice is spiritually appropriate, discernment demands critical analysis of oppressive structures. . . . For Christians hungry for faith that transforms both self and society, this book is your roadmap."

—**Tripp Fuller, Host, Homebrewed Christianity**

"Keefe-Perry brilliantly weaves together lived experience, pedagogical wisdom, and theological insight to guide us toward a more liberative understanding of how we are called to live, work, serve, and have our being. . . . An essential resource for educators, ministers, those discerning their own call, and those wondering how vocation is shaped by the intertwining of faith and freedom."

—**Lakisha R. Lockhart, Associate Professor, Union Presbyterian Seminary**

"*Tending Call* fills a missing piece in the literature of spiritual formation, offering a clear, justice-oriented framework to help people discern God's call for their lives in the thick of this complex world. I will be using this book in my own theological education classrooms, and I'll also be purchasing it as a gift for any friend trying to discern their next best steps in life or ministry."

—**Anastasia Kidd, Director of Contextual Education, Boston University School of Theology**

"What can it mean both to lament and yet to hope? And how might we weave that journey throughout our lives? These questions require complex engagement with a range of theological insights and theoretical frames—and you will find all of that in this magnificent book."

—**Mary E. Hess, Professor of Educational Leadership, Luther Seminary**

"This wonderful book combines vision and spiritual wisdom with common sense and practical advice. It will accompany you as you 'tend your call' and equip you to walk alongside others discerning their vocations. The compassionate companionship it offers is extremely precious in today's complex world."

—**Heather Walton, Professor, University of Glasgow**